ESSENTIALS OF EXAMINATION SYSTEM

Evaluation, Tests and Measurement

By the Same Author

- Theory and Principles of Education
(Philosophical and Sociological Bases of Education)
- Development and Planning of Modern Education
- Landmarks in the History of Modern Indian Education
- Essentials of Educational Technology: Teaching Learning: Innovations in Education
- Essentials of Educational Psychology
- Teaching of History: A Practical Approach
- Teaching of Social Studies: A Practical Approach
- Teacher and Education in a Developing Society
- Role of UNESCO in Education

ESSENTIALS OF EXAMINATION SYSTEM

Evaluation, Tests and Measurement

J.C. Aggarwal

Deputy Director of Education (Retd.)
Directorate of Education, Delhi

VIKAS® PUBLISHING HOUSE PVT LTD

VIKAS® PUBLISHING HOUSE PRIVATE LIMITED
E-28, Sector-8, Noida-201301 (UP), India
Phone: +91-120-4078900 • Fax: +91-120-4078999
Registered Office: A-27, 2nd Floor, Mohan Co-operative Industrial Estate, New Delhi-110044
E-mail: helpline@vikaspublishing.com • Website: www.vikaspublishing.com

SALES AND BRANCH OFFICES OF VIKAS® AND S CHAND AND COMPANY LIMITED

Chennai : Ph: 044-2363 2120, chennai@schandpublishing.com
Guwahati : Ph: 0361-2738 811, 2735 640, guwahati@schandpublishing.com
Hyderabad : Ph: 040-4018 6018, hyderabad@schandpublishing.com
Jalandhar : Ph: 0181-4645 630, jalandhar@schandpublishing.com
Kolkata : Ph: 033-2335 7458, 2335 3914, kolkata@schandpublishing.com
Lucknow : Ph: 0522-4003 633, lucknow@schandpublishing.com
Mumbai : Ph: 022-2500 0297, mumbai@schandpublishing.com
Patna : Ph: 0612-2260 011, patna@schandpublishing.com

Essentials of Examination System
ISBN: 978-81259-0051-1 Product Code: V7EES69TEDU10ENAA97O

First Edition 1997
Reprinted several times between 1997 and 2018, 2022 (Twice)
Reprint 2025

PRINTED IN INDIA
By Vikas Publishing House Private Limited, Plot 20/4, Site-IV, Industrial Area Sahibabad, Ghaziabad-201010 and Published by Vikas Publishing House Private Limited, E-28, Sector-8, Noida-201301

Contents

Preface

The book attempts to provide a detailed survey and indepth analysis of the crucial issues relating to examinations, evaluation and measurement including testing at the school and college level. Aspects like smooth conduct of examinations, setting good question papers, balanced provision of different types of questions, marking scheme, moderation and scaling of examination results, grades and marks, multiple set of question papers, question banks, open book examination system, internal evaluation semester system and classroom testing etc., are discussed in detail.

The volume surveys the history of examination and evaluation reforms since 1902. An exercise is made here to assemble extensively and arrange in a chronological order source materials on the subject. It contains twenty-one vital documents which include Committees and Commissions, Seminars and Workshops. It may be noted that these documents have indicated the directions of reform. Beginning with the report of the University Education Commission (1948-49), it ends with the deliberations of the conference of the Boards of School Education on Semesterisation and Examination Reforms (1992).

A wide coverage is provided to the efforts made by the Association of Indian Universities, Boards of Education, University Grants Commission and the Department of Education, Ministry of Human Resource Development, Government of India, to improve the system of evaluation and measurement.

The four-country comparison of the examination and evaluation system of India, U.K., U.S.A. and U.S.S.R., has the advantage of compactness, clarity and comprehensive treatment. Such a comparative study as the book has essayed, enables one to see the problem in a global perspective as well as to comprehend and evaluate the native system with reference to those of most advanced countries.

Where needed, text is supplemented by diagrams and tables.

The comprehensive bibliography is intended to serve as a reliable guide to those who would like to take up advanced study on the subject.

The book is specifically geared to the needs of B.Ed., M.Ed., M.Phil. and M.A. (Education) students of different universities. Nevertheless its practical suggestions for classroom teachers entitle it to be used for in-service teacher education programmes and orientation courses for educational administrators, planners and supervisors.

By virtue of its extensive and indepth treatment, it will be equally useful in the Middle-east and South Asian Countries.

The author is grateful to all the authors and publishers whose books he has made use of in the preparation of this publication.

J.C. Aggarwal

Chapter 1

Origin, Concept and Functions of Examinations : An Overview

1.1. ORIGIN OF EXAMINATIONS IN INDIA

In his preface to the book *Examinations in Ancient India* (1993), S. Narain observes that the process of examination development began when the Vedas were composed. Elements of some kind of testing methodology are also traced in the age of Upanishads. The concept of an examination came into play clearly when Panini (4th century BC), the great grammarian of ancient India graded his students on the basis of errors made in reciting the text of scriptures.

Teachers in the Vedic period were autonomous in their functioning and they followed various methods for admission. However, a teacher was the sole pedagogic authority to decide whether the student was fit for admission and also to decide whether the student had completed his study.

According to Narain, the extensive study of the old literature provides a glimpse that the undermentioned kinds of tests and modes of examination were followed by the ancients:

1. Screening test for admission.
2. Entrance test for higher education.
3. Continuous assessment for grading of students.
4. Terminal examination.
5. External check on evaluation standard.

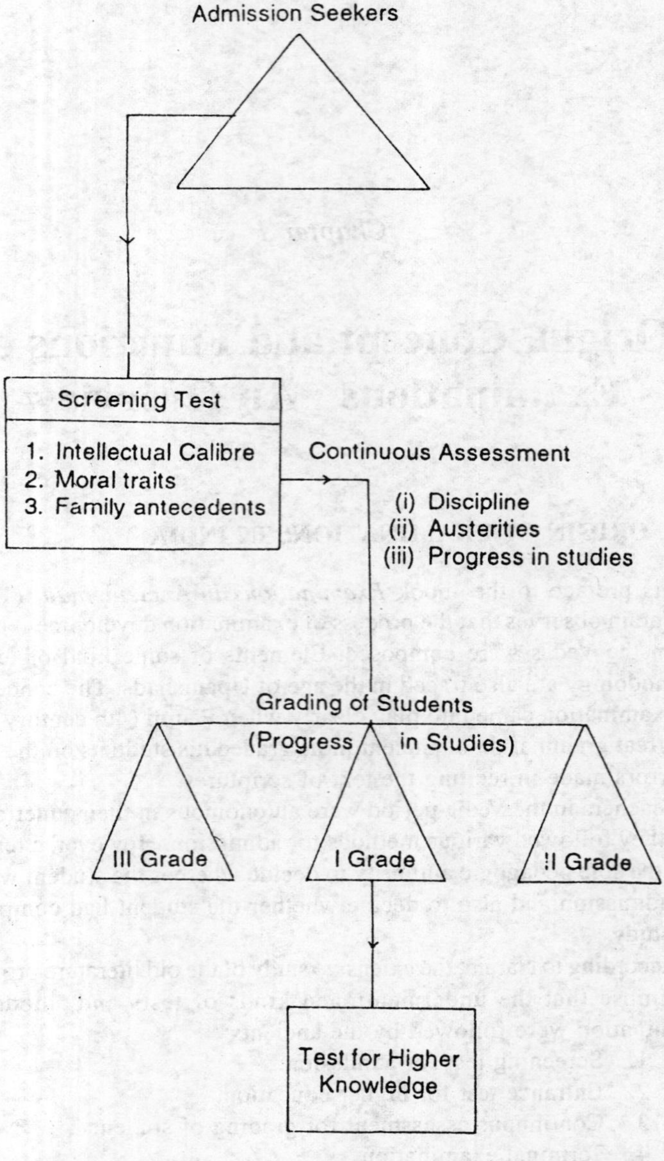

Fig. 1.1. Examination and Evaluation Model of Ancient India.

The common practice was that the 'Acharya' would ask the aspirant for education a few questions to adjudge his moral standard, sincerity and suitability to receive education.

After having been granted studentship, it was compulsory for the student to live with the teacher. Under the ancient system, all the three processes of education i.e. teaching, learning and evaluation were entirely integrated. The 'Acharya' was the teacher as well as the evaluator and exercised full supervision over the students who were treated as his family members. Evaluation of a student was a continuous process and it was almost a daily affair—in fact moment to moment affair.

The Acharya graded his students into the following categories:

1. 'Maha Prazanan' grade—students of high ability.
2. 'Madhyama Prazanan' grade—students of medium ability.
3. 'Alpa Prazanan' grade—students of low ability.

Students placed in the 'Maha Prazanan' grade were only allowed to pursue higher knowledge.

External check on evaluation standard was exercised through learned assemblies where the 'snataka' (graduate) was asked some questions and the answers given by him provided a glimpse of the standard of education he had received from the Acharya.

Panini, the author of the famous book *Ashtadhyayi* appears to be a pioneer in introducing the system of termination examination and grading. A student who committed one error in the examination was called *Aikanyika* i.e. one error student. Similarly one who committed two errors was given the grade of *Divanyika,* the two error student and so on. There were 12 grades and the student who committed 12 errors was called *Dwadasanyika* i.e. 12-error student. The errors were in respect of repetition of the Vedic hymns.

EXAMINATION AND EVALUATION IN ANCIENT INDIAN UNIVERSITIES

Taxila or Takshila University (150 BC to 180 BC)

This is considered to be the oldest of the ancient Universities dating the Ramayana period. Situated about 20 miles West of Rawalpindi (now in Pakistan), it had many famous teachers to whom students flocked from far off places. From the stories in various Jatakas, it appears, admission was open to all with no admission test. Students were at liberty to terminate their studies at their option.

Nalanda University (450 A.D. to 850 A.D.)

An institution of higher learning situated near the present Patna in Bihar where students from all parts of India and from distant countries like East Indies, Turkistan, Mongolia, China, Korea and Tibet came to study. In the middle of the 7th century A.D. the number of students in the University was almost 10,000. Every day about 1500 teachers delivered discourses on diverse subjects.* There was a big rush for admission to this university. As such, admission to the university was regulated through an entrance test. According to Hieun Tsang, only two or three out of ten aspirant students could get admission. There were six *Dwar Pandits* (Scholars of eminence at the gate), one at each college of the university to put oral questions to a student aspirant for admission to judge his aptitude and basic knowledge.

Mithila University (Ramayana Period to about 14th century A.D.)

This is said to be the first ancient Indian University to have introduced the system of 'Graduate Examination'. The system was called 'Salorkha Priksha' method (Needle Examination Method). Under this system, the candidate was put to test by asking him to explain a page of the manuscript. The page was chosen by piercing a needle revolving through the manuscript. The student who could explain the given page chosen through piercing the needle was awarded the Degree of Mithila University.

Mithila's earlier name was Videha under the famous philosopher—King Janak. In the time of the Upanishads it was a stronghold of Brahmanical culture and learning.

Nadia University (12th century A.D.)

A great centre of learning located on a site close to the modern town of Krishan Nagar in West Bengal, followed the dialectical method of evaluation.

Origin of the present system of examination in India.

With the establishment of the universities of Bombay, Calcutta and Madras in 1857, the matriculation examination began to be conducted by the universities. However in due course, universities abandoned their college entrance examination in favour of State Boards of Education.

It is of interest to note that till 1877, the matriculation examination was not open to girls.

External examinations came to dominate the entire educational process till 1921.

---

* (Education imparted at Nalanda was free).

The Indian University Commission of 1902 recommended that the School Final Examination should be conducted by the Education Departments and not by the Universities. The Government of India Resolution on Educational Policy, 1904 accepted this recommendation.

With the advent of the British rule in India, there was a specific shift in the educational system. The British rulers thought in terms of their basic interests. This is evident from the purposes for which universities were established in 1857. These purposes were "to ascertain by means of examinations the proficiency acquired by students" and "to provide a test of eligibility for government service." In due course, examinations began to serve the purpose of eligibility for admission of students to higher classes in schools and universities.

1.2. ORIGIN OF EXAMINATIONS IN CHINA AND OTHER COUNTRIES

According to Kuo (1915), a Chinese scholar as quoted by Charles W. Harris in *Encyclopaedia of Educational Research* (1960), the Great Shun, a model emperor of antiquity (of China) whose reign ended in 2205 B.C. examined his officers every third year and gave them a promotion or dismissed them from service. This was at a time when letters were newly invented. The competitive examination system of ancient China, which developed from precedents such as this, was closely related to the educational system and helped it serve its primary purpose of providing men of ability for the services of the State. However, the details of this system are not precisely known. With the passage of time the system of examination was improved in China.

"He who shall excel at tablet writing shall shine like the sun." This inscription is found on the walls of an ancient school in Mesopotamia, in the time of Hammurabi, around 2000 B.C. The word 'excel' denotes an element of comparison with others and in this word we can probably see the institution of an examination. This makes clear that examinations have existed throughout history, whether as forms of trials of skills or professional tests or public disputations.

Plato (427 B.C. - 347 B.C.) in Greece and Quintilian (38 B.C. — 86 A.D.) in Rome criticised examinations.

The Spartans conducted examinations as early as in 500 B.C.

In ancient Athens, emphasis upon athletic development led to some sort of examination or evaluation by means of games and contests.

In England, written examinations for educational purpose, probably made their appearance around 1770 at Cambridge and Oxford. The School Certificate Examination in Scotland came into being in 1888.

Charles W. Harris (1960) states that European Universities from their beginning also emphasised examinations as the basis for the awarding of degrees and honours. The Cambridge Tripos is a well-known example of such examinations.

In the U.S.A., in the middle of the nineteenth century Horace Mann was responsible for development of an examination system in American schools. J.M. Rice was another reformer during the early decades of the twentieth century. He produced substantial literature of research studies on the statistical properties of written tests of all kinds.

D. Starch and E. C. Elliott did a lot of work on the use of objective tests during the early period of the twentieth century.

By about 1930, a majority of educators in the U.S.A. began to rely more heavily on the objective tests.

About the origin of examinations, M. Mascarenhas in his book, *Examinations: An Informative Update* (1991) states that they arose out of the need of a teacher to give a public manifestation of the effectiveness of his teaching through a display of the talents of his students, or it arose from the compulsions of a student to win fame through public debates. Later, in an evolving scientific age with greater specialisation, nations needed to be properly equipped to take over these areas in the interests of preparing the country face a better tomorrow. But specialists could only be selected by a credentialling system that followed an examination. The examination, therefore, was an instrument of liberation: "it either gave the individual a run for his talents and the approbation of society, or it gave the country a relevance in the cavity of nations and enabled it to take care of the problems arising out of a multiracial, technocratic or stagnant society."

1.3. MODERN CONCEPT OF EXAMINATIONS

The Dictionary of Education (1959) by Good defines examination as "(1) an appraisal of ability, achievement, or present status in any respect; (2) The instrument used in making such an appraisal."

H. C. Barnard and J.A. Lauwerys in *A Handbook of Educational Terms* (1967) explain the concept of an examination as "A test of knowledge acquired, or more generally a means of assessing intellectual capacity or ability. There are normally three types of examination: (1) a set of questions designed to check a pupil's progress on the results of a course of instruction; (2) a means of qualifying candidates for a certificate or degree in which they are required to attain a certain standard for a pass or honours; (3) a competitive test on the strength of which a scholarship or other award is made to the successful candidate. Examinations may be conducted by means of written answers to set questions or by local methods."

International Dictionary of Education (1978) by G. Terry Page and J.B. Thomas explains the concept of examination as "(1) Assessment of ability, achievement or present performance in a subject. (2) Instrument of assessment can be long essay or mixed form of assessment. May be used for qualifying for entrance to professions and higher education."

A Dictionary of Education (1981) by Derek Rowntsee explains the concept of examination in these words, "A formal assessment of a student's learning, used particularly at the end of a course. Although many teachers bemoan the distorting influence examinations can have on teaching and learning, when used wisely they can assess student qualities that would otherwise go unobserved. An examination usually involves one or more of the following features: All students are given the same task to perform (perhaps with some degree of choice); its precise nature; will not be made clear until the moment they begin upon it; they will be given a time-limit and they will not be allowed to consult references or one another; they will perform in the presence of an invigilator; and they will be expected to experience some sense of urgency or stress. Now-a-days many examinations relex one or more of these restrictions (e.g. students may be given advance notice of the questions or may be allowed to use certain reference materials, but the last mentioned feature usually remains."

1.4. THE PLACE OF EXAMINATIONS

Examinations have been in existence from times immemorial. "To close down examinations would be to give the signal for educational saturnalia," observed Sir Michael Sadler. J. C. Mathur emphasises the value of examinations when he writes, "Even in the idealised picture of society portrayed in H.G. Wells' Utopia, examinations find an important place." "Nevertheless examinations—and specially external examinations—have a proper place in any scheme of education," writes the Secondary Education Commission. Examinations are good servants as they help to evaluate the achievements of our students. They are a great touchstone for measuring the amount of knowledge acquired or the degree of skill achieved.

1.5. FUNCTIONS OF EXAMINATIONS

1. **To Evaluate the Achievement of the Students.** The abilities and the achievements of the students must be evaluated. Examinations are conducted to discover whether or not the child had been able to acquire a certain amount of knowledge or skill.

2. **To Measure Personality.** They are used to test the power of clear thinking, quickness of mind, calmness and perseverance.

3. **To Measure the Efficiency of Teachers and of the School.** They provide a suitable occasion for the authorities to measure the efficiency of the teachers. The efficiency of the institution is also measured through the examinations. They provide a proper occasion to the teachers to know whether or not their methods of teaching are appropriate.

4. **To Help in Diagnosis.** They help parents to know the progress of their children. They help to discover the specific weak points of an individual or class and thus give an opportunity to the teachers as well as to the taught to remove these defects.

5. **To Act as Incentive.** Stimulation to work hard is provided to the students through the institution of examinations. Some objectives are placed before the students and for the realisation of those objectives the students develop in them the habits of constant hard work.

6. **To Help in Prognosis.** The examinations have a prognostic value also. With this device the aptitudes of the students are determined.

7. **To Provide Uniformity of Standard.** The external examinations facilitate the problem of uniformity of standards attained by the students of different institutions.

8. **To Help in Guidance.** They facilitate the work of grouping individuals for the purpose of teaching by bringing those together who have more or less the same attainment.

9. **To Measure Fitness for Admission to Higher Courses.** They are designed to determine the capacity and fitness of the candidate to pursue higher courses of general or professional study or training. Examinations which serve this purpose are called Entrance or Qualifying Examinations.

10. **To Help in Selection by Competition.** The examinations are also conducted to select the best candidates for appointment to public service or for award of prizes and scholarships.

11. **Study of Every Subject.** The students study all the subjects including what are known as 'dull ones' for fear of examinations.

12. **Parents' Point of View.** Examinations provide an opportunity to the parents to know where their wards stand and whether money spent on them is being utilized properly.

13. **To Certify Competency.** A technological society needs qualified doctors, engineers and scientists etc. and the examination system certifies their presence even if inadequately.

14. **To Link Schools with the World.** Examinations fulfil an important role in linking schools with each other and with the world.

1.6. CRITICISM OF EXAMINATIONS

Examinations have disturbed the examinees almost from the day of their origin. They have been a way of life from time immemorial. 'A necessary evil' is how an examination is termed. In the absence of anything worthwhile to substitute it, it has endured. Of course, different names have been given to examinations with varying emphasis on one or the other aspect of them. Terms like measurement, evaluation and testing have come into vogue. Nevertheless, the institution of examinations has enjoyed a robust health.

The 'child-centred examination' seems to be an ideal approach in the context of internal examinations of the educational institutions. But how to achieve this objective is a hard nut to crack. G. H. Bantock has observed in *Culture, Industrialisation and Education* (1968) that the examination came to be the final arbiter of justice so much so that in the U.K., parents even demanded examinations because they were convinced that an independent examination was an impartial judge. But now this judge has come under cloud !

J. Krishnamurthi, (1973) puts the problem in these words, "When you compare B with A, openly or secretly, you are destroying B. B is not important at all for you have in your mind the image of A who is bright, clever, and you have given him a certain value. The essence of all this competitiveness is comparison: comparing one picture with another, one book with another, a person with another. This comparison is measurement between what is and what should be you give marks to the student and so force him to compete with himself, and the final misery of all this comparison is the examination."

Examinations distort knowlege in that they make the student believe that only what is examined is important, that knowledge can be compartmentalised, that a knowledge of facts alone is important and that the mastery of a subject requires only the learning of an accumulation of facts.

First Voice against the System. A Calcutta Principal in 1871 said that because of the examinations, "Education is cramming of a large amount of ill digested knowledge" and the students were reduced to "Mere machines of memory"

The Hunter Commission and the Calcutta University Commission have in very unambiguous terms denounced the system and pointed out its short-comings.

Sri S.N. Mukerji, Chairman, Examination Section, All India Educational Conference, 1944, observed: "The conclusion is irresistible that education in India dominated by external control and tutelage in the form of fragmentary and unscientific examination has resulted in the perpetuation of medicority and retardation of genius, facts which are necessary concomitants, if not inevitable consequences, of the prevailing system."

The University Education Commission, presided over by Dr. Radhakrishnan wrote, "For nearly half a century, the examination has been recognised as one of the worst features of Indian Education."

The Secondary Education Commission, summarizing the glaring shortcomings of our examination very aptly and emphatically stated, "External examinations are exercising a restricting influence over the entire field of education to such an extent as almost to nullify its real purpose."

W.H. Ryburn strongly criticises them when he writes, "It goes without saying that examinations are the enemies of creative work, at least as they are usually conducted."

The main defects of examinations are as under:

1. **Lack of Definite Aim.** Our examinations are not geared to the realization of specific objectives. The same test serves different purposes like passing a course, admission to the next course, passport to employment, discovering individual capacities, securing scholarship etc., with the result that it becomes invalid for any purpose.

Sultan Mohiyuddin writes, "Business firms wanting empolyees look at the results of the examination, the high schools base their admission on it, and government accepts it as a passport to all departments of service; there are no specific, mental or moral traits, and disabilities that the ordinary examination seeks to discover and measure, and there is, therefore, no definite guidance it can offer to the professions, business houses and higher educational institutions."

2. **Element of Chance.** Element of chance plays an important role and decides the fate of large number of students. It is often found

that some students prepare a few selected questions and leave everything to chance. If perchance, the same questions are set in the examination, they pass with credit. The question arises, have they actually attained the requisite standards? Perhaps not ! Now take the case of another student who has been regular in his work throughout the year. He might not secure as good marks as the one mentioned above. Should we conclude that the former are more intelligent than the latter?

3. **Lowering of Educational Standard.** According to the Secondary Education Commission (1952-53), the examination determines not only the content of education but also the methods of teaching, in fact, the entire approach to education. The efficiency of a teacher is judged by the pass percentages of his results. The teachers adopt the trick of the trade to improve their results. 'Idea of exam.' the sole aim and 'Cram' the only method, dominates the entire educational system. The students do not feel interested in a subject unless it is included in the examination scheme. They are more interested in notes and guides rather than in text-books with the result that they ignore habits of independent study. Stress is laid on spoonfeeding and pupils are encouraged to memorise facts and vomit them out in the examination.

Again to quote the Secondary Education Commission, "The present system of examination does not test anything except memory and a certain kind of verbal felicity."

Thomson called them, "a presumptuous attempt to gauge the depth of human ignorance."

Valentine rightly observed, "There is a grave danger of certain studies being crammed and spoilt by the prospect of an examination ahead."

P.C. Wren quotes Sir Oliver Lodge, "External examinations which have to be prepared for specially are hampering to the teacher. They tend to keep his attention directed to some artificial aim—rather than to the immediate object of his work—namely the drawing out and development of the minds committed to his care."

4. **Lowering of Moral Standard.** Examinations teach the students different ways of becoming dishonest. Books are smuggled in the examination centres and attempts are made on the life of the supervisors who try to catch the students who use unfair means.

5. **Ignoring Qualities of Character.** They fail to provide any measures to test the originality, initiative, truthfulness, honesty, sociability of an individual and thus they fail to test real education. Sultan Mohiyuddin writes, "Training in originality and independence of thought, correctness of judgement or reasoning, responsiveness to noble ideas

and sentiments and enjoyment of beautiful things—these cease to be the aims of teacher's effort for they are not judged by the traditional examination. Examination is the sole aim and cram the sole method.

6. **Element of Subjectivity.** Subjective attitude of examiners influence the marks of individuals and leads to a great variability in marking. Vernon points out, "The same script might receive a different mark if read after instead of before dinner."

Dr. R.K. Singh says, "Our examinations are subjectively weighed and subjectively scored and are not, therefore, dependable indices of pupils'achievements." The Harvard University Commission in England says, "Where the panel of readers (examiners) is large, where thousands of answer books are being rated, where physical conditions of weather and health are not always under control, and where practically all judgements are subjective, it would be indeed strange if discrepancies in ratings are not numerous, if mistakes are not frequent and costly."

7. **Putting Heavy Mental Strain.** Most of the students are in the habit of working strenuously just near the annual examination and this severely tells upon their health, leads to mental dyspepsia and discourages the formation of healthy mental habits.

8. **Developing Frustration.** Failures in examinations lead to frustration and even to suicides in some cases.

9. **Causing Large Incidence of Failure.** The Education Commission (1964–66) observes, "The matter about which the public at large is most deeply concerned is not the irrationality of the scoring procedures, or the inefficiency of the administrative processes, but the large incidence of failures in the external examination at the end of the school stage. An analysis of the results of the different Board examinations for the last five years show that about 55 per cent of the candidates appearing for the high school examination and about 40 per cent of those appearing for the higher secondary school examination fail regularly every year. In the case of the private candidates the percentage soars up to 70 per cent or even more. Failure often has a demoralizing effect on the unsuccessful candidates. The failure of such large numbers of students, particularly after they have been screened year after year by means of annual and other school examinations, is a sad reflection on our methods of education as well as on our system of examination."

"We also believe that with the proposed improvement in the curriculum, instructional materials and methods of teaching, and the reorientation in the training of teachers, the incidence of examination failures will be reduced. But we do not think that a student should be branded as a total failure, if he passes in certain subjects but is unable to make the grade in others. There is no reason why he should carry with him the stigma of being declared as unsuccessful candidate if he has partially succeeded in his educational effort."

10. **Promoting Supremacy of Textbooks.** Examinations tend to promote the supermacy of textbooks. The students begin to assume that the expectations of the examiners in no way differ from the conclusions reached in the textbook. In this way critical thinking loses its validity.

11. **Dehumanising Effect.** The examinations which are basically meant to evaluate quality, have become a means of qualification of human beings and a tool for dehumanisation.

12. **Certificate Inflation.** Too much reliance on examinations has resulted in what may be called a 'certificate inflation.'

13. **Disappearance of the Process of Education.** The most deplorable aspect of the matter is that students, parents and teachers are concerned only with examination marks and not with the means by which the marks are obtained. The real processes of education are losing significance. This accounts for irregular attendance, indifference to the value of scholarship and complete loss of love for learning.

As a matter of fact, the examinations have met with heavy criticism from all quarters. This criticism is due to the excessive development of the examination system and a large number of students subjected to it. Candidates complain against the examination system because of its mental strain; the teachers against the examination because of its harmful influence on school work; the parents denounce it because of its injurious effect on the physical and mental health of the children; the practical psychologists speak ill of it because of its unreliability and invalidity and the educational theorists attack it because of its lack of definiteness in aim and purpose.

EPITHETS GIVEN TO EXAMINATIONS

1. An enemy of true education.
2. An incubus.
3. A blood sucker.
4. A bane of educational system.
5. A necessary evil.
6. A glorification of memory.
7. A begetter of rivalry and strife.

8. A dead hand of education.
9. A growing tyranny.
10. A presumptuous attempts to gauge the depth of human ignorance.
11. An obstacle to learning.

1.7. REMEDIAL MEASURES

1. To minimise the subjective element, new type of objective tests should be introduced alongwith the essay type of questions.

2. Questions put should be thought-provoking and evenly distributed over the entire course. Difficult as well as easy questions should find a place in the question paper.

3. Due consideration should be given to the work of the students done in the class. The teacher's recommendations should be given their due importance. He should be trusted and given a fair opportunity to know and study closely the pupils in his charge.

4. Cumulative records should be maintained in respect of all the students.

5. The paper-setters and examiners for external examinations should be drawn from the teachers who actually teach subjects in schools.

6. Standard of marking should be prescribed so as to minimise the variability in marking.

7. The system of permitting private candidates to take the examination should be discouraged.

8. The system of compartmental examinations should be introduced at the final public examination.

9. In place of numerical marking the system of symbolic marking be adopted. Five-point scale seems to be the best type of symbolic marking scale *i.e.*, 'A' stands for excellent, 'B' for good, 'C' for fair and average, 'D' for poor and 'E' for very poor.

10. Examinations should be regarded as means and not ends. They should be conducted in such a manner that they become effective instruments of education. They should serve as stimulus to learn new facts, gain new experiences, discover weak points and estimate progress.

11. Oral examinations should be held in addition to the written ones. Some qualities like candidate's alertness, intelligence, special interests, mental outlook, his personal qualities of mind and character and his mastery of acquired knowledge can be better tested by *viva voce* tests than by written examinations.

12. An examination should have only one definite aim before it and that aim must be clearly known to the teacher and the examinee.

13. A well-conducted examination should test both the actual attainment and capacity for future achievements. A combination of the traditional examination and carefully constructed intelligence test, therefore, supplies a more reliable means of selecting candidates for higher courses of study than the traditional examination alone.

14. External examination need not be compulsory for all the students of Class X or Class XI/XII. A student may choose to leave the school with the school certificate only without appearing for the external examination, and seek a job or even an entry into some vocational course on the basis of the certificate and the school records. It must be recognized, however, that since admission to institutions of higher secondary education as well as of higher education will be selective, the authorities controlling such institutions will lay down their own rules of eligibility for admission. A student seeking entry into these institutions may have not only to pass the external examination in the subjects laid down and secure the prescribed grades but also submit himself, if necessary, to certain admission tests required by the institution.

The certificate issued by the Board on the basis of the results of the external examination at the end of the lower or higher secondary stage, should give the candidate's performance only in those subjects in which he has passed but there should be no remark to the effect that he has passed or failed in the whole examination. The Board, however, should issue a statement alongwith the certificate showing his marks or grades in all the subjects.

15. The candidate should be permitted to appear again if he so desires, for the entire examination or for separate subjects in order to improve his performance.

16. On the completion of the course, at the end of the lower or higher secondary stage, the student should receive a certificate also from the school giving the record of his internal assessment as contained in his cumulative record card. This certificate may be attached to that given by the Board in connection with the external examination.

17. The technical competence of paper-setters should be raised through an intensive training programme sponsored by the State Boards.

18. The question paper setters should be oriented to testing not merely the acquisition of knowledge but the ability to apply knowledge and the development of problem-solving abilities.

19. The nature of the questions asked should be improved.

20. It is essential that scientific scoring procedures should be devised so that there may be optimum reliability in the assessment of the candidate's performance.

21. With the ever-increasing number of students appearing for the Board examinations, the task of getting the answer scripts properly valued and processing the results efficiently within a given time is becoming more and more difficult. It is necessary that this process should be mechanized so as to make it more accurate and expeditious.

1.8. NEW APPROACH TO EXAMINATIONS

H.S. Srivastava, Head Examination Reform Unit, NCERT (1977), states the new approach to examinations in these words, "In functional terms, the new approach to examinations conceives of the abolition of the practice of declaring students as pass or fail, as also that of declaring the overall results of students in terms of divisions. Instead, it prescribes the declaration of the levels of achievement and proficiency of students in different subjects separately and in terms of grades. The scheme also attacks the sanctity of public examinations, the irreversibility of their results as also the omnibus use of the same for a variety of purposes. The new scheme is founded on the principle that evaluation ought to be used for the improvement of pupil performance rather than its mere assessment. Thus, unit teaching and testing, diagnosis of strengths and weaknesses of students, guidance through remedial and enrichment programmes for the optimum scholastic and non-scholastic growth of pupils' personality became the corner stones of the new strategy of evaluation."

1.9. EXAMINATIONS OF TOMORROW

Srivastava, Singh and Anand (1978) visualise the picture of examinations of tomorrow as, "Once the role of evaluation in teaching and learning is appreciated by the teachers, students and administrators, the importance of the external examination would be relegated to the secondary position. Such examinations can be used to compare the standards of different institutions, and select students for admissions and job. When the school becomes the agency for conducting the examinations and teachers are agents of this change, the validity of the students' evaluations would not be challenged. Then the teachers who teach will assess the performance of their wards. Students will not devise ways and means to get grades which they do not deserve. Certificated marks would no longer serve as meal tickets for the examinees; nor would the admissions to the institutes of higher learning be ensured on the basis of certifications. Once the teacher becomes the arbitrator of the curriculum *viz-a-viz* evaluation, external examinations held by the Boards would be replaced by teachers' evaluation in the school. Ultimately, the external, examinations would have to be abolished altogether. How soon this will become a reality, depends on the Boards' realisation of the necessity for this change and the extent to which the teachers are able to develop technical competence and exhibit integrity of the present day paper setters and examiners. The sooner this responsibility is handed over by the examination agencies and taken over by the class teachers, the better it will be for all those who are involved in the teaching-learning process."

Chapter 2

Types of Examinations

2.1. CLASSIFICATION ON THE BASIS OF TYPE OF QUESTIONS

Examinations may be classified on the basis of type of questions i.e. essay type, objective type, and oral type. This may be illustrated as under:

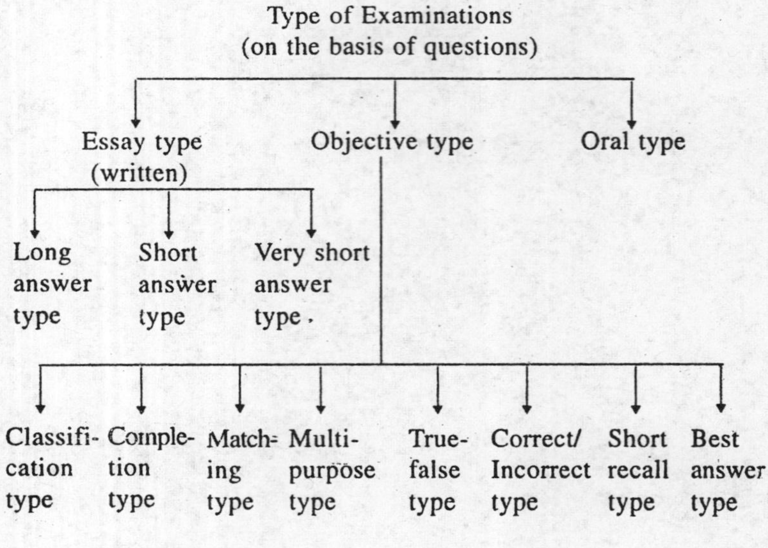

An ideal system of examination combines different types of questions judiciously and rationally in a balanced manner.

2.2. EASSY TYPE EXAMINATIONS OR ESSAY TESTS

Essay tests have a long history that dates back to more than four thousand years. W.E. Coffman in an article entitled "Essay Examinations", published in a book *Educational Measurement* (1971), edited by R. L. Thorndike observes that essay tests were in use earlier than 2300 B.C. Until the turn of the 20th century, they were almost the only form of written examination.

Very few attempts have been made to define and clarify the concept of essay tests. They have been used so widely that it is assumed that everybody understands their meaning.

Robert L. Ebel and David A. Frisbie in their book *Essentials of Educational Measurement* (1986) writes, "An essay test presents one or more questions or other tasks that require extended written responses from the persons being tested."

Gilbert Sax in *Principles of Educational and Psychological Measurement and Evaluation* (1989) states, "Essay test is a test containing questions requiring the student to respond in writing. Essay tests emphasise recall rather than recognition of the correct alternative. Essay tests may require relatively brief responses or extended responses."

William Wiersma and Stephen G. Jurs in their book *Educational Measurement and Testing* (1990) writes, "Essay item is an item that requires the student to structure a rather long written response upto several paragraphs."

It is very difficult to give an exact and perfect definition of an essay test. Usually an essay test refers to any written test that requires an examinee to write several paragraphs or passages. However, answer may constitute even a sentence or a paragraph also in some cases. Weidemann (1933), observes that an essay type question may use the following eleven words, signifying the simple to higher mental processes.

(a) What, Who, When, Which and Where.

(b) List	(c) Outline	(d) Describe
(e) Contrast	(f) Compare	(g) Explain
(h) Discuss	(i) Develop	(j) Summarise and
(k) Evaluate.		

Classification of Essay Questions

According to Norman E. Godman (1985) essay questions may be subdivided into two broad types—extended response and restricted response.

In extended response question, no restriction is placed on the student as to the points he will discuss and the type of organisation he will use. An extended response type of essay question permits a student to demonstrate his ability to

(i) recall factual knowledge;
(ii) evaluate his factual knowledge;
(iii) organise his ideas;
(iv) present his ideas in a coherent and logical way.

An example of an extended response question: Describe at length the state of affairs in the Golden Age of the Gupta Period.

Restricted Response. In restricted response, the student is restricted as to the form and scope of his answer because he is specifically told the context in which his answer is to be made. For example: Describe in not more than 100 words the state of literature in the Golden Age of the Gupta Period.

Restricted response questions tend to be more objective while the extended type questions tend to be more subjective.

The restricted response questions are more useful in measuring more specific learning outcomes but they cannot measure learning outcomes which stress integration. The extended response questions are more useful in measuring complex behaviours which cannot be done by other types of tools but how accurately they do so is controversial.

W.S. Monroe and R.E. Carter(1993) list the following types of questions:

1. Analysis.
2. Application of laws, principles and rules to new situations.
3. Cause or effect.
4. Classification.
5. Comparison of two ideas or things in general.
6. Comparison of two things on a single basis.
7. Criticism as to the adequacy, correctness or relevance of a statement.
8. Decisions for and against.
9. Explanation of the use or exact meaning of some word, phrase or statement.

10. Evaluation recall-basis given.
11. Formulation of new question—problems and discussions raised.
12. Illustration of examples.
13. Inferential thinking.
14. New methods of procedure.
15. Outline.
16. Reorganisation of facts.
17. Selective recall—basis given.
18. Statement of an author's purpose in the selection or organisation of material.
19. Statement of relationships.
20. Summary of some unit of the textbook or of some article.

Merits of the Essay Tests

1. Abilities like logical thinking, critical reasoning and systematic presentation, etc. can be best evaluated by the essay type of tests.

2. They provide an opportunity to the students to show their originality of thought as they are permitted freedom of response.

3. They help to develop good study habits such as preparing outlines and summaries, organising arguments *for* and *against* a topic.

4. They provide opportunities to students to develop abilities such as to organise ideas effectively, to criticise or justify a statement and to interpret, etc.

5. They can be successfully employed for evaluating the performance of students in all the school subjects.

6. It is relatively easier to prepare an essay type test than to prepare an objective type test.

7. It is relatively easier to administer an essay type test.

8. It takes relatively lesser time to mark an essay type test.

9. Guessing is eliminated to some extent.

10. The students cannot guess the answer because they have to supply it.

11. They give examinees freedom to respond within broad limits.

12. They can measure divergent thinking.

13. They require less time for typing, duplicating or printing. They can be written on the blackboard also if the number of questions and students is not very large.

14. It is more economical to use essay type tests than objective tests.

15. They can measure complex learning outcomes which cannot be measured by other means.

16. They stress integration and application of thinking and problem solving skills.

17. They can be used as an instrument for measuring and improving expression skills and language of the examinees.

18. They are more helpful in evaluating the quality of the teaching process.

19. Students focus on learning broad concepts and articulating relationships, comparing and contrasting.

20. They set better standards of professional ethics for teachers because they require more time in assessing and scoring.

21. They provide less scope for the use of unfair means.

Limitations/Demerits of Essay Type Tests

1. They generally stress the lengthy enumeration of memorised facts.

2. They have limited content validity because only a sample of questions can be asked in an essay type test.

3. They are difficult to score objectively because the examinees have wide freedom of expression.

4. There is the lack of consistency in judgements even among competent examiners.

5. They have 'halo' effect which implies that the examiner's judgement in evaluating one characteristic is influenced by another characteristic. A well behaved student on account of his behaviour may get more marks.

6. They have 'question to question carry effect'. A student who gives the best answer in the beginning of the answer book is likely to get more marks in the subsequent question and *vice versa.*

7. They have 'examinee to examinee to carry effect' which means that a particular student may get marks not only on the basis of what he was written but also on the basis of the answer of the previous student.

8. The examiners may be influenced by the language of the examinees. The quality of handwriting of the examinees may also influence the examiner. The length of the answer rather than the depth of the content may also influence marking.

9. Some examiners are too liberal in marking and some too strict.

10. Sometimes it is said that the 'mood' of the examiner also influence marking. Immediate happy events in the family or the job may motivate the examiner to be more generous. A quarrel in the family may lead to the award of low marks.

11. Essay type of tests may not provide a true picture of the comprehension level of the examinee. Some students cram answers and write the same in the examination and get good marks.

12. They are time consuming both for the examiner and the examinee.

13. The speed of writing may influence the performance of the students. Students who are slow in writing may not be able to provide answers to all the questions in the limited time table allotted for the paper. This results in low scores although the students may be knowing the correct answers of all questions.

Suggestions for the Essay Type Tests

As Coffman (1971) has pointed out, "Essay examinations are still widely used in spite of more than a half century of criticism by specialists in educational measurement and evaluation."

There is no doubt that inspite of their limitations, the essay type questions have come to stay and are being extensively used. It is, therefore, very essential that all possible efforts are to improve them so that the desired results are achieved to the maximum. Suggestions for improved essay type tests are categorised under the following two heads:

1. Suggestions for constructing a good essay type test.
2. Suggestions for scoring essay type tests.

Suggestions for Constructing a Good Essay Type Test

(i) The test constructor or the paper setter as he is commonly called should prepare ideal answers to all the questions given in the essay type test. It becomes all the more essential when different examiners are required to examine the answer books. This step is needed to ensure two things:

(a) The approximate time required to complete the paper and

(b) To provide uniformity to marking by different examiners.

(ii) The expected length of the answer of each question should be indicated on the paper.

(iii) While preparing questions, it should be kept in mind that the maximum subject matter content is covered.

(iv) There should be no overall choice in the question paper. Choice should be given for each question or it should be sectionwise.

(v) Questions should be such as they require the examinees to show a reasonable command over the essential knowledge of the subject matter being evaluated.

(vi) Questions should be so worded that all the examinees interpret them in the same as the examiner wants.

(vii) It is sometimes advocated that questions requiring opinion should not be asked as in case of different opinion by an examinee from that of the examiner, an examinee may suffer.

(viii) Questions should be very explicit so that the examinee may know the intention of the examiner in asking the question and accordingly he may give the answer.

(ix) The examiner should clearly indicate the weight of each part of the question so that the examinees may determine the time to be devoted to each part of the question.

(x) The number of questions may be large and the expected answers within reasonable limits.

(xi) The use of essay type questions should be restricted to those learning outcomes which cannot be measured by objective type items so satisfactorily.

(xii) Reasonable amount of time should be allowed to ensure that the essay type test does not become a test of speed in writing. It should be a power test rather than a speed test.

(xiii) It should be a balanced paper in the sense that it includes different types of questions: essay type, short answer and very short answer type.

(xiv) It should include a variety of questions to assess abilities like knowledge, understanding, analysis, synthesis and application.

(xv) The questions should not be too general, vague and comprehensive. They should define the task for the candidate and indicate clearly the scope of the answer.

(xvi) A large number of short and more specific questions requiring short or limited answers should find a prominent place in the paper and be preferred to a few long and general questions.

(xvii) The time allowed for the examinations should be carefully considered in relation to the amount of writing required on the part of the students. The examinations should be so timed that the students are usefully engaged for the whole duration.

(xviii) The questions may be arranged in order of difficulty, *i.e.*, from the easier to the more difficult.

(xix) Clear instructions to the students regarding the number of questions to be attempted, marks given to each question, or part thereof, and marks reserved for any special purpose, such as diagrams, neatness, etc., may be given in the beginning of the question paper.

(xx) As far as possible, equal marks may be allotted to each question.

(xxi) Question paper may be reviewed before it is handed over to the person concerned. Quite a few points may strike the paper setter on this second reading. A paper setter should safeguard his reputation as a setter by taking all the care that is possible at the beginning.

Suggestions for Scoring Essay Type Questions

1. The examiner should prepare a scoring guide for sub-examiners which may contain an outline for the ideal answer.
2. Normally no weightage should be given to hand-writing, spelling and better language in papers other than language ones.
3. When any weightage is given to any aspect in a language paper, it should be clearly indicated in the paper.
4. The identity of the examinee should be kept secret from the examiner so that 'halo effect' does not affect scoring.
5. The examiner should go through a sampling of the answer books of the examinees before he actually starts marking the answer books so that he may have a general idea of the quality of the answers.
6. It is sometimes suggested that a particular question of all the examinees should be evaluated at one time. Then the second question of all the examinees and so on. The present practice of scoring all questions of one examinee may be abolished.
7. To avoid fatigue, only a reasonable number of answer books should be marked in one setting by an examiner.
8. There should be consistency in assessment.

Measures for Tackling the Problem of Memorisation

1. Identification of instructional objectives of the subject matter or topic in question.
2. Giving proportionate weightage to each of the instructional objectives in the framing of the question paper.
3. Framing questions testing different objectives equivalent to the weightage given to each.

Measures for Tackling the Element of Subjectivity

Preparing a policy statement of the question paper by the examining agency and passing it onto the paper setter. The policy statement may cover the following aspects:

(a) Weightage to major areas of content.
(b) Weightage to objectives of each area of content.
(c) Weightage to different forms of questions *i.e.* essay, short answer and objective type.
(d) Weightage to differnt forms of objective type questions.
(e) Elimination of overall options.
(f) Providing options to individual question or within a part of the question paper. Options should be comparable in respect of objective to be tested, content area covered, form, difficulty level, expected time for answering it, etc.
(g) Wording questions specifically so as to delimit the scope and length of the answer.
(h) Preparation of a scoring key and a marking scheme.

Steps to overcome the Issue of Poor Coverage of the Contents

(i) Giving proportionate weightage to the major area of content.
(ii) Including increasing number of short-answer and objective type tests for covering as large an area of content.
(iii) Eliminating overall options in the question paper.

Steps to Overcome Administrative Problems

1. Appointment of those persons as paper setters who are well-versed with the concept and techniques of evaluation.

2. Moderation/reviewing of the question paper so as to ensure that no question is out of syllabus and also to ensure the balanced nature of the questions.

3. Introduction of mechanised process of results.

4. Introduction of a system of grading in place of giving marks.

MARKING SCHEME

With a view to minimise subjectivity in marking answer scripts, a marking scheme must be prepared and circulated to all the examiners. According to C.B.S.E (1991), a good marking scheme should have the following highlights.

1. It is a three column statement showing serial number of questions, their expected outline answers and the marks allotted to each value point under them.

2. In respect of long answer questions or essay type questions the expected outline answers should:

(*a*) be complete and cover all possible or major areas as demanded by the questions.

(*b*) clearly indicate each expected point or the parts under the outlined major areas.

(*c*) provide direction as to whether all points will count towards a complete or correct answer or a set of points will be adequate enough for full credit. If so, it be clearly reflected.

(*d*) indicate marks for each expected point. Marks so distributed over expected points or their sets should be equal to the total marks assigned for a question.

3. In respect of short answer questions a complete answer may be provided with its break ups wherever necessary alongwith the break up of marks.

4. Out of total marks assigned for a question, each point so enumerated may be assigned marks according to their significance in the answer.

5. In some solutions, apart from the content other qualities of answer may also matter significantly, particularly in long answer or essay type questions. There could be logical approach, coherence, lucidity of expression, the style of presentation etc., some marks may also be set apart for such overall qualities of answer which cannot be usually covered in enumeration of the content points.

6. The scheme of marking needs to be comprehensive enough not to leave any points unexpected and thus should provide clear guidelines in respect of the break up of marks over different points or parts of the answer.

7. If a question entails some other points beyond one's expectation a provision may also be made to take them into account and suitably reward them. This may need redistribution of marks within a question at the level of Head Examiners.

Short-Answer Type Test

Meaning. In a simple language it may be stated that a short-answer type test is between an essay type test and an objective test. Here we mention a few definitions given by experts to have a comprehensive view.

Anthony J. Nitku in his book, *Educational Tests and Measurement* (1983) states, "Short-answer items require the examinee to respond to the item with a word, short phrase, number or a symbol."

Robert L. Ebel and David A. Frisbee in their publication, *Essentials of Educational Measurement* (1986) write, "A short-answer test item aims to test knowledge by asking examinees to supply a word, phrase, or number that answers a question or complete a sentence."

Norman E. Granland in, *Measurement and Evaluation* (1985) observes, "The short-answer item that can be answered by a word, phrase, number a symbol."

K. D. Hoppkins, J.C. Stanley and B.R. Hopkins in their book, *Educational and Psychological Measurement and Evaluation* (1990) write, "The short-answer test is an objective test in which each item is in the form of a direct question, a stimulus word or phrase, a specific direction, a specific problem or an incomplete statement or question. The response must be supplied by the examinee rather than merely identified from a list of suggested answers supplied by the teacher."

William Wiersma and Stephen G. Jurs in their book, *Educational Measurement and Testing* (1990) provide this definition, "Short-answer items are considered objective items in that the correct response can be secured objectively. That is, preferably there is a single correct answer so that equally important scores would agree on the correctness of a response."

Merits of Short-Answers Tests

1. It is easy to construct them as they measure only simple learning outcomes.
2. They are very useful for the recall of simple memorised facts and figures.
3. They are useful to test the lowest level of cognitive taxonomy i.e., knowledge of terminology, classification etc.
4. A large area of subject matter can be covered by the inclusion of a large number of short-answer questions.
5. Marking is relatively objective as compared with essay type of questions.
6. There is very little scope for the influence of handwriting and spelling etc. on marking.

Limitations and Shortcomings

1. They are not suitable for measuring complex learning outcomes.
2. They are not suitable for judging the power of analysing and reasoning of the students.

Suggestions for Improving Short-Answer Tests

1. The intended answer should be thought first and then an appropriate question formed.
2. Questions should not be picked up exactly from the textbook.
3. Sufficient number of short-answer questions should be asked to cover the content.
4. A direct question is more desirable than an incomplete sentence.
5. Language of the question should be simple.
6. A scoring key should be prepared.
7. The number of words the answer should contain must be specified.

2.3. NEW TYPE OR OBJECTIVE TESTS

The traditional system or examination or the essay type of examination has come under heavy fire. Students denounce it because of its heavy strain; the parents criticise it because of its injurious effect on the physical and mental health of the children; the teachers complain because of its harmful effect on school work; the practical psychologist speaks ill of it because of its unreliability and invalidity and the educational theorist attacks it because it lacks definiteness in aim and purpose.

To mitigate some of the evils of the essay type examinations, objective tests seem to be very useful. Modern educationists lay much stress on this type of tests to supplement the traditional type of tests.

Objective tests are of a large variety. However, only seven or eight types of objective tests are commonly used.

Definition and Meaning

R.L. Ebel and D.A. Frisbie (1986) define an objective test as "one that can be provided with a simple predetermined test of correct answers so that objective opinion or judgement in the scoring procedure is eliminated."

Lou M. Carey (1988) defines an objective test as "objective test items require students to work or select a correct or best answer. These items are called objective because they can be scored more objectively than any other type of item used to measure students' performance... selected response items include alternative response, matching, keyed and multiple choice items."

Gilbert Sex (1989) regards a test objective if "it has a clear and unambiguous scoring criteria. Because multiple choice and true-false tests can usually be scored objectively, they are sometimes referred to as objective test.

W. Wiersma and S.G. Jurs (1990) state, "Objective items are items that can be objectively scored, items on which persons select a response from a list of options."

ALTERNATE-RESPONSE TYPE TEST ITEM

Definition and Meaning

In the words of A. J. Nikto (1983), "A true-false item consists of a statement or proposition which the examinee must judge and mark as either ture or false."

According to N.E. Gronlund (1985), "The alternative response test item consists of a declarative statement that the pupil is asked to mark true or false, right or wrong, correct or incorrect, yes or no, fact or opinion, agree or disagree and the like. In each case there are only two possible answers. Because the true-false option is the most common, this item type is most frequently referred to as the true-false item."

Hopkins, K.D., Stanley J.C. and Hopkins B.R. (1990) observe, "The true-false test, a form that is very popular with classroom teachers has been the object of more criticism than any other form of objective test."

In the alternate-response test, out of two responses only one is correct. A student chooses one of the two responses and judges the truth or otherwise of the statement. Some of the common variations of the alternate-response tests are:

(a) True-False *(b)* Yes-No *(c)* Right-Wrong *(d)* Correct-Incorrect.

Examples:

(i) Lord Buddha was born before Jesus Christ. True/False

(ii) The Aryans built beautiful temples. Right/Wrong

(iii) The Vedas are the religious books of the Hindus. Yes/No.

(iv) Kanishka was a great writer. Correct/Incorrect

Merits of Alternate-response Test Items

1. It is easy to construct them.
2. They are capable of sampling very quickly a wide range of the subject-matter.
3. They are more suitable for young children who have poor vocabulary.
4. They are more reliable per unit of testing time.
5. They can be scored objectively.
6. They can be scored quickly.
7. They are adaptable to most content areas.
8. They are easy to construct.
9. They are time-savers because they allow for frequent testing.
10. They can measure the higher mental processes of understanding, application and interpretation.
11. They provide a simple and direct means for measuring the outcomes of formal instruction.

Limitations

1. Generally they emphasise rote memorization.
2. The examinees are not required to apply principles to new situations.
3. Several facts are not entirely true or entirely false. They, therefore, cannot be measured through these items. These tests do not admit the possibility of intermediary position.
4. Since there are only two choices, they allow a high degree of guessing.
5. They are largely limited to learning outcomes in the knowledge domain.
6. They expose students to error which is psychologically not desirable.
7. They may motivate the students to study and accept only oversimplified statements of factual details.
8. These can be attempted even by those who know nothing of the subject matter.

Writing Good True-False Items

1. Be sure that the item as written can be classified unequivocally as either true or false.

2. Avoid ambiguous and indefinite terms of degree or amount *e.g.* frequently, greatly etc.

3. Avoid the use of negative statements and particularly double negatives.

4. As a rule, limit true-false statements to a single idea.

5. Keep true and false statements approximately equal in length.

6. Employ a random occurrence of true and false statements to avoid giving irrelevant clues.

7. Avoid double negative statements.

8. The direction regading the answers should be very clear.

9. Long and complex statements should not be used because they measure reading comprehension also and which may not be the objective of the examiner.

10. Each statement should be unequivocally true or false. It should not be partly true or partly false.

11. Such true and false items should be constructed as they measure important instructional objectives.

12. The item should be expressed clearly and concisely.

MATCHING TYPE TEST ITEM

Definition and Meaning

A. N. Nitko (1983): A matching exercise presents the pupil with a list of premises, a list of responses and a set of directions for matching the elements of these two tests."

N.E. Gronlund (1985): "The matching exercise consists of two parallel columns with each word, number or symbol in one column being matched to a word, a sentence or phrase in the other column. The items in the column for which a match is sought are called premises and the items in the column from which the selection is made are called responses."

R.L. Ebel and D.A. Frisbie (1986): "Matching test items occur in clusters composed of a list of premises, a list of responses and directions for matching the two. In many clusters the distinction between premises and responses is simply in the names given to them. The two lists can be interchanged without difficulty."

L.M. Corey (1988): "Matching items are another popular selected response format. These items require students to match information in two columns. Items in the left hand column are called premises and those in the right hand column are called responses. Students are required to locate the correct response for each premise."

Hopkins K. D., Stanley J.C. and Hopkins, B.R. (1990): "A matching exercise typically consists of two parallel columns, with each word, number or symbol in one column being matched to a word, sentence or phrase in the other column. The items in the column for which a match is sought are called premises and the items in the column from which the selection is made are called responses."

W. Wiersma and S.G. Jurs (1990): "An item consisting of a two-column format—premises and responses that requires the student to take a correspondence between the two."

There are several varieties of matching tests. In the traditional format, a matching test consists of two columns. The examinee is required to make some sort of association between each premise and each response in the two columns. He pairs the corresponding elements and records his answers.

Example: Under column A, names of certain books are given and under column B, names of certain authors are given. Write down the names of right authors under column C.

A	B	C
Bhagvad Gita	Kalidasa	
Indica	Ashvagosha	
Buddha Charitam	Lord Krishna	
Ragu Vansam	Kalhan	
Raj Tarangini	Megasthenese	

Merits of matching tests. 1. Many questions can be asked in a limited time because they require little reading time.

2. Reliability of the test increases as they afford us an opportunity to have a large sampling of the content.

3. Scoring is comparatively easier.

4. Matching tests can be constructed relatively easily and quickly.

5. There is less scope for guessing as compared with true-false tests.

6. A good deal of space can be saved.

7. Pupils usually have less reading to do.

Limitations of matching tests. 1. They are not well adapted to testing for the acquisition of knowledge or understanding of and ability to use relatively complete interpretative ideas.

2. They may encourage serial memorisation rather than association

if sufficient care is not taken in their construction.

3. It is at times difficult to get clusters of questions that are sufficiently similar so that a common set of responses can be used.

4. Generally they provide clues.

Guidelines for constructing matching tests. 1. Keep each list relatively short — 12 as the maximum.

2. Each matching test should consist of homogeneous items.

3. Avoid an equal number of premises and responses. Have one or two more responses than premises. This will minimise guessing.

4. All items of the test should be on the same page.

5. Do not mix statements or responses highly dissimilar in character.

6. Avoid using matching test for testing small units of the subject matter.

MULTIPLE CHOICE TYPE TEST ITEM

Definition and Meaning

According to N.E. Gronlund (1985), "A multiple choice item consists of a problem and a list of suggested solutions. The problem may be stated as a direct question or an incomplete statement and is called the stem of the item. The text of suggested solutions may include words, numbers, symbols, or phrases and are called alternatives (also called choices or options). The pupil is typically requested to read the stem and the list of alternatives and to select the one correct or best alternative."

In the words of R.L. Ebel and D.A. Frisbie (1986), "A multiple choice item has two parts: the stem consisting of a direct question or an incomplete statement and two or more options consisting of answers ons or completion of the statement."

(1989) observes, "Multiple-choice items consist of two a stem and number of options, or alternatives. The stem is a question o statement that is an vered or completed by one of the alternatives. All incorrect or I appropriate alternatives are called distractors or foils and the student's task is to select the correct or best alternative from all the options."

A multiple item consists of two parts:

1. The 'stem' which contains the problem.
2. Options or Responses i.e. list of suggested answers.

The stem may be stated as a direct question or an incomplete statement.

The incorrect responses are often called 'distractors' and the correct responses as the 'key'.

From the list of responses provided the student selects the one that is correct or the best.

Forms of Multiple Type Test

(a) The correct answer form. It contains three or more choices but only one of them is correct.

(b) The best answer form. One or more or all choices may be correct but one of them is the best answer. The examinee is required to select the best one.

(c) The multiple response form. The correct answer may consist of more than one choices and the examinee is asked to identify all those which are correct.

(d) The incomplete statement form. The stem is incomplete and can be completed by the correct choice. The examinee is asked to select the correct one.

(e) The substitution form. The word outlined in the stem is to be substituted by the correct response. Responses are given and the examinee is asked to select the one which can substitute the desired word.

(f) The combined response form. The choices are different phrases or sentences of a paragraph. The examinee is required to correct order of the phrases or sentences.

Examples. Certain alternatives are given against every statement. Put tick mark against the correct ones.

Stem: 1. **Question Variety.** Which of the following invented the telephone?

Responses or options: (a) Bell *(b)* Morse *(c)* Edison *(d)* Faraday.

Stem: 2. **Incomplete Variety.** The telephone was invented by

Responses: (a) Morse (b) Bell (c) Edison *(d)* Faraday.

Other examples: (1) Kalidasa was a statesman/ dramatist/warrior

(2) Hieun Tsang was a Buddhist/Hindu/Muslim.

3. **One Correct Answer Type:** A multiple choice type question may be in the correct answer form.

For example: Put a cross against the correct answer.

Mahatma Buddha went into forests because:

(i) he was asked by his father to do so.

(ii) he wanted to find out the truth.

(iii) he wanted to become a seer.

(iv) he was tired of his family life.

Merits of Multiple Choice Test Items

1. They can measure cognitive levels better than true-false items because examinees do not score for merely knowing whether the statement is true or false but for knowing which is the correct answer.

2. They can measure from the most elementary knowledge level to the most complex level, understanding and judgement and ability to solve problems.

3. A substantial amount of subject matter can be tested because the examinees do not require much time for writing the answer.

4. They are objective in scoring because the key for the correct answer is prepared alongwith the test.

5. They reduce the effect of guessing because there are three or four choices.

6. Their format is helpful in item analysis to find out the area of weakness of the examinees.

7. These can be written in several forms which provides opportunities for measuring different kinds of thinking.

8. They can be easily adopted for machine scoring.

Limitations

1. They do not permit the examinees to express their own views.
2. They cannot measure attitudes or motor skills.
3. It is difficult to find four choices for each item out of which three may be plausible incorrect answers.
4. They cannot evaluate the ability to organise and present ideas.
5. They require more time to construct.
6. They check only limited knowledge.
7. Element of guess work is not entirely eliminated.

Writing Good Multiple-Choice Question

1. Be sure the stem of the item clearly formulates a problem. The stem implies the portion that contains the question or problem. It should be worded in such a way that the student clearly understands what problem or question is being asked before he reads the answer choices.

Example: Where is the Taj Mahal located?

A. Delhi B. Agra C. Calcutta D. Fatehpur Sikri

2. Include as much of the item as possible in the stem and keep options as short as possible.

3. Include in the stem only the material required to make the problem clear and specific.

4. Use the negative sparingly in the stem of an item.

5. Use novel material in formulating problems to measure understanding or ability to apply principles.

6. Be sure that there is one and only one correct or clearly best answer.

7. Be sure no unintentional clues to the correct answer are given.

8. Use the option 'none of these' or 'none of the above' only when the keyed answer can be classified unequivocally as right or wrong.

9. Avoid the use of 'all of these' in the typical multiple choice item.

10. The stem should consist of a statement that contains a verb.

11. Repetition of words in the options should be avoided.

12. Unfamiliar and difficult symbols and vocabulary should be avoided.

13. There should be only one correct or best answer in every item.

14. Questions and sentences should be kept as short as possible.

15. As far as possible, direct question form should be used.

16. Arrangement for the answers to be written in the right hand margin should be made.

SOME EXAMPLES OF VARIOUS FORMS

Simple Recall Test. Write in one word the answer of the following:

(a) What is the per capita income in India?

(b) What is the per capita income in the U.K.?

(c) What is the exchange value of the Indian rupee in terms of the dollar?

Best Answer Test. Put Tick (√) mark against the best answer.

(*a*) Alexander did not proceed further because

(i) he did not know the route.

(ii) his forces refused to go further.

(iii) he was defeated by some king.

Completion Test. Fill in the blank by appropriate word(s) in the following:

(i) Only hardwork can.....good result.

(ii) You should refrain.....doing undesirable things.

Classification Test. In each line, underline the word that does not belong there.

Example: Harbour, trade, exports, import, mountains.

(a) Tulsidas, Kabir, Surdas, Ashoka.

(b) Calcutta, Madras, Bombay, Delhi.

(c) Cat, horse, cow, tree.

Merits of Objective Type Tests

Percival Symonds discuss merits of objective type tests as under.

First Advantage. "The new type examinations are more objective in their scoring, since the responses of pupils are controlled, and since there can be no doubt as to the correctness or incorrectness of their responses."

They are free from the personal factor of the teacher. The mood of the examiner in no way affects scoring. Each question which is asked has only one possible answer. 'Contrast the achievements of Mahmud Ghaznavi with Mohd. Gori' is a legitimate thought-provoking assignment in the essay type of examination, but there is a great scope for a variability in marking.

Second Advantage. "They may be very comprehensive and can be made to cover a great deal more material than the old type of examination. Since the pupil does very little writing, he can devote his time to thought and can thereby answer a great many questions than when he has to write his answers out at length."

Chance element is very predominant in the essay type of examination. Only a limited number of questions are set out of the wide field that has been covered. It is not uncommon to find students preparing fifteen or twenty questions in a subject and securing very high marks and students preparing forty questions but failing miserably. How does it happen and how could it be avoided? The answer is very simple. This happens simply because the number of questions set in the paper is so small that quite a major portion of the course covered remains untested. On the other hand, a large number of questions which are set in a new type of test eliminate the element of chance and cover a wide field of course.

Third Advantage. "They are very easy to score as compared with the older type of examination. Notwithstanding the fact that the tests are more comprehensive, they may be scored in less time and with less labour. This itself is a sufficient reason to make them attractive to all teachers."

A key of the various questions may be prepared and then anybody can mark the question papers.

Fourth Advantage. "Pupils like them. There is no question as to the accuracy of marks they receive. There is no chance for the teacher to show favouritism or personal bias. The pupils, relieved of much writing, find these tests less tiring."

The pupils like the new type of tests because they think that marking will be fair and judicious. Even the students may be asked to mark the papers themselves if key is supplied to them. The general complaints of leniency of marking in one case and hard marking in the other are eliminated.

Fifth Advantage. "They are more educative for the pupils. Let your pupils score their own tests directly after they take them by exchanging papers with their neighbours. It is then that their interest is at white heat. After the papers have been scored, the questions may be discussed. The pupils readily see where they need further study."

Besides the five advantages given by Symonds, we might add some more.

Sixth Advantage. The new type of tests discourage cramming and encourage thinking, observation and scrutiny.

Seventh Advantage. They are more reliable. Same results will be secured whoever may be the examiner. An essay type of question paper cannot give the same results if it is given to different examiners.

Eighth Advantage. Objective tests can be standardised by applying beforehand to a large number of students of the same age group before the actual examination. On the basis of the results of these standardised tests, the authorities of a particular institution can compare the standard of their institution with other institutions of the same area.

Limitations. Symonds gives two main limitations of new-type examinations.

First Limitation. "The pupil does not have an opportunity to show his ability to organise his thought. He has nothing to do except check over the truth and falsity of statements or fill in the missing words or incomplete sentences. Pupils miss the valuable experience of making comparisons, giving explanations or giving definitions. They are not asked to summarize the material or to make applications of principles, and, of course, these are valuable abilities which we do not want to neglect."

Second Limitation. "These new types of examinations are not diagnostic in that they do not tell where the pupil's reasoning process goes wrong or where he stops reasoning altogether and starts guessing."

Besides, the following limitations may also be noted:

Third Limitation. It is commonly said that new type of tests fail to check cramming. Once the test is standardised the teachers will coach their pupils on the test, thus making it very little helpful. There is every possibility that 'keys' or 'guides' to these tests may find their way in the market. General knowledge guides have already made their entry in the market.

Fourth Limitation. It is often argued that use of new types of tests is very expensive.

Fifth Limitation. Like the essay type of tests, these also fail to test the character-building aspects.

Principles of Construction of New Type of Tests

1. Prepare a list of all the topics falling within the scope of the examination.
2. Keep in view the most significant items in each topic.
3. Every item should have only one correct answer.
4. Easy questions should come first and then moderate and in the end the most difficult ones.
5. Include different types of objective tests, i.e., Recognition, Recall etc.
6. Frame definite and brief questions.
7. Give reasonable time to the students to answer the paper. Ruch suggests the following time:

   Recall Type—4 to 8 items per minute.

   True-False type—10 to 15 items per minute.
8. Give clear instructions.

CHARACTERISTICS AND COMPARISON OF THE OLD AND NEW-TYPE TESTS

1. The number of questions in the essay or old type of tests is very small, generally five or six questions in the paper.

   There are a large number of questions in the new type tests.
2. Answers required in the old type of tests are large.

   The answers are so short in the objective tests as can be written in a word or two or at the most in a sentence.
3. Essay type questions are usually broad, general and indefinite. The examinees are at a loss to know how much they will have to write as answers.

   Objective questions are specific, narrow and definite.
4. In essay-type tests personal factors like bias, temperament, whims, etc., of the examiner influence marking.

   Scoring becomes objective in the new type of tests.

5. In the answer of the essay test there is scope for partial credit. Answers may be partially wrong and right.

In the new tests, there is no provision for partial credit. Answers must either be right or wrong and hence full or no credit.

6. In the essay tests examinees have to devote a long time.

Questions can be answered in a short time in the new tests.

7. In the essay tests, questions are selected at random and the entire course is not covered. Some chapters or questions are completely ignored.

The entire course can be covered by comprehensive questions in new tests.

8. Essay tests put premium on expression. Students hardly find any time to think over the question.

New tests put premium on thinking.

9. Pupils having linguistic skill are at an advantage in the essay tests.

New tests are advantageous to the intellectually smart students.

10. It takes a short time to frame questions in the essay tests.

It takes a long time to frame questions in the new tests.

11. Students find it easier to prepare essay questions. They can safely omit many portions of the subject-matter in the essay tests.

Students have to devote a longer time to prepare as they have to go through the entire course for clear conceptions.

12. Essay tests are very suitable for testing composition, skills and knowledge of the subject.

New tests are not suitable for testing composition and skill as well as appreciation of the subject.

13. In the essay tests there is relatively less scope for 'guessing' questions. Students prepare themselves from 'Made Easy' books.

In the new type there is more scope for guessing answers.

14. Essay tests take a longer time in examining scripts.

Short answers take less time to examine scripts.

15. Printing cost is small in the case of essay tests.

Since there are many questions, printing is costly in the new tests.

16. Answer scripts cost much as answers are very lengthy in the case of essay tests.

Answers being very short and usually can be written on the question paper itself, this makes the answer scripts less costly.

17. There is less scope for adopting unfair means by the students in the examination hall in the case of essay type questions.

There is enough scope for adopting unfair means in the new tests.

Summing Up

The Indispensable Nature of Essay Tests. Essay-type tests govern a wide field of learning-thinking and reasoning, study skills and work habits. Essay tests measure the functional aspects or the application of knowledge. We can evaluate through them the logical reasoning power of the students. The essay tests help us to test the power of expression, verbal facility, use of vocabulary and style of writing. They also help us to evaluate the capacity of the students to organise knowledge, to evaluate thoughts and to create new thoughts. The objective tests fail to evaluate these powers.

The Indispensable Nature of New Tests. The new type tests cover the subjects as fully as possible and they offer better and more adequate facilities of sampling knowledge than the traditional type. They also help the teacher to find out where teaching has been defective or learning inadequate. Scoring becomes very objective. Personal preference of the examiners do not matter and subjective factor is completely eliminated and this increases reliability of the tests. In these respects tests have an upper hand over the essay type tests.

Combination of Essay and Objective Tests. From the above it is quite evident that both type of tests are complimentary to each other. The shortcomings of the essay type of tests are overcome by the new type of tests and *vice versa.* Hence a judicious combination of the two is advisable. Essay type examinations or new type tests do not serve our purpose either singly or independently. A happy combination of these two, therefore, is the first essential to be achieved in the reform of the traditional examination system. We may have the following merits of the combination of the two types:

1. The objective tests will make evaluation more reliable by eliminating the subjective element inherent in essay type tests.

2. Objective tests will cover a wide area of the subject-matter and fill up the gaps left by the essay type tests.

3. The two types of tests measure two different faculties, the essay type tests measure the functional aspect and the objective tests measure the theoretical aspect.

4. The scores obtained in the two tests can be correlated and thus

the degree of reliability found. This will also check subjectivity.

Limitations of the Two. These tests are tests of knowledge. The various behaviour patterns remain untested. These fail to test the totality of the child's development of personality and character.

These tests should be supplemented by other tests like personality tests, intelligence tests etc. The views of the teachers who guide the students and watch them should be given their due place.

2.4. ORAL EXAMINATIONS

The historical origin of oral examinations is lost in antiquity. Oral examinations date back to the beginning of human language. Oral examinations seems to have been in vogue during the Vedic period. Rote learning was the chief method of acquiring knowledge and oral method as the method of examination. Socrates (4th century B.C.) used this method. Until the availability of inexpensive pencils and paper tests after the middle of the 19th century in the U.S.A., oral examinations were a standard practice in American schools. Similar was the case in other countries.

Concept of oral examinations. Oral examination is a face-to-face question-answer activity between the examiner and the examinee. The examiner asks questions and the examinee attempts to answer them. The examiner probes into with further questions or accepts the answer. Finally, the examiner judges the quality of the answers and grades the examinee accordingly. Sometimes more than one examiner participate in the panel.

Forms of Oral Examinations

Important forms of oral examinations are—interview, viva-voce, quiz contest, panel discussion or group discussion. Each of these can be used as a teaching-learning technique and as an evaluation technique.

Objectives of Oral Examinations

1. To probe into pupil's insight that directs and focuses on pupil's skill in appreciating and critically analysing a topic.
2. To identify and analyse pupil's presence of mind as exposed through oral questioning.
3. To evaluate pupil's cognitive, affective and psychomotor abilities.
4. To evaluate pupil's spontaneity and mannerism.

5. To evaluate the soundness of the knowledge acquired by the student through various forms of questions.

6. To upgrade the teaching-learning process by shifting the emphasis from mere transmission of information to the development of abilities that would help the pupil in his later life.

7. To boost pupil's analytical and divergent approach to problem's that need critical enquiry.

8. To supplement the information obtained through other evaluation techniques.

9. To diagnose pupil's limitations and weaknesses and to take remedial action.

Limitations of oral Examinations

1. They tend to be subjective.
2. They are usually unplanned.
3. There may not be uniformity in maintaining the standards by the examiner or examiners.
4. Gradually the sampling of the pupil's knowledge and understanding becomes very narrow.
5. Oral examinations are time consuming.
6. Students who are shy in nature are likely to be adversely affected by the presence of the examiner.
7. Oral examinations may work to the advantage of the highly articulate students.
8. Lot of pressure may be put on the examiner to award more marks.
9. Oral examinations may open doors of prejudice, partiality and discrimination.
10. Several influences may work to lower the validity of the oral examinations.
11. Oral examinations are very expensive.

Issues Involved in Oral Examinations

A national seminar conducted by the NCERT in September 1987 deliberated upon the following eleven issues.

1. In what form can oral examination be introduced as an appropriate strategy for reforming examination and implication thereof?
2. What should be the thrust and focus of oral examination in the present context of examination reform?
3. What weightage may be given to oral examination in the
   (*a*) internal and/or
   (*b*) external examinations?

4. School stages at which oral examinations will be the most appropriate technique?

5. Subjects for which oral examinations will be the most appropriate technique?

6. Administrative and organisational infrastructure required for introducing oral examination at school stage as a part of internal and/external examinations.

7. If introduced, in what respects teachers are to be oriented?

8. In what form questions for oral examinations may be set and type of questions to be developed for use in oral examinations?

9. With the introduction of oral examination what shift can be visualised in the teaching-learning process and what will be the implications of this shift on (*a*) teachers; (*b*) students; (*c*) method of teaching; and the courses of studies?

10. How evaluation of responses under oral examination should be done and what weightage should be given to some of the inputs such as presentation of the subjects; insight over subject matter and showing the presence of mind in answering questions?

11. How to achieve higher reliability in marking the responses obtained through oral examinations?

Issuewise Recommendations

1. Qualitative improvement in education is possible only when examination evaluates different skills—written, oral and practical of the pupils. Writing as well as speech are the two important vehicles of communication and both of them should be developed in a balanced manner and evaluated appropriately.

2. Oral examination should be introduced in the school system as a supplementary/complimentary tool to the written test. All pupils would need to be exposed to this system by use of varied forms of oral examinations in order to allow pupils to speak what he/she thinks or knows.

3. Subjectwise specific areas which are most amenable to evaluation through different forms of oral examination need to be identified. Oral examination may be resorted to in those areas for measuring pupil achievement and diagnosing difficulties on the spot.

4. One of the terms/periodical assessments in schools should be through oral examinations with proportionate weightage in the composite marking scheme.

5. The present written examinations are bookish and mainly operate at reproduction level. The main thrust of oral examinations should be on the ready responsiveness of the pupil. Pupil should have facility in communication to say what one thinks. Thus, the focus should be on grasping, observation and imagination.

6. The main focus should be to develop the ability to express without fear or faltering. The examinee should be able to marshall the relevant points without wavering.

7. The following aspects in languages could be emphasised in evaluating oral expression:

(*i*) Pronunciation (to speek with correct articulation, pronunciation and intonation).

(*ii*) Grammatical correctness (to speak grammatically correct language).

(*iii*) Vocabulary and usage (to make an appropriate use of words, phrases and idioms).

(*iv*) Thought content and its organisation (to express rich and relevant thought content in an organised way).

(*v*) Delivery (to speak fluently).

(*vi*) Manners and gestures (to use appropriate physical gestures for what is being expressed in speech).

(*vii*) Effect (to speak effectively).

8. Listening and reading aspeets have also to be focussed in the oral examinations.

9. In non-language subjects, a pupil's quickness in supplying correct and precise answers, clarity of thought, presence of mind, etc. are to be focussed in oral testing.

10. In view of the fact that NPE 1986 envisages Continuous Comprehensive Evaluation at all stages of education inclusive of the school stage, it would be in the fitness of things to make a judicious allocation of weightage to oral tests in both internal and external examinations. Maximum possible weightage would be given to oral examinations during the first two years of schooling and as we go up the educational ladder, it could be reduced gradually in subsequent stages.

11. The following suggestive weightage to oral examinations varying from subject to subject but having greater emphasis in language subjects was recommended by the national level seminar.

Classes	I and II	50% to 60%
Classes	III to V	30% to 40%

Classes	VI to VIII	20% to 30%
Classes	IX to X	15% to 25%
Classes	XI & XII	10% to 20%

5% weightage in practical examination through oral questioning.

12. Oral examinations should be introduced from Class I and should form an integral part of evaluation till the end of class XII.

13. Languages are highly amenable to the use of oral examination as a technique of evaluation. It can also be made an effective tool of evaluation in other subjects such as Social Sciences, Physical Sciences, Mathematics and Fine Arts, etc.

14. Oral examinations in languages and non-language subjects could be suitably distributed among the periodical assessments in schools.

15. Under the present circumstances, introduction of oral examination at public examinations may not be feasible but its utility for the external examination could not be ruled out after a successful field trial. Attempts may be initiated to introduce oral examination at public examination also on an experimental basis in a phased manner.

16. Contact points in each state may be established and with the help of willing teachers, oral examinations should be tried out on an experimental basis as a measurement device.

17. Question banks suited to this examination should be developed on all topics in languages and non-language subjects most amenable to oral examinations.

18. The teachers should be given comprehensive orientation in the conceptual, structural and operational aspects of oral examinations. Indepth orientation programmes for teachers making them well acquainted with the pattern of examinations may help in bringing about objectivity in the marking of responses.

19. The role of a teacher is important in organising oral examinations. He should be a man of integrity, and very fair in conducting oral examinations and giving grades to the pupil on the spot. A teacher should develop an attitude of self-reliance and self-sufficiency among students.

20. One of the purposes of oral examination will be probing the pupils from the known to the unknown and thus questions testing narration, intensive discussion, etc. should be framed for questioning pupils. However, rigidity should be avoided. Questions set for oral examinations should be at once thrilling and searching in order to assess the pupil's personality from different angles. Depending upon responses, challanging questions should be designed on the spot.

21. Specific areas in each subject which are most amenable to oral testing need to be identified for developing behavioural outcomes for framing questions.

22. A wide variety of situations should be used keeping in view the linguistic aspects to be evaluated in languages. The non-standardised, informal and criterion referenced procedures have to be chosen to elicit worthwhile responses from pupils.

23. Situations for narration, description and explanation should be selected in testing in oral expression. Some of the situations could be *(i)* Conversation-to establish a rapport with the examinee; *(ii)* Short speech; and *(iii)* Answers to questions to test an examinee's skills in oral expression.

24. The techniques used are *(i)* reading aloud; picture story card; *(ii)* prepared questions; *(iii)* conversation on a prepared topic; *(iv)* general conversation; *(v)* general questions; *(vi)* questions on pictures and role playing, etc. The themes which are usually chosen would be from day-to-day life experiences, immediate environment, current affairs and hobbies and interests of pupils. All these techniques need not to be used in the same oral examination. A suitable technique may be selected for use in oral examination.

25. The oral examinations in non-language subjects provide an opportunity to know precisely what the examinee actually knows on a particular content area about which he may be questioned. Such oral questions should be divided into three categories and should be written on well designed sample tickets.

Category I Consisting of general type of questions at recall level;
Category II Consisting of specific type of questions at understanding level; and
Category III Consisting of questions for judging the merit and excellence of the pupils at application level.

All questions in each category should be possible of equal difficulty level and discriminative power. Oral questions selected for the purpose on sample tickets should be prepared by experts. Atleast one question from each category should be put to an examinee. Maximum 6-8 minutes may be spent on each pupil.

26. Sample questions may also be prepared and circulated to all schools. However, the pattern of questions for oral examinations may be decided by the concerned schools. In language and non-language subjects, the following type of questions alongwith the suggestive precentages should be developed so that uniformity and objectivity are maintained.

		Non-language	*Languages*
(*a*)	Objective type questions	20%	10%
(*b*)	Very short answer questions	20%	10%
(*c*)	Short answer questions	30%	30%
(*d*)	Expression testing questions	30%	50%

27. Oral test can be either structured or unstructured. The structured oral test is divided into three above mentioned categories. An oral test whether structured or unstructured requires careful planning in order to have valid and reliable assessment. All the steps of test construction are to be followed in oral examinations also. These steps are indentifying behavioural outcomes to be assessed, specific aspects and content of oral expression to be evaluated, specifying test items to be used, laying down instructions for the examiners conducting the test, preparing guidelines for assessing the pupil's performance, etc.

28. The teachers should be fully aware of the proper technicalities of oral examinations. The teachers will have to be oriented in respect of the following:

(*a*) Propriety and importance of oral examinations.
(*b*) Areas (subject content) of the oral parts.
(*c*) Exposure to the methodology and pedagogy of skills to be developed through the strategy of the oral examinations.
(*d*) Acquaintance with the nature of questions for oral examinations.
(*e*) Expression skills-linguistic contents and ideational content.

Teaching learning progress should provide ample scope for students' oral work and performance in oral examination.

29. The following points will act as guidelines in achieving higher reliability in this examination.

(*i*) Higher reliability in the oral examination will primarily depend upon the integrity of the teacher. If possible more than one examiner should be appointed to conduct the examination.
(*ii*) Systematisation of oral examination, examiners' experience, training, alertness, tact, awareness and knowledge will reduce biases in marking the responses.
(*iii*) Adequate sampling of content and specifications will help in achieving higher reliability. Subjectwise blue-prints need to be developed for framing a variety of questions.
(*iv*) Weightages to different aspects to be evaluated should be determined in advance in order to have uniformity in marking by the same examiner or by more than one examiner.

(*v*) Recording of marks awarded by each examiner should, for the sake of confidentially, be made in a separate sheet and the final award should be made out of the average of these marks to ensure higher reliability.

Researchable Areas on Oral Examinations

The national seminar suggested that the following research studies can be carried out by the investigators in the area of oral examinations. The studies may be conducted at the National/State/Region/District levels and also at Pre-Primary/Primary/Upper Primary/Secondary/Higher Secondary/Graduate/Post Graduate/Doctoral levels with required modifications in the titles.

The list consists of a few suggested topics and it may be noted that it is not exhaustive.

1. A comparative study of performance of students in oral and written examinations.
2. A comparative study of the reliability of the scores obtained by the students on oral and written examinations.
3. A comparative study of the achievement scores of the students on oral examination and essay type of examination/short answer type of examination/objective type of examination.
4. A critical study of historical perspective of oral examinations.
5. A study of oral examinations in pre-independent and post-independent eras.
6. Attitude of teachers towards oral examination as a strategy of examination reform.
7. Attitude of parents/students/teachers towards oral examination — A study.
8. A comparative study of the achievement of students in oral and written tests in languages/non-language subjects.
9. Oral examination as an instrument of diagnostic evaluation.
10. A survey of the present status of oral examinations.
11. A comparative study of the status of oral examinations in the schools managed by Govt./Private/Voluntary organisations.
12. A study of oral examinations in traditional schools.
13. A comparative study of oral examinations in India and U.S.S.R U.K./U.S.A.
14. An enquiry into the opinion of teachers about the weightage to be given to oral examination in the internal and external examinations.

15. Administrative, organisational and academic aspects responsible for the success or failure of oral examinations.
16. A study of organisational climate conductive to/hindering the oral examinations.
17. Relative merits and demerits of different scoring procedures adopted in the valuation of oral examinations.
18. Identification of competencies of teachers for conducting oral examinations skillfully.
19. A comparative study of the effect of oral and written examinations on cognitive/affective domains.
20. A study of strategies to achieve higher reliability in scoring the responses obtained through oral examinations.
21. A comparative study of the effectiveness of oral and open book/closed book/practical examination.
22. A study of suitability of the type of questions for oral examinations.
23. A study of suitability of the situations for oral examinations.
24. A study of feasibility of oral examinations at external examinations.
25. A comparative study of suitability of oral examinations at different levels of education (pre-primary/primary/secondary/higher secondary/graduate/post-graduate stages).
26. A study of the effect of home work and no home work on oral examinations.
27. The effect of certain psycho-social variables (e.g. personality, achievement, motivation, anxiety, etc.) verbal fluency, memory on oral examination results.
28. An enquiry into the opinions of teachers about the types of questions in question bank for oral examinations.
29. A survey of specific learning outcomes expected through oral examinations.
30. A study of various socio-psychological factors amenable to oral examinations.
31. An investigation into administrative implications for introducing oral examinations.
32. A study of the role of examiners and examinees in oral examinations.
33. Impact of oral examinations on learning process of students.
34. An investigation of factors motivating to introduce oral examinations.

35. A study of establishment reliability and validity of oral examinations.
36. Relative merits and demerits of different situations used in oral examinations.
37. A comparative study of time and cost benefit analysis of oral and written examinations.
38. A critical study of the conduct of oral examinations in schools with special reference to the given syllabus in few states.
39. A study of test types and assessment principles used in oral examinations in foreign languages at 16+ in the U.K. and lessons to be drawn for India.
40. A study of utility of language laboratory for improving oral communication skills and expressions.
41. A comparative study of the aspects of evaluation of oral expression in mother tongue and foreign language.
42. Personality of the teachers and its impact on oral examinations of their students.
43. Effectiveness of oral examinations with or without the use of computer in evaluation.
44. A study of factors relating to teachers, students, parents and public responsible for the misuse of oral examinations.
45. A comparative study of the awareness of the uses of oral examinations among administrators, academicians and students.
46. A comparative study of oral examinations as an instrument for manifestation of pupil's creative and aesthetic consciousness.
47. An enquiry into the opinions of teachers about the importance of oral examination for evaluation of pupils' creative and aesthetic excellence.

Chapter 3

Reforms in Examinations

3.1. SOURCES OF ERROR AND THEIR RECTIFICATION

V. Natarajan in his monograph *Sources of Error in Examinations* (1979) lists the following sources of error in examinations and their rectification.

1. Error due to subjectivity in marking (Mark-Remark error).
2. Error due to biased sampling of topics.
3. Error due to biased sampling of abilities.
4. Error due to choice of questions.
5. Error due to arbitrary time limits.
6. Error due to examination conditions.
7. Error due to assumption in addition of marks.

1. **Subjectivity in Marking: (Mark-remark error)**

(*a*) Variation in marks between different markers on the same occasion.

(*b*) Variation in marks between different occasions for the same marker.

This error can be minimised by:

1. designing marking schemes agreed to by all examiners.
2. adjusting marks on the basis of different markers' norms (scaling).
3. using objective type tests.

2. **Error in sampling of topics:** Any test or examination (especially at the end of a semester or a year) is only a sample of an infinite number of questions that can be asked. The sample must be representative. If the sampling is defective, variations in scores will result.

This is minimised by (*a*) sampling the subject through a table of specifications or Blue print; (*b*) testing the *whole subject*—usually by objective type tests.

3. **Error in sampling abilities:** Attainment tests if not carefully prepared may be reduced to tests of memory. Variations in observed scores will result if other abilities are tested without reference to teacher and student preparation. To minimise this source of error.

(a) the test is to be prepared to an agreed list of abilities reflected in teaching/learning.

(b) a variety of types of test items must be used.

4. **Error due to allowing a choice of questions:** A test/exam. may permit students to choose *five* out of *ten*. There are different ways of choosing five out of ten questions. This variation in the test produces a spurious variation in test scores.

Minimised by allowing no choice—a typical procedure with objective type tests.

Minimised by allowing internal choice only in essay questions and not in objective type and short answer.

5. **Error due to arbitrary time limits:** In measuring *attainment*, introduction of an arbitrary time limit produces a variation in observed scores which are not related to a variation in student attainment.

Minimised by: (*a*) pretesting to find the optimum time required to finish the paper—a typical procedure with objective type tests.

(*b*) prevalidating questions/items with the help of subject experts/evaluation experts.

6. **Error due to examination conditions:** Spurious variations in observed scores are caused by random and systematic variations in examination conditions and student expectation. This is minimised by standardising examination conditions and instructions and giving candidates a clear idea of what is required of them.

7. **Error due to assumption in addition of marks:** In adding individual marks to obtain a final test score for one student, it is assumed that the marks are of equal weight and are scalar. These are invariably false and lead to variation in observed scores. This is minimised by:

(1) ensuring that each mark is equal in weight (mark/item in an objective test);

(2) ensuring that each mark awarded correlates with the final test score to give linear vector addition.

3.2. GOALS AND ISSUES IN EXAMINATION REFORMS

According to Srivastava, Singh and Anand (1978) the main targets of a programme of examination reform ought to be:

- To so reform examinations that they help in improving the quality and standards of education instead of acting as a hindrance to it.
- To make examinations accurate, in order that the decisions made on the basis of their results are valid, reliable and dependable.
- To de-emphasise the over-importance attached to examinations by society.
- To reduce the undue strain of examinations (on children, parents and society) the unreliable results of which frequently cause frustration.
- To eliminate mis-education which is the cause of a multitude of maladies like indiscipline, malpractices and fall in moral standards among students.
- To ultimately eliminate public examinations of the present type and replace them by continuous and comprehensive evaluation done by schools.
- To conduct common examinations for the comparison and improvement of educational standards in schools rather than merely for grading, classification and certification of students.
- To institute selection tests for admission to institutes of higher education or professional training.
- To dispense with the traditional practice of declaring students as pass or fail and to introduce a system of giving an examinee a clearance certificate for an examination as a whole or in parts.
- To discourage the use of external examinations as a screening device for every purpose.
- To replace marks by grades and to give students an opportunity to improve their grades by appearing at subsequent examinations.
- To discontinue the use of raw scores in the determination of a student's results and to institute appropriate scaling procedures.
- To try the experiment of having autonomous schools which give their own certificates.
- To create a social climate against malpractices in examinations.

The Specific Genesis

The genesis of the reform programme ought to be the

evaluation of pupil growth, in both academic and non-academic areas (like interests, attitudes, personal and social qualities, participation in co-curricular activities, etc.) rather than the academic areas alone.

The reckoning year-round continuous evaluation for judging students' real merits to replace dependence on arbitrary end-of-the-year evaluation.

elimination of chance element and subjectivity from examinations as far as possible through appropriate academic and administrative measures.

de-emphasis of memorization, by incorporating testing situations demanding, understanding, application of knowledge, and critical thinking.

use of a variety of techniques and tools of evaluation.

functional and meaningful declaration of results for meaningful use by students, teachers and parents.

wide uses of test results for purposes of guidance, academic prediction and curriculum evaluation.

improvement of the mechanics of conducting examinations.

introduction of concommitant changes in curriculum, instructional materials and instructional methodology.

Issues Involved in Examination Reforms

Broadly speaking issues involved in examination reforms may be classified under the following two heads:

1. Academic; 2. Administrative.

Academic. Academic issues may be listed as under :

(*i*) Improving questions by making them specific in terms of objectives, content and language.

(*ii*) Improving question papers by giving proportionate weightage to objectives, content areas, different forms of questions, limiting options, etc.

(*iii*) Improving scoring procedures by developing marking scheme with suitable instructions to examiners.

(*iv*) Improving interpretations of scores by providing data like state average, percentile rank and other derived scores.

(*v*) Extending the techniques of evaluation to oral examinations, observation, check lists, rating scales, etc.

(*vi*) Bringing about concomitant changes in curriculum, textbooks, instructional materials and methods.

Administrative. These include:

(*a*) Framing suitable rules for admission to an examination.

(*b*) Appointing paper setters and moderates with appropriate qualifications.

(*c*) Developing scientific mechanism of conducting examinations.

(*d*) Appointing superintendents and invigilators for the smooth conduct of examinations.

(*e*) Deploying suitable machinery for checking unfair means.

(*f*) Evolving suitable methods regarding declaration of results, their publications and issues of certificates.

(*g*) Developing scientific mechanism for re-evaluation of answer books.

3.3. HURDLES IN THE EXAMINATION REFORM

1. Resistance to change by the State Departments of Education and Boards of Secondary Education, as it involves a reorganisation of the administrative machinery and procedures.

2. Resistance to change by the teachers, because of their unpreparedness for taking up the challenges of the new system and because it requires some additional work.

3. Resistance to change by the students, as examinations after the reform are likely to become valid and reliable and would require more precise and regular study.

4. Resistance to change by unscrupulous elements, as malpractices are likely to lose ground in improved examinations.

5. Resistance to change by vested interests, which are desirous of maintaining the *status quo* which protects their powerful positions and even financial gain.

6. Lack of suitable sample evaluation material for providing illustrations of the nature of the reform envisaged.

7. Paucity of financial support, as the reform measures in examinations will necessarily be more expensive than the traditional ones.

8. Inadequate training of the teachers for keeping up with the changed situation.

3.4. FUNCTIONAL DIMENSIONS OF EXAMINATION REFORM

Efforts to achieve the above goals of the programme may be made through the reform of both the *external public examinations and evaluation in schools.* Multidimensional improvements required in each of the above two areas of evaluation are described below.

Written Examinations. The reform of written examinations will mainly consist of improvements in the questions, question papers, scoring procedures, mechanics of conducting examination.

Practical Examinations. The reform of practical examinations will mainly cover the evaluation of both the product and process of performance.

Oral Examinations. The reform of oral examinations will mainly consist of the comprehensive coverage of various linguistic abilities and the institution of effective measures for objective scoring.

Observational and other Techniques. The inclusion of observational and other techniques in the programme will be particularly necessitated by the incorporation of the non-scholastic aspects of pupil growth (like interests, attitudes, personal and social qualitites etc.) in the comprehensive programme of evaluation in schools. These techniques will further need to be adapted to the resources and needs of our institutions.

Activities in the Programme

The activities which need to be taken up centrally for pursuing the programme could be classified under the following categories:

1. Research studies and investigations of a functional nature in the area of
   - (*a*) External examination
   - (*b*) Evaluation in schools
2. Training and extension programmes for training leaders in educational evaluation at the
   - (*a*) State level
   - (*b*) National level
   - (*c*) International level
3. Development of literature and evaluation material
   - (*i*) Conceptual literature in educational evaluation
   - (*ii*) Sampling evaluation materials in
     - (a) scholastic areas of pupil growth
     - (b) non-scholastic areas of pupil growth

(*iii*) Periodical publications
(*a*) Examination abstracts
(*b*) Evaluation Newsletter
(*iv*) Report of conference, seminars and workshops.

4. Test library (Item bank)
(*a*) Test items
(*b*) Unit tests
(*c*) Full tests

5. Coordination of state level examination reform programmes undertaken by various reform agencies.

6. Clearning house functions in regard to information at
(*i*) State level,
(*ii*) National level,
(*iii*) International level.

7. Consultative services to the collaborating educational agencies in regard to the development and implementation of their programmes.

Among the chief state agencies collaborating in these programmes are:

(*i*) State Boards of Secondary Education
(*ii*) State Departments of Education
(*iii*) District Institutes of Education and Training
(*iv*) State Evaluation Units
(*v*) State Institutes of Education
(*vi*) State Councils of Educational Research and Training
(*vii*) Colleges of Education
(*viii*) University Departments of Education.

3.5. QUESTION PAPERS

Need and Significance of Question Papers

A variety of techniques and tools have been designed to measure the performance of the learners. These tools have their specific uses although they play complimentary role to each other. Among the important devices are—written tests, oral tests, practical tests, project work, interviews, checklists, questionnaires etc. In internal and external examinations, question papers for written examinations, practical examinations for practice oriented subjects and oral examinations, where verbal expression is most significant, stand out prominently.

A question paper includes a variety of questions. A question is a task given to the student to organise or reorganise his information, ideas, opinions, beliefs, etc. which provide an evidence of the things learnt by the student. It is, therefore, very important to give a careful attention to the structuring of questions and their assemblage into a question paper.

Each type of question—essay type or long answer question, short answer and objective type—has a specific role to play.

Main Characteristics of a Good Essay Question Paper

1. It gives appropriate weightage to instructional objectives.
2. It provides balanced weightage to the content units.
3. It accords due weightage to all types of questions.
4. It includes internal options in place of external options.
5. It does not show large variations in the difficult levels of questions.
6. The language of questions is easy, simple and understandable.
7. All questions in the question paper are well worded and measure desired objectives.
8. It contains questions relevant to content.
9. Its arrangements of questions is suitable.
10. It has a proper format.
11. There is complete compatability between English and Hindi and regional language versions of the question paper.
12. It contains clear general instructions to students.
13. It indicates the scope and credit for each question.
14. Normally a question paper should have 15% easy, 70% average and 15% difficult questions.

Main Characteristics of a Good Question (All forms of Questions)

1. It measures a single specific objective or a learning outcome. An essay type question may test cognitive domain (knowledge, understanding or application).
2. It samples a significant content area.
3. It states the subject matter in a correct and accurate way.
4. It is within the scope of the syllabus or textbook.
5. Its form is suitable.
6. It is set at the desired level of difficulty.
7. It is well within the comprehension of the pupils.
8. It can be attempted within a reasonable length of time.
9. It provides an appropriate testing situation.
10. It sets the task pinpointing almost a definite answer.
11. It is worded in a clear, precise, simple and unambiguous language.

12. It excludes difficult and unfamiliar word or term.
13. It is concise enough and avoids unnecessary reading load.
14. It is free from superfluous words or terms.
15. It communicates the intent of the item written effectively.
16. It is translated into regional languages without distorting sentence structure and its import.
17. It uses the most appropriate directional word (e.g. classify, enumerate list etc.).

3.6. MODERATION OF EXAMINATION RESULTS

Moderation of examination results plays a pivotal role in determining the results. In common parlance moderation has come to mean the award of some grace marks to a candidate in an examination. The marginal and boderline cases usually come under the purview of moderation. Moderation ensures that candidates with the minimum total do not fail on account of a small deficit in one or two subjects. It is generally assumed that such a procedure is necessary to help those students who fail but are better than those who pass.

A Monograph on Moderation of Examination Results (1986) explains the rationale of moderation as follows.

Most public examining bodies measure a candidate's performance by assigning marks to his answer script. Let us take a hypothetical situation. There is a paper of three hours carrying 100 marks and the examiners are asked to award numerical scores while assessing the answer scripts. The marks can range from 0 to 100. This is called the 101 point scale because, including 0, there are in all 101 units of measurement. The implicit meaning of having such 101 steps in marking is that a candidate who scores 46 marks is superior to one who scores 45 marks and so on. Such an inference could be correct if the marks are a "true" mark. Unfortunately, the marks given by an examiner is a "raw" mark, subject to several uncertainties (listed below) and needs moderation.

(*i*) The first uncertainty is about the thing to be measured i.e. the candidates' performance. This is invariably ill-defined. The marks may be a measure of the candidate's ability or knowledge or memory or intelligence or power of expression or a combination of one or more of these characteristics. No one really knows what the examiner has really measured. Therefore, the marks assigned may vary from one examiner to another.

(*ii*) The second uncertainty arises from the assumption that there is a true mark for each script. Such true marks can only be assigned by an ideal examiner who does not exist. The actual examiner at best, makes only an estimate of the true marks. This estimate is therefore, a 'raw' mark and is subject to considerable error. For some typical papers set at universities, experts have carried out a statistical analysis. Such a statistical analysis has shown that when an examiner assigns marks to a script, there is a 50 percent chance that his error is greater than 5 percent. This means that when a candidate is awarded raw marks of 41, his/her true marks may be either above 46 or below 36 in 50 percent of the cases. Under these circumstances, the 101 point scale where candidates are distinguished in steps of one mark loses all its significance.

(*iii*) It is quite often that certain marks are laid down as the minimum required for passing, for getting a second class or for getting a first class. This arbitrary minimum is meaningless. It may result in candidates who do not deserve a pass passing and *vice-versa.*

(*iv*) Unfortunately, the public in our country has not been kept informed of the inaccuracies of our current marking scheme. Many of them take the 'raw' marks assigned by an examiner as 'true' marks and use it for a variety of purposes. Thus a candidate getting 60 percent marks is regarded as superior to a candidate getting 59.9 percent marks. This causes a considerable measure of frustration.

(*v*) It will be seen from the above that the 101 point scale of marking together with the arbitrary minimum for a first, second or pass class is scientifically unsound. It was adopted when our scientific knowledge about examinations was inadequate. Even with improved information becoming available about the reliability of such marks, we still continue giving marks on the 101 point scale and furnishing these marks to the student. The unscientific nature of this work and the harm if does to the student is really unbearable.

3.7. SCALING QF EXAMINATION RESULTS

The seminar on scaling of examination result conducted by the NCERT from 22 to 26 December 1979 at the NIE Campus, New Delhi made the following recommendations.

1. In the public examinations conducted at Secondary and Higher Secondary stages a large number of candidates appear for the examination. The examining bodies have to appoint quite a large number of examiners, sometimes the number running into four figures, to examine a paper thus resulting in inter-examiner variability in the case of essay type and short answer type questions where objectivity in scoring poses real problems. It has been proved by empirical researches that answers to such questions are marked differently by different examiners and sometimes this variation is quite large, in spite of the best efforts by way of providing scoring keys and other detailed instructions.

Therefore, to reduce the adverse effect of inter-examiner variability it is recommended that scaling of marks be resorted to by the Boards' decisions regarding which may be taken in individual cases after proper study and deliberation.

As a pre-requisite to scaling it is necessary that the lots of answer-scripts to be sent to different examiners in a subject are properly randomized to reduce institutional bias, if any. Boards, where central evaluation is being done, can do it easily with a little extra effort. In other Boards also randomisation may be tried.

Research studies for minimizing inter-examiner variability may be taken up by all the Boards in order to avoid hardship to candidate due to eratic examiners. The NCERT may initiate and design these studies and then act as a clearing house for dissemination of research findings to all concerned.

2. For an efficient introduction of scaling the use of computer is a basic necessity. Some examining agencies are already using computer for processing their results as also for conducting research studies. They can easily utilize this facility for the scaling of marks as well other agencies conducting large scale examinations.

3. Since scaling requires ready availability of expert guidance at the various stages of processing of examination it is highly desirable that the Boards may set up academic wings manned by personnel with requisite qualification. Wherever such wings are already existing they should be suitably strengthened if necessary.

4. To make scaling of marks acceptable to public it is necessary to highlight its advantage in a layman's language as against the vagaries or raw marks.

5. (*a*) The concept of cut-off scores at pass and other division levels is also closely linked with the issue of scaling of marks. At present some sort of *ad hoc* adjustments is resorted to boost pass percentages,

particularly when the result in a particular paper or subject is very low. In these cases grace marks are added. Sometimes they are fixed and at others proportionate. This, in a way, makes the cut-off scores floating. It will be better if the whole issue of floating or fixed cut-off scores is reconsidered in the context of scaling. Also empirical criteria may be developed regarding floating as compared to *ad hoc* adjustments here or there.

(*b*) In orděr to avoid the J-effect at various cut off points it will be desirable that no intimation be sent to examiners regarding these. They may be required to mark the answer-scripts as objectively as possible according to the scoring key and other instructions provided. Decisions regarding the cut-off scores may be taken after looking into the distributions in a more-scientific manner than is being done at present.

6. Scaling will be useful when the question papers contain essay and short answer type questions. In case a question-paper is of a mixed type, i.e., it contains questions belonging to all the types *viz.* essay, short-answer and objective, then the objective type questions should form a separate part of the paper and need not be subjected to any scaling.

It is also useful between the question papers including the Practical in the same subject where marks of these question papers are to be added. It is again useful when marks obtained in different subjects are to be equalled. This problem may be analysed in two parts:

(*i*) Compulsory subjects
(*ii*) Optional subjects.

As regards scaling between marks obtained in compulsory subjects there is no theoretical objection and it should be done. But in case of optional subjects scaling should be done between subjects which belong to one group of subjects *e.g.*, Humanities, Sciences, Commerce, etc. between group scaling may be at times misleading.

7. For scaling between languages there will be two situations. In the first situation where languages are considered as subjects, scaling may be done as between any two other subjects. In the second situation where different languages are used as media of examination it would be better to appoint examiners who know two languages, one of which is a common language known to all examiners. Distributions of common media marks may be used to scaling marks for other media. But a general caution shall be necessary. In case the number of candidates using a particular language is less than 50, scaling is to be avoided.

8. (*a*) Situations, where the practice of internal and external

assessment is in vogue and two are added to get an aggregate, the ranks in the internal assessment given by the class teacher may be converted into numerical marks on the basis of external examination results. For a group of candidates, the candidate getting first rank in internal assessment may be assigned the marks obtained by the first ranker of that group in external assessment. This pertains to scaling within institution. A precaution will have to be taken regarding ranks by avoiding 'tied' ranks.

(*b*) For 'between institutions' scaling of internal assessment, it is felt that scaling according to external assessment criterion will defeat the very purpose of internal assessment. As such no scaling may be done.

9. There are different methods of scaling, the easiest one being the linear transformation using 'mean' and 'standard deviation'. What these 'means' and 'standard deviations' should be is a question of detail. If all scaling is done to common mean of say 50 and a common standard deviation of 15, then many problems arising out of use of different means and standard deviations (determined on the basis of the total population in a paper) shall be sorted out automatically. Of course, adjustment of relative weights (of paper and also subjects in the total curriculum) shall have to be kept in view.

10. As regards the question, whether scaling should be done for all examiners or some only is debatable. Again, the idea of two stage scaling may be considered which means that firstly, the Head Examiner may have a look at the assessment of the sub-examiners and if he finds that a particular sub-examiner is very stiff or very liberal be may make necessary adjustment in the scores as he deems fit and subsequently the marks may be scaled for the total group.

11. **Scaling between Boards.** It is recommended that the NCERT may take up studies in which information from organisations conducting All India Examinations may be obtained. These examinations may be for admissions or appointments. This information may be used to scale the marks allotted by different Boards. These scaling criteria (between Boards) may be revised from time to time.

12. **Scaling within Board for every Examination.** This shall prove useful to know any marked deviations from the general trends of results. If there are minor deviations scaling is not necessary. But in case the deviations are very marked it may become a must.

13. The NCERT and other agencies engaged in educational research as also the Boards of Secondary Education should initiate and undertake

various studies related to scaling of marks and disseminate this information for the benefit of all the examining agencies.

3.8. GRADES AND MARKS

The manner in which the results of an examination should be furnished has engaged the attention of experts all over the world. It appears that in a majority of the examinations in the advanced countries of the world, the trend is towards adopting what is called a five-point scale. In this technique, all the candidates who appear for the examination are grouped into five grades: grade 1 signifying the best and grade 5 the weakest of candidates. Grouping is also done in five grades.

In our country, the current practice in most of our Public Examinations is to measure the candidate's performance by assigning marks to an answer script. Suppose there is a paper of three hours carrying 100 marks. The examiners are asked to award numerical scores while assessing the answer scripts. The marks can range from 0 to 100. This is called the hundred and one point scale because including 0, there are in all 101 units measurement. The implicit meaning of having such 101 steps in marking is that a candidate who scores 46 is superior to one who scores 45 and so on.

It is generally believed that grading system is more rational than the marks system. In view of the element of subjectivity, marking system is considered to be inferior to the grading system.

A Monograph on Grading in Universities (1976) gives the following reasons in favour of grading over numerical marking.

1. Numerical marking provides a very inaccurate measurement for

(*a*) The standards of examiners differ widely. There is a standard error of measurement ranging from 5 to 20 marks in different subjects.

(*b*) Examiners, by indulging in evaluation rather than measurement, distort results by giving an unusually great number of 35 marks (when 35 is passing mark) and none at all of 34 and 33.

(*c*) Examiners in different subjects use different ranges. In some the full scale of 0 to 100 is used, while in many others, scales used are all different.

(*d*) Marks given by examiners are not scaled.

(*e*) Marks in different subjects are added up when they should not be. The most important of all these is that it is impossible to have comparability amongst different disciplines (even in different papers in the same discipline) with the result that there is a great irrationality in the choice of subjects by students. This does not reveal the actual aptitude of students but the ease with which high marks can be secured. Finally, everyone tends to take marks as absolute and attach a kind of arithmetic value judgement that is to say, if three students A, B and C score 58, 61, and 57, they think that 61 is more than 58 and 58 is more than 57. In reality if the S. Errors of measurement is taken as 5 marks, then the true marks of the student with 58 marks is either (58–5)=53. or (58+5)=63. For every 2 out of 3 cases, his true marks which will fall within the range of 53 to 63 includes all the three students marks. In a sound grading system, all these students are said to belong to the same group of achievement and given a letter grade. Here a single individual mark has no meaning but there is a range of marks to be replaced by a single letter grade.

A grading system ensures fulfilment of the following objective:

(*a*) Evaluation which is mainly judgement based on measurement is uniform if all the universities agree to adopt the 7 points scale grading system and establish relationship between various grades and their meaning in qualitative terms. It is possible also for teachers and examiners to do what is called 'direct grading' and this has been found to possess merits over the process of initial marking and conversion into grades.

(*b*) Comparability amongst various disciplines and within various subjects in a particular discipline is possible with the grading system. Top students in Mathematics (and those securing 95% and above) will be given a letter grade of 0 as also the top students of History (and those securing 58% and above). If students discover that an equally good student of Mathematics or History is likely to get a high grade (no matter what maximum marks they get) the choice of subjects will be rational and dependent more on their aptitude than on the fact that in some subjects getting a higher grade is easier than in others.

(*c*) If all universities adopt the same 7 points scale, then students can move from one university to another much more easily.

(*d*) Grading system takes the emphasis away from marks.

(*e*) Teachers employing many procedures for evaluating achievement (test, oral recitation, quiz, project work, lab/ practical work, assignments, tutorials, checklist, rating scales, etc.) will find that a grading system is much more meaningful and feasible than the marking system. It is recommended to various universities wanting to implement a 7-point scale grading system, that wherever possible, 'there shall be 'direct grading'. Direct grading requires a thorough understanding of the meaning of each letter category in terms of their quality and it is much more meaningful in the case of answers which are long. One of the guidelines that can be given, when randomization of scripts is adopted, is that for every randomized group, certain percentages can be thought of to constitute each letter grade.

O	Outstanding	3%
A	Very good	7%
B	Good	22%
C	Average	36%
D	Below Average	22%
E	Poor	7%
F	Very poor	3%

3.9. OPEN BOOK EXAMINATION SYSTEM

Concept of open book examination system. In the open book examination system students have the freedom to consult the textbooks, reference books and other reading material to answer questions set by examining agencies or the educational institutions. Of course, this can be done within the prescribed time.

Objectives of open book examination system. A brochure entitled *Open Book Examination System* (1982) lists the following general objectives of the open book examination system:

1. To reduce considerably if not remove altogether the emphasis laid on memory in the existing system.
2. To make the examination more comprehensive in nature by providing for testing of higher cognitive abilities.
3. To inculcate regular study habits among students.
4. To upgrade the teaching-learning process by shifting the emphasis from mere transmission of information to the development of abilities that would help the students in their later life.
5. To remove the 'fear psychosis' among students and help them develop positive attitudes towards examinations.
6. To rid the examination system of the several stresses and strains that afflict it at present.

Further it pointed out that the following abilities and skills can be acquired by the students through the open book examination system:

(*i*) Competency to consult reference books.
(*ii*) Development of self-study habits.
(*iii*) Development of the abilities of the examinees to marshall

(*iv*) Development of habits to spend more and more time in libraries and meditate on what they have read to encourage creative abilities.

(*v*) Development of the capacity to present relevant materials in a logical sequence.

(*vi*) Development of the ability of self-exploration and self-appreciation.

Advantages Claimed over Traditional System of Examination

1. The system is free from pre-examination tensions.

2. Copying and other malpractices would become unnecessary.

3. Bazari notes become irrelevant and as a consequence the racket in guide writing and publishing would become unprofitable.

4. The emphasis is shifted from memorising to the reviewing of the material and as much more well directed and varied efforts become necessary to meet the examination challenges which is not possible in the traditional closed book examination system.

Limitations. 1. The development of self-study habits may not be attained by this system. Rather the students may not have any incentive to study before the examination because of their access to reference books and other materials at the examination centres.

2. The concept of standard textbooks and reading material may vary from place to place and person to person.

3. In the context of growing number of students appearing in the examinations, it may be difficult to provide enough reading material for consultation.

4. The reduction of malpractices may not be achieved because of the possibility of consultation among students in the examination halls will be made easier.

5. The problem of training teachers to prepare students for this type of system and of preparing question papers poses serious difficulties.

Suggestions for the Implementation of the Open Book Examination System

1. The open book examination system should be tried out experimentally at an internal examination only.

2. To begin with open book system should be assigned a maximum of 20–25 % weightage.

3. In the beginning open book system may be introduced at the 10+2 stage.

4. Number of students in the classes should be controlled.

5. Adequate financial allocation should be made for the enrichment of libraries.

6. Question banks suited to this system should be developed in all subjects.

7. Related conceptual material on open book examination should be disseminated.

8. Reference material and teachers' handbooks should be prepared through workshops.

9. Indepth orientation programmes for teachers should be organised. These programmes should cover:

(*i*) Preparing objective based questions.

(*ii*) Methodology of developing library usage habits.

(*iii*) Paper setting and type of question to be set in the open book system.

(*iv*) System of evaluation of answer scripts in the open book examination.

10. Training students in the use of library material.

3.10. QUESTION BANKS

The question bank is a planned library of test items pooled through cooperative effort for the use of evaluators, teachers and students. It is an inbuilt feed-back mechanism for improvement of questions. A question bank serves a number of purposes. Questions from the question bank can be used by teachers at the pre-testing stage, for the development of a lesson and for revision purposes.

Questions from the question bank can be used for the measurement of the pupils' achievement. Questions can also be made use for diagnosis of the pupils' difficulties.

Question banks should be established in various subjects.

As for the location of question banks, these can be set up at the DIETS, Teacher Training Schools and Colleges, State Evaluation Units, Boards of Secondary Education, SCERTS and NCERT.

Questions for the question banks, as far as possible, should be prepared by practising teachers in workshops conducted by experts.

Enrichment of questions by updating, discarding, replacing, modifying and adding new questions should be a continuous process.

The Association of Indian Universities, New Delhi has prepared a Question Bank Series. The type of questions, objective type, short answer and long answer type that could be on a particular topic are included in the volumes. These are aids for teaching and preparing for examinations including the competitive and entrance tests. Question banking takes into account all the techniques of testing and evaluation. Each title contains anything between 2000 and 6000 items of varying degree. Question Banks are available in the following subjects.

Undergraduate Level

1. Mathematics
2. Physics
3. Chemistry
4. Zoology
5. Botany
6. History
7. Geography
8. Psychology
9. Educational Psychology
10. Economics
11. Commerce
12. Political Science
13. Foods & Nutrition
14. Plant Pathology
15. Soil Science
16. Banking & Accountancy
17. Sociology
18. English Languages & Literature
19. Physiology
20. Pharmacology
21. Automobile Engineering
22. Law of Contracts
23. Anatomy
24. Constitutional Law
25. Electrical Power System
26. Agronomy

Hindi Editions

27. Zoology (जन्तु विज्ञान)
28. Chemistry (रसायन शास्त्र)
29. History (इतिहास)

Post Graduate Level

30. Mathematics

3.11. MULTIPLE SETS OF QUESTION PAPERS

The multiple set of question paper scheme was introduced by the Central Board of Secondary Education, Delhi (CBSE), in the year 1992. There were four different sets of question papers in some selected subjects for Delhi schools only. In 1993, the Board changed the policy and conducted the examination with three sets of question papers in which about 70 percent of the questions were common but they shuffled in their order. The main objective of the scheme was to minimise malpractices in the examinations. During the conduct of examinations in March 1991, reports appeared in the press regarding incidents where parents scaled the compound walls of an examination centre to smuggle in copying material, sale of cyclostyled and photocopied answer sheets outside centres and use of public address system to dictate answer to the questions.

The CBSE claimed that with the introduction of multiple set of question paper scheme it was able to control copying. However, the introduction of this scheme has been described by the Division Bench of High Court, Delhi as arbitrary, unreasonable and having no rational relationship with the objective to be achieved, i.e. elimination of mass copying. The Bench observed that the CBSE had not obtained the views of concerned persons and organisations before introducing such a standard.

Regarding the educative value of multiple sets, Dr. B.M. Gupta of the NCERT in an article 'Educational Relevance of Multiple Sets' published in *Journal of Indian Education* (September 1993) has observed, "Examination results can make or mar the career of the students. The entire future of the students depends on how they fare in the Boards's examination. Hence the question papers are of critical importance to them and also to the parents, teachers, principals, schools and actually to the whole teaching-learning system. Therefore, the continuance/introduction of multiple sets of question papers need to be based on sound educational and academic reasonings supported by research studies. A research study should prove that all the multiple sets of question papers are 'equally capable' of measuring the academic achievement of the examinees. The argument that the multiple sets of question papers curb mass-copying may not work in the long run. It is felt that malpractices in examinations are more of a social, psychological and administrative nature rather than purely an academic and educational problem. Use of multiple sets of question papers for the eradication of the menace may not be the right medicine for the virus. The real problem calls for hard decisions, legal remedies, courage and conviction. Since the examination results are very much tied up with the physical, mental and career growth of the examinees, besides their social and psychological adjustments, it will be appropriate if such a research study is undertaken and the results of the study are made known to all. A public debate should be held before introducing the innovation. The assumption that the multiple sets of question papers eliminate or reduce malpractices in examinations also requires to be proved beyond doubt."

Chapter 4

Semester System and Internal Assessment (Examination)

4.1. SEMESTER SYSTEM

Meaning of the Word Semester. The *Shorter Oxford English Dictionary* gives the following meaning of the word semester.

"A period of term of six months, especially in German Universities and some United States' Colleges, the college half year."

It is thus clear that the semester signifies the division of academic year into two parts. Division of the academic year also implies that courses are designed to cover one semester (instead of a year) and that final examinations are held twice a year.

A Monogrpah on Semester System for Universities (1984) lists the following merits associated with the system:

(*a*) The quantities of content in various subjects would be proportioned suitably into semesters.

(*b*) This helps students to achieve their objectives in a better way.

(*c*) There is greater freedom to change the subjects and the combinations even in the middle of the course.

(*d*) There is flexibility to choose the number of courses in every semester between two and seven.

(*e*) Continuous assessment being an important component of semester system encourages the students to work systematically throughout the course.

(*f*) There is increased self reliance on the part of students in respect of schedule evaluation and performance improvement.

(*g*) Shortage of attendance in a subject is no bar to the student taking examinations in other subjects where attendance required is fulfilled.

(*h*) Continuous internal assessment with more emphasis on abilities that are not vested by a semester examination forms an integral part of the system.

(*i*) It is, therefore, necessary to keep internal assessment and external semester examination marks/grades separate.

(*j*) Students have the opportunity to discuss their answers in all accepted tools of internal evaluation. This adds to reliability.

(*k*) One of the components of internal assessment, namely periodical tests, prepares students continuously for the final examination, thereby eliminating the fear of the unknown.

(*l*) Semester system does include improved methods of assessing student performance in semester examination, making increased use of objective type testing.

(*m*) A Question Bank, if made available, will help in the effective implementation of semester system.

(*n*) In a semester system, there is increased rapport and relationship between teachers and students.

There are several other features which, though they are not necessary concomitants of the semester system, are often associated with it. Those of major importance are the "CREDIT SYSTEM", the system of "LETTER GRADES", greater reliance on home study, INTERNAL ASSESSMENT, and use of Question Bank, improved Methods of Assessment etc.

Credit

The Credit-System is basically a system for simplifying what has been called "academic book keeping". A student earns his diploma by accumulating a specified number of academic credits instead of attending for a specified number of years. Thus a part-time student may spread out his studies over several more years than normal, while a specially brilliant may occasionally take a heavier than normal load and shorten his education by a semester or so. A university usually prescribes that a certain minimum number of credits must be obtained in the student's main department. The distribution of the remaining credits may be unrestricted, or it may be restricted in accordance with any scheme which the university may desire. For example, one university may require that almost all of the non-departmental credits be taken in courses which the department considers supplementary or relevant to the main while another may want to burden students by requiring, in addition to the main, minimum of atleast six credits each in pure sciences, social sciences, humanities and modern language. It is thus evident that the credit system has the effect of adding considerably to the flexibility allowed by the semester organisation of the academic schedule.

The semester credit hour is defined as a unit for expressing quantitatively the content of a course at the level of higher education. The most widely accepted meaning of a credit is that a student earns one credit by attending one 50 minutes period of lecture class instructions and doing 2 to 3 hours of home study, each week throughout one semester (15–18 weeks). Thus the terms 'credit' and 'semester hours' are often used interchangeably. The credit system allows great flexibility in fitting course time to the particular subject taught. Most semester courses carry 2 to 4 credits each.

Credits do not always require a particular number of class periods. Since one hour of theory class is expected to be supplemented by 2 to 3 hours of home study, it is considered equivalent to three hours of laboratory practical work. Similarly, 2 or 3 credits per week may be allowed for a thesis which involves no class-attendance at all. A full time student making normal progress will complete 30 to 32 semester credit hours of course work in an academic year of 9 months. To obtain a bachelor's degree in a three year college, a student must normally accumulate 90–94 semester hours.

Another feature incidentally associated with the semester system is a greater reliance of home study. Since a great deal more can be covered in an hour of reading than in an hour of speech the lecturer does not expect to "cover the course" in his lecture and in fact the lectures often contain only supplementary material not available in books. The student is expected to read and study 300–600 pages every week of the semester (Except examination week). Thus a student in full time attendance is generally required to attend 15 or 16 hours of lecture classes/week which is supplemented by home study, and this amounts to 40 to 50 hours/week for an average student.

The main advantage of organising courses on the credit system is the flexibility it permits to students, intensively as also extensively to cover a wide range of subjects. The course can be adjusted to the needs and abilities of the individual students. The selection of a course is done with utmost care and in consultation with the adviser concerned. The adviser ensures that preparatory courses are taken in the first or second semester. It is also ensured that nearly 2/3rds of the course credits is from the subject in which the student intends to major at the end of the first two years of general education programme. The student is also allowed to offer some courses for which no credit may be given. Generally speaking a student is required to offer not less than 9 credit courses and not more than 16 credit courses in one semester.

Precautions to be taken before the Implementation of the Semester System

Teaching is a highly complex and sophisticated science requiring not only the knowledge of a particular discipline but also the ability to analyse, synthesise, evaluate, communicate, demonstrate, show application, draw analogies and finally promote learning in the class rooms, laboratories and field. While few individuals possess this facility without the benefit of training, it has been proved beyond doubt that good teachers can be made and are being made out of training: so, before the implementation of the semester system, teachers must undergo training for some period to understand the details regarding the semester system, acquire skills and competencies to adopt the system.

However, modern educators feel that good teaching is that which ensures effective learning. The premium must therefore be on effective learning, so before the implementation of the semester system students must be made to know some details about the semester system.

A rational and scientific semester system implementation has certain implications on Syllabus (Curriculum), Teaching methods, Evaluation methods etc.

The framing of the syllabus for semester system is not done by simply breaking the old traditional syllabus into two halves. The areas like content and ability have to be taken into consideration.

In terms of content. Content areas for the earlier semesters have to be lower order involving information; complex areas may be included for the later semesters.

In terms of ability. Similarly, the preliminary areas must deal with the simpler abilities, like comprehension and knowledge, while the later ones must deal with more complicated intellectual abilities like application, analysis, synthesis and evaluation. By and large, there must be a built-in continuity in respect of both content and abilities.

Teaching methods. The traditional method, i.e., lecturing must be given secondary importance and more number of hours have to be allotted for assignment, tutorial, discussion and project, laboratory work, home study because intellectual abilities of higher order like Application, Analysis, Synthesis, Evaluation and affective abilities like Interest, Motivation, Attitudes, Team work are all developed only by these methods.

One other important implication of semester system is that better and effective methods of student performance during and at the end of the semester are to be adopted. Internal continuous assessment for abilities and skills that are not tested by end semester examinations, must be given proper weightage and there should be increasing objectivity in the tools of evaluation.

Basic Psychological Principles for the Success of Semester System

1. Involvement of implementers in decision making and giving their views on various issues.
2. A consensus design of semester system must be evolved.
3. A proper training programme for teachers in semester system implementation is to be held.
4. Information must be passed onto teachers/students/parents/ administrators about semester system sufficiently in advance.
5. Implications of adopting a semester system on administrative practices, record keeping procedures etc. must be studied and prepared for.
6. Adequate preparation time must be allowed.
7. A few volunteers and other well established colleges must be allowed to experiment and evaluate.
8. A systematic 'system evaluation' must be instituted and results reported to people concerned.
9. Modifications and improvements are effected based on results of evaluation.

4.2. INTERNAL ASSESSMENT

A Monograph on 'Internal Assessment for Universities (1984) stress upon the following fundamentals of internal assessment.

1. Internal assessment is continuous periodic and internal. This means that assessment is done in relation to certain abilities and skills in certain

subject areas periodically and continuously. This has to be planned at the time of curriculum development, syllabus interpretation and clarifying objectives of learning. This is internal in the sense that the teacher/ instructor is to assess and no external agency comes in.

2. Internal assessment does not necessarily replace end examination. Internal assessment should not be taken as something to replace the end examination. Both have a part to play in the best planned evaluation systems. Very often the end examination is to be taken as a part of the internal assessment.

3. Internal assessment does not mean a few mid term examinations in place of a final examination.

4. Internal assessment demands that the outcomes of learning a particular subject, must be spelt out first and then there is the choice of suitable meaningful, valid and reliable evaluation tools to match these abilities and skills.

A few outcomes of learning are:

(*a*) Knowledge
(*b*) Comprehension — (translation, interpretation, manipulation, extrapolation)
(*c*) Application — (problem solving closed and open ended, new situations)
(*d*) Analysis
(*e*) Synthesis
(*f*) Evaluation
(*g*) Drawing, sketching skills
(*h*) Handling instruments
(*i*) Communication skills (reading, writing talking)
(*j*) Social skills: Team work, Leadership
(*k*) Personal — (Regularity, Hardwork, Inventiveness, Originality, Initiative).
(*i*) Interest
(*m*) Positive/Scientific Attitude
(*n*) Appreciation
(*o*) Creativity.

Some of the tools of evaluation suitable for measuring these outcomes, are given below:

1. Quiz announced.
2. Quiz unannounced.
3. Short duration objective type tests (10 to 15 minutes for periodical achievement of cognitive abilities).

4. Short answer/Problem solving (15 minutes to 30 minutes for periodical achievement of cognitive abilities).
5. Long answer essay (30 minutes to 60 minutes for periodical achievement of higher order cognitive abilities).
6. Class assignments/Tutorial (Once in a week for developing higher order abilites and checking on them).
7. Home assignments (Once in a week or fortnight to develop skill in producing drawings, sketches, essays, flow diagrams, charts, maps, illustration etc.).
8. Guided individual projects (Given twice in a semester or 4 times in an academic year to bring in new meaningful and relevant that world of work would offer in his/her subject).
9. Guided group projects are additional to (8) above to develop leadership qualities, teamwork discipline etc.
10. Lab./Field/Practical work (periodically to develop and assess practical skills in handling instruments, experimenting, reporting, concluding).
11. Observation (periodically (once in a fortnight) to assess personal qualities of regularity, hardwork, inventiveness, innovativeness, initiative, originality etc.).
12. Check lists/Rating scales (periodically once in a fortnight) to assess personal qualities of regularity, hardwork, inventiveness, initiative, originality etc.).
13. Rating scale for interest (3 times in a semester or 6 times in a year to rate his interest in the subject).
14. Rating scale for attitude (3 times in a semester or 6 times in a year to rate his attitude (positive and scientific in the subject).
15. Group Discussion (Once in a month to assess his originality, creativity, initiative, communication skills etc.).
16. Seminar (Once in a semester or twice in a year to develop, assess originality, creativity, discipline, communication skills, initiative).
17. Thesis/Dissertation (once in a year to develop critical thinking, analysis, synthesis, evaluation, performing skills, communication skills etc.).

5. The main purpose of introducing internal assessment is to integrate teaching and evaluation and to test those skills and abilities which cannot be tested through a written examination at the end of a course.

For this, teachers must identify the abilities/skills they want to develop in their students in their own subject areas and then allocate weightage to the selected abilities/skills. They are also to make a choice of method, design the schemes, taking into consideration the possible constraints of time, effort, finance and acceptability. Very low weightage must be given to simple recall of knowledge and information, in internal assessment.

6. The question of giving weightage to internal assessment and end examinations (external) is important. In a unitary university/autonomous college, this question does not arise since a design of internal assessment can be done including the end examination as a part of it. In an affilliating type of university, dealing with a good number of colleges, the question of fixing up weightage for internal assessment and end university examination exists and this can be tackled in one or the other of the ways:

(1) Internal assessment and external end university examination marks or grades can be shown separately. In as much as internal assessment is for abilities/skills that are not tested by end university examination, it is meaningless to add the two. At the same time, there can be an argument that unless, students see the importance of internal assessment in their final marks or grade, the motivation and interest for internal assessment will be lacking if not absent. If, however, grading system is adopted, internal and external can be shown separately.

(2) Some universities will still require a proportion of internal assessment marks to account for and be added to the external university examination marks. Various percentages have been adopted and are being adopted. While it will be difficult to say what percentage is ideal, it is worthwhile to quote the work of F.W. Starr "Combining internal and external for Education Courses". He tried all kinds of percentages and finally recommends a 50-50 for internal and external to correlate well with all other combinations.

In cases where the internal marks are added to external examination marks, there will be a tendency on the part of a few affiliated colleges to boost up their students' internal marks. Also the range of marks in internal will be low while the range of marks will be fairly high in external. It can be shown that the real weightage of internal to external will depend upon the relative ranges of marks. In such a case, some sort of scaling of internal marks will have to be resorted to.

Chapter 5

Unit Test

5.1. MEANING, CHARACTERISTICS, ELEMENTS AND CONSTRUCTION OF A UNIT

Professor H.C. Morrison (1871—1945) of the University of Chicago is the originator of unit approach to teaching. He has explained the Unit Method in detail in his book, *The Practice of Teaching in Secondary Schools* (1926). The unit method is very popular and frequently used in the U.S.A. The unit approach is based on the growing acceptance of the Gestalt-Organismic-Field Theories of learning which emphasise the 'wholeness' nature of learning. This approach is contrary to the older atomistic conception of learning according to which learning was a matter of adding one small item of knowledge to another bit by bit. The new approach is based upon the assumption that effective learning takes place in an environment in which the goals are clearly perceived and every phase of the operational procedure is viewed as a relational part of the total learning situation. The underlying assumption is that the learner reacts to the situation as a whole and not to parts in isolation.

Meaning of a Unit.

Few terms in modern educational usuage have been more extensively used with so much of disagreement as regards their meaning as has been the term 'unit'.

According to Morisson, "Unit is a comprehensive and significant aspect of the environment of an organised Science and Art."

In the words of Bossing, "A unit consists of comprehensive services of related and meaningful activities so developed as to achieve pupil purposes, provides significant educational experiences, and results in behavioural changes."

The Dictionary of Education defines a unit as "an organisation of varied activities, experiences and types, learning around a central problem, purpose, developed cooperatively by a group of pupils under teacher leadership, involves planning, execution of plans and evaluation of results."

James High defines unit approach in *'Teaching Secondary School Social Studies'* as, "It is more than a mere technique and is often called the unit approach rather than method. The primary requisite is a point of view that will allow the imaginative instructor to arrange and organise all available and pertinent information around a nuclear idea and then select and provide references, aids and activities that will enable his students to master the basic material."

According to Wesley, 'Unit is an organised body of information and experience designed to effect significant outcomes of the learner.'

Jarolimek John defines unit "as a means of organising materials for instructional purposes which utilises significant subject matter content, involves pupils in learning activities through active participation intellectually and physically and modifies the pupil's behaviour to the extent that he is able to cope with new problems and situations more competently."

Richard Survey has pointed out in *Social Studies Instruction in Elementary School* as, "A teaching unit in social studies is a comprehensive instructional plan specifying the 'what', the 'how' and 'when' of teaching a big idea."

According to East S. Johnson, "Unit is a segment of experience which is cut out for study, within it, i.e. method employed. It is my understanding that every unit is a 'project'. It is a project in the sense that one projects enquiry into it. Furthermore, every unit has a topic, theme or careful tendency or whatever name you choose to call it, otherwise it could have no unity. Every unit is a 'contract' in the sense that the student enters upon a contract or obligation to study how the things which it contains are related, how they work, how cause and effect are identified and related and how a conclusion is reached. Every unit is also a 'problem', a problem of significance and meaning in some unknown or less than thoroughly known phase of human experience."

Hanna, Hageman and Potter state, "A unit can be defined as a purposeful learning experience focused upon behaviour of the learner and enable him to adjust to a life situation more effectively.

Main Characteristics of a Unit

1. A unit is a purposeful learning activity or experience.
2. A unit is around a central problem.
3. A unit has a significant content.
4. A unit is comprehensive enough to have scope and unity.
5. A unit is developed cooperatively by a group of pupils.
6. A unit is developed under the guidance of the teacher.
7. A unit involves pupils in learning intellectually and physically.
8. A unit modifies the pupil's behaviour to the extent that he is able to cope with new problems and situations more competently.
9. A unit emerges out of the pupil's experience.
10. A unit provides opportunities for creative experiences.
11. A unit is flexible and provides opportunities in adopting instruction to individual differences of children.
12. A unit is a logical useful division.
13. A unit is evolutionary or functional.

Elements of a Teaching Unit

A good teaching unit has nine elements but the sequence of those elements is not fixed. Following sequence is generally followed :

1. **Overview**. This implies the consideration of the needs of the students while formulating the objectives of teaching unit.

2. **Inventory or background**. This element is concerned with exploring the entering behaviour of the students. The teacher is required to establish the behaviour repertoire by linking the new knowledge with the previous knowledge of the students.

3. **Presentation**. This element is concerned with providing new experiences to the learners. It includes an analysis and presentation of the elements of teaching units in a logical sequence so that they are helpful to the students. With a view to encourage students' participation in teaching, question-answer strategy is employed.

4. **Motivation**. This element of the teaching unit is concerned with the creation of motivational situations to facilitate learning.

5. **Summarisation**. This element of the unit is concerned with providing a summary of the unit.

6. **Drill**. This element provides an opportunity to the students for drill or practice which enables them to retain longer what is learnt.

7. **Review**. This implies giving the salient features of the unit orally.

8. **Organisation**. This element involves giving assignments to the students to organise their learning experiences of their own.

9. **Evaluation**. This element of the teaching unit consists of ascertaining how far the teacher has been successful in achieving the objectives of the lesson, i.e. to what extent students have grasped, the content and developed meaningful behaviour.

5.2. UNIT TEST

Tests are usually conducted at the following stages:

(1) During teaching a lesson.
(2) At the end of teaching a daily lesson.
(3) At the end of a teaching unit.
(4) At the end of the term.
(5) At the end of the year.

A unit test is a short test given at the end of a teaching unit. A unit test in basically a miniature test. It is different from a full test mainly in regard to the limited content area (unit) on which it is based. Questions are of the same type. Time for the test is about 45 minutes and total marks allotted 25.

Why a Unit Test. Total reliance on the end-of-the-year examination is not considered desirable. It is only the continuous evaluation which makes instruction more purposeful and acts as a means of improving instruction as well as pupils' achievement through regular feedback. Unit testing followed by needed corrective measures makes teaching, learning and testing an integral process. A unit test serves the following purposes:

1. To ascertain the effectiveness of teaching-learning.
2. To find out strengths and weaknesses of individual learning.
3. To assess the progress of learning.
4. To help the teacher in modifying his plans.
5. To motivate the students.
6. To provide opportunity to the student for self-evaluation.
7. To use as home assignments.
8. To use for remedial instruction.
9. To use as a teaching device.

Construction of a Unit Test

Following are the important considerations to be kept in view in the construction of a unit test.

1. Selection of objectives.

2. Weightage to objectives.
3. Weightage to different areas of content.
4. Weightage to different forms of questions.
5. Weightage to difficulty level.
6. Scheme of options, if any.
7. Sections in the question paper.
8. Selection of test items.
9. Grouping of test items.
10. Questionwise anaysis (before the test is given).
11. Critical evaluation of the test (before the test is given).
12. Marking scheme and scoring key.
13. Instruction to examiners.
14. Item analysis (after the test is given).

Should Options be given in the Unit Test?

As far as possible options should not be provided in a unit test on account of the following:

1. The main objective of a unit test is to have 'complete' evaluation of an instructional programme of a unit. This objective is not served if options are given.
2. It is very difficult to set two alternative questions of the same level or standard.
3. The scheme of options is likely to develop some wrong practices among students. They may omit some portions of the content.

5.3 BLUE-PRINT OF A UNIT TEST

A blue-print of a unit test serves as a guide. It is a three-dimensional chart showing the weightage given to objectives of instruction, content and forms of questions in terms of marks. Just as we cannot think of an engineer without the blue-print of a building to be built, similarly we cannot think of a teacher without a blue-print of a unit test in evaluation.

Marking Scheme. A marking scheme indicates the following:

1. The number of points or steps expected in an answer.
2. An outline of each point or step expected in the answer.
3. The weightage to each point or step.

A marking scheme is useful in the following ways:

(1) A marking scheme helps the examiner to bring about a uniformity of standard in assessing.

(2) A marking scheme increases the objectivity of the test. The whims of the examiners cannot influence scoring.

(3) Several examiners may be judiciously involved in assessing answer books.

Limitations of Unit tests. The construction of a unit test demands a lot of energy, resources and time. In the prevailing situation when classes are overcrowded and teachers overburdened, it becomes very difficult to construct and use unit test.

5.4. AN ILLUSTRATIVE MODEL UNIT TEST

The following model has been selected from the models prepared in a workshop conducted by NCERT and published in a book *Sample Unit Tests in History* (1985). The model includes the following particulars:

1. Unit on Social and Cultural Awakening during 19th Century.
2. Blue print of the Unit Test.
3. Unit Test.
4. Scoring Key and Marking Scheme.
5. Question-wise Analysis.

BLUE PRINT

Subject: Social and Cultural Awakening during 19th Century — Class : XII
Maximum Marks : 25 — Time : 40 Mts.

S.	*Objective*	*Knowledge*				*Understanding*				*Application*				*Skill*		*Total*
No.	*Form of question* *Content Unit*	*E*	*SA*	*VSA*	*O*	*E*	*SA*	*VSA*	*O*	*E*	*SA*	*VSA*	*O*	*E*	*SA*	
1.	Condition of Indian Society										2(1)					2
2.	Contributions of Raja Ram Mohan Roy		2(1)				2(1)									4
3.	Contribution of other Reforms		2(1)	2(2)	1(1)		2(1)	2(2)				1(1)				10
4.	Results and effects of reform movements	5(1)					2(1)		2(2)							9
	Sub-Total:	5	4	2	1		6	2	2		2	1				25
	Total:		12				10				3					25

Notes : Figures within brackets indicate the number of questions and figures outside the brackets indicate marks.

Summary	*Type of Questions*	*No. of Questions*	*Marks*
(E)	Essay	1	5
(SA)	Short Answer	6	12
(VSA)	Very Short Answer	5	5
(O)	Objective	3	3
	Scheme of Options	: Nil	
	Scheme of Sections	: Nil	

Unit : Social and Cultural Awakening during 19th Century

Marks : 25 *Class: XII*

Time: 40 Mts.

General Instructions:

I. All questions are compulsory.

II. Marks allotted to each question are indicated against it.

III. In the Q. No. 1 to 3 four alternative A, B, C and D are given, out of which only one is correct or the best. To answer those questions, write the letter indicating the correct response alongwith the number of questions.

IV. Answer to Q. No. 10 to 14 should not exceed a sentance, a word or a phrase.

V. Answer to Q. No. 4 to 9 should not exceed 40 to 50 words each.

VI. Answer to Q. No. 15 should not exceed 150 words.

VII. Answers have to be written on the answer book provided.

Questions

1. With a view to oppose the monopoly of Sanskirt studies being enjoyed by the then priestly class of India during 19th Century, Iswar Chandra Vidya Sagar. 1

A. evolved a new technique of teaching Sanskrit.

B. helped in the establishment of a new college.

C. opened the gates of Sanskrit college to all castes.

D. introduced the study of Western thought in the Sanskrit College.

2. The impact of western ideas was felt much earlier in Bengal than in western India because: 1

A. Western India was brought under effective British control as late as 1818.

B. Western Indian society was much more conservative.

C. Western India lacked leadership who could awaken consciousness.

D. Western India was late in realising the necessity of starting social reforms.

3. Devendra Nath Tagore revitalised Brahmo Samaj in the light of the fact that he wanted to 1

A. Combine the best in the traditional Indian learning and new thought of the west.

B. Put into practice the ideas of Ram Mohan.

C. Promote a systematic study of India's past through the activities of Brahmo-Samaj.

D. Spread a national outlook among the intellecutals of Bengal.

4. Our religion is in the Kitchen. Our God is in the cooking-pot and our religion is "Do not touch me. I am holy. We are just do not touchiest". (Vivekanand)

What two inferences do you draw from the above statement of Swami Vivekanand? 2

5. Raja Ram Mohan Roy organised a historic agitation against the inhuman customs of *Sati.* Cite two arguments which he put forward before the people to convince them not to follow this evil practice. 2

6. Which two major activities during 19th Century were supported by all the Reform Movements to uplift the condition of women in India? 2

7. Raja Ram Mohan Roy's religious reform movement indirectly aimed also at the political upliftment of the country. Prove it by citing any of his two ideas or teachings. 2

8. Henry Vivian Derozio, the leader of Young Bengal Movement drew his inspiration from the French Revolution. Which principles of the French Revolution did Derozio try to spread among his followers? 2

9. Which two activities of Swami Vivekanand go to prove him a great humanist? 2

10. What was that main point on which Raja Ram Mohan Roy and Swami Dayanand had different views? 1

11. Gopal Hari Deshmukh was an outstanding champion of new learning and social reforms in Maharashtra during the 19th Century. Cite his one such teaching which has become one of the main features of our Constitution. 1

12. By whom and when was Rama Krishna Mission founded? 1

13. Which teaching of Theosophical Society is needed much in todays' world? 1

14. Name the college founded by Sir Sayyid Ahmed Khan which later grew into a university.

15. Which three main problems did the social and religions reforms of the 19th century in India had to face? 5

OR

In which four ways did the religious reform movements prove very useful for the country? 5

5.5. SCORING KEY AND MARKING SCHEME

Sl No.	*Expected Out-line Answer*	*Marks allotted to each point*	*Total Marks*
1.	C	1	1
2.	A	1	1
3.	A	1	1
4.	(*a*) irrational thinking in Indian religion.	1	
	(*b*) conservatism.	1	
	(*c*) caste system and untouchability. (Any two)	1	2
5.	(*a*) cited the authority of the oldest sacred Indian books that the Hinduism at its best was opposed to the practice.	1	
	(*b*) reasoned out the practice on humanity	1	2
6.	(*a*) movement for widow remarriage.	1	
	(*b*) education of women.	1	
	(*c*) abolition of polygamy. (Any two)	1	2
7.	(*a*) caste system hindered the development of patriotism.	1	
	(*b*) criticised oppressive activities of zamindars in Bengal.	1	
	(*c*) Indians should take western education for nationalism. (Any two)	1	2
8.	(*i*) think freely and rationally.	1	
	(*ii*) question authority.	1	
	(*iii*) have liberty, equality and truth. (Any two)	1	2
9.	(*a*) appealed the educated people to serve the poor and ignorant.	1	
	(*b*) served the people in times of famine and flood etc.	1	
	(*c*) was shocked by the poverty, misery and sufferings of the people.	1	
	(*d*) collected wealth from western countries.	1	2
10.	Education.	1	1
11.	Advocated secular values.	1	1
12.	Swami Vivekanand, 1896.	1	1
13.	Brotherhood.	1	1
14.	Anglo-Oriental College Aligarh.	1	1

15.	(*a*) Family members opposed them.	$1^1/_2$	
	(*b*) Orthodox people of their community opposed them.	$1^1/_2$ each point	5
	(*c*) Religious people were against them.	2	
	OR		
	(*i*) Awakening against social evils.		
	(*ii*) Development of education.		
	(*iii*) Rise of Nationalism.		
	(*iv*) Democratic Development.		
	(*v*) Renaissance in the field of literature.	$1^1/_4$ for each point	
	(*vi*) thinking and attitude of the people changed. (Any four).		5

5.6. QUESTION-WISE ANALYSIS

Sr. No.	*Objective*	*Specification*	*Content unit*	*Form of questions**	*Marks Allotted*	*Estimated difficulty level* +
1.	Knowledge	Recalls	Contribution of Reforms.	0	1	C
2.	Understanding	Selects the facts	-do-	0	1	B
3.	-do-	-do-	-do-	0	1	B
4.	Application	Draws Inference	-do-	SA	2	A
5.	Knowledge	Recalls	Contribution of Raja Ram Mohan Roy.	SA	2	C
6.	Understanding	Identifies relationship	Results and effects of Reform movements.	SA	2	B
7.	-do-	Selects facts.	Contribution of Ram Mohan Roy.	SA	2	B
8.	-do-	Compares	Contribution of other Reformers.	SA	2	B
9.	Knowledge	Recognises	-do-	SA	2.	C
10.	Understanding	Compares	-do-	VSA	1	B
11.	Understanding	Selects	-do-	VSA	1	B
12.	Knowledge	Recalls	-do-	VSA	1	C
13.	Application	Selects relevant facts.	-do-	VSA	1	A
14.	Knowledge	Recalls	-do-	VSA	1	C
15.	Knowledge	Recalls	Results and effects of Reform movement	E	5	C

*O	for Objective type	+ A	Difficult
VSA	for Very Short Answer type	B	Average
SA	for Short Answer type	C	Easy
E	for Essay type.		

Observations on the Unit Test. The last question and its marking scheme does not appear to be quite rational and scientific as for three problems, five marks are allotted. Likewise, in the alternative question for 'four ways', five marks are given. Such fractions could be avoided by framing the question more rationally and scientifically. On the whole, it may be considered a model unit test.

Chapter 6

Examination System in India

6.1. INTERNAL AND PUBLIC EXAMINATIONS

Class Examinations/Internal Examinations. In our schools we have different classes/grades. Thus, at the primary stage we may have four or five classes (I to IV/V). At the upper primary or middle stage, we may have three or four classes (V to VII or VI to VIII). At the secondary stage we have two classes (IX and X). At the senior secondary stage we have three classes (IX to XI). At the higher secondary stage we have two classes (XI and XII). According to the new pattern of education we have 10+2+3 classes. The duration of instruction in each class is one year. Promotion from one class to next class is made mainly on the results of written examinations which are held atleast once in a year in the school. Usually apart from annual examination, monthly/ bimonthly or quarterly tests are also held and some weightage is given to these tests. Such examinations are called class examinations or school examinations or internal examinations.

External/Public Examinations

In some States in our country, there is a common examination conducted for all the students of a region at the end of the primary and upper primary (middle school) stage. Almost invariably, there is an examination conducted by a Board at the end of high school or secondary stage and higher secondary stage for the pupils of all the schools in the region/state.

Examinations are also conducted by the Central Board of Secondary Education Delhi and the Anglo Indian Board in respect of schools affiliated to them. Similarly universities conduct examinations for all students of all the colleges affiliated to them. All such examinations are called Public Examinations or External Examinations. These are called external examinations as these are conducted not by the teachers who teach the students but by an external organisation other than the school or college. To pass a Public Examination, it is often necessary to obtain minimum pass marks in all the subjects prescribed for the examination or a certified number of specific subjects. Failure in one or two subjects may lead to the student being required to appear in those subjects at a supplementary examination. Marginal failures in one or more subjects are often condoned, on the basis of certain rules or through discussions in committees, by the award of grace marks. In addition to the declaration of results in terms of pass and fail, the common practice is to classify candidates into three divisions: first, second and third. Successful candidates are issued mark sheets and certificates. These certificates are recognised by all the Boards and Universities on reciprocal basis for admission to various classes and also by different departments/organisations in states for purposes of eligibility for various posts.

India has 41 Boards of Inter/Secondary Education conducting public examinations at the end of ten and twelve years of schooling. These Boards are autonomous bodies and have their own statutes. Usually each State Board has jurisdiction limited to its affiliated schools located in the State/Union Territory. A few States have more than one Board. (Table 1)

Table 1. Number of Boards (1993-94)

S. No.	*State/Union Territory*	*No. of Boards*	*S. No.*	*State/Union Territory*	*No. of Boards*
1.	Andhra	1	12.	Madhya Pradesh	2
2.	Arunachal Pradesh	0	13.	Maharashtra	6
3.	Assam	2	14.	Manipur	1
4.	Bihar	2	15.	Meghalaya	1
5.	Goa	1	16.	Mizoram	1
6.	Gujarat	1	17.	Nagaland	1
7.	Haryana	1	18.	Orissa	2
8.	Himachal Pradesh	2	19.	Punjab	1
9.	Jammu & Kashmir	1	20.	Rajasthan	2
10.	Karnataka	2	21.	Sikkim	0
11.	Kerala	1	22.	Tamil Nadu	5

S. No.	State/Union Territory	No. of Boards	S. No.	State/Union Territory	No. of Boards
23.	Tripura	1	28.	D. & Nagar Haweli	0
24.	Uttar Pradesh	1	29.	Daman & Diu	0
25.	West Bengal	2	30.	Delhi	1
26.	A & N Islands	0	31.	Lakshadeep	0
27.	Chandigarh	0	32.	Pondicherry	0

Source: Selected Educational Statistics 1993-94. Government of India, Ministry of Human Resource Development. (Department of Education, New Delhi, 1994)

The Central Board of Secondary Education, Delhi had 3857 schools affiliated to it in 1993-94. These schools are located across the length and breadth of the country. A few of these schools are also located outside the country, e.g. in Abu Dhabi, Bahrain, Kabul and Moscow etc. The Central Board conducts public examinations at the end of class X and class XII.

6.2. LOW RELIABILITY AND VALIDITY OF EXAMINATIONS

Among the important factors, mention may be made of the following:

1. Inter-examiner variability i.e. examiners differing widely in their standard of marking.
2. Distorted distribution of marks on account of concentration of frequencies of marks at pass-mark.
3. Variation in the distribution of marks in different subjects i.e. different subjects having different means standard deviations and pass percentages.
4. Year to year variation in the mean and standard deviation of marks in the same subject as well as in the pass percentage.
5. Board to Board variation in average marks and pass percentages.
6. Inadequate sampling of curriculum content in the question paper.

Various Measures of Overcoming the Low Reliability and Validity of Examinations

1. Improvement in the question paper.
2. Uniformity in the standard of marking.
3. Scaling of marks of different examiners.
4. Conversion of marks into grades.

6.3. MALPRACTICES ADOPTED IN EXAMINATIONS

Broadly speaking malpractices adopted may be categorised under three categories:

1. Malpractices adopted before the commencement of the examinations.
2. Malpractices adopted during the conduct of examinations.
3. Malpractices adopted after the conduct of examinations.

1. Malpractices adopted before the Commencement of the Examinations

1. *Pupils:*

(*a*) Trying to procure the expected or anticipated questions through various sources.

(*b*) Writing out the answers on slips of papers of the expected questions.

(*c*) Preparing the answers for anticipated questions on additional sheets stealthily secured from the examination centre.

(*d*) Keeping written slips of the expected answers in their pockets, in their shoes, in geometry boxes, sleeves, etc.

(*e*) Writing the answers on limbs, palms, thighs and other parts of the body.

(*f*) Writing the answers on pads in an invisible script.

(*g*) Conspiring with their friends to throw paper balls containing answers, shouting the answers from outside and arranging loudspeakers giving out answers.

(*h*) Threatening the lives of invigilators.

(*i*) Preparation to carry knives and daggars, chilli powder in their pockets with an intention to make use of in emergency.

(*j*) Detaching the papers of the expected questions from the textbooks with an intention to carry them to the examination hall.

(*k*) Conspiring with the invigilators to assist them in the examination hall to the maximum extent.

(*l*) Drawing maps, diagrams, writing formulas, technical words, etc. on walls and desks.

2. *Teachers*:

(*a*) Teachers prepare the answers to the questions brought by the pupils and thus encourage them in malpractices.

(*b*) They accept other types of presentations, promising the pupils to help them in the examination hall.

(*c*) Teachers leak out question papers sometimes misguiding the pupils with an imaginary question paper.

(*d*) Give hopes to the pupils that they would be the invigilators, thus violating many a time Official Secret Act.

(*e*) Teachers take initiative to help their wards who are having special coaching under them by getting themselves appointed as invigilators, in that particular centre where their wards take the examination.

(*f*) Teachers supply additional answer sheets to the pupils in excess with an intention to encourage them to write the answers at home.

3. *Parents*:

(*a*) Canvass the invigilators to help their children in the examination hall.

(*b*) Encourage short cut methods in allowing their children to secure question papers both from reliable and unreliable sources.

(*c*) Try to find out the names of paper setters, invigilators, examiners, etc., so as to help their children in the examination and thus giving them a wrong lead for malpractices.

(*d*) Try to influence the persons at various levels of examination.

Preventive Measures suggested for minimising Malpractices.

Student Level:

(*a*) Proper precautions are to be taken to kee the question papers strictly confidential.

(*b*) A thorough check of the pupils before they enter the examination hall and prevention of any written matter or manuscript to be carried into the halls.

(*c*) Proper check and supervision over the distribution of additional sheets and roomwise accounts of additional sheets are to be maintained. On additional sheets the students should note the subject and the Roll No. immediately. The Chief Superintendent should maintain a correct account of the additional sheets.

(*d*) If any written matter is detected on any part of the body, the pupils should be sent out of the examination hall besides suitable punishment to be inflicted later.

Teachers:

(*a*) Teachers should be advised to discourage undesirable methods adopted by the students while preparing for the examination. They could guide the students, but not encourage malpractices in the examination.

(*b*) Such of those invigilators, who are found violating Offical Secret Act, should be immediately reported to the District Education Officer by the Chief Superintendent and disciplinary action should be taken against them, as an experimental measure.

(*c*) Invigilators could also be appointed from persons other than the teaching community to facilitate judicious supervision.

As the invigilators would be drawn from other departments also, malpractices could be prevented to some extent.

Parents: (*a*) Parents should be advised to exercise careful supervision over the studies of their children, rather than adopt shortcut methods in the eleventh hour.

Miscellaneous

(*a*) Hundred yards around the examination centre should be enclosed as a prohibited area. Strict vigilance by the police is desirable.

(*b*) Wide publicity should be given regarding drastic measures to be adopted in cases when the students are found carrying knives, daggers, etc.

(*c*) Frequent shift of invigilators from room to room during the examination should be made. Proper care in the selection of invigilators is to be taken. Such of the invigilators who are found conspiring with the students should be severely dealt with.

(*d*) The school building should be got whitewashed before the commencement of the examination and students not allowed to enter the examination hall.

Malpractices Practised during the Conduct of the Examination

(1) Copying from slips of paper.
Copying from slips of textbooks.
Copying from slips of neighbours' answer books.
Copying from slips of other sources.

(2) Copying with the help of external agencies, such as teachers, peons, watermen, parents and through other members engaged in the examination work.

(3) Copying from paper balls received from outside.

(4) Writing the answers received from outside agencies, such as loudspeakers, shoutings, etc.

(5) Copying the objective type of answers by means of code language or gestures.

(6) Writing the answer with the help of invigilators, teachers and Chief Superintendent.

(7) Exchanging answer scripts with their friends.

(8) Under the pretext of easing oneself, the students look into the textbooks or paper slips and gather information. Near the urinals boys meet each other and exchange the answers.

(9) Exchanging question papers on which answers are written.

(10) Sending the question paper out immediately after the distribution of question papers; consequently answers are dictated by others from outside.

(11) Due to improper seating arrangements, the candidates being in close proximity to each other copying is encouraged.

(12) The teacher writes the answers on the black board and the students copy them in toto.

(13) Mass copying is attempted with the help of teachers.

(14) Threatening the invigilators with daggar and knives both inside and outside the examination hall for purpose of copying.

(15) Connivance at copying by the invigilator.

(16) Insertion of additional sheets on which answers are written at home.

Suggestions for Preventing Malpractices during the Conduct of Examinations

(1) Prohibiting the entry of persons other than the bonafide candidates to an area within a reasonable distance from the place where public examinations are being held.

(2) Use of multiple question papers.

(3) Deployment of flying squads.

3. Malpractices after the Examinations.

(1) Making efforts to insert additional material or make corrections in the answer books.

(2) Finding out the original roll numbers so as to locate answer sheets having secret codes assigned to them.

(3) Approaching the examiners and offering inducements to enhance the marks secured.

(4) Threatening examiners of dire consequences in case they refuse to oblige.

(5) Changing answer sheets.

(6) Faulty tabulation.

(7) Ineffective administrative machinery.

Checking Malpractices after the Examinations

(1) Introducing the system of spot evaluation.

(2) Careful selection of personnel.

(3) Careful computerisation of results.

6.4. OPERATIONAL STEPS IN THE MANAGEMENT OF PUBLIC EXAMINATIONS

Operational steps related to public examinations could be broadly divided into the following parts:

1. Pre-examination modalities.
2. Conduct of examinations.
3. Post-examination modalities.

1. **Pre-examination Modalities.** These include:

(*i*) Curriculum development and prescribing syllabi.

(*ii*) Recognition and affiliation of schools for pursuing the courses prescribed and for sending their students for the examinations conducted by them.

(*iii*) Announcement of prescribed/recommended books.

(*iv*) Announcement of the dates of examinations.

(*v*) Receipt and scrutiny of applications sent by the schools and private candidates regarding the eligibility of candidates and appropriateness of the subject combinations offered.

2. **Conduct of Examinations:**

(*i*) Selection of paper setters and reviewers if any.

(*ii*) Setting and moderation of question papers.

(*iii*) Printing and packing of question papers—confidential nature of printing work.

(*iv*) Selection of examination centres.

(*v*) Appointment of superintendents and invigilators and other staff for the fair conduct of examinations at centres.

(*vi*) Arrangement for the safe delivery of the question papers at the centres.

(*vii*) Supply of stationary to centres.

(*viii*) Distribution of question papers to examinees under the supervision of the centre superintendent.

(*ix*) Posting of police personnel at the centres.

(*x*) Packing of answer scripts and sending them to Board's Office.

(*xi*) Deployment of special squads for checking unfair means.

(*xii*) Assignment of fake or fictious or secret roll nos. to answer books at the Board's Office.

(*xiii*) Appointment of examiners and head examiners.

(*xiv*) Preparing marking schemes and distributing them to concerned persons.

(*xv*) On the spot evaluation—evaluation at some specified centres where head examiner and examiners mark the scripts.

3. **Post-Examination Modalities.** These include:

(*i*) Tabulation of marks and their scrunity.

(*ii*) Moderation of marks.

(*iii*) Conversion of fake roll nos. to original roll numbers.

(*iv*) Declaration of results through press/centres/schools etc.

(*v*) Checking of totals etc. in case of complaints.

(*vi*) Re-evaluation of answer scripts—this is done by a very few examining bodies.

(*vii*) Awarding of certificates indicating grades and or marks/divisions in individual subjects as well as overall performance.

6.5. ENSURING FAIR CONDUCT OF EXAMINATIONS: RECOMMENDATIONS OF A SEMINAR

A national seminar conducted by NCERT on the theme 'Management of Public Examinations' from 16–20 October, 1978 made the following recommendations.

1. It has been observed that the syllabi prescribed by the Board of Secondary Education in various subjects do not provide sufficient guidance about the scope of different topics. The seminar, therefore, recommends that steps may be taken immediately to see that the topics included in the syllabus of each subject are spelt out in sufficient details. It further recommends that objectives in terms of specifications, may also be stated as an integral part of syllabus in each subject so that paper setters, textbook writers, teachers and pupils, could clearly visualize the expected learning outcomes.

2. As setting of question-papers is a very responsible job, the seminar recommends that it should be entrusted only to persons who, in addition to being experts in the subjects concerned, possess the necessary technical competence. For this purpose, the Boards of Secondary Education may organise training programmes for paper setters in the concept and techniques of evaluation immediately so as to ensure that question papers set in their examinations are of a very high quality both in respect of content and technique.

3. For getting question papers set on scientific lines, the Boards of Secondary Education should develop and supply to the paper setters designs of question papers indicating the weightage to instructional objectives, areas of content, different forms of questions, alongwith the scheme of sections and the pattern of options. Based on these designs the Boards should also get prepared blue-prints of question-papers, sample question papers, their scoring keys and marking schemes which may be circulated to schools well in advance so as to enable teachers prepare their students for the improved examinations.

4. A good question paper should ensure a balanced and adequate coverage of the syllabus. This is not possible through the use of essay type questions only. The Seminar, therefore, recommends that objective type, very short answer type and short answer type questions, may

also be incorporated in the question papers. The objective type and very short answer type questions should, however, be placed in a separate section with a separate time limit for answering.

5. Setting of question papers on scientific lines demands expertise in pedagogy and a proper understanding of prevailing school situation besides that of content. The seminar, therefore, recommends that the Boards of Secondary Education should henceforth entrust this job to a team consisting of a practising teacher, an evaluation expert and a subject-matter expert. The team should develop blueprints based on the design supplied by the Board, question papers based on these blueprints, detailed marking scheme and question–wise analysis.

6. The Seminar recommends that the Boards of Secondary Education may organise orientation workshops/courses for teachers, headmasters, educational inspectors and others concerned with school education, in the concept and techniques of evaluation with a view to conducting the examination efficiently. Similar courses workshop may also be conducted by the NCERT for those who manage public examinations so as to equip them with the necessary competence to gear the system to the emerging needs of improved examinations.

7. The Boards of Secondary Education should develop confidential question banks for the exclusive use of paper-setters. The paper-setters should have the freedom of setting question from outside the book also. Only such questions as have been properly tried out should be included in the question banks. The Boards may also encourage the schools to develop their own question banks for their home examinations.

8. The existing practices, pursued by most of the Boards for maintaining uniformity of scoring standards by different examiners are not adequate. The seminar, therefore, recommends that coordination meetings of examiners with the chief examiners in each paper may be organised before scoring is started. This is essential for developing a common understanding among the examiners about the evaluation of different levels of answers, particularly in respect of long answer questions. This process will be facilitated if spot evaluation of scripts is introduced which will also help in maintaining secrecy of assessment and minimisation of malpractices related to the evaluation of answer-scripts.

9. Mechanisation accelerates the processes involved in the management of public examinations, ensures accuracy, makes easily possible analyses which otherwise may take a long time at a tremendous cost, and facilitates storage and retrieval of data. The seminar, therefore,

recommends that the Boards of Secondary Education which have not yet introduced mechanisation may do so as early as possible.

10. It was noted by the seminar that the practice of awarding grace marks was being followed by all the Boards of Secondary Education, decisions regarding which are mostly taken on an *ad-hoc* basis. It is strongly recommended that relevant statistical procedures may be utilised for arriving at decisions in this regard.

11. The seminar observed that in spite of various measures adopted by the Boards for minimising inter-examiner variability (issuing of common detailed instructions for marking of scripts, holding meetings of examiners, scrutiny of samples of marked scripts by chief examiners, supervised assessment of scripts, randomisation of scripts etc.) considerable variations persist. In order to minimise these, this seminar recommends that scientifically developed statistical procedures for scaling up and scaling down the scores awarded by those examiners whose means fall outside the limits of tolerance, may be adopted. Due care may be taken to see that proper randomisation of answer scripts is done before they are passed onto the examiners for evaluation.

12. As public examinations, in addition to being valid and reliable, are also to act as powerful instruments of improving teaching and learning, the seminar recommends that the Boards of Secondary Education may regularly undertake the analysis of the performance of candidates in different papers which may cover item-analysis of different questions, error analysis and analysis of content and objectives as reflected on the performance. The findings may be fed-back to the paper setters, examiners, teachers and students. In addition to the aforesaid analysis of performance, the Boards may also undertake to analysis of the results in different subjects as also of the examination as a whole for maintenance and improvement of standards.

13. The Boards of Secondary Education are taking a variety of measures for maintaining secrecy at different operational stages. The seminar recommends that these may be compiled and circulated by the NCERT to the Boards confidentially.

14. The seminar observed that a variety of measures are being adopted by the Boards for combating malpractices in public examinations. The NCERT may compile the information and circulate it to all the Boards for their use.

15. Keeping in view the magnitude of malpractices in examinations, the need of arousing social conscience against these cannot be over-emphasised. To create a proper climate against this social evil, which

has almost completely vitiated the educational process, the Boards should make all possible efforts to ensure the cooperation of the community in general and of the leaders of public opinion in particular.

16. At present the Boards of Secondary Education are almost exclusively engaged in the time-targetted routine tasks connected with the conduct of examinations and their man-power has hardly any time for academic work. It is recommended that strong academic units may be set up in the Boards to attend to the academic work related to examinations so as to improve their quality and also to positively influence the total educational process.

17. With the increasing pressure of numbers and the growing complexity of the management of public examinations, it has become essential to make a systematic study of the administrative processes of the work of the Boards, with a view to increasing their speed and efficiency. The Boards may, therefore, initiate steps to take professional help in the area of management from specialised agencies for accomplishing this task.

Chapter 7

Research in Examinations

7.1. RECOMMENDATIONS OF A SEMINAR

The National Seminar on Research in Examinations organised by the NCERT from 23 to 27 October, 1978 at St. Paul's School, Darjeeling (West Bengal) made the following recommendations.

Recommendations

(1) The seminar strongly feels that there is need for *co-ordination* of the activities, specially of research, of different agencies concerned with examinations and, therefore, recommends that action may be initiated immediately to establish the necessary machinery.

(2) In spite of the fact that a number of innovations have been introduced for improving the measurement quality of examinations, the impact has not been commensurate with effort invested into it. It is also well known that a variety of *social, psychological* and *pedagogical* factors may be responsible for this situation. Research may, therefore, be undertaken immediately into the *societal context* of examinations for developing a proper perspective and for identifying the appropriate agencies.

(3) Research for developing a *model for continuous evaluation* of the examination system may be undertaken by the NCERT in collaboration with some Boards of Secondary Education. This research, in addition to the psychometric aspects, may cover the psychological, sociological, pedagogical, economic and other aspects as well.

The programmes of the Boards with whose collaboration the aforesaid model is developed, may be evaluated on the basis of the model in order to help them in the improvement of their existing practices. The

NCERT may provide the necessary assistance in this regard.

(4) The Boards of Secondary Education may be helped by the NCERT in *developing evaluation models for validating a change* both *before and after* its introduction. This model should cover all the different implications of change *viz.* psychological, pedagogical, economic, etc. Only such changes may be institutionalized which do not produce any adverse side-effects.

(5) It is now being increasingly recognised that new types of programmes and teaching learning strategies are required for meeting the emerging needs and challenges of our educational system. The existing system of examinations cannot cope up with these demands. Research in the development of new strategies as alternative to the present system of examination may, therefore, be undertaken immediately.

(6) The NCERT may study the papers submitted to the seminar and prepare a classified list of the problems at the M.Ed./Ph.D. on which research in examinations could be undertaken on institutional levels. The list, when ready, may be placed before a small group for finalization. This may then be published and circulated to Universities, Boards of Secondary Education, Teachers's Colleges and Institutions interested in the area of examination research.

(7) The NCERT in collaboration with other agencies and organisations should prepare reports, both technical and popular, of research in examinations, and circulate them to various agencies and institutions concerned with examinations.

(8) The NCERT may also offer research grants for the conduct of studies on various problems identified in this seminar through its ERIC Programmes.

7.2. SUGGESTED RESEARCH PROJECTS/STUDIES ON RESEARCH IN EXAMINATIONS

1. A comparative study of the existing practices related to various aspects of external examinations conducted by various boards (from the prescription of syllabus and paper setting to declaration and feedback of the results).

2. Standardization of procedures for conduct of examinations, format of tests, answer-sheets, scoring sheets, tabulation, recording and reporting procedures.

3. A study of the rules and regulations of different boards for allowing students to appear privately.

4. A study of the patterns of expenditure incurred by the examining agencies, on the various components of the examination system (like paper setting, evaluation of scripts, computerisation, etc.) by different boards.

5. Development of a model for continuous evaluation of the programmes of the boards of secondary education (both measurement aspects and non-measurement aspects).

6. A comparative study of the standards of different boards of secondary education in India.

7. A study of the impact of examination reform in a board on the teaching-learning process where reform has been introduced in the public examination.

8. A study of the impact of reform in external examinations as reflected in the lower classes in the schools.

9. A study of the errors committed by students in different subjects at the board examinations.

10. An analytical study of the complaints of students and teachers about the difficulties of question paper and other aspects.

11. Indepth study of the background factors in respect of selected schools showing consistently good and poor results at the board examinations for the last 10 years.

12. A comparative study of the effectiveness of the mastery learning approach and the traditional approach with respect to achievement of pupils at the elementary stage.

13. An experimental study of the innovations in evaluating students at the elementary stage.

14. An experimental study of remedial teaching as a motivational device for learning.

15. A study of commercial help books, guides, etc. in use for preparation for examination in a subject in some selected areas.

16. Job analysis of teachers at primary, secondary and college level with special reference to evaluation procedures and maintenance of records.

17. A follow up case study of the high achievers as related to their job performance.

18. A study of the successful employees in relation to their academic achievement in different examinations.

19. A comparative study of the impact on scholastic achievement and mental health of students whose mother tongue is or is not the medium of instruction.

20. A study of the level of aspiration and actual achievement by different categories of students against the correlated factors.

21. A study of the students expectations of their achievement before the examination and immediately after the examination as related to the actual achievement on that examination.

22. A study of the pre-examination behaviour of students on internal and external examinations.

23. A study of the various types of co-curricular activities organised in different institutions and their contribution to the cognitive and non-cognitive development of students.

24. A critical study of the scaling procedures adopted by examining agencies in India and abroad.

25. A study of the effectiveness of co-ordination among examiners working under a chief examiner.

26. A study of grading practices followed by different examining agencies and their corresponding impact on teaching, learning and testing.

27. A study of the relative effectiveness of scales with different points to minimise inter-examiner reliability and optimise scale points.

28. An investigation into the validity and reliability of various types of judgements (norm referenced, criterion-referenced and self-referenced).

29. An investigation into the causes of resistance on the part of the students, teachers, supervisors and administrators to the introduction of internal assessment in schools and colleges (liberal and professional).

30. A study of the existing measures adopted to reduce subjectivity in internal assessment and to develop appropriate procedures to minimise subjectivity.

31. A study of examination feedback mechanisms and their implications for teaching and learning in schools.

32. A status study of the measures adopted in checking existing malpractices in school examinations.

33. A psycho-sociological study of the malpractices in examinations.

34. A comparative study of standards of evaluation courses B.Ed. programmes of various universities.

35. Construction of predictive batteries for selection to primary and secondary teacher's institutes.

36. Development of procedures for selection of teachers for employment.

37. Development of institutional question banks in various subjects on a co-operative basis.

38. Development of batteries of diagnostic test in different subjects at the elementary stage of education.

39. Development of criterion-referenced tests in sciences and mathematics for elementary schools.

40. Development of a battery of tests for identifying potential talent at the elementary stage.

41. Development of tests of selected concepts in different subjects at different taxonomic levels.

42. Construction of sequential tests at elementary level for use in ungraded schools.

43. Development of National Tests in different subjects for awarding national merit scholarships and for comparison of standards.

44. A study of different systems of evaluation of script in different universities.

45. Study of student's performance on different forms of questions (objective type, short answer type, essay type) given in question papers of different subjects in the external examination conducted by a board.

46. A study of the relationship between marks obtained on different questions and overall marks with respect to the other of questions attempted by these students in examination.

47. An experimental study for the development of evaluation instruments in affective and psychomotor domains.

48. An experimental study to judge the effectiveness of illuminative evaluation in appraising the affective outcomes of learning.

49. A study of the procedures of evaluating students in work experience and vocational education.

50. A diagonistic study of assessment of practical work in science subjects in home examinations.

51. Development and standardisation of procedures of evaluating students in games and sports.

52. A study of the curricular validity and reliability of practical examinations conducted by the boards and the institutions.

Chapter 8

History and Present Status of Examination Reforms in India

8.1. HISTORY OF EXAMINATION REFORMS SINCE 1902

Strong criticism of the examinations first came with the observations of the Indian University Commission in 1902. It stated, "Examinations as now understood are believed to have been unknown as an instrument of general education in ancient India nor do they figure prominently in the Despatch of 1859. Today, however they have grown extravagantly as that instruction is confined within the rigid framework of the prescribed courses, and all forms by training, not tested by written examinations, are liable to be neglected and teachers and pupils are tempted not to concentrate upon genuine study as upon questions likely to be set by examiners."

The Government Resolution on Educational Policy, 1913 observed that examinations as mere tests of achievement did not help either mental development or the growth of character. It was necessary, therefore, to keep a record of the progress and conduct of each pupil for atleast two or three years before the public examination.

The Calcutta University Commission, 1917, generally known as Hunter Commission, was of the opinion that admission to the university on the basis of the Matriculation Examination was the cause not only of the unmanageable numbers at the university but also created undue pressure of work at the university. It, therefore, recommended that a new institution known as Intermediate College be started which would provide the logical link between the school and the university. The admission tests for the university would now mean the passing of intermediate examination and not the matriculation examination.

The Auxiliary Committee of the Indian Statutory Commission, popularly known as the Hartog Committee (1929), found fault with the examination system in vogue and observed, "The whole system of secondary education is still dominated by the ideal that every boy who enters a secondary school should prepare himself for the university, and the immense number of failures at the Matriculation and in the University examination indicate a great waste of effort."

The Central Advisory Board of Education, formed in 1920, abolished in 1923 and revived in 1935, suggested a public examination at the end of the elementary school stage in which the discovery of promise rather than actual attainment should be the aim.

Report of the Wardha Education Committee, popularly known as Zakir Husain or Basic Education Committee Report, stated in 1937, "The system of examinations prevailing in our country has proved a curse to education. A bad system of education has been made worse by awarding to examinations a place out of all proportion to their utility. As a measure of the work of individual pupils or the schools, by a consensus of experts opinion examinations are neither valid nor complete. They are inadequate and unreliable, capricious and arbitrary. The purpose of the examination can be served by an administrative check of the work of the schools in a prescribed area by means of a sample measurement of the attainment of selected groups of students conducted by the inspectors of the Education Boards. The introduction of this check up by sample testing will add greatly to the efficiency of the school system and will in fact lengthen the teaching term of the final class by atleast six weeks, the time now usually wasted on memorising 'notes' and 'revisions' which precede the ordeal of examinations. The promotion from grade to grade should be decided exclusively by the teaching faculty of the school on the basis of careful records of the pupils' work."

The Kher Committee (1938) recommended that there should be no external examinations in a basic school. It also recommended that at the end of a course, a school learning certificate should be given.

The Sargent Report (1944), also recommended that no external examination need be held. At the end of basic school course a school leaving certificate based on any internal examination should be given. Promotion from class to class should be determined by the school though the results of the internal examinations should be subject to the supervisions inspection.

The University Education Commission (1948-49) headed by Dr. S. Radhakrishnan, on the subject of examinations stated, "For nearly half a century, examinations, as they have been functioning, have been recognised as one of the worst features of Indian Education Commissions and Committees have expressed their alarm at their domination over the whole system of education in India. The obvious deficiencies and harmful consequences of this most pervasive evii in Indian education have been analysed by successive University Commissions since 1912. With most of their criticism we are in agreement and do not wish to dilate on the patent defects and dangers of this system. We only note that while the magnitude of the problem has been growing at an alarming rate, nothing constructive in the way of reform has happened." Among other things the Commission recommended the use of objective tests.

The Secondary Education Commission 1952-53, under the Chairmanship of Dr. Lakshman Swami Mudaliar too found fault with the examination system. It pointed out, "Examinations dictate the curriculum instead of following it, prevent experimentation, hamper proper treatment of subjects and sound methods of teaching, foster dull uniformity and encourage average pupil to concentrate too rigidly on too narrow a field and thus help him develop wrong values in education. Pupils assess education in terms of success in examinations. Teachers, recognising the importance of the external examinations to the individual pupils, are constrained to relate their teaching to an examination which can test only a narrow field of the pupils' interests and capacities and so invariably neglect the qualities which are more important though less tangible." The Commission further observed, "All circumstances conspire today to put an undue and unnatural emphasis on examinations, especially the external examinations, and they have come to exercise a restricting influence over the entire field of Indian education to such an extent as almost to nullify its real purpose." Its important recommendations on examination reforms were as under:

1. Introduction of objective type tests.
2. Keeping school records for assessing all round progress of pupils.
3. Symbolic marking in place of numerical marking.
4. Number of external examinations to be reduced.
5. In the final assessment due credit to be given to internal tests and school records.

6. Only one public examination at the completion of the secondary school course.
7. Introduction of a system of compartmental examination at the final public examination.

As a result of the recommendations of the Secondary Education Commission, the All India Council for Secondary Education, Government of India, started a comprehensive programme of examination reform.

The Assessment Committee on Basic Education (1955–56) was of the view that examination in Basic Schools should be wholly internal and based on assessment of continuous progress of students on cumulative records.

In February 1956, the Bhopal Seminar on Examination Reform recommended the establishment of an expert body to be known as the Central Examination Unit (CEU).

Around the same time, Dr. B.S. Bloom, the Chief Examiner of the University of Chicago conducted several courses in India on examination reforms and popularised the concept of behavioural objectives in evaluation.

The Committee on Rural Higher Education (1954–57) under the Chairmanship of Shri B. Mukherjee, stressed the need for assessment on cumulative records of practical and social activities of the students.

The Study Team on General Education (1955–57) with Dr. S. Bhagavantam recommended that passing an examination in the prescribed General Education courses should be made a requisite condition in the case of all students before graduation.

The Three-year Degree Course Estimates Committees (1956) under the Chairmanship of Shri C.D. Deshmukh recommended that there should be a public examination at the end of pre-university class.

The Examination Committee (1957) appointed by the U.G.C. under the Chairmanship of Shri. S.R. Dongerkery, made several recommendations regarding examination reforms at the University level. *Inter-alia*, it recommended the use of methods of evaluation other than essay type examinations such as multiple-choice tests, short answer tests, open book tests, *viva voce*, etc.

All these efforts led to the setting up of a Central Evaluation Unit (CEU) in 1958. State Evaluation Units also came into being. On 1st September 1960, the National Council of Educational Research and Training (NCERT) was established by the Ministry of Education. The Central Evaluation Unit became a part of NCERT. In 1966, CEU was renamed as the Examination and Evaluation Unit (CEU). Later on with the amalgamation of the Department of Curriculum, Methods and Textbooks, it came to be known as the Department of Curriculum and Evaluation.

By 1964, State Evaluation Units had started functioning in 12 States and one Union Territory.

Satisfactory solution to various problems of education including examinations remained eluded. This led to the appointment of a Commission known as Education Commission 1964-66 or the Kothari Commission under the Chairmanship of Dr. D.S. Kothari. The Commission went into all aspects of education and made several recommendations on reforms in examinations. It observed, " It is now agreed that evaluation is a continuous process, forms an integral part of the total system of education, and is intimately related to educational objectives. It exercises a great influence on the pupils study habits and the teacher's method of instruction and thus helps not only to measure educational achievement but also to improve it. The techniques of evaluation are means of collecting evidence about the student's development in desirable directions. These techniques should, therefore, be valid, reliable, objective and practicable." The Commission further stressed that "a natural corollary of the acceptance of the new approach will be to improve the written examination in such a way that it becomes a valid and reliable measure of educational achievement." The Commission was of the view that several important aspects, of the student's growth could not be measured by written examinations. It, therefore, laid stress on other methods such as observation techniques, oral tests and practical examinations.

The Kothari Commission made the following recommendations on examination reform:

1. Classes I to V to be treated as an ungraded unit.
2. Observation techniques and oral tests to be used at the primary stage.
3. No external examination to be held at the end of primary stage.
4. Standardised tests to be conducted to assess the standard of performance of primary schools.
5. External examination need not be compulsory for all the students of class X or class XI/XII.
6. Certificate to be given by the school to the students at the end of a stage, indicating the record of internal assessment as contained in the cumulative record card.

7. Board's certificate at the end of the lower or higher secondary stage to give the student's performance only in those subjects in which he has passed but no remark to be made to the effect that he has passed or failed in the whole examination.
8. Internal assessment to be made very comprehensive.
9. National Board of School Education to be set up at the Centre.
10. Establishment of experimental schools with the right to hold their own final examination at the end of class X.

In 1967, a Committee of Members of Parliament that considered the 1964–66 report recommended that there can be no public examinations at the end of classes X and XII. The Committee also suggested a draft for the National Policy on Education.

On the role of the examinations, the National Policy on Education 1968 observed, "A major goal of examination reforms should be to improve the reliability and validity of examinations and to make evaluation a continuous process aimed at helping the student to improve his level of achievement rather than at 'certifying' the quality of his performance at a given moment of time."

Notwithstanding the efforts to reform the examination system, considerable concern was expressed in different quarters about the malpractices, eruption of violence, etc. during the progress of public examinations held in the different parts of the country. The Central Advisory Board of Education, Ministry of Education and Social Welfare, Government of India, appointed Committee on Examination. The Union Education Minister was its Chairman and Director NCERT its Member-Secretary.

The Committee made its observations and recommendations under the following heads:

1. Amending legislation passed in the relevant laws pertaining to the powers of the Boards of Examinations.
2. Conducting examinations.
3. Use of examination results.
4. Budgeting for research in examinations.
5. Malpractices adopted before the commencement of the examinations.

6. Preventive measures for minimising malpractices.
7. Malpractices practised during the conduct of examinations and preventive measures.

The Education Commission 1964–66 had recommended the introduction of a uniform pattern of 10+2+3 in the entire country. This recommendation was incorporated in the Education Policy 1968. In 1973, the Government of India appointed a National Committee on 10+2+3 Educational Structure. The Committee gave its recommendations in September 1973 on the implementation of the New Pattern of Education. Regarding examinations, the Committee made these observations:

1. There should be a public examination at the end of class X and another at the end of class XII or at the completion of the Vocational Course.
2. In the examination at the end of class X subjects of Moral Education, Physical Education and Craft or Trade need not be examined externally.
3. The practical examination should include a *viva voce,* and passing in the practical examination should be obligatory on the part of every student.
4. In the examinations in languages, particularly in the home examinations, provision should be made for oral test.
5. For practical and administrative considerations, it is desirable to make the State Board of Higher Secondary and Vocational Education (by whatever name it is called) be responsible for conducting public examinations for both the academic and the Vocational Courses.
6. The new scheme should provide a continuous internal assessment throughout the course of studies. The marks of the students after moderation, where necessary, should be incorporated in the Board's certificate in a separate column parallel to the one in which the result of the examination is given under the existing practice.
7. The result of internal assessment should be expressed in terms of grades on a five-point scale.

8. A scheme of continuous internal assessment of each student of the vocational stream similar to one for the academic stream should be prepared and incorporated in the scheme of examination.
9. Facilities should be provided in class XI and XII to enable the students to prepare and pass the examination in one or more subjects at one time.

While the 1968 Policy on Education was being implemented, the NCERT published *"The Curriculum for the 10 Year School: A Framework"* in 1975. It stated, "Gradually as the system of internal assessment takes root, and personal biases leading to the lowering of standards are brought under check, the external public examination at the end of class X will become redundant and should be abolished. It would be necessary for each Board/State to evolve a phased programme of accomplishing this." This remained only a pious hope.

Far reaching political changes took place in the country during the year 1977. With the formation of the Janata Government in March 1977, the Education Minister appointed a Review Committee with Shri Ishwarbhai Patel as its Chairman. On the subject of examinations, the Committee stated, "The weightage to be given to internal assessment and external evaluation should be determined by each examining body."

Three more documents on the reforms of education appeared. A National Education Conference convened by the All India Nai Talim Samiti in New Delhi in December 1977 recommended the new structure of education as 8+4+3—eight years of free and compulsory education, four years of secondary education and three years of University education. It recommended that in States which have so far provided for only seven years of elementary education, the structure may be 7+5+3. However, matriculation examination may be conducted after the completion of ten years of school education for those students who cannot afford to complete the full period of secondary education. The National Review Committee for the Plus 2 Curriculum (1978) under the Chairmanship of Dr. Macolm S. Adiseshaih dealt with the vocationalisation of education. The National Review Committee recommended that in those States where the universities have already adopted the semester system, the same may also be introduced in classes XI and XII.

A document titled *Education for Our People* (1979), prepared under the leadership of J.P. Naik on behalf of the Trustees of the J.P. Institute of Human Rights, Bombay, made several suggestions for reconstructing education in the country.

The movement of educational reforms launched during the Janta Dal Government at the Centre, led to the formulation of Draft National Policy on Education, 1979. On examination reforms, the Policy observed, "Examinations, especially public examinations should be made more objective and reliable. Evaluation should enable the teacher to see the effectiveness of his instruction and enable the pupils to judge the results of their learning efforts. It should thus act as an instrument of improving and learning processes including the content of courses and methods of teaching." With the fall of the Janata Government in 1979 the Draft National Policy on Education lost its significance.

A Working Group on Autonomous Schools (1981) with Fr T.V. Kunnunkal, Vice Chairman, Central Board of Secondary Education (CBSE) as Convener, recommended that autonomous schools to be established should develop their own syllabi at the secondary stage in all the subjects (within the Scheme of Studies of the Board) and hold own examination in place of the Board's examination. The Autonomous Schools Committee will initiate certain moderation procedures to ensure that the marking norms of the school do not vary in any significant measure from those of the Board *vis-a-vis* other schools.

In 1983, a Working Group on Curriculum Load was constituted by the NCERT. The Working Group felt that the present system of examination with its emphasis on memorisation is responsible to a great extent for the problem of curriculum load.

Dissatisfaction with the system of education continued to grow. Realising the gravity of the situation, the then Prime Minister, Rajiv Gandhi in his broadcast to the nation on January 5, 1985, declared that a new education policy would be formulated that would equip the country both scientifically and economically to enter the 21st century. Accordingly the Ministry of Education prepared a document *Challenge of Education: A Policy Perspective* in August 1985. This document presented a 'Status Report' on Education. On the issue of examinations it observed that the prevailing system was out of tune.

There was a nation-wide discussion on the above mentioned document and it resulted in the formulation of the National Policy on Education, 1986. The Policy stated, "As a part of sound educational strategy examinations should be employed to bring about qualitative improvement in education. The objective will be to recast the examination system."

For implementing the National Policy on Education a Programme of Action, 1986 was prepared by the Ministry of Human Resource Development (Formerly known as Ministry of Education). The programme included a comprehensive strategy to bring about reforms in the system of education. Spot evaluation of answer script was one of the important measures. It included several short-term and long terms steps. It also envisaged the establishment of a National Testing Service.

In 1988, in accordance with the directions contained in the NPE 1986, NCERT prepared the National Curriculum for Elementary and Secondary Education — A Frame Work. On evaluation and examination, it observed, "By and large the public examinations at the terminal stages of school education have dominated the Indian scene, the ill effects of which on the learners have been widely recognised by experts and layman alike." It further stated, "Dominance of the public examination apart, even the year-end evaluation in schools is modelled after the external Board examination and hence a great deal of importance is given to the one-shot examination at the cost of continuous and comprehensive internal evaluation. Thus the entire curriculum transaction is not only determined but also adversely affected by its dictates, the teachers gear their teaching to satisfy exam-requirements rather than the needs of learners and their growth and development in various areas of learning." The document suggested the following steps for the reform of evaluation and examination.

1. Minimum levels of learning should be attained by the learners.
2. Grades in place of marks should be given.
3. Proper records of growth and developement of the learners should be maintained.
4. Due weightage should be given to essay type questions, short answer questions, objective type questions and oral tests.
5. Open-book examination may be tried out on a large scale.
6. Provision for improvement in grades should also be made.

7. Semester system from the secondary stage may be introduced.

8. Educational Testing Service should be established at the district level.

The Programme of Action for the implementation of the National Policy on Education 1986 could not be undertaken effectively as there was a change of government at the Centre in 1989. The short-lived Janata Government headed by Shri V.P. Singh, Prime Minister of India, appointed a Committee in May 1990 to review the NPE, 1986 formulated by the Congress Government under Shri Rajiv Gandhi. The National Policy Education Review Committee (NPERC) is popularly known as Ramamurti Review Committee after the name Acharya Ramamurti who was the Chairman of the Committee. The Committee made a detailed survey of the reforms being made at the school and higher level.

In its recommendations (R. Nos. 267 and 268), the NPERC particularly made four points, namely:

(*i*) The examination reforms should be construed as a package.

(*ii*) The package as a whole should be implemented instead of in piecemeal and *ad hoc* implementation of individual elements.

(*iii*) Implementation of the package suggested by the NPERC bristled with practical problems such as the vast diversities in the education system and the wide spread apprehensions about the credibility of the internal evaluation process.

(*iv*) The need to constitute a high level National Examination Reforms Commission to coordinate and monitor the progress in Examination Reforms at various levels. The recommendations of the Ramamurti Committee were examined by a Committee headed by Janardhana Reddy. The Committee is also known as CABE (Central Advisory of Education) Committee, 1992. This Committee was constituted by the Congress Government at the fall of the Janata Government.

The Janardhana Committee made the following observations on the recommendations of NPERC. "The reading of the recommendation as a whole would make it appear that the NPERC was itself undecided about the immediate feasibility or acceptability of the package suggested by it. Given the diversity of the educational institutions, it would not be realistic to prescribe a single package of reforms across the board. Some of the reforms like introduction of semester system may be relevant for higher education rather than for school stage. Facilities for multiple entry and exit, and transfer of grade from one instituion to another are not immediately feasible, atleast in the school stage, and call for a degree of uniformity in curriculum and medium of instruction, which are difficult to achieve in a continental nation like ours. Therefore, the endeavour should be to strive for the best achievable results rather than plan for the best unobtainable package. Examination reforms have necessarily to be contextual and evolutionary.

The essentiality of examination reforms cannot be overstated. We do feel that rather than leaving examination reforms to the individual initiatives and inclinations of the examining bodies, a strong and coordinated effort should be made by the Centre and the State Governments in this area. The idea underlying the constitution of an Examination Reforms Commission is appealing. However, rather than creating yet another institution, we suggest that the NCERT and the UGC should play a lead role in promoting and guiding examination reforms in school and higher education systems respectively. *Inter alia,* the following measures are suggested:

(*i*) Preparation of a status report of examination reform measures undertaken by the examining bodies.

(*ii*) Preparation of a National Examination Reform Framework to serve as a set of guidelines to the examining bodies which would have the freedom to innovate and adapt the framework to suit the specific situation.

(*iii*) Developing an effective mechanism for coordination, monitoring and evaluation of the implementation of the examination reforms by the different examining bodies.

(*iv*) Documentation and dissemination of innovations and measures for examination reforms."

(See also Chapter 22 for detailed recommendations of Committees and Commissions)

8.2. STATUS OF EXAMINATION REFORMS AT SCHOOL AND COLLEGE LEVEL

The Ramamurti Report 1990 made a detailed survey of the steps being taken by different States regarding evaluation and examination reforms. These are presented below in Tables 1 and 2.

Table 1. *Status of Implementation of Examination Reforms at The School Level*

Sr. No.	*Steps for Examination Reforms*	*Boards/States which have introduced Reforms*
1.	Development of policy statement (designs) for each question paper.	Andhra Pradesh, Assam, Gujarat, Kerala, Maharashtra, Punjab, Rajasthan, CISCE, J&K, M.P., Manipur, CBSE, Haryana, Tripura, Karnataka, Goa, U.P., West Bengal.
2.	Appointment of paper setters from among those trained in evaluation.	Andhra Pradesh, Gujarat, Kerala, Maharashtra, Orissa, Rajasthan, CISCE, J&K, M.P., Manipur, Tamil Nadu, Haryana, Goa, U.P., West Bengal.
3.	Appointment of panels of paper setters for each question paper.	Andhra Pradesh, Assam, Kerala, Gujarat, Maharashtra, Rajasthan, CISCE, Tripura, Goa, U.P.
4.	Allocation of definite proportionate percentages of marks in question papers for testing different abilities.	Andhra Pradesh, Assam, Gujarat, Maharashtra, Kerala, Rajasthan, CISCE, J&K, M.P., CBSE, Haryana, Manipur, Tripura, Karnataka, Goa, U.P.
5.	Ensuring an effective coverage of the syllabus through the question papers.	Andhra Pradesh, Assam, Gujarat, Kerala, Maharashtra, Rajasthan, CISCE,CBSE, J&K, Manipur, M.P., Haryana, Goa, U.P.
6.	Introduction of specific pinpointed questions in the question paper.	Andhra Pradesh, Assam, Gujarat, Karnataka, Kerala, Maharashtra, CISCE, CBSE, Haryana, Tripura, Goa, U.P., West Bengal.

(1)	*(2)*	*(3)*
7.	Inclusion of short-answer questions in the question papers, besides the essay-type ones.	Andhra Pradesh, Assam, Gujarat, Karnataka, Kerala, Maharashtra, Manipur, Orissa, Punjab, Rajasthan, Tamil Nadu, CISCE, CBSE, Haryana, Tripura, Goa, U.P., West Bengal.
8.	Introduction of objective type questions (multiple choice) in the question papers.	Andhra Pradesh, Gujarat, Karnataka, Kerala, Maharashtra, Manipur, Orissa, Punjab, Rajasthan, Tamil Nadu, CISCE, Tripura, Goa, U.P.
9.	Use of question banks for setting question papers.	Gujarat, Rajasthan, CISCE, Goa, Bihar, CBSE, Haryana, West Bengal.
10.	Abolition of overall options in the question papers.	Andhra Pradesh, Assam, Gujarat, Karnataka, Kerala, Orissa, Rajasthan, CBSE, U.P.
11.	Development of marking scheme alongwith each question papers by the setter himself.	Assam, Gujarat, Karnataka, Kerala, Punjab, Rajasthan, CISCE, CBSE, U.P., Goa, Maharashtra, West Bengal.
12.	Division of question papers into two separate sections for fixed response and free response questions with fixed separate time limit.	Andhra Pradesh, Gujarat, Kerala, Karnataka, Punjab, Rajasthan, Tamil Nadu, CISCE.
13.	Introduction of centralised spot evaluatioin of scripts.	Andhra Pradesh, Assam, Gujarat, Karnataka, Kerala, Tamil Nadu, CISCE, CBSE, Tripura, Goa, U.P.
14.	Introduction of mechanical processing of examination results.	Andhra Pradesh, Gujarat, Kerala, Karnataka, Maharashtra, Rajasthan, CISCE, CBSE, U.P.

(1)	*(2)*	*(3)*
15.	Scaling of subject-wise results for making them comparable.	Gujarat, Kerala, CISCE.
16.	Allowing students to clear the examination in parts.	Andhra Pradesh, Karnataka, Kerala, Rajasthan, Punjab, CBSE.
17.	Permitting students to improve their grades by appearing at subsequent examinations.	Andhra Pradesh, Karnataka, Kerala, Rajasthan, Punjab, CBSE.
18.	Reckoning both the product and performance in evaluation of practical work in science subject.	Assam, Gujarat, Kerala, Punjab, Maharashtra, Rajasthan, CISCE, Tripura, CBSE, U.P.
19.	Incorporation of both academic and non-academic areas of pupil growth in the scheme subject.	Rajasthan, Tamil Nadu.
20.	Issue of separate certificate of internal assessment alongwith that of external examination.	Rajasthan.
21.	Analysis of question papers in details as feedback for paper setters.	Rajasthan
22.	Analysis of answer-scripts of the examination locating common errors, correlation in score and functional value of item, etc.	Rajasthan.
23.	Autonomy to schools in curriculum, teaching, text-books and evaluation etc.	Rajasthan.

The following statement further presents information on the status of implementation of examination reforms in the universities:

Table 2. *Status of Implementation of Examination Reforms at the University Level*

Sr. No.	*Item*	*No. of Universities*
1.	Universities which have introduced internal evaluation at different levels.	74
2.	Universities which have developed question banks.	74
3.	Universities which have adopted grading systems for various courses.	45
4.	Universities which have introduced semester system.	71
5.	Universities which have initiated steps to divide syllabus into units/areas of content.	56
6.	Universities which have decided that choice in answering questions should be restricted to each units of syllabus.	50
7.	Universities which have agreed to hold examinations without fulfilling the requirements of minimum lectures/tutorials, laboratory sessions etc.	52

Chapter 9

Definition, Meaning, Purposes and Nature of Evaluation

9.1. EVALUATION, MEASUREMENT, TESTING AND APPLIED TERMS

It would be of interest to know what *A Critical Dictionary of Education* (1982) has to say on these terms. "Educational discourse has many words that relate to the broad task of judging the worth of a person, programme, or piece of work, including, 'evaluating' 'measuring', 'assessing', 'appraising', 'examining', 'testing', 'marking', 'grading' and 'scoring'. Such words, are often confused : one person's 'testing', is another person's 'assessing', and 'marking' in one country may be 'grading' in another. Nevertheless, these words are not all synonymous. 'Scoring' is usually applied to the act of checking responses to objective questions (a task that may be completed by a machine). 'Marking' and 'grading' (British and American Equivalents) indicate that a teacher is judging the worth of written scripts submitted by students, either in examination conditions or as a part of cause requirements. 'Testing' and 'examining' usually suggest the application of a standardized (as in tests of basic skills) or teacher-devised instrument to gauge the progress of students during the end of a course of study. 'Assessing' and 'appraising' are general terms that may indicate a variety of intentions and activities, such as measuring progress in a strict experimental sense, estimating certain qualities in a programme, or judging the worth of an educational activity. On different occasions, therefore, both these words have been used as synonyms for very different terms : 'measuring' on the one hand, or 'evaluating' on the other.

The differences between measuring and evaluating are important. Measuring generally has a very precise denotation : assigning numerals to objects or events according to rules. Consequently, those interested in measurement typically search for observable indications or properties of objects or events under study, apply rules to those basic properties, and then allocate a number to the result, often using statistical techniques. Thus, in measuring creativity, researchers identify a particular range of behaviours that are thought to indicate creativity, apply a test that requires students to demonstrate those behaviours, and then derive and rank a series of scores based on the results of that test. Consequently a number indicating relative creative ability may be attached to each student. An important aim is that all experiments will obtain the same result."

The International Dictionary of Education (1977) explains these concepts as :

Evaluation. "Value judgement on an observation, 'performance test', or indeed any 'data' whether directly measured or inferred. For example, if a pupil gains a score of 32 on a test of education, this measure is evaluated by placing a meaning on it relative to a standard, norm or some other situation. Thus, the score may be 'above average', 'fail' or indicative of below or above average effort on the part of the individual, or again that the score is 'good' for his/her age, but 'average' for his/her particular class."

Assessment. "In education, the process by which one attempts to measure the quality and quantity of learning and teaching using various assessment techniques, assignments, projects continuous assessment, objective type tests."

Measurement. "Act of finding dimensions of any object and the quality found by each act."

The Dictionary of Education (1982) explains the concept evaluation and assessment as, "Evaluation in often used interchangeably with assessment. This is because there is a considerable overlap in their meanings. Both involve measurements designed to describe the amount of certain attributes. Both involve procedures for obtaining these measurements which can involve tests as well as less objective instruments such as rating scales. There is a tendency, however, for evaluation to be used in a more general way, involving a wide range of measures with a great acceptance of subjective judgements. There is also a tendency for evaluation to be used more when the subject of the evaluation is not a person (or group of persons) but the success of a course of teaching or method of teaching. Assessment is therefore used more usually in situations where the procedures involve more objective instruments, and when these instruments are measuring personal attributes."

Panton, M.Q. (1985) in an article 'Evaluation, Assessment and Measurement' published in *The International Encyclopaedia of Education* (Husen and Posthethwatle (Editors-in-chief) states that in the minds of many educational practitioners the words evaluation, testing and measurement appear to be used 'interchangeably'. In the United States during the 1970's and now increasingly in other parts of the English speaking world, evaluation is being used 'with less and less regard to its original meaning. Panton further observes, "What evaluation, assessment and measurement have in common is testing. Each frequently (but not always) makes use of tests, but none of them is synonymous with testing, and the type of tests required for each of the three processes may be different." The author defines these terms as given below:

Measurement. The regulatory definition of "assigning a numerical quantity to..." will serve in most educational applications. While instruments such as rulers and stop watches can be used to determine height, speed, and so on, many intellectual capacities or other quantities of educational interest must be measured indirectly. Thus tests are typically used to measure such dimensions as level of intelligence, the ability to apply a given principle in a variety of situations, the proportion of material learned or forgotten. Measurement is rarely carried out for its own sake. It may be included in an assessment or evaluation, but is more to be regarded as a basic research procedure."

Assessment. "As far as possible the term assessment should be reserved for application to people. It covers activities included in grading (formal and nonformal), examining, certifying, and so on. Student's achievement on a particular course may be assessed. An applicant's attitude for a particular job may be assessed. A teacher's competence may be assessed. Throughout the world, most educational systems find it appropriate to record student's achievement in some way, whether with a number, a letter code, or a comment such as 'satisfactory' or 'needs improvement.' Such assessments are based on the internal synthesis of a wide variety of evidence, and although they often include test results, they rarely have much in common with scientific measurement. These procedures are increasingly being labelled 'Student evaluation' in the United States."

Evaluation. "In general, it would seem preferable to reserve the term educational evaluation for application to abstract entities such as programmes, curricula and organisational variables. Just as assessment may be characterized as a routine activity in which most educators will be involved, evaluation is an activity primarily for those engaged in research and development."

A Critical Dictionary of Educational Concepts (1986) explains the concept assessment as: "Students may be assessed for a number of different reasons and in a number of different ways. We may for example, wish to test the level of student attainment, to gather data to aid inquiry into our teaching or for purposes of accountability, to make predictions concerning the student's future, to set standards, or to motivate students. The range of types of assessment runs from the conventional written essay, through oral tests or practical projects, to various types of objective tests."

9.2. RELATION BETWEEN EVALUATION AND MEASUREMENT

Stevens (1951) explains the difference between evaluation and measurement in these words, "In its broadest sense, measurement is the assignment of numerals to objects, or events, according to rules. We measure height and weight following certain rules and then assign some numerical value to the measurements. We do not assign numbers in all cases of measurement, especially when using criterion-referenced measuring instruments. Here the symbols assigned may be equivalent to (+) or (–) since the measuring instrument sets a single standard and the individual either meets or fails to meet the absolute standard set by the objective. When evaluating data we go beyond the concept of measurement and make a judgement about the measurements taken."

Dubois, Alverson and Staley (1979) explain the distinction between evaluation and measurement in these words, "As with any assessment process, the evaluation of entering behaviour involves the collection and evaluation of data. Psychologists working in the field of tests and measurement use the term measurement to refer to the collection portion of the process."

A Dictionary of Education (1981) explains the concept measurement as "Fundamentally we can say that measurement entails certain rules and procedures for assigning numbers to attributes in such a way that the numbers represent the quantity of the attribute. It is necessay to be clear that it is not the object, organism or event itself which is being measured. For example, we don't measure a 'piece of wood' but we measure one of its attributes such as its length or weight. In educational measurement we are faced with attributes that do not lend themselves to such intuitive procedures (as used in physical sciences).

According to D.L. Stuffebeam (1968), measurement may be defined as the assignment of numerals to entities according to rules.

In the words of Lester O. Cron and Others, "Evaluation is a broader term than measurement. Evaluation not only is concerned with the determination of learning results but it also involves value judgement of the desirability of these results. It is a continuous process in which various techniques of testing or measurement can be utilised. Evaluation is a cooperative activity in which the principal, the teacher, the pupils and the parents participate."

H.H. Remmen and N.L. Gage point out, "It is the felt need that has caused the shift from the term 'measurement' implying mathematically precise mensuration of knowledge — to the term 'evaluation' which widens the areas to be studied to include subjective opinions and qualitative changes as well as objective and quantitative changes to include changes in attitudes, appreciation and understandings as well as acquisitions of knowledge and skills."

Ebel and Frisble (1991) explain the concept of measurement and testing in these words, "Measurement is the process of assigning numbers to individuals or their characteristics but does not require that value judgements be made about the numbers obtained from the process. We measure achievement with a test by counting the number of test items a student answers correctly, and we use exactly the same rule to assign a number to the achievement of each student in the class. Measurements are useful for describing the amount of certain abilities that individuals have. Tests represent one particular measurement technique. A test is a set of questions, each of which has a correct answer. All tests are a subset of the quantitative tools or techniques that are classified as measurements. And all measurement techniques are a subset of the quantitative and qualitative techniques used in evaluation. Tests that measure relevant school learning with precision are the most useful tools available to teachers for most classroom summative evaluation needs."

Prof. Adediran A Taiwo (1995) distinguishes measurement and evaluation in these words, "While measurement is concerned with only the amount, quantity or frequency of a variable, evaluation matches such an amount, quantity or frequency with relevant criteria for the purpose of making some value judgement about the measured or the observed amount. ...In essence, the term evaluation involves both quantitative and qualitative description of events, behaviours, things, parameters, or variables as well as value judgement of things or events being described. It, therefore, follows that any time one talks of evaluation, be it in the realm of achievements of students, the effectiveness of a teaching method or the appropriateness of a curriculum, one is concerned with both numerical and verbal description as well as value judgement of what is being described."

Evaluation is a comprehensive and continuous process which covers every aspect of an individual's achievement in the educative programme. It is an integral part of education in which students and teachers are partners. It signifies a wider process of judging students' progress in various aspects. Measurement, on the other hand, implies only a precise quantitative assessment of instructional outcomes.

Evaluation is integrated with the entire task of education and not only with examinations, tests and measurement.

Evaluation encompasses tests and measurement but also goes beyond them.

Evaluation depends upon measurement but is not synonymous with it.

Measurement is a quantitative determination of *how much* an individual's performance has been, while evaluation is a qualitative judgement of *how good* or *how satisfactory* an individual's performance has been.

Measurement describes a situation; evaluation judges its worth or value.

Measurement is only a tool to be used in evaluation. By itself, it is meaningless, but without it evaluation is likely to be of little significance.

Sound evaluation is based upon the results of accurate and relevant measurement. It is also to be remembered that not all uses of a test or measurement in education can be considered evaluation, for evaluation is always in the light of some particular goal, purpose or value.

Evaluation is not only quantitative but also qualitative and includes value judgement. Mathematically it may be said that:

Evaluation = Measurement (quantitative description of students' achievements) + Qualitative description of students' abilities

+ Value judgements about students' achievements and abilities.

The difference between evaluation and measurement may be explained with the help of the following examples:

(1) A teacher measures Mohan's height to be 180 cm. He evaluates his height when he says that he is 'long'.
(2) A teacher measures Sita's achievement in Economics to be 50%. He evaluates his achievement when he says that Sita's achievement in Economics is 'satisfactory'.
(3) A teacher measures the size of a classroom and finds that it is 4m × 3m. He evaluates the classroom dimensions when he reports that the classroom is 'too small' for 40 students.
(4) Bharat and Mohan study in the same class. In the first test they obtain 50 and 70 marks respectively in English. In the second test, both of them obtain 80 marks. Now in the second measurement (test scores), achievement in English is the same, yet the evaluation will differ. When the teacher states that the rate of progress of Bharat is comparatively better than that of Mohan.

Measurement helps in evaluation. This may be clarified by taking one example. Rahul and Bharat study in the same class. They take two tests. In the first test, they obtain 45 and 65 marks respectively in Civics. In the second test, both of them obtain 80 marks. Now, in the second test, the measurement (test scores) of their achievement in Civics is the same, yet the evaluation will differ, when the teacher says that the rate of progress of Rahul is comparatively better than that of Bharat.

9.3. EVALUATION, MEASUREMENT AND TESTING

Evaluation, measurement and testing have similar meanings and are closely related with each other. Nevertheless, these terms are not synonymous.

Anthony J. NiHKo in his book *Educational Tests and Measurement* (1983) makes the following distinction, "Tests are systematic procedures for observing persons and describing them with either a numerical scale or a category system. Thus tests may give either qualitative or quantitative information."

"Measurement is a procedure for assigning numbers to specified attributes or characteristics of person in a manner that maintains the real world relationship among persons with regard to what is being measured."

"Evaluation involves judging the value or worth of a pupil on an instructional method or on an educational programme. Such judgements may or may not be based on information obtained from tests."

N.E. Gronlund defines these terms in the book *Measurement and Evaluation* (1985) as under:

Test. "An instrument or systematic procedure for measuring a sample of behaviour. (Answer the question "How well does the individual perform either in comparison with others or in comparison with a domain of performance tasks"?)

Measurement. "The process of obtaining numerical description of the degree to which an individual possesses a particular characteristic. (Answer the question, "How much?") Evaluation: "The systematic process of collecting, analysing (classroom) and interpreting information to determine. The extent to which pupils are achieving instructional objectives. (Answer the question, "How Good"?)

Robert L. Ebel and David in their book *Essentials of Measurement* (1986) observe, "All tests are a subset of the quantitative tools or techniques that are classified as measurements. And all measurement techniques are a subset of the quantitative and qualitative techniques used in evaluation."

William Wiersma and Stephan G. Jurs in their publication *Educational Measurement and Testing* (1990) define these terms as under:

Test. "(It) has a narrower meaning than either measurement or assessment. Test commonly refers to a set of items or questions under specific conditions. When a test is given, measurement takes place: however all measurement is not necessarily testing."

Measurement. "For all practical purposes assessment and measurement can be considered synonymous. When assessment is taking place, information or data are being collected and measurement is being conducted."

Evaluation. Evaluation is a process that includes measurement and possibly testing but it also contains the notion of a value judgement. If a teacher administers a test to a class and computes the percentages of correct responses, measurement and testing have taken place. The scores must be interpreted which may mean converting them to values like As, Bs, and Cs and so on or judging them to be excellent, good, fair or poor. This process is evaluation because value judgements are made."

The term test is the narrowest of the three terms. A test is a device or procedure for confronting a subject with a standard set of questions or tasks to which the student responds independently and the results of which can be treated in such a way so as to provide a quantitative comparison of the performance of different students. As a result of a test, a measure is obtained. An observation, a rating scale or any other device that allows to obtain information in a quantitative form is an instrument of measurement. Measurement is an act or a process that involves the assignment of a numerical index to whatever is being assessed. The last stage in the process of gathering, using and interpreting all relevant and accurate information is that of evaluation. Evaluation allows one to make a value judgement. Mathematically, it may be stated that:

Evaluation = Quantitative description of learner's achievement
+ Qualitative description of learner's abilities
+ Value judgements about achievements and abilities.

A test results in a measurement which ultimately leads to evaluation.

Encyclopaedia of Educational Research (1960) edited by Chester W. Harris states, "No important distinction is made between the terms tests and examinations in ordinary speech in the United States. In educational usage either term ordinarily refers to a series of questions or tasks designed to measure the knowledge or skill of an individual. Sometimes the term test is used loosely to include not only instruments which are intended to measure maximum capability, such as achievement tests, aptitude tests, and intelligence tests but also instruments intended to describe typical behaviour, such as personality, interest and altitude inventories.

A Handbook of British Educational Terms (1963) defines assessment as, "The evaluation of the work of a pupil or a candidate by an examination. This may be by means of marks or by a literal scheme—e.g., (in descending order of merit), A, B, C, D, E to which plus or minus signs may be added."

According to Derek Rowntree (1981) assessment is the process whereby one person (usually a teacher or examiner) attempts to find out about the knowledge, attitudes or skills possessed by another (the learner). This may involve him in merely observing the student as he sets about normal learning activities; or he may need to create special assessment activities, e.g. quizzes, examinations, oral tests etc. In the USA, the term evaluation is usually used instead of assessment.

9.4. BRIEF HISTORY OF EVALUATION

Chester W. Harris (1960) traces the history of the concept evaluation to the thirties of the twentieth century. It emerged as a "reaction against the relatively narrow information – and skill – centred educational measurement of the previous decades." It was observed that the educational tests developed in the first quarter of the twentieth century had tended to focus on the tangible and easily measurable fields of knowledge and skill only and they neglected other aspects of education. A strong movement developed under the leadership of Alvin C, Eurich, Ralph W. Tyler and J. Wayne Wrightstone to broaden the various areas of appraisal – attitudes, interests, ideas, ways of thinking, work habits and personal and social responsibility.

In the decade just before World War II the Progressive Education Association in the USA carried out a number of major evaluation projects.

The American Council on Education made large scale cooperative efforts to improve evaluation procedures in the post-war era.

The work of Ralph W. Tyler during the 1930's laid the foundations of the evaluation movement as we know it now. Probably Tyler's contribution was his insistence of defining the goals and objectives in behavioural terms and making them the basis of instrument development in education and evaluation.

In India, the work related to evaluation began in the 1960's.

9.5. DEFINITION AND MEANING OF EVALUATION

Evaluation poses a problem to the educator for it has been a shifting concept. As observed by J.C. Merwin (1969), "Concepts of evaluation have changed over the years. They have changed on relation to such issues as who is to be evaluated, what is to be evaluated, and how evaluations are to be made."

With a view to comprehend the meaning of the term evaluation, some of the important definitions are given below. (Definitions given in the beginning of this chapter are not repeated here).

Encyclopaedia of Modern Education (1943) by Harry N. Rivlin reads, "The term evaluation frequently is used to refer to a great many informal situations in which one or more persons consider what value has followed from some particular experience. For instance, a class of children with their teacher may look back over the unit of work they are completing and consider what value the activities of the unit have had for them as a class and as individuals. Evaluation is used significantly in curriculum improvement.

Ralph Tyler (1950) defines evaluation as "the process of determining to what extent the educational objectives are being realised."

Encyclopaedia of Educational Research (1960) explains the concept of evaluation as, "Evaluation in education signifies describing something, in terms of selected attributes and judging the degree of acceptability or suitability of that which has been described. The "something" that is to be described and judged may be any aspect of the educational scene, but it is typically, (*a*) a total school programme, (*b*) a curricular procedure, or (*c*) an individual or a group of individuals. The process of evaluation involves three distinct aspects: (*i*) selecting the attributes that are important for judging the worth of the specimen to be evaluated, (*ii*) developing and applying procedures that will describe these attributes truly and accurately, and (*iii*) synthesising the evidence yielded by these procedures into a final judgement of worth."

Scriven (1967), points to the judgement nature of evaluation and defines it as the assessment of merit or worth.

The concept of Evaluation in Education (1963) of the NCERT considers evaluation as the "process of determining:

- the extent to which an objective is being attained,
- the effectiveness of the learning experiences provided in the classroom,
- how well the goals of education have been accomplished."

Cronbach and Others (1980) perceive evaluation as a systematic examination of educational or social programmes.

Stuffebeam and others (1971) regard evaluation as providing information for decision making.

Derek Rowntree *in A Dictionary of Education* (1981) states that in the U.K., this term (evaluation) tends to mean identifying the effects and judging the effectiveness of some learning experience (e.g., a lesson) or a course, or a complete curriculum. In the US, the term is also used for what we in the UK call assessment (of student attainment). Assessing student attainment before and after the learning experience might be an important part of evaluation but so too are interviews with teachers, administrators, students, parents and other people in the community, critical analysis of teaching materials, observation of teaching and learning activity, and so on. Some evaluations incline more towards a quantitative approach while others emphasise the qualitative aspects. Some will combine the two approaches.

Nyberg, D. (1981) states, "The teacher is like a banker who should also control evaluation which is the currency of the classroom (and greater educational) economy. The evaluations are loan notes that the student repays with interest and which may be called in by the bank at any time. In this system of exchange it is very likely that if the student shows great interest i.e. pays a lot of attention, then the loan of a positive evaluation is secure."

According to Dr. K. Sudha Rao (1986), "Educational evaluation is a process of estimating and appraising, the degree and dimension of students' achievements. Further, it is also a process of estimating and appraising the proficiency level of the particular educational practice, which is being conducted. It is a way of appraising the application of educational theory in practice."

Husen, Torsten and Postpethwatte, T. Neville (1988) observe that "the problem of defining evaluation is almost as large as that of teaching." According to these writers, successful performance assessment involves three phases or steps, all of which are essential. (*a*) The standard task or set of tasks. The first step in the assessment of human performance is the definition of the work or tasks the candidate for evaluation is to perform. (*b*) The documentary record. This means that those elements in the behaviour or performance of a candidate on which the score will be based must be recorded in scorable and permanent form. (*c*) The scoring key. There must be a procedure for deriving a criterion score from the record which will yield score that are equal when based on records of equal quality, no matter who does the scoring.

9.6. CHARACTERISTICS OF EVALUATION

Evaluation is a continuous process. The Education Commission 1964–66 observed, "It is now agreed that evaluation is a continuous process, forms an integral part of the total system of education, and is intimately related to educational objectives. It exercises a great influence on the pupil's study habits and the teacher's methods of instruction and thus helps not only to measure educational achievement but also to improve it. The techniques of evaluation are means of collecting evidence about the student's development in desirable directions. These techniques should, therefore, be valid, reliable, objective and practicable."

Evaluation includes Academic and Non-Academic Subjects. Clara M. Brown states, "Evaluation is essential in the never ending cycle of formulating goals, measuring progress towards them and determining the new goals which emerge as a result of new warnings. Evaluation involves measurement which means objective qualitative evidence. But it is broader than measurement and implies that considerations have been given to certain values, standards and that interpretation of the evidence has been made in the light of the particular situation."

Evaluation in its broader concept includes examination of academic and examination of non-academic aspects of education. The term 'evaluation' is a newly introduced term. According to Wrightstone, "Evaluation is a relatively new technical term, introduced to design a more comprehensive concept of measurement than is implied in conventional tests and examinations – evaluation involves the identification and formulation of a comprehensive range of the major objectives of a curriculum. This definition is in terms of pupil behaviour, and the selection or construction of valid, reliable and practical instruments for appraising the specified phases of pupil behaviour." In examination and measurement the emphasis is upon the academic subjects only whereas evaluation includes all the changes that take place in the development of a balanced personality and measures the qualities of head, hand, health and heart of an individual.

Evaluation is a Procedure for Improving the Product. Wiles defines evaluation as, "Evaluation is a process of making judgements that are to be used as a basis for planning. It consists of establishing goals, collecting evidence concerning growth or lack of growth towards goals, making judgement about the evidence, and revising procedure and goals in the light of the judgements. It is a procedure for improving the product, the process, and even the goals themselves."

Discovering the Needs of an Individual and Designing Learning Experiences. Chester T. McNernly observes, "The purpose of any programme of evaluation is to discover the needs of the individuals being evaluated and then to design learning experiences that will solve these needs... Evaluation is an important and delicate process not only from the standpoint of determining the needs and growth of programmes and individuals but also from the stand-point of what it does to the individuals being evaluated.....An evaluation cannot adequately be made by using a single check list, an isolated anecdotal record, or a battery of examinations; a complete evaluation will require the use of many techniques."

Evaluation in Terms of Purposes. Thomas H. Briggs and Joseph Justman write that evaluation is "a process by which the values of an enterprise are ascertained." Further they write, "Evaluation should be conceived primarily in terms of educational purposes which the programme of supervision is intended to serve."

(*i*) If the purpose is to stimulate teachers to improve their techniques of class-room instruction, evaluation must concern itself with ascertaining the extent to which such improvement is being affected.

(*ii*) If the purpose is to enrich and vitalize the course of study, evaluation must seek to determine whether the pupils are really deriving greater educational value from the "enriched" and "vitalized" programme than they did formerly.

(*iii*) If the purpose is to re-establish faculty *'esprit de corps'* and school morale, the objectives of evaluation will be to assess in various ways the degree of improvement in personal and professional attitudes in human relations, and ultimately, therefore, in efficiency of teaching and learning.

(*iv*) If an important purpose of the supervisory programme is to promote greater educational attention to individual needs of pupils, evaluation will necessarily concern itself with estimating the success with which guidance procedures, differentiated programme of study, courses and units of learning experience, individualised teaching and learning procedures, and other educational measures designed to achieve greater satisfaction of individual needs are operating.

Shane and McSwain conceive evaluation, "as a process of inquiry based upon criteria co-operatively prepared and concerned with the study, interpretation, and guidance of socially desirable changes in the developmental behaviour of children....It is a process within the child as a result of which he responds to the psychological interpretations he makes of his school-community environment."

Correlation between the Educational System and the System of Evaluation. Evaluation cannot be done in a vacuum. It is always with reference to the objectives of a particular system of education. Evaluation has to be very comprehensive in a system of education which aims at the many-sided development of the personality of a child. "The school of today concerns itself not only with the intellectual pursuits but also with the emotional and social development of the child, his physical and mental health, his social adjustment and other equally important aspects of his life — in a word, with an all-round development of his personality", writes the Secondary Education Commission. In the light of these objectives of the system of education, a comprehensive programme of evaluation would include:

1. Evaluation of the academic subjects.
2. Evaluation of the skills.
3. Evaluation of the physical development.
4. Evaluation of the moral development.
5. Evaluation of the social development.

Evaluation as a complex process. In modern times evaluation tends to become a complex process. It needs scientific techniques and tools. It needs the corporate efforts of teachers, pupils, parents and the administrative staff. It involves an element that brings cohesiveness or coordination in the whole activity.

Decision Taking and Evaluation

Persons involved in the enterprise of education have to take a number of decisions at every step. During the course of a school day, the principal, the teachers and other school personnel take several decisions regarding academic and administrative matters about students. They also assist students to take many decisions for themselves. Whosoever takes a decision, however important or trivial, he should see to it that it is based on:

(*a*) as much information as possible;
(*b*) as accurate information as possible;
(*c*) as relevant information as possible; and
(*d*) as latest information as possible.

For educational decision makers, accurate judgements and inferences are absolutely necessary. This involves the use of tests, measurements and evaluation. Evaluation is done for several purposes. For each purpose a separate type of decision is required. The evaluation decision also determines the type of tests to be used for evaluation. Thus, there is a close relationship between the purposes of evaluation, evaluation decisions and types of tests to be used for them.

Differential Vs. Uniform Evaluation

In evaluation situations, we tend to overlook the fact that there are individual differences among students. We feel satisfied with using a uniform yardstick for all students at a particular point of time. We do not usually take cognizance of the fact that the rate of learning of different children may be different, the learning situations may vary from class to class and student to student and resource inputs may not be the same. Evaluation has to take care of and cater to the needs of such extensive and intensive differences and promote self-paced learning by providing for individual differences instead of prescribing uniform group evaluation.

Full Vs. Partial Evaluation

Full evaluation must take into account all the three aspects i.e. cognitive, affective and psycho-motor. The traditional system of examination evaluates only cognitive abilities. Even in cognitive area external examinations often to do not go beyond the evaluation of memorisation or convergent thinking. These drawbacks can be overcome through evaluation at the school level.

9.7. MAIN GENERALISATIONS ABOUT EVALUATION

A publication of the NCERT entitled *Reforming Examinations: Some Emerging Concepts* (1978) lists the following generalisations:

1. Evaluation is a function of the learner and instruction and, therefore, good evaluation is one which is done by the teacher, of the taught as an individual.
2. Evaluation provides quality control at every stage of the teaching learning process and, therefore, evaluation would be treated as an integral part of the teaching-learning process.
3. Since evaluation provides feed-back about the rate of the pupil's learning and the effectiveness of instruction, evaluation should be done unitwise after teaching every unit.
4. As the purpose of teaching is learning by students, focus of teachers' evaluation should be on improvement of pupils' achievement and not on judging their achievement. Therefore, diagnostic testing and remedial teaching should go side by side.
5. Pupils' achievement is the outcome of the integrated process of learning within a given set of conditions. Evaluation of pupils' learning should, therefore, be also integrated with regard to both the process and product of learning.
6. Keeping in view the obsolesence and explosion of knowledge, the new curriculum stresses the learnability aspect more than the knowledge aspect. Emphasis in evaluation should, therefore, shift from testing of rote memory to that of problem solving abilities and attitude development.
7. For appraisal of the total development of the learner, it is essential that evaluation should not be limited to scholastic achievement alone, but it should encompass all aspects of pupils' development. As such evaluation techniques will have to be extended beyond written and practical examinations to include oral testing, observations, checklists, rating scales and interviews.
8. Since independent learning by students is considered an

important method of learning in the new curriculum self-assessment by pupils of their own learning should be practised in the evaluation system of an institution, so that cooperative assessment of the teacher and the learner is encouraged.

9. Since it is impossible to achieve 100 percent or even near to 100 percent reliability of the various tools used for evaluating pupils, it is desirable that students should be classified broadly into 5 to 7 grades rather than using 101 point scale as at present.
10. As every pupil learns at his own rate he should be judged in terms of his own capacities and goals and not in terms of the standards of his class, institution or the board of secondary education. As such passing of a student in all the subjects at a time cannot be considered essential.
11. The grades of every pupil indicate only his level of performance which may be satisfactory or unsatisfactory in terms of his own standard. Thus, a grade howsoever low it may be, cannot be taken as failure but as an indicator of his present level of achievement.
12. Given more time and proper remedial teaching a student can improve his achievement. Therefore, a student should get the opportunity of improving his grade in one or more subjects, if he so desires.
13. The more accurately and meaningfully the evidence about pupils' growth in different aspects of his development is reported to students, teachers, parents, employers and institutes of higher learning, the more appropriate and reliable would be the decision taken for classification, certification and selection of students for different purposes. Therefore, regular recording of pupil performance in various areas of development is a prerequisit to every evaluation programme.

9.8. COMPONENTS OF EVALUATION

Following are the five components of evaluation:

1. Specifying learning outcomes.
2. Collection of evidence about pupils' growth through reliable data gathering devices.
3. Analysis and interpretation of performance or pupil's growth.

4. Diagnostic appraisal i.e. indicating the level of performance rather than the judgement on the performance.

5. Redefining and readjusting the instructional objectives on the basis of feed-back.

9.9. PURPOSES, NEED AND FUNCTIONS OF EVALUATION

According to J.H. Ahman and M.D. Glock (1954) the overall purpose of evaluation will be "to provide information to enable each pupil to develop according to his potential within the framework of the educational objectives of the school."

According to Bloom (1971), the main purposes of evaluation are:

(*a*) To discover the extent of competence which the student has developed in initiating, organizing and improving his day-to-day work and to diagnose his strengths and weaknesses with a view to further guidance.

(*b*) To predict the educational practices which a particular student-teacher can best participate in or organize.

(*c*) At the end of a career to certify the students' degree of proficiency in a particular educational practice.

The Committee on Examinations (1970-71) appointed by the Central Advisory Board of Education, Ministry of Education and Social Welfare outlined the purposes and need for evaluation in these words, "In a Welfare State, children have to be educated according to their age, aptitudes and abilities. For this purpose evaluation becomes a necessary tool in the educational process. In this way, it has a positive function. Whilst our present system of examinations attempts to assess scholastic attainments, it should nevertheless have also a predictive function to help pupils choose courses of study suited to their talent and potential so that they may develop into useful citizens. Unfortunately, in our country, the negative function of an examination is emphasised more than its positive role, and the objective generally is to find out what a pupil is really unfit for, thus creating a fear and a failure complex. This overemphasis on the negative aspect does incalculable harm to the whole educational process and leads to highly undesirable consequences. It may be mentioned here that world education opinion is against the practice of declaring a student as having 'failed' in a subject or in an examination."

According to Dr. S.K. Mitra, Director NCERT (1977), "under the new approach to schooling, evaluation occupies a very important position in the total curriculum. Emphasis on teacher's evaluation of their pupils, continuous assessment through unit-wise testing, introduction of grading in place of numerical marking, use of evaluation as feedback for improvement of teaching and learning are important features which seek to shift the emphasis from external examinations to internal assessment by teachers."

In order to achieve the ultimate objective of education, we may identify the following main four purposes of evaluation.

1. Classifying students in classes or sections of a class according to their demonstrated knowledge or ability in some subject areas.
2. Diagnosing the individual student's educational weaknesses in order to plan remedial work for him and to revise teaching strategies.
3. Assessing pupils progress from time to time.
4. Predicting students' future academic success or otherwise.

Overall purposes of evaluation are as under:

1. Evaluation appraises the status of and changes in pupil behaviour.
2. Evaluation discloses pupil's needs and possibilities.
3. Evaluation aids pupil-teacher planning.
4. Evaluation expands the concepts of worthwhile goals beyond pure achievement.
5. Evaluation serves as a means of improving school-community relation.
6. Evaluation familiarizes the teacher with the nature of pupil learning, development and progress.
7. Evaluation relates measurement to the goals of the instructional programme.
8. Evaluation facilitates the selection and improvement of measuring instruments.
9. Evaluation appraises the teacher's competence.
10. Evaluation appraises the supervisor's competence.
11. Evaluation serves as method of self-improvement.
12. Evaluation serves as a guiding principle for the selection of supervisory techniques.

9.10. FACTORS PLAYING MAJOR ROLE IN POPULARISING THE CONCEPT OF EVALUATION

1. Child-study approach.
2. Emphasis on individualisation of instruction.

3. The greater breadth and more functional nature of the curriculum.
4. Availability of a variety of appraisal instruments.
5. Specification of instructional objectives.
6. Limitations of traditional system of examination.

9.11. BASIC TERMS IN EVALUATION

Behaviour:

Any visible activity displayed by a learner (student) — mental, emotional and physical reactions and responses. Thus, these reactions or responses are behaviours.

Content. The subject-matter to be assimilated, digested or grasped by the students.

Criterion. A standard by which terminal behaviour is evaluated.

Entering Behaviour. The state of behaviour of the learner before taking up an instructional programme.

Evaluation Procedures. The means of determining the extent to which the learning of activities have been effective.

Instructional Behaviour. The kinds of behavioural changes we wish to bring about in the learner .

Learning. A more or less permanent change in behaviour which occurs as a result of instruction and practice.

Learning Activities. Activities including arrangement of teaching aids, explanations, questioning, observation and reading, writing, listening etc. which lead to learning.

Learning Experiences. Interactions of the learners and the situations provided to the learner in the teaching-learning process for modifying the behaviours of the learners.

Learning Outcomes. Changes in student's behaviour arising out of classroom instruction.

Terminal Behaviour. Behaviour expected of the learner to be able to demonstrate at the time the influence of classroom instruction/ programme over him ends.

Chapter 10

Evaluation in the Overall System of Education

10.1. TOTAL SCHEME OF EVALUATION

Evaluation has to be very comprehensive in a system of education which aims at the many-sided development of the personality of a child. "The

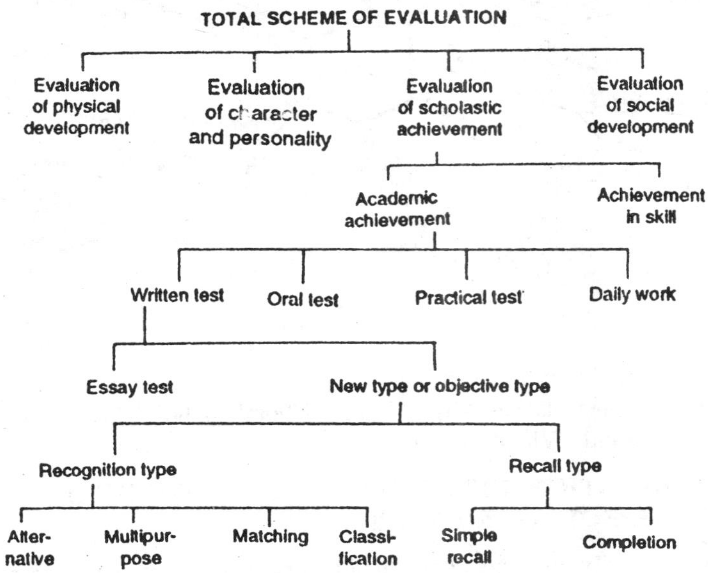

Fig. 10.1. Total Scheme of Evaluation.

schools of today concerns itself not only with the intellectual pursuits but also with the emotional and social development of the child, physical and mental health, his social adjustment and other equally important aspects of his life; in a word, with an all-round development of his personality", writes the Secondary Education Commission. In the light of these objectives of education, a comprehensive programme of evaluation would include elements as shown in Fig. 10.1, in the total scheme of evaluation.

10.2. EVALUATION DESIGN

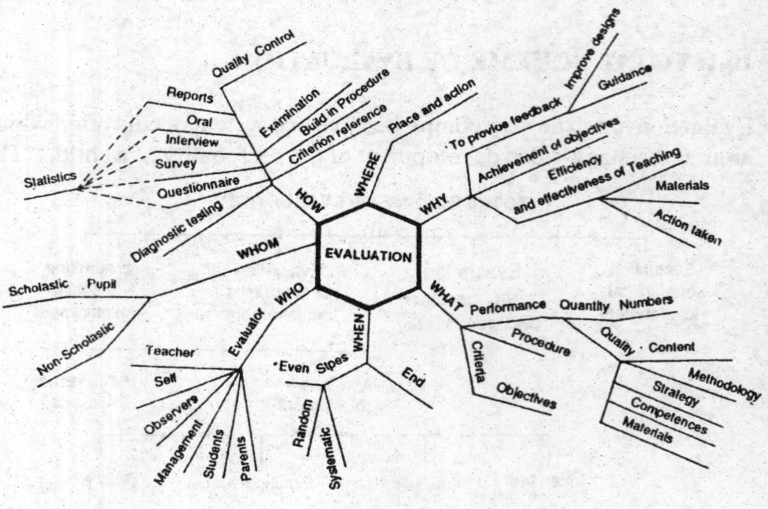

Fig. 10.2 presents the 'Why', 'What', 'Whom', 'Who', 'How', 'Where', and 'When' of evaluation.

10.3. RELATIONSHIP OF EVALUATION WITH OTHER ASPECTS OF EDUCATION

Schematically the concept of educational evaluation may be presented by showing the relationship among objectives, content (subject-matter, learning activities and evaluation procedures (testing).

The inter-relationships of these four aspects of evaluation clearly indicate that the process of evaluation is a continuous one and involves continual appraisal of objectives of the teaching-learning process and of the testing procedures used by the classroom teacher.

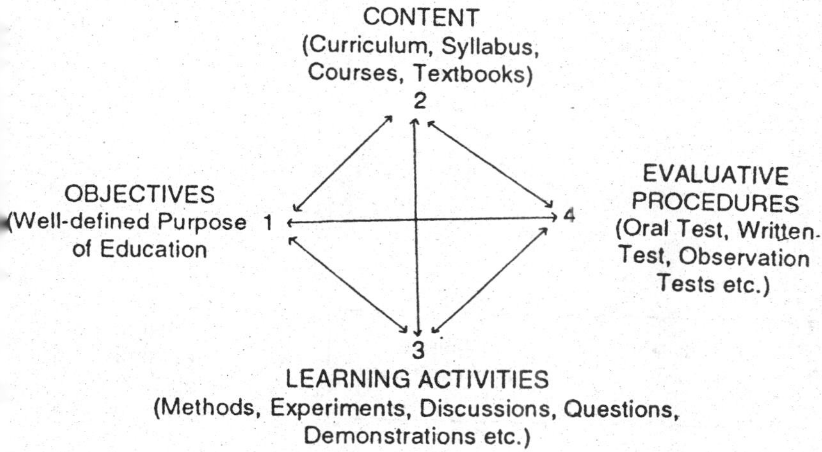

Fig. 10.3. Schematic View of Evaluation.

10.4. INTER-RELATION OF OBJECTIVES AND EVALUATION

The inter-relation of objectives, instruction or the learning experiences and evaluation in a programme of teaching may be expressed through the Fig. 10.4.

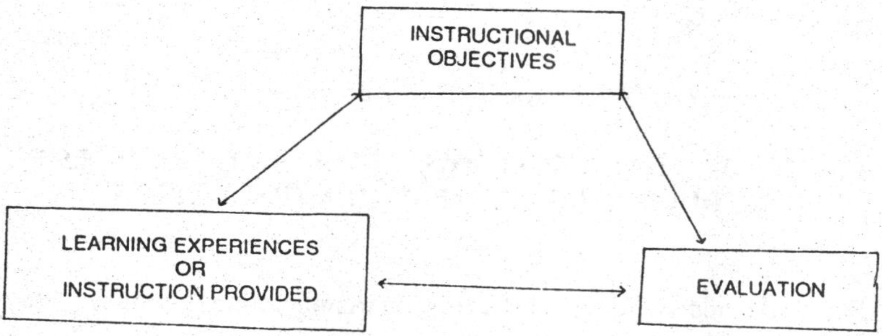

Fig. 10.4. Interrelationship of Objectives, Instruction and Evaluation.

10.5. FLOW CHART OF EVALUATION

Flow Chart of evaluation is shown in Fig. 10.5.

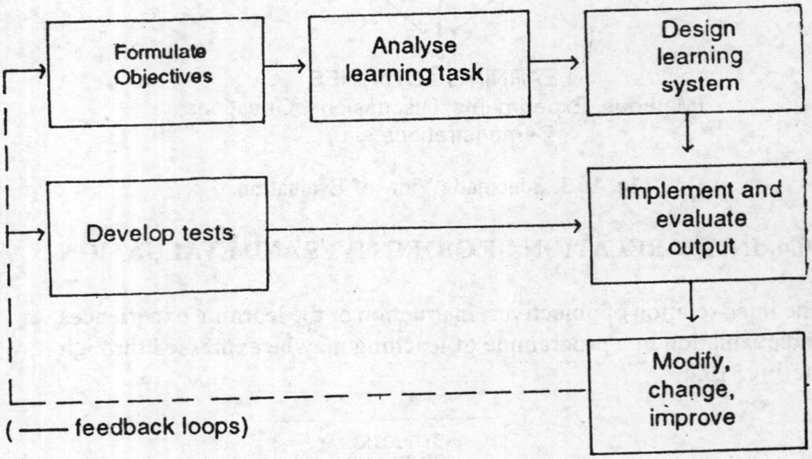

Fig. 10.5. A system flow chart of Evaluation.

10.6. FLOW CHART FOLLOWED BY A TEACHER IN THE INSTRUCTIONAL SYSTEM AND EVALUATION

Fig. 10.6 and 10.7 present the flow charts in the instructional syster and evaluation.

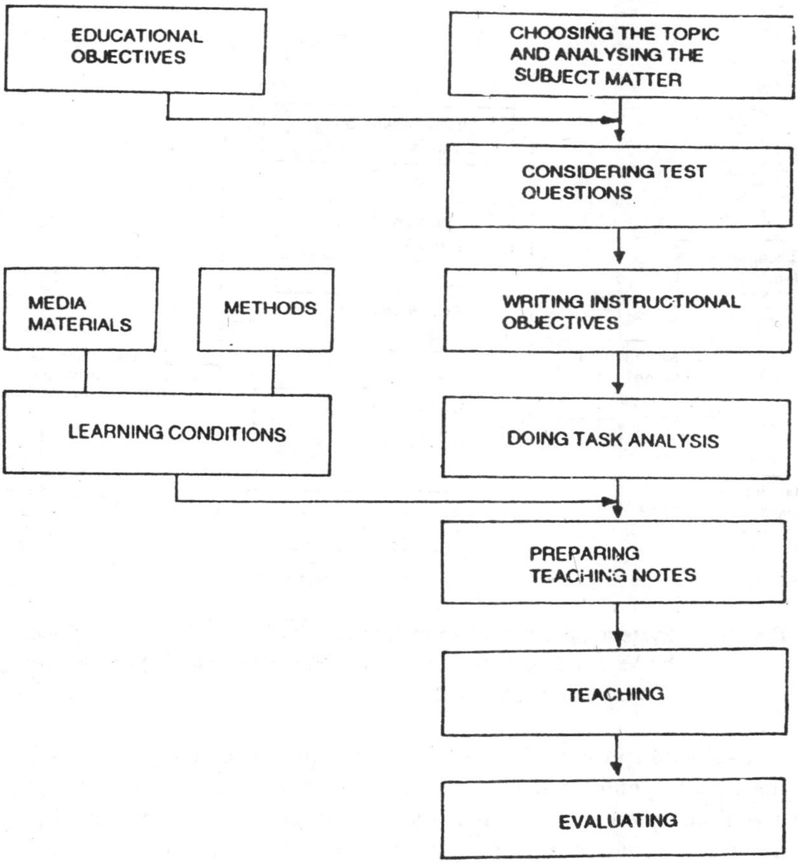

Fig. 10.6. Flow chart showing in detail the path followed by a teacher in an instructional and evaluation system.

10.7. HOW EVALUATION IS HELPFUL

Evaluation and the teacher.

To a teacher with a clear concept of evaluation, changes in the behaviour of the pupils, in their thinking, feeling and actions are the basis for both of his instruction and assessment. Evaluation oriented teacher has two essential tasks i.e. to adopt a child-centred approach and to individualise instruction.

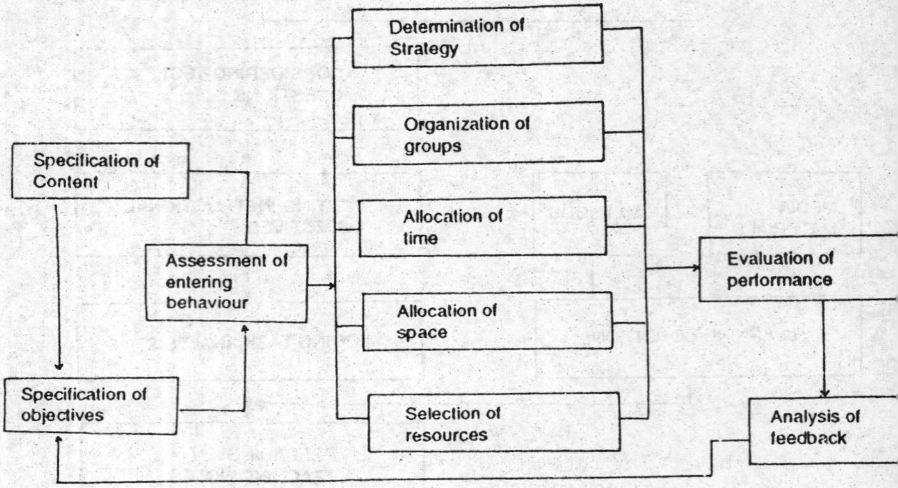

Fig. 10.7. Systematic approach to Instruction and Evaluation (as developed by Vernon S. Gerlach and Donald P. Ely in *Teaching and Media:* A systematic approach).

Evaluation provides the teacher with adequate knowledge concerning the students' entry behaviour. The importance of readiness to learn is a well-accepted fact. For teaching effectively, the teacher must find out where a student is, from where to start and where to go. A teacher, therefore, must have estimates of a student's ability for learning and of what he currently knows.

Knowledge of a student's entry behaviour obviously helps the teacher in setting, refining and clarifying realistic objectives for each student.

Evaluation helps the teacher to organise appropriate learning activities for the students to realise the objectives.

Evaluation helps the teacher to find out the extent to which objectives are realised.

Evaluation helps the teacher to improve his classroom procedures and methods of teaching-learning in the light of feedback.

Evaluation and Students.

Evaluation helps the students in a number of ways.

1. *Awareness of objectives.* Statements of clear objectives enable the students to know clearly what the teacher expects from them and they cooperate with him in realising the objectives.

2. *Increasing motivation.* Knowledge about their performance serves as a motivating factor to the students and ultimately facilities learning.

3. *Encouraging study habits.* Evaluation being a continuous process encourages students to develop good study habits. Students pay daily attention to their work and understand that today's work cannot be postponed till tomorrow.

4. *Greater chances for increasing abilities and skills.* Constant feedback makes students aware of their strengths and weaknesses. There is enough evidence to show that such feedback improves subsequent performance. Student learn while preparing for evaluation, while being evaluated and after the completion of a particular phase of evaluation.

Evaluation and the Administrators Planners and Supervisors

Evaluation helps the administrators and others associated with the various aspects of education to take appropriate decisions in planning curricular and co-curricular programmes. Evaluation helps in proper placement of students in ability-grouping or in achievement grouping. Evaluation is useful in enabling the educational personnel to determine the effectiveness of instruction and learning activities.

Reporting student's progress. Evaluation serves as a basis for summarising and reporting the progress of students and institutions.

Evaluation and guidance. For guidance — educational, personal and vocational, systematic, evaluation serves an important basis.

Evaluation and parents. A systematic and continuous programme of students' evaluation keeps the parents well-versed with the performance of their children and they endeavour to take appropriate action for their further improvement.

Functions of Evaluation

1. To make provision for guiding the growth of individual pupils.
2. To diagnose the weaknesses and strength of pupils.
3. To locate areas where remedial measures are needed.
4. To provide a basis for a modification of the curriculum and courses.
5. To provide a basis for the introduction of experiences to meet the needs of individuals and group of pupils.

6. To motivate pupils towards better attainment and growth.

7. To test the efficiency of teachers in providing learning experiences and the effectiveness of instruction and classroom activities.

8. To improve instruction.

9. To bring out the inherent capabilities of a pupil, such as attitudes, habits, appreciation and understanding, manipulative skills in addition to conventional acquisition of knowledge.

10.8. STEPS INVOLVED IN EVALUATION

Following steps are involved in evaluation:

1. Identifying and defining general objectives.
2. Identifying and defining specific objectives.
3. Selecting teaching points.
4. Planning and implementing of suitable learning programmes and activities.
5. Appraising and assessing the achievements.
6. Using the results as feedback.

1. Identifying and defining general objectives. The first step is to determine what to evaluate. What kind of abilities and skills should be developed when a student studies a subject or subjects for one year? The process of identifying and defining educational objectives is very complex and challenging as there is no single clear-cut procedure which suits all teachers. Some prefer to begin with the lists of objectives suggested by curriculum experts, some with the course content and some with general aims. Whatever be the procedure, the focal point is the product—the student's behaviour at the end of a course of study. Therefore, general objectives should be stated in terms of his knowledge, understanding, skill, application, attitudes, interests and appreciation, etc.

2. Identifying and defining specific objectives. Every topic or unit must have specific objectives which would provide direction to teaching-learning process. They will also be useful in planning and organising appropriate learning activities and in planning and organising appraisal procedures too. Specific objectives determine two things: One, the various types of learning situations to be provided by the class teacher to the learners; Second, the method to be employed to evaluate both—the objectives and the learning experiences.

3. Selecting teaching units. The third step in the process of evaluation is to select teaching points through which the objectives can be realised. This includes two elements—framing the content i.e. curriculum, syllabi and courses and content analysis. The first element is decided by the philosophers and educationists and the second by the teachers. The teacher has to analyse the subject matter into teaching point.

4. Planning suitable learning activities. Here the teacher will have to plan the learning activities for the pupils so that the objectives may be substantially, if not completely are obtained. The teacher may employ a variety of methods and techniques of teaching learning—Dalton method, Heuristic method, Project Method, demonstration, excursion, field trip, discussion, lecturing etc.

5. Appraisal. The teacher may plan an oral test or a written one. He may administer essay type test, short-answer test or an objective type test or he may conduct a practical test. In any case, he will select a test or tests through which he can best find out the achievement of the students in the light of objectives set forth.

6. Using the results on feedback. The results of evaluation will enable the teacher to introspect and to reorganise learning activities.

10.9. GUIDANCE VIEW OF EXAMINATIONS AND EVALUATION

According to the guidance view examinations and evaluation should serve the following purposes:

1. They should help to measure pupils' strength and weakness in a learning situation and lead to constructive planning.
2. They should help us to classify students in more homogeneous groups so that they may profit most from class instruction.
3. They should continually measure the day-to-day achievements of the students.
4. They should develop wholesome attitudes in the minds of the students for themselves.
5. They should measure the power of understanding, critical thinking and appreciation of the students.
6. They should measure intelligence, special abilities and interest of the students.
7. They should measure the extent to which the students are co-operative, reliable, courageous—the qualities which a man of character should possess.

The term evaluation or appraisal is being substituted for testing and examining children. Evaluation makes use of all usable techniques.

(See also Chapter on Psychological Tests)

10.10. PRINCIPLES OF EVALUATION

1. Considering interrelationship of objectives, instruction or learning experiences and evaluation.
2. Determining and clarifying what is to be evaluated.
3. Selecting evaluation techniques in terms of the objectives to be served.
4. Combining a variety of evaluation techniques for comprehensive evaluation.
5. Knowing the strenghts and limitations of various evaluation techniques.
6. Taking evaluation as a means to an end, not an end in itself.

10.11. MODERN EVALUATING TECHNIQUES

Fairly exhaustive methods have been designed by educationists to evaluate the various aspects of child's growth. Following are the commonly used techniques:

1. Intelligence Tests.
2. Achievement Tests.
3. Aptitude Tests.
4. Personality Tests.
5. Tests of Attitude and Behaviour.
6. Rating Scales.
7. Questionnaries and Check Lists.
8. Interview.
9. Anecdotal Records
10. Autobiographical Method.
11. Pupil's Dairy.
12. Case History.
13. Sociometric Techniques.
14. Projective Techniques.

(See also chapters 12 to 16)

10.12. EVALUATION OF PRACTICAL WORK

Practical work is an integral part of science teaching, work experience and socially useful productive work. In languages and social studies also, stress is being laid on practical work in the form of projects. As such evaluation of practical work in these subjects is equally important for assessing pupil's growth in the psycho-motor domain. A casual scrutiny of the available instruments for measuring performance in these subjects would reveal the inadequacy of the system.

Evaluation of practical work serves a number of purposes:

1. It supplements the written examinations to provide comprehensive evidence of pupil's development.
2. Practical application of theory brings in realism.
3. Practical evaluation provides opportunities for developing the fundamental skills related to vocations of a practical nature.

Improvement of Evaluation of Practical Work

Improvement is needed in the following aspects:

1. Improving the validity of practical examinations.
2. Improving the reliability of practical examinations.
3. Improving the usuability of practical examinations.

1. Improving the validity of practical examinations. The following steps need to be given due attention:

(*i*) Formulation and specification of objectives of practical work in terms of product of performance and process of performance.

(*ii*) Defining the question papers taking care of the following aspects:

(*a*) Proper sampling of skills.

(*b*) Proportionate weightage to different types of skills.

(*c*) Weightage to skills in relation to functional understanding.

(*d*) Adequate coverage of various content areas of the prescribed syllabus.

(*e*) Proportionate weightage to different content areas.

(*iii*) Setting exercises appropriate to the skills/functional understanding tested.

(*iv*) Using appropriate directions for completing the task.

(*v*) Maintaining the appropriate level of difficulty of each task.

2. Improving the reliability of practical examinations. The following measures may be adopted:

(*a*) Increasing the number of exercises/tasks.

(*b*) Listing clearly the tasks in terms of the processes of performance and the products of performance.

(*c*) Ensuring uniformity of testing conditions for conducting the practicals.

(*d*) Issuing uniform instructions to examiners.

(*e*) Using simple and unambiguous language in all questions.

(*f*) Ensuring comparability of question papers.

3. Improving the useability of practical examinations. In this context, following points may be emphasised:

(*i*) Providing clear directions to the examinees.

(*ii*) Apportioning time limit for different exercises and tasks.

(*iii*) Organising experiments and other exercises/tasks is a manner that lends better supervision and saves time.

(*iv*) Providing for scoring sheet which is time saving and convenient for recording of observations.

(*v*) Insisting on marking immediately after observing a particular process or product of observations.

(*vi*) Using a reporting proforma useful for interpretation and use of evidence of pupil's performance.

10.13. EVALUATION OF NON-SCHOLASTIC ASPECTS OF PUPIL'S GROWTH

A national seminar organised by the N.C.E.R.T. from 8 to 12 October, 1979 made the following recommendations on making effective evaluation of Non-scholastic aspects of pupil's growth.

1. Educationists, the world over, are expressing a grave concern over the bookish nature of the present day education dominated by examinations which tend to evaluate mostly the cognitive outcomes of education only. This is particularly true of the Indian scene. The seminar strongly recommends that educational policy-makers, planners, administrators and teachers should take a serious note of this lacuna and take proper steps to ensure that adequate attention is paid to the development and evaluation of both the cognitive and non-cognitive aspects of pupil growth. This is possible only when the schools pay adequate attention to the development and scientific evaluation of both these aspects in an integrated and balanced manner.

2. Since the foundations of personality are laid in early childhood it is very important that developmental evaluation of non-cognitive aspects of growth should start as early as possible. The Education Departments and the Boards of Secondary Education should ensure that proper facilities are provided in the educational institutions so as to make possible the development and evaluation of these aspects of pupil growth. For this purpose it would be necessary to develop systematic and realistic programmes for various types of institutions and to ensure that they are sincerely executed. The importance of cocurricular activities in the fostering of non-scholastic objectives of

education is too well known to need reiteration by this seminar. It is, therefore, recommended that at least six periods per week must be provided for cocurricular activities in all secondary and higher secondary schools. The proportion could be even large in primary schools. The planning and execution of these activities need to be done in a manner that participation of each and every pupil in some worthwhile activity is duly made possible.

3. Appreciating the role of education in shaping the personality of the child the seminar recommends that evaluation in schools should be used more for developmental purposes than for simply reporting, promoting from class-to-class and certification. This is particularly true to the non-scholastic aspects of growth,scientific assessment of which poses serious theoretical and practical problems. The seminar therefore, recommends that the evaluation done in these areas should be used for formative purposes only and should not be quantified to be used for promotion from class-to-class.

4. The seminar considered in detail the role of class-room instructional programmes in the development of non-scholastic aspects of growth. It was agreed that in each subject area specific objectives of the psychomotor and effective domains should also be identified and included in the evaluation scheme. Similar exercise may be done in the cocurricular area as well. In addition, programmes conducive to the development of these objectives should also be identified and executed in both the areas in a systematic manner.

5. Training of teachers in the development and evaluation of non-scholastic aspects of pupil growth is very crucial, more so because of the elusive and non-tangible nature of these aspects. The Departments of Education, Boards of Secondary Education and the Universities should undertake in-service programmes on an extensive scale and also incorporate to relevant topics and activities in the preservice programmes. Availability of adequate facilities for training in this area should be made an essential condition for recognition of training institutions at all levels.

6. The role of the supervisor in the proper execution of educational programmes in India cannot be ignored. For successful implementation of any innovative project, involvement of administrators and the headmasters is a must and therefore orientation of these categories of staff in the supervision of work in the non-scholastic aspects of growth should receive proper emphasis in their training and orientation programmes.

7. The present state of affairs in education in India is an inevitable outcome of quantitative expansion at the cost of quality control. To restore education to its pristine glory it is necessary that serious notice is taken by the Central and the State Governments and the local communities of the existing inadequate facilities in most of the schools and ernest efforts are made to improve them early so as to make possible a satisfactory implementation of educational programmes. The wide gap between the stated objectives of education and their actual implementation in schools for want of adequate facilities need to be appreciated early enough and remedial measures taken accordingly.

8. Instructional materials and manuals make a significant contribution to the successful implementation of educational programmes. There is a great need for development of such materials in the forms of teacher's guides, students' guides etc. and their circulation to schools. The Department and the Boards of Secondary Education should get such materials developed with the help of Teachers' colleges and other experts in adequate quantities for the guidance of teachers and students. The role of mass media in this area need also be recognised.

9. To give due importance to the development and evaluation of non-scholastic aspects of growth in the school time-table it is necessary that the periods devoted by teachers to this work should be counted in their work-load.

10. For an effective implementation of any programme of development and evaluation of non-scholastic aspects of growth it is essential that good work done by teachers in this area should receive due recognition for which the Department and the Boards can undertake a variety of steps such as holding seminar reading programmes, issuing of special certificates of recognition to outstanding teachers and providing for the assessment of the work in this area in the confidential report forms of teachers.

11. The need for research and development activities in the non-scholastic area of pupil growth is too obvious to be dilated upon. The National Council of Educational Research and Training, the State Institutes of Education, Colleges and the Departments of Education in the Universities should appreciate this need and undertake Systematic and Scientific research in this area. A beginning in this respect has

been made by the National Council of Educational Research and Training which needs further intensification at all levels.

10.14. MASTERY LEARNING INSTRUCTION (MLI) AND EVALUATION

Meaning and Significance of Mastery Learning. Mastery learning is defined as a teaching learning approach which asserts that under appropriate instructional conditions, all students can learn most of what is taught in schools. Appropriate instructional conditions are — if instruction is approached systematically; if the students are helped when and where they have learning difficulties; if they are given sufficient time to achieve mastery; and if there is some clearcut criteria of what constitutes mastery.

According to B.S. Bloom (1968), most students can master what teachers teach them. The instructional variables can be easily manipulated so that almost all students achieve the prescribed degree of mastery.

Studies by J.H. Block (1971, 1974) indicate that in many subject areas, all students can achieve some defined level of mastery. It has been found that even gifted students need individual methods of study suited to their personality, rather than the conventional stereotyped techniques of teaching.

T.R. Guskey (1980, 1987, 1988) concluded (through the synthesis of researches on mastery learning) that mastery approach has allowed many teachers to dramatically increase the number of students in their classrooms who learn, and learn very well what they as teachers have set out to teach. Therefore, if systematically practised, mastery learning strategy could be of immense help to the teachers and administrator in arresting the rising rate of dropouts by raising achievement, self-concept and attitude towards schooling of the learners.

Mastery Learning Strategy (MLS) was first used by F. S. Keller (1968) in the late sixties of the 20th century. Since then it has become very popular in several advanced countries. It is estimated that half of the total courses in the USA are based on the mastery learning concept and such courses are offered in the form of 'learning packs' using individualized instruction.

The studies conducted in India by Das Gupta (1977, 1980), Mathur

(1977, 1980, 1981) and Kishore (1981, 1982) and others have proved that from the points of view of consolidation, achievement, recall and favourable student response, the mastery learning model based on the individualized system of instruction has shown promise.

In the mastery learning strategy, the student is motivated to interact at his own pace with a given learning segment. He consolidates his learning by getting his difficulties removed individually by taking individual guidance from his instructor and the fast-pacers.

With a view to motivate the student to learn, the course material is broken into small segments and each segment has an interesting introduction, a list of behavioural objectives, a suggested procedure for learning and a set of self-assessment exercises.

In this learning strategy, the student is allowed to proceed onto the next learning segment when he passes a criterion test. The criterion test is to be passed by the student with a minimum cut-off score of more than 80% marks indicating the mastery of his on-going learning segment.

If a student is unable to pass the criterion test, he is given individual guidance by the instructor and peer-tutors. The student repeats the learning segment and takes retests until he passes the criterion test.

The mastery learning model places focus on the following aspects:

1. Behavioural objectives. The specific objectives for learning a study unit are made clear to the learner; so that he knows what is expected of him from the course of study.

2. Small learning segments. The subject matter of a study unit is broken into several blocks each followed by self-assessment questions which work as learner's own evaluation checks.

3. Self-pacing. The learner learns the study unit at his own speed. The time for learning a study unit is different for different learners while the degree of mastery is the same.

4. Individual attention. As and when a student is unable to understand a portion of the study unit, he takes the individual help from a fast-pacer or instructor.

5. Criterion-referenced testing. A minimum level of performance is specified which indicates the mastery of the study unit and readiness for learning new material.

The criterion-referenced tests are used primarily in the courses based upon the mastery learning concept. A student pursuing such a course

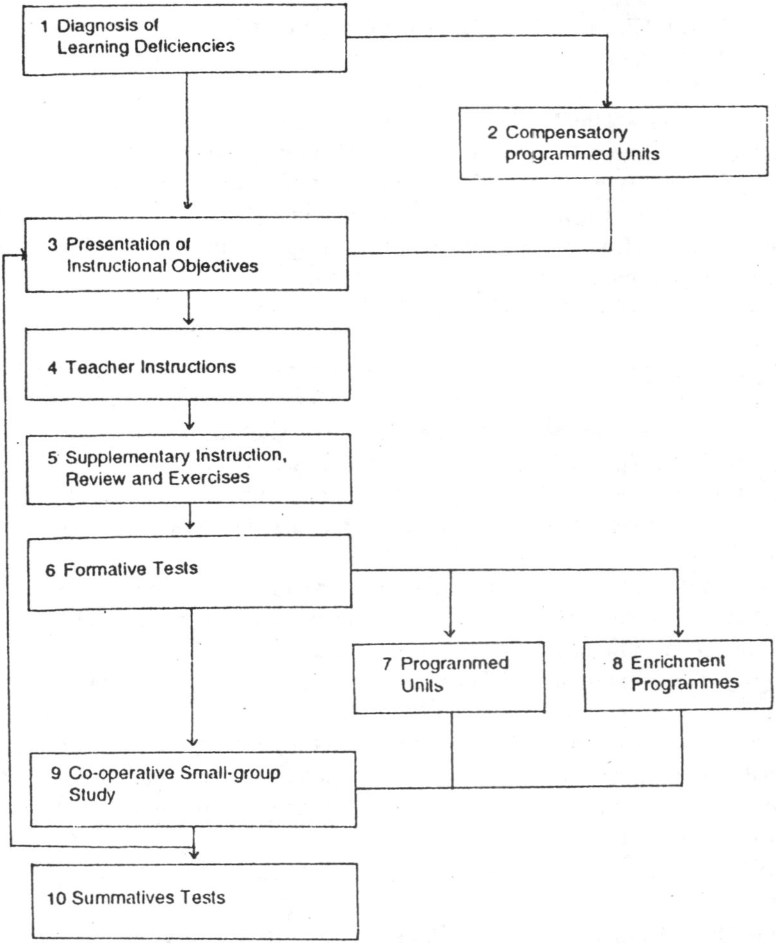

Fig. 10.8. Major principles of instruction for mastery learning.

is asked to consolidate a given subject matter at his own pace of learning assisted by an instructor. The relationship between the criterion-referenced test and mastery learning procedure is shown below:

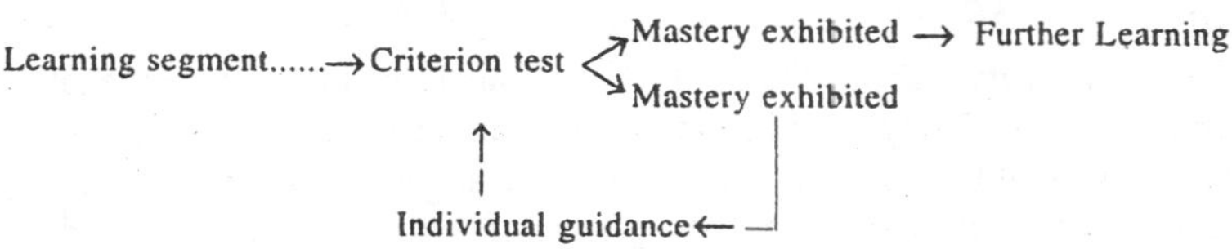

Relationship between mastery learning and criterion testing.

10.15. MINIMUM LEVELS OF LEARNING AND EVALUATION

Introduction. The National Policy on Education (NPE) 1986 emphasised the need for laying down Minimum Levels of Learning (MLLs) for each stage of school education as a prerequisite for setting performance goals for the teachers. This was visualised so that these could serve as effective guides for organising teaching—learning experiences and evaluating pupil achievement.

Concept of MLLs. The concept of MLLs can be approached in a number of ways.

1. MLLs may be stated as expected learning outcomes.
2. MLLs may be seen in terms of observable terminal behaviours.
3. MLLs are expected outcomes in areas such as knowledge, comprehension, application, analysis, synthesis and so on.
4. MLLs may be described in terms of learning competencies expected to be mastered by every child by the end of a particular class or stage of education.

It may, however, be remembered that the above mentioned approaches are not mutually exclusive. The basic issue is that MLLs should present what children should have learnt by the end of every stage of education.

Need for specifying MLLs. There are five important concerns which necessitate the need for specifying MLLs.

Firstly, laying down of well-defined levels of learning is expected to introduce a proper sense of direction for teachers as well as students.

Secondly, it is expected that it would provide a greater element of accountability in the system.

Thirdly, there will be a clearly defined set of criteria for measuring student progress.

Fourthly, it is expected that MLLs will provide an effective tool for programme formulation for school improvement.

Fifthly, it is expected that from the point of equity, all children, irrespective of the environment they come from and the schools they attend, reach a minimum level of learning before they finish a stage of education.

Role of evaluation. About the role of evaluation in this context, the working group on Early Childhood and Elementary Education set up for Formulation of Eighth Five Year Plan (1989) stated, "Students should have a well-defined goal of acquiring a mastery level, particularly in subjects which serve as the basic tools of learning. Parents seem to feel dissatisfied with the levels of learning being achieved in schools and would feel happier with a testing system introduced. Teachers too need to know more clearly about the expected outcomes in the courses they teach. Educational administrator would have in the system of tests of learners, the instrumentality to appraise the performance of institutions and teachers."

According to the Committee on Minimum Levels of Learning at Primary Stage (1991) set up by the Department of Education, Ministry of Human Resource Development, evaluation at the primary stage should be essentially used for two mutually reinforcing purposes:

(i) To improve students' learning through the diagnosis of their performance, identifying specific inadequacies in mastering one or more competencies or sub-competencies and taking appropriate remedial measures to enable all learners to reach the mastery level.This is a kind of formative or supportive evaluation and is to be carried out by the teacher or NFE (Non-formal Education) instructor as part of the process of teaching and learning.

(ii) To carry out summative assessment for various other types of decision-making by policy-makers and planners, administrator and community members besides teachers. These decisions may be related to promotion, comparison of performance between schools, blocks, districts or states, maintaining or raising the overall levels of learning, etc.

10.16. TRENDS IN EXAMINATIONS AND EVALUATION

As a result of reform movement in examinations and evaluation, following major trends are disconcernible:

1. Use of more scientific and systematic methods instead of arbitrary methods.
2. Stress on performance in both academic and non-academic areas.
3. Continuous evaluation in place of periodic examinations.
4. Use of a variety of techniques and tools instead of a few techniques and tools of evaluation.
5. Wider uses of test results in place limited uses.
6. Emphasis on improvement of achievement rather than measurement of achievement.
7. Treatment of testing in relation to other elements of the curriculum rather than treating testing in isolation.

8. Preferring grades to marks.
9. Awarding subjectwise grades in place of overall grades.
10. Clearing the examination in parts and not at one stroke.
11. Improving grades through subsequent attempts.
12. Providing opportunities for re-evaluation.
13. Spot evaluation at specified centres in place of marking by examiners at their residences.
14. Deployment of special squads for checking unfair means.
15. Declaring the use of unfair means as an offence.
16. More flexible and purposeful form of question papers than the traditional one.
17. Apart from testing memorisation, questions include for evaluating abilities like understanding, critical thinking, application of knowledge and skills etc.
18. More coverage of the syllabus.
19. Inclusion of a variety of questions in the question paper.
20. A large number of questions in place of a few questions.
21. Replacement of overall options to internal options.
22. Specifically worded questions in place of large questions.
23. More objective scoring.
24. Use of multiple sets of question papers.

Chapter 11

Evaluation and Instructional Objectives in Behavioural Terms

11.1. EDUCATIONAL OBJECTIVES AND INSTRUCTIONAL OBJECTIVES

There is a lot of confusion regarding the use of terms like aims, goals, outcomes, objectives etc. Quite a large number of educators use these terms synonymously. However, some educators use it differently. Following points of comparison will make the distinction clear between aims and objectives.

Aims	*Objectives*
1. Aims are the directions in education. They are the end-view of the possible achievement.	1. An objective is a point showing the possible achievement in a direction.
2. Aims are the directions given to the entire educational system within and without the classroom.	2. Objectives are confined to the classroom.
3. The aims of education cannot be changed from subject to subject.	3. Objectives may be changed from subject to subject. Objectives of teaching sciences, will differ greatly from the objectives of social sciences.

Aims	*Objectives*
4. The achievement of aims of education is beyond the scope of school programmes. There are other agencies of education also.	4. Objectives of instruction can be achieved.
5. Aims are broader.	5. Objectives originate from aims.
6. In the day-to-day work aims being broad and wide hence little significance.	6. Objectives being specific become meaningful.
7. Aims being very broad and wide are not very helpful in selecting the content of a subject.	7. Objectives being quite specific help in the selection of the subject matter and also teaching-learning activities.

Educational aims and objectives provide direction to instructional aims and objectives.

Some Illustrations of Aims and Objectives

Aims	*Objectives*
1. To develop international brotherhood.	1. The pupils acquire the knowledge of the location and culture of other countries.
2. To eradicate illiteracy.	2. The adults acquire the knowledge of 3 R's.
3. To create good and intelligent citizens.	3. Pupils understand the relationship between rights and responsibilities.
4. To establish a harmonious balance between the head and heart.	4. Pupils acquire basic knowledge of arts, literature and science.
5. To develop spiritualism among students.	5. Pupils learn how to lead a virtuous life.

According to Srivastava and Shouri (1989), the educational objectives serve the following functions:

1. Provide the desired directions to educational activities.
2. Determine the nature of educational activities.

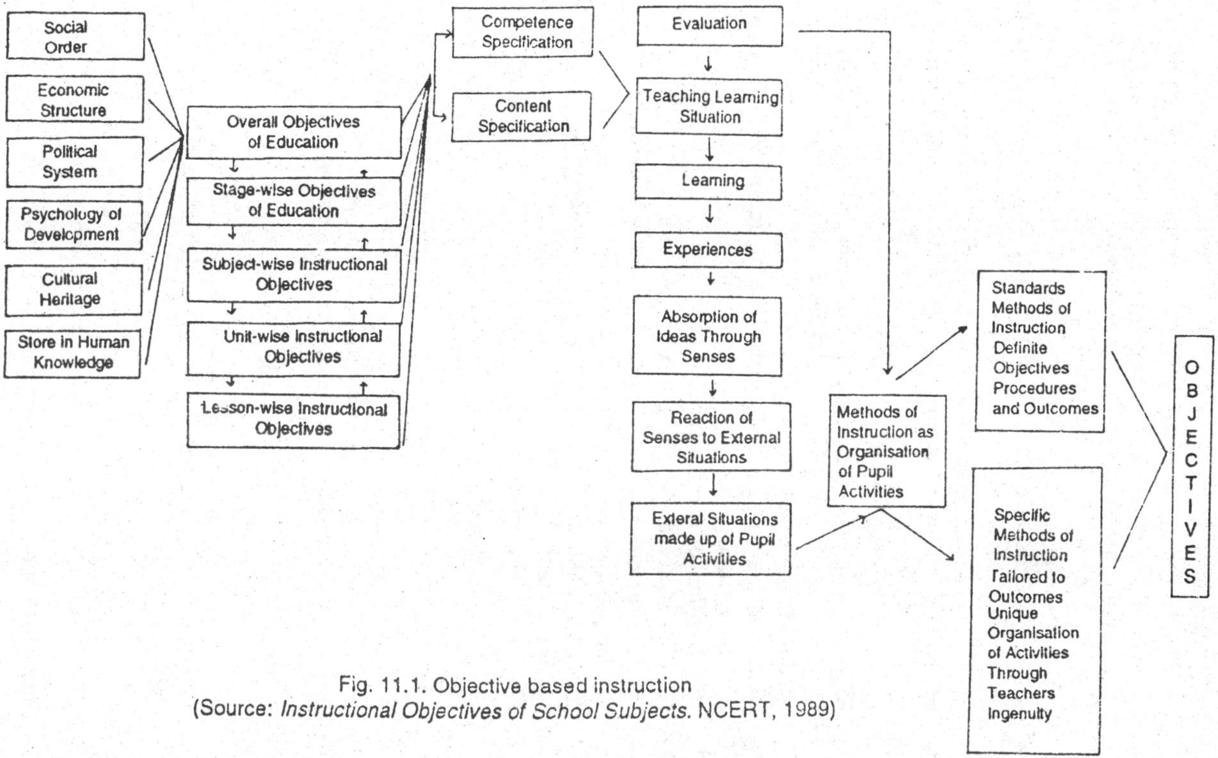

Fig. 11.1. Objective based instruction
(Source: *Instructional Objectives of School Subjects*. NCERT, 1989)

3. Provide a basis for systematising or planning an educational programme.
4. Decide the points of emphasis in an educational activity.
5. Give unity and coherence to an educational programme.
6. Provide the basis for the measurement of growth and thus guarantee valid evaluation.
7. Help distinguish between various aspects of learning.
8. Help focus attention on proper attributes of teaching and evaluation.
9. Help grade learning experiences and also evaluation material.
10. Help maintain a balance between different aspects of an educational programme.
11. Help fix priorities in an educational programme.
12. Guide educational decisions in curricular and co-curricular areas.
13. Guide in the selection of relevant content.
14. Guide improvements in education.
15. Give meaning to and clarify the structure and content of curriculum.
16. Help make learning functional.
17. Help articulate learning in various fields.
18. Help discover or evolve proper learning situations.
19. Help define educational processes.
20. Help make the intangibles in education tangible.
21. Help identify weaknesses and strengths of pupils in learning.
22. Facilitate communication among educational workers.

The work on determining levels of objectives may follow the following pattern:

Overall Objectives of Education

↓

Stagewise Objectives of Education
(Primary, Secondary and University etc.)

↓

Subjectwise Objectives
(Social Studies, Hindi, Maths etc.)

↓

Classwise Objectives
(Classes I, VI, IX, XI etc.)

↓

Instructional Objectives

Instructional objectives are also formed as learning outcomes.

Educational Objectives and Instructional Objectives Compared

Educational Objectives	*Instructional Objectives*
1. Philosophy determines educational objectives.	1. Psychology is the basis of instructional objectives.
2. Educational objectives are very broad.	2. Instructional objectives are very specific.
3. All school subjects may have common educational objectives.	3. Each school subject has specific teaching or instructional objective.
4. Educational objectives include instructional objectives.	4. Instructional objective form a part of educational objectives.
5. Examples of educational objectives are: development of character, emotional and national integration, democratic values, secularism etc.	5. Examples are : Behaviour patterns of a man of character — characteristics of a man of character —how he conforms to a situation in honesty etc.

11.2. MEANING AND SIGNIFICANCE OF INSTRUCTIONAL OBJECTIVES

Examinations or evaluation or tests are the mileposts along the road of learning and are supposed to tell the teacher and the learner (student) the degree to which both have been successful in their achievement of the course objectives. An instrumental objective may be defined as an intent communicated by a statement describing a proposed change in a learner—a statement of what the learner is to be like when he has successfully completed a learning experience. There are several objectives to be achieved through instruction and accordingly several learning experiences are provided. The statement of objectives of a teaching programme must denote 'measurable' attributes 'observable' in the learners. As Robert E. Mager has said, "An instructor will function in a fog of his own working until he knows just what he wants his students to be able to do at the end of the instruction."

Objectives provide direction to classroom teachers. They indicate the way to follow. They help the teacher in instructional planning, and guiding students' learning. They also provide a criterion for evaluating the outcomes of the learning experiences. The evaluation of what has been achieved may be useful in determining what should be achieved. In other words refinement of objectives can be done on the basis of the achievement of objectives.

Sources of Objectives. The sources of objectives of education are many and varied, and also interrelated. They are determined by a number of factors such as cultural, economic, environmental, historical, philosophical, political, psychological, religious and sociological.

The Central Board of Secondary Education (CBSE) has envisaged the following learning outcomes in a brochure *Improving Question Papers in Schools* (1991).

1. Learning outcomes denote direction of change in the behaviour of students occurring as a result of teaching-learning.
2. Accomplishment of an outcome necessitates development of several specific skills or mental processes which have got to be perfected through a series of exposures at the teaching-learning stage.
3. The mental processes or specific skills acquired are more enduring than the subject matter and become part of human nature or the style of thinking.
4. The content/subject matter serves only as a means to accomplish these outcomes.
5. The learning outcomes and their related specific skills should be exploited both for purposes of teaching as well as testing.
6. The learning outcomes and the mental processes have to be related to small points of content to devise a teaching or testing situation.

11.3. TAXONOMY OF INSTRUCTIONAL OBJECTIVES

Blooms Taxonomy of Instructional Objectives in Behavioural Terms

The word taxonomy is derived from a Greek word 'taxis' — plural, taxa — meaning 'arrangement', 'division'. It is orignally associated with biology. It refers to a system of classifying animals and plants, typically by division, class, order, family, germs and species. In education it just means any systematic organisation. One of the most famous is B. S. Bloom's (1956) taxonomy of educational objectives which categories large number of elements within the cognitive and affective domain and seeks to relate those to specifiable and observable learning objectives.

Prof. B. S. Bloom of the University of Chicago (USA) is considered to be a pioneer in this field. He was the editor of the first volume of *Taxonomy of Educational Objectives* (1956) produced by an American Committee of College and University Examiners. He presented his taxonomy related to cognitive domain, Karathwohe related to affective domain (1964) and Harrow related to psychomotor domain. Prof. Bloom has shifted the emphasis from content to the objectives in the examination and evaluation system. He advocated that tests should be objective-centred rather than content-centred. Each test should evaluate one specific objective. He made efforts to write objectives in behavioural terms. In describing the behaviour that is required of a student when he demonstrates his mastery of the subject or the skill, it is important to identify in very clear terms, exactly what he will do. This involves stating how he will recognise the cue or situation which will cause him to commence action or behaviour, as well as how he will recognize that the action has been successfully accomplished.

The Hierarchy of Taxonomy

It can be depicted in the following manner.

Hierarchy

Knowledge (K)	→	Comprehension (C)	→	Application (A)	→
Analysis (AN)	→	Synthesis (S)	→	Evaluation (E)	→

Taxonomy of Educational Objectives in the Cognitive Domain (Bloom)

1. Knowledge Objective. Knowledge is defined as recall of specifics and universals, recall of methods and processes or the recall of a pattern, structure or setting. This objective stresses the psychological process of remembering.

(*a*) Knowledge of specifics include:
- (*i*) Knowledge of terminology
- (*ii*) Knowledge of specific facts.

(*b*) Knowledge of ways and means of dealing with specifics:
- (*i*) Knowledge of conventions
- (*ii*) Knowledge of trends and sequence
- (*iii*) Knowledge of classifications and categories
- (*iv*) Knowledge of criteria
- (*v*) Knowledge of methodology.

(*c*) Knowledge of the universals and abstractions in a field:
- (*i*) Knowledge of principles and generalisations
- (*ii*) Knowledge of theories and structures.

2. Comprehension
- (*i*) Translation
- (*ii*) Interpretation
- (*iii*) Extrapolation.

3. Application. It involves the application of a concept to new or unfamiliar situations.

4. Analysis. It implies the breaking down of a communication into its constituent elements or parts so that relative hierarchy of ideas is made clear.
- (*i*) Analysis of elements
- (*ii*) Analysis of relationships
- (*iii*) Analysis of organisational principles

5. Synthesis. It refers to putting together of elements and parts into a whole.
- (*i*) Production of a unique communication.
- (*ii*) Production of a plan or a proposed set of operations.
- (*iii*) Derivation of a set of abstract relations.

6. Evaluation. It refers to the judgements about the values of materials and methods for given objectives.
- (*i*) Judgement in terms of internal evidence
- (*ii*) Judgement in terms of external criteria

Above mentioned objectives are clarified as under:

1. Knowledge. It is defined as the remembering of previously learned material. It represents the lowest level of learning outcomes in the cognitive domain.

2. Comprehension. It is defined as the ability to grasp the meaning of material. The learning outcomes go one step beyond the simple understanding of material and represent the lowest level of understanding.

3. Application. It is the ability to use learned material in new and concrete situations. Learning outcomes in this area require a higher level of understanding than those under comprehension.

4. Analysis. It refers to the ability to breakdown material into its component parts so that its organisational structure may be understood. Learning outcomes here represent a higher intellectual level than comprehension and application because they require an understanding of both the content and the structural form of the material.

5. Synthesis. Synthesis refers to the ability to put parts together to form a new whole. Learning outcomes in the area stress creative behaviour, with major emphasis on the formulation of new patterns or structures.

6. Evaluation. Evaluation is concerned with the ability to judge the value or material (Statement, novel, poem, research report) for a given purpose. Judgements are to be based on definite criteria.

Objectives and Mental Process or Ability in Bloom's Taxonomy

Objective	*Mental Process or Ability*
1. Knowledge	1. Recall
	2. Recognize
2. Comprehension	1. See relationship
	2. Cite example
	3. Discriminate
	4. Classify
	5. Interest
	6. Verify
	7. Generalize
3. Application	1. Reason
	2. Formulate
	3. Establish
	4. Infer
	5. Predict
4. Analysis	Analyse
5. Synthesis	Synthesize
6. Evaluation	Evaluate

Cognitive Objectives and Associated Words

Objective	*Associated Action Verbs*
1. Knowledge	1. Define 2. State 3. List 4. Name 5. Write 6. Recall 7. Recognise 8. Label 9. Underline 10. Select 11. Reproduce 12. Measure.
2. Comprehension	1. Identify 2. Justify 3. Select 4. Indicate 5. Illustrate 6. Represent 7. Name 8. Formulate 9. Explain 10. Judge 11. Contrast 12. Classify.
3. Application	1. Predict 2. Select 3. Assess 4. Explain 5. Choose 6. Find 7. Show 8. Demonstrate 9. Construct 10. Compute 11. Use 12. Perform.
4. Analysis	1. Analyse 2. Identify 3. Conclude 4. Differentiate 5. Select 6. Separate 7. Compare 8. Contrast 9. Justify 10. Resolve 11. Breakdown 12. Criticise.
5. Synthesis	1. Combine 2. Restate 3. Summarize 4. Precise 5. Argue 6. Discuss 7. Organize 8. Derive 9. Select 10. Relate 11. Generalize 12. Conclude.
6. Evaluation	1. Judge 2. Evaluate 3 Determine 4. Recognize 5. Support 6. Defend 7. Attack 8. Criticise 9. Identify 10. Avoid 11. Select 12. Choose.

Affective Domain

"The affective domain includes those objectives which are concerned with changes in interests, attitudes and values and the development of appreciations and adjustment."

Affective taxonomy is divided into five major classes arranged in an hierarchical order on the basis of the level of involvement. A condensed version of affective domain taxonomy is presented in the table shown on page 175.

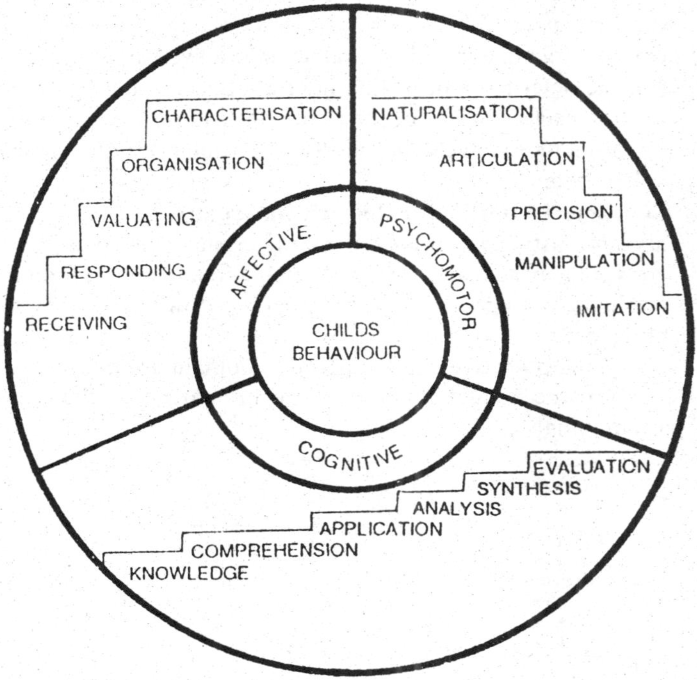

Fig. 11.2. Objectives of cognitive, Affective and Psychomotor Domains. (NCERT).

TABLE : Condensed version of the Affective Domain Taxonomy of Educational Objectives (Krathwohl et al. 1964)

(1) **Receiving (attending).** This means that the learner should be sensitised to the existence of certain phenomena and stimuli. This includes awareness, willingness to receive and controlled or selected affection.

(2) **Responding.** This is concerned with responses that go beyond merely attending to phenomena. A person is actively involved in attending to them.

This includes acquiescene in responding, willingness to respond and satisfaction in response.

(3) **Valuating.** This includes acceptance of a value, preference for a value and committment to or a conviction in regard to a certain point of view.

Contd...

(4) **Organization.** For situations where more than one value is relevant, the need arises for
  (*a*) the organization of the values into a system,
  (*b*) the determination of the interrelationship among them, and
  (*c*) the establishment of the dominent and pervasive value.

  It includes conceptualisation of a value and organisation of a value system.

(5) **Characterisation by a value or value complex.** At this level, the already existing values are organized into some kind of an internally consistent system and control the behaviour of an individual, who attains an integration of his beliefs and attitudes into a total philosophy.

If the objectives in the affective domain are attended to and are achieved, the evaluator will be in a position to predict the behaviour of an individual.

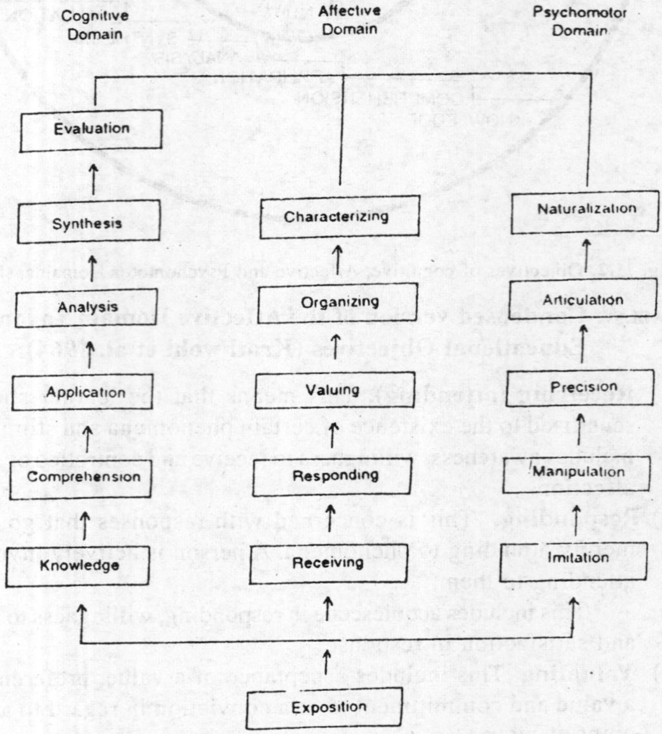

Fig. 11.3. CAP classification of instructional objectives.

Psycho-motor Domain

The psycho-motor domain includes those objectives which are concerned with manual and motor skills.

Simpson (1966) and Kibler (1970) are the pioneers in the field of taxonomy of objectives in the psycho-motor domain.

Dr. R.H. Dave of the NCERT has proposed a taxonomy in the psychomotor domain. The educational objectives proposed under this domain are :

(1) *Imitation* of an action, performance;
(2) *Manipulation of an act.* This includes differentiating among various movements and selecting the proper one;
(3) *Precision in reproducing a given act.* This includes accuracy, proportion and exactness in performance;
(4) *Articulation among different acts.* This includes co-ordination, sequence and harmony among acts.
(5) *Naturalisation.* Here a pupil's skill attains its highest level of proficiency in performing an act with the least expenditure of psychic energy. The act becomes so automatic that it is attended to unconsciously.

11.4. SPECIFICATION OF THE BEHAVIOURAL OBJECTIVE OUTCOMES

The broader objectives should be broken down into specific ones to a limit where they stand fully clarified and delimited. This step is often known as specification of the objective or behaviour outcomes. For example : The statement of an objective in History would be 'To develop interest in the study of History'. The specification of this objective would be to demonstrate the achievement of the above objective, the student:

1. Collects coins and other types of historical material.
2. Prepares illustrative material aids, etc.
3. Participates in historical dramas and presentation of historical facts.
4. Visits places of historical interest, archaeological sites, museums and archives.
5. Reads historical documents, maps and charts.

6. Plays an active role in the activities of the History Association
7. Writes articles on historical and other related topics.

Writing Statements of Objectives

Following points should be kept in view while writing statements of objectives:

1. The statement of an objective should indicate a worthwhile objective appropriate to the age and physiological and psychological abilities and needs, etc. of the students. For example at the school stage, the objective such as to 'prepare economists' or 'to prepare scientists' is not worthwhile. The worthwhile objective may be 'to acquire the skills essential for the study of Economics'.
2. The statement of an objective should be related to human ability which can be developed or achieved through instruction. For instance one of our objectives in languages will be 'to acquire the ability of expressing oneself orally'. Objectives like 'to change the shape of lips or tongue' should not be a statement of an objective.
3. The statement of an objective should mention the content or the subject matter through which a particular ability is to be developed. For example: Do not write 'the pupil acquires knowledge' and write 'The pupil acquires knowledge of the soil of Deccan region.'
4. The statement of an objective should be in the form of student's achievement and not in the form of teacher's intention. For example: Do not write 'To develop a scientific temper among students' and instead write 'The student develops a scientific temper.' Here emphasis is on the student as instruction has to be 'student or child centred.'
5. The statement of an objective should be written in the form of achievement of a student and not in the form of achievement of a group of students. For example: Do not write 'The class develops the ability of appreciating the literature of mother tongue.' Write 'the student develops his ability of appreciating the literature of mother tongue.'.
6. The statement of an objective should contain only one ability to be developed or modified. For example: Do not write 'The student reads English silently with comprehension and writes English

correctly.' Write (1)'The student reads English silently with comprehension' and (2) 'The student writes English correctly.'

7. Objectives should be so stated that there is a clear indication and even distinction among learning situations required for realising different behaviour changes. For example, learning situations for memorising certain facts would be basically different from the ones needed for critical thinking.
8. The list of objectives as a whole should be comprehensive enough to cover different outcomes of an educational programme.
9. The statement of an objective should contain verbs as shown in the example. 'The pupil *comprehends* the information represented on a daily weather chart.'

Examples of Important Action words used in the Specification of Objectives/Behavioural

A : Acquires, Advances, Analyses, Applies, Appreciates, Arranges.
B : Bends, Bisects, Blows, Brings, Bruhes, Brids.
C : Catagorise, Changes, Clarifies, Classifies, Collects, Compares, Completes, Composes, Computes, Concludes, Connects, Constructs, Contrasts, Cooperates, Copies, Counts, Criticises.
D : Decides. Deduces, Defines, Demonstrates, Derives, Describes, Detects, Differentiates, Discovers, Discriminates, Discusses, Displays, Distinguishes, Distributes, Divides, Draws.
E : Estimates, Evaluates, Expands, Explains, Expresses.
F : Fills, Finds, Forms, Formulates, Frames.
G : Gathers, Generalises, Gives, Graps, Groups.
H : Handles, Harmonizes, Holds.
I : Identifies, Illustrates, Includes, Indicates, Inserts, Integrates, Interprets.
J : Joins
K : Knows, Knights
L : Lists, Locates.
M : Makes, Manipulates, Marks, Matches, Measures, Modifies, Multiplies.
N : Narrates, Notes.
O : Omits, Operates, Organises, Outlines.
P : Points, Paraphrases, Participates, Performs, Plots, Predicts, Prepares, Presents, Produces, Pronounces, Proposes, Proves, Provides, Punctuates.

Q : Questions, Quotes.

R : Reacts, Reads, Recites, Reconstructs, Records, Reduces Relates, Reorganises, Repeats, Rephrases, Reports Reproduces, Responds, Reserves.

S : Says, Selects, Separates, Sets, Shows, Signifies, Simplifies. Speaks, Specifies, Spells, States, Substitutes, Substracts Suggests, Summarizes, Supplies, Supports, Synthesizes.

T : Tabulates, Tallies, Tells, Traces, Translates, Tries.

U : Underlines, Uses.

V : Verifies.

W : Writes.

X : X-rays, Xeroxes.

Y : Yields, Yelps, Yap.

Z : Zealously, Zips, Zooms.

SPECIFICATION OF OBJECTIVES

1. Knowledge Objectives

(*a*) The student is able to recognize.

(*b*) The student is able to recall.

2. Understanding Objectives. The student is able—

(*i*) to see relationship between — and —

(*ii*) to discriminate between — and —

(*iii*) to classify—

(*iv*) to interpret—

(*v*) to verify

(*vi*) to generalize.

3. Application Objectives

(1) The learner is able to reason out—

(2) The learner is able to formulate hypothesis for—

(3) The learner is able to establish hypothesis for—

(4) The learner is able to infer about—

(5) The learner is able to predict about—

4. Creativity

(*a*) The learner is able to analyse—

(*b*) The learner is able to synthesize

(*c*) The learner is able to evaluate—

11.5. GUIDELINES FOR WRITING OBJECTIVES

1. Keep in mind the entry behaviour of the learner.

2. Give thought to the element of content, topic or the learning experiences to be provided to the learner.

3. Keep in mind the teaching or learning objective.

4. Select appropriate mental processes or abilities for writing objectives.

11.6. INSTRUCTIONAL OBJECTIVES IN HISTORY

1. To acquire the knowledge of concepts, terms, facts, events, symbols, ideas, problems, trends, personalities, chronologies generalizations, etc. related to the study of History.
2. To develop the understanding of facts, terms, principles, events, trends etc. related to the study of History.
3. To develop the ability of critical and logical thinking.
4. To develop practical skills useful in the study and understanding of historical phenomena.
5. To develop interests in the study of History.
6. To develop healthy social attitudes.

Instructional Objective No.1. To acquire the knowledge of concepts, terms, facts, events, ideas, problems, trends, personalities, chronologies, generalizations, etc. related to the study of History.

Behavioural Outcomes. To demonstrate the achievement of the above objective, the student:

(*a*) recalls facts, concepts, terms, events, etc.
(*b*) recognises facts, concepts, terms, events etc.
(*c*) shows information on maps, charts, diagrams, etc.
(*d*) reads information presented in various forms.

Instructional Objective No. 2. To develop an understanding of facts, terms, principles, events, trends etc. related to the study of History.

Behavioural Outcomes. To demonstrate the achievement of the above objective, the student.

(*i*) classifies facts, concepts, terms etc.
(*ii*) compares and contrasts the events, trends, concepts etc.
(*iii*) discriminates between the significant and insignificant, important and less important causes, events, etc.
(*iv*) identifies relationship between causes and effects, means and ends, etc.
(*v*) arranges facts, trends, etc. in a particular known order.
(*vi*) detects errors in the statements and rectifies them.
(*vii*) summarises.

(*viii*) interprets the maps, charts, extracts, etc. from the different sources of History.

Instructional Objective No. 3. To develop the ability of critical and logical thinking.

Behavioural Outcomes. To demonstrate the achievement of the above objective, the student.

(1) identifies the problem.
(2) analyses the problem.
(3) interprets problems with implications.
(4) sets up hypothesis.
(5) selects relevant facts, principles etc.
(6) establishes relationships.
(7) advances arguments in support of contentions.
(8) draws inferences and generalizations.
(9) verifies the inferences.
(10) predicts.
(11) evaluates.

INSTRUCTIONAL OBJECTIVES IN ENGLISH

Dr. Mamta Agarwal (1988) of the NCERT suggests the following instructional objectives of English:

Objective I:	The student acquires the knowledge of the elements of English language.
Objective II:	The student comprehends English when spoken at normal conversational speed.
Objective III:	The student reads English silently with comprehension.
Objective IV:	The student speaks English correctly and effectively.
Objective V:	The student writes English correctly and effectively.
Objective VI:	The student develops an interest in English.

Objective I : The student acquires the knowledge of the elements of English language.

Specifications : The student—

(1) Recognizes characteristic English speech sound, stress, intonation pattern and rhythm in sentences.
(2) Recognizes content words, structural words, sentence patterns, spelling, capital letters and marks of punctuations.

(3) Recalls content words, structural words, sentence patterns, spelling, capital letters and marks of punctuation.
(4) Recognizes difference between correct and incorrect grammatical forms.

Objective II : The student comprehends English when spoken at normal conversational speed.

Specifications : The student—

(1) Grasps the significance of different stress and intonation patterns in the English Language.
(2) Grasps the meaning of words, phrases, and sentences in context.
(3) Grasps the simple idea or ideas in a piece of connected speech.
(4) Follows the sequence of ideas expressed or event narrated—live or over the radio or T.V.
(5) Grasps relationships between objects, persons, ideas, events, etc., occurring in speech or in passages read out to him.
(6) Grasps the substance or the central idea of a connected speech.

Objective III : The student reads English silently with comprehension.

Specifications : The student—

1. Has reasonable speed.
2. Grasps the meaning of words, phrases, and sentences from the context.
3. Grasps the ideas conveyed in a passage.
4. Locates key words, phrases, and sentences in a passage.
5. Locates important facts and ideas.
6. Identifies relationship between objects, ideas, events, facts, characters, etc.
7. Follows the sequence of ideas, facts, etc.
8. Compares objects, ideas, events, facts, characters, etc.
9. Distinguishes between related words and ideas.
10. Interprets ideas, events, traits of character, etc.
11. Infers meanings, ideas and messages in a passage.
12. Infers the mood of the author or character.
13. Gets at the central idea of a piece.
14. Evaluates events, actions, ideas, feelings, and views.

Objective IV : The student speaks English correctly and effectively.

Specifications : The student—

1. Uses proper pronunciation, stress, and intonation.

2. Uses appropriate pauses in speech.
3. Uses appropriate words, phrases and sentences.
4. Uses a variety of sentences.
5. Presents ideas in a proper sequence.
6. Has reasonable speed and flow in speech suited to the situation.
7. Uses conventional greetings and formulae.

Objective V : The student writes English correctly and effectively.

Specifications : The student—

1. Writes a neat and legible hand with a right-hand or perpendicular drift and reasonable speed.
2. Speaks correctly.
3. Uses capital letters and marks of punctuation.
4. Uses appropriate words, idioms and structures.
5. Uses of variety of sentencses.
6. Makes appropriate use of connectives such as and, but, so, therefore, otherwise etc.
7. Presents only relevant ideas and facts.
8. Avoids unnecessary repetitions.
9. Organises ideas, facts into paragraphs.
10. Introduces, develops and ends a subject well.
11. Displays imagination in writing.
12. Follows the techniques of different forms and formates of written expression.

Objective VI : The student develops an interest in English.

Specifications : The student—

1. Reads English books, newspapers and magazines on his own.
2. Listens to radio and television broadcasts and sees films.
3. Listens to speeches, debates, discussions, plays, songs, etc.
4. Takes part in debates, discussions, plays, etc.
5. Makes use of a dictionary and other reference books.
6. Collects or remembers lines from poems and quotations from prose.
7. Speaks English outside the class when there are opportunities.
8. Writes reports, stories, letters, poem, etc. in English on his own.

The objectives from I to V operate at all the stages of teaching English within the range of the vocabulary and grammatical structures prescribed for that stage. These objectives have been arranged in a hierarchical order, e.g. objective I, the knowledge of the elements of language is the simplest and the basic objective to be developed and tested because the subsequent objectives of English require its use. Then comes the objective of comprehension (listening and reading) and after that comes expression (oral and written), because the ability of comprehension is subsumed in the ability of expression, that is to say that expression is not possible without comprehension. Though from the point of view of language learning the order of objectives should have been listening, speaking, reading and writing, but, here these skills have been rearranged from the point of view of mental processes involved. Thus listening and reading being the receptive skills have been put under comprehension and speaking and writing have been grouped under expression.

11.7. NCERT TAXONOMY OF INSTRUCTIONAL OBJECTIVES

The NCERT has been using the following taxonomy (condensed form of Bloom's taxonomy)
(*a*) Knowledge (*b*) Understanding / Comprehension (*c*) Application

The specification of these objectives is given below:

1. *Knowledge (The pupil)*
   (*i*) Recalls (*ii*) Recognises
2. *Understanding (The pupil)*
   (*i*) Translates (*ii*) Cites examples
   (*iii*) Identifies relationship (*iv*) Detects error
   (*v*) Compares (*vi*) classifies
   (*vii*) Interprets (*viii*) Explains
3. *Application (The pupil)*
   (*i*) Analysis (*ii*) Hypotheses
   (*iii*) Suggests methods and materials to test hypotheses (*iv*) Establishes relationships
   (*v*) Reasons (*vi*) Generalises or draws conclusions
   (*vii*) Predicts (*viii*) Judges adequacy, consistency and relevance etc.

RCEM (Regional College of Education Mysore) Approach

In RCEM approach, there are four categories in place of six given by Bloom.

Objectives	*Mental Processes or Mental Abilities*
1. Knowledge	1. Recognise
2. Understanding	2. Recall
	3. See relationships
	4. Cite example
	5. Discriminate
	6. Classify
	7. Interpret
	8. Verify
	9. Generalise
3. Application	10. Reason out
	11. Formulate hypothesis
	12. Establish hypothesis
	13. Infer
	14. Predict
4. Creativity	15. Analyse
	16. Synthesise
	17. Evaluate

Creativity replaces Bloom's Three categories of analysis, synthesis and evaluation.

EVALUATION OF RCEM APPROACH

Merits

1. Since the approach is developed in Indian setting it suits our schools.
2. It is applicable to cognitive, affective and psychomotor objectives of teaching and learning.
3. It lays stress on mental abilities or processes in writing objectives in behavioural terms. Therefore, it is capable of shifting focus from product to process in the writing of objectives.
4. It provides a list of 17 mental abilities or processes associated with instructional objectives.
5. Seventeen statements help us in writing objectives in school subjects.
6. This approach enables the teacher and the learner to seek their goals more easily and satisfactorily.
7. This approach makes the task of evaluation and test construction quite simpler and objective.

Limitations:

1. This approach is more suitable to cognitive objectives than the conative or affective objectives.
2. This approach does not make a clear-cut distinction among objectives belonging to the three domains of behaviour.
3. This approach is not very helpful in objectives concerning the development of skill, appreciation, interest in some of the subjects.
4. The approach is based on the erroneous assumption that the human learning can be explained through seventeen mental abilities or processes.
5. It is a very challenging and tedious task to match the content element with the appropriate mental ability or process.

Criteria for Stating Objectives in Well-defined Terms or Statements:

1. Using such verbs in writing objectives that can describe the behaviour to be observed.
2. Specifying conditions in which the learner performance occurs.
3. Specifying the minimum level of performance of the learner.
4. Covering objectives of all the three domains–cognitive, affective and conative (psychomotor).
5. Covering objectives of different levels of learning outcomes.

11.8. EVALUATION OF TAXONOMY OF OBJECTIVES

Merits:

1. It can be useful in translating into practice the principle of comprehensiveness of evaluation by ensuring proper coverage of various aspects of pupil's growth : cognitive, affective and psychomotor.
2. The evaluation may prove useful in arriving at the meaningful synthesis of various dimensions of pupil's growth.
3. Identification of areas of inter-relationship among the three domains may be of particular significance in this regard.
4. The logical nature of classification may be helpful in identifying and grading teaching-learning situations which can be an important source of selecting appropriate testing situation too.
5. Curriculum development and preparation of instructional material can profit such a scheme of classification in several ways.
6. Preparation and analysis of textbooks based on well defined objectives may prove to be a great improvement.

7. The classification through its well defined criteria can provide a bridge for further communication among teachers, between teachers and evaluators, curriculum and research workers, psychologists and other behavioural scientists.
8. The evaluation of the evaluation devices in terms of their validity may be facilitated.
9. The taxonomy has opened new avenues for research in education.
10. Tools of evaluation can become very objective.

Drawbacks and Limitations of Stating Behavioural Objectives

Following arguments are usually given against the use of behavioural objectives:

(1) Though easier to operationalize, trivial objectives may be stressed at the expense of important ones.
(2) Pre-specifying objectives may prevent the teacher from capitalizing on the unexpected.
(3) Educational outcomes other than stated pupil behavioural changes lose significance.
(4) Measurability being mechanistic, it becomes dehumanizing.
(5) Planning how students will behave in undemocratic manner.
(6) It is perhaps not realistic to expect teachers to state measurable goals.
(7) It is very difficult to identify measurable outcomes in certain subjects.
(8) Measuring denotes accountability and is thus threatening.
(9) Stating goals in measuring terms is a difficult and time-consuming task.
(10) Evaluators are likely to ignore important goals other than pre-specified ones.

Lewtom (1973) and Kelly (1977) have criticised this method of classifying educational objectives as under :

1. Bloom's three-fold classification is somewhat artificial as in practice all the three—cognitive, affective and psycho-motor, are closely interrelated.
2. There is not always agreement on the appropriate classification for certain behaviours.
3. In this classification, there is a tendency to overstress 'measurable behaviour' and to disregard the importance of those aspects of pupils' work which are not 'measured'.

4. Bloom's classification is not applicable to all areas of the curriculum and to all circumstances of learning.
5. It is a difficult exercise to formulate objectives to match Bloom's higher category. It requires lengthy preparation in order to produce anything worthwhile.
6. Formulating objectives of instruction in direct relation with the particular content of lesson.
7. Correlating objectives with the evaluation process.

A WORD OF CAUTION

While landing the role of objectives in evaluation, Prof. C. L. Anand (1986) has struck a note of dismay in these words, "It is also sometimes felt that the terminology used in the statement of objectives especially of the type based on the Bloom's taxonomy is mostly a kind of educational jargon and many teachers refer to it simply because it is fashionable to do so. In fact they themselves may not be very clear about them and hence they become more of a hinderance than help to them. A good deal of work has by now been done in respect of the development of objectives of education by the NCERT, the SCERT and a host of professional bodies at various levels. But unfortunately many of these curriculum objectives are referred to rather mechanically with little relation to the pupil behaviour or ability and the type of content involved. Therefore, despite this widespread attention to the statements of the objectives of education and even of the individual subjects for each class or grade, the impact of such statements on the curriculum or on what actually takes place in classroom is generally much less than what it otherwise ought to be."

Chapter 12

Summative and Formative Evaluation

Honer, M. Seriven (1967) coined the terms of summative and evaluative evaluation.

12.1. SUMMATIVE EVALUATION

Definition and meaning. According to A.J. Nikto (1983), "Summative evaluation describes judgements about the merits of an already completed programme, procedure or product."

N.E. Gronlund (1985), observes, "Summative evaluation typically comes at the end of a course (or unit) of instruction. It is designed to determine the extent to which the instructional objectives have been achieved and is used primarily for assigning course grades or certifying pupil mastery of the intended learning outcomes."

In the views of Ebel, R.L. and Frisbie (1986), "Summative evaluation is conducted at the end of an instructional segment to determine if learning is sufficiently complete to warrant moving the learner to the next segment of instruction."

In the words of Gilbert Sax (1989), " A summative evaluation can provide evidence that the programme is satisfactory and should be continued for next year's students or that student learning and learning attitudes are so negative that a new programme is needed."

W. Wiersma and S. G. Gurs (1990) state, "Summative evaluation is done at the conclusion of instruction and measures the extent to which students have attained the desired outcomes."

A perusal of the above definitions shows that the summative evaluation has the following chief elements.

1. There should be some instructional programme before summative evaluation.
2. The instructional programme should be for the attainment of some objectives.
3. Summative evaluation is done at the end or completion of a particular instructional programme whose duration may vary from a semester to whole year.
4. Summative evaluation should check whether there has been earning or not. If the answer is yes, then what is the quantity and quality of the learning in relation to pre-determined objectives.
5. Summative learning provides feedback to the classroom teacher for the success or failure of the programme or and of the student.

Chief Characteristics of Summative Evaluation

1. It lends to the use of well-defined evaluation designs.
2. It focuses on analysis.
3. It provides descriptive analysis.
4. It tends to stress local effects.
5. It is unobtrusive and non-reactive as far as possible.
6. It is concerned with broad range of issues.
7. Its instruments are reliable and valid.

12.2. FORMATIVE EVALUATION

Definition and Meaning

In the words of A.J. Nitko, (1983), "Formative evaluation is concerned with judgements made during the design and or development of a programme which are directed towards modifying, forming or otherwise improving the programme before it is completed."

According to N. E. Gronlund (1985), "Formative evaluation is used to monitor learning progress during instruction and to provide continuous feedback to both pupil and teacher concerning learning successes and failures. Feedback to pupils reinforces successful learning and identifies the learning errors that need correction. Feedback to the teacher provides information for modifying instruction and prescribing group and individual remedial work."

In the views of R. L. Ebel and D. A. Frisbie (1986), "Formative evaluation is conducted to monitor the instructional process, to determine whether learning is taking place as planned."

Gilbert Sax (1989) states: "Formative evaluation takes place during instruction by letting the teacher or evaluator know if students are meeting instructional objectives, if the programme is on time and if there are ways that the programme might be improved. Formative evaluation helps current students to learn more effectively."

W. Wiersma and S. G. Jurs write, "Formative evaluation occurs over a period of time and monitors student progress."

Following are the implications of the above definitions for the classroom teacher :

1. Formative evaluation is done during an instructional programme.
2. The instructional programme should aim at the attainment of certain objectives during the implementation of the programme also.
3. Formative evaluation is done to monitor learning and modifying the programme if needed before its completion.
4. Formative evaluation is for current students.

Characteristics of Formative Evaluation:

1. It relatively focuses on molecular analysis.
2. It is cause seeking.
3. It is interested in the broader experiences of the programme users.
4. Its design is exploratory and flexible.
5. It tends to ignore the local effects of a particular programme.
6. It seeks to identify influential variables.
7. It requires analysis of instructional material for mapping the hierarchical structure of the learning tasks and actual teaching of the course for a certain period.

12.3. DIFFERENCE BETWEEN THE SUMMATIVE AND FORMATIVE EVALUATION

In the beginning these terms applied for the evaluation of curricular work only.

M. Seriven explains the difference between these terms as follows in his book *Evaluation Thesaurus* (1980), "Formative evaluation is conducted during the development or improvement of a programme or product (or person). It is an evaluation conducted for in-house staff and normally remains in-house but it may be done by an internal or external evaluator (preferably) a combination. Summative evaluation, on the other hand, is conducted after completion of a programme (or a course of study) and for the benefit of some external audience or decision maker (e.g. funding agency or future possible users) though it may be done by an internal or an external evaluator or by a combination."

Gloria, Hitchok and others (1986) state the difference between the summative and formative evaluation in these words, "It is fairly straight forward to produce an 'ideal' type of either a summative or a formative profile. It is far more difficult to combine the two into one unified system. The underlying philosophies of the two appear difficult to reconcile."

Following are the main differences between these two types of evaluation.

1. They differ in purpose, nature and timing.
2. Summative evaluation is the terminal assessement of performance at the end of instruction but formative evaluation in the assessment made during the instructional phase to inform the teacher about progress in learning and what more is to be done.
3. The summative evaluation limits the use of profiles and record of achievement but they are regularly used informative evaluation.
4. The main consideration in summative evaluation is the determination of the extent to which the examinee has mastered the knowledge and skills associated with a course. On the other hand, the main consideration informative evaluation is to reveal the processes by which the examinee achieved these outcomes.
5. In summative evaluation, the assessment is done to test learning outcomes against a set of objective criteria without revealing the details of the route to the teacher which the student followed in reaching that point. Formation evaluation takes the form of a dialogue between the student and teacher in which the task is determined by both.

Broad Differences between Formative and Summative Evaluation

Characteristics	*Formative*	*Summative*
Purpose	To monitor progress of students by getting feedback	To check final status of students
Content focus	Detailed	General
	Narrow scope	Broad scope
Methods	Daily assignments	Tests
	Observations	Projects
Frequency	Daily	Weekly, quarterly etc.

Alkin (1974) pointed out that a formative evaluation study uses a great variety of instruments which are either locally developed or standardized, it relies on observation and informal data collection devices, mostly locally chosen. In contrast, summative evaluation studies tend to use well defined evaluation designs, as unobtrusive and non-reactive as possible, they are comparative and concerned with a broad range of issues, for example, implications, politics, costs, competing options. The instruments used in summative evaluation are publicly accepted, reliable and valid instruments, reflecting concerns of the sponsor and of the decision maker.

Formative tests are administered at the completion of each unit of learning and help students to pace their learning and put forth necessary effort at the appropriate time. They provide immediate and continuous feedback to the student via instruments that are essentially brief, so that they do not take up inordinate amounts of instructional time. Thus, it forces and reinforces learning mastery by providing data that can direct remedial teaching. Summative evaluation are in real sense 'final' tests of students' achievement typically covering relatively large blocks of instructional material. In formative evaluation, scoring is based on criterion reference approach but in summative evaluation, scoring is generally norm referenced though it can be criterion referenced also. Informative evaluation, the method of reporting scores is individual pattern of pass-fail scores on each task in hierarchy, whereas in summative evaluation, attainment is reported in terms of total scores.

Scriven adheres to the view that there are no basic logical and methodological differences between formative and summative evaluation.

Both are intended to examine the worth of a particular entity. Only timing, the audience requesting it, and the way its results are used can indicate whether a study is formative or summative. Moreover, the same study may be viewed by one client as formative and by another one as summative.

Chapter 13

Internal Assessment and Evaluation

13.1. MEANING AND SIGNIFICANCE OF INTERNAL ASSESSMENT AND EVALUATION

Education is not only concerned with the acquisition of knowledge but also is concerned with the development of desired attitudes, interests, skills and various personal and social qualities. External examinations/ public examinations fail to assess the development of these qualities. Even in the area of assessment of acquisition of knowledge, it has come under heavy criticism. Evaluation by teachers through teacher made and standardized tests, observation, and other techniques is called for and this is known as internal assessment—assessment done internally by the teachers teaching in the same institution. External examination or assessment is organized and conducted by an external agency, other than the school.

Internal assessment mitigates a major defect of the external examination. In place of basing results on the assessment at any one time, internal assessment can be as continuous as desired.

Internal evaluation enables us to diagnose pupils' difficulties in learning. It points out the potentialities of an individual and provides opportunities to find out the needs, goals and interests and aptitudes of an individual and shows him the way for their development. This has a motivating effect and this in turn induces him to utilise his resourcefulness which is otherwise cramped.

Since internal evaluation is continuous, it builds regular study habit among students.

By assessing both the tangible and intangible attainments of students, internal evaluation supplements external assessment.

Internal evaluation by the teacher with responsibility provides motivation to students.

Internal evaluation by providing a comprehensive picture of students' learning, helps in the improvement of the teaching-learning process.

Objectives of the affective domain (appreciation attitudes and interests) and psycho-motor domain (skills), require for their achievement a long process of continuous observation, testing and recording etc. Obviously such a process can only be followed in internal evaluation.

Internal evaluation provides a continuous feedback for undertaking diagnostic and remedial teaching and other measures.

Limitations and Shortcomings of Internal Evaluation:

1. It can be misused by the teachers.
2. It requires experienced, honest and sincere teachers.
3. Its reliability and validity are questionable in view of several elements of subjectivity.
4. It cannot replace external examinations. It can only supplement them.
5. It requires a lot of time to undertake several activities related to internal evaluation.

13.2. PLANNING INTERNAL SCHOOL EVALUATION PROGRAMME

As observed by the Education Commission 1964-66, "Internal assessment should be built into the total educational programme and should be used for improvement rather than for certifying the level of achievement of the student." Obviously a school evaluation programme is expected to cover all areas of growth and development i.e. scholastic as well as non-scholastic. One of the chief defects of external examinations is that they neglect the evaluation of the pupil's growth in non-scholastic areas. It may be remembered that education aims at developing the ability of applying the acquired knowledge to new situations, to inculcate desirable interests and to develop desirable, personal and social qualities leading to a balanced and harmonious development of pupil's abilities and accomplishments in the cognitive, affective and psychomotor domains. Therefore, a comprehensive school evaluation programme is expected to take note of this fact.

Steps in the Development of the Programme:

1. Determination of the areas to be evaluated.
2. Identification and selection of tools and techniques of evaluation for each area.
3. Development of tools of evaluation.
4. Determination of the periodicity of evaluation.
5. Implementation of the programme.
6. Recording of results.
7. Using results for instructional decisions.

1. Areas to be evaluated. These are as under:

1. Scholastic achievement.
2. Personal and social attributes, attitudes, work habits, etc.
3. Physical and health development.
4. Performance in skill areas.
5. Products produced by the students.

2. Techniques and tools of evaluation. These includes—

(1) *Techniques*

(*a*) Written examination
(*b*) Oral examination
(*c*) Practical examination
(*d*) Interviews
(*e*) Observation
(*f*) Projective techniques
(*g*) Sociometric techniques.

(2) *Tools*

(*a*) Tests – These include (*i*) intelligence tests, (*ii*) Teacher made tests (*iii*) Standardized achievement tests (*iv*) Unit tests (*v*) Terminal tests (*vi*.) Annual tests (*vii*) Diagnostic tests.
(*b*) Anecdotal records.
(*c*) Check lists.
(*d*) Cumulative records.
(*e*) Interview schedules.
(*f*) Inventories.
(*g*) Questionnaires.
(*h*) Rating scales.

3. Development of Tools. Sometimes teachers themselves may be required to develop some of the tools. These need not be very sophisticated. Nevertheless, these tools should be valid, reliable and practicable.

Blue-print of the Internal Evaluation Programme

I. SCHOLASTIC ASPECTS

Area	*Periodicity*	*Techniques and Tools*
(*a*) Curricular area	1. Monthly tests 2. Term tests 3. Annual test	(i) Written Examinations (ii) Oral examinations (iii) Practical examinations (iv) Standardised achievement tests
(*b*) Intelligence	Once at the beginning of the four school stages i.e. Primary, Middle, Secondary and Sr. Secondary	Standardised paper-pencil and performance tests of abilities and intelligence.

II. NON-SCHOLASTIC TESTS

A. Personal and Social Habits.		
(*i*) Cleanliness habits	Once in every term	Anecdotal records
(*ii*) Cooperative attitude		Observation
(*iii*) Discipline		Rating scales
(*iv*) Emotional stability		
(*v*) Industriousness		
(*vi*) Initiative		
(*vii*) Punctuality		
(*viii*) Regularity		
(*ix*) Social service		

B. Interests. Once in each term.

(*i*) Artistic	(*i*) Anecdotal records
(*ii*) Literary	(*ii*) Interest inventories
(*iii*) Musical	(*iii*) Observation
(*iv*) Scientific	(*iv*) Rating Scale
(*v*) Vocational	

C. Attitudes. Once in each term.

(*i*) Towards studies	(*i*) Anecdotal records
(*ii*) Towards schoolmates	(*ii*) Interviews
(*iii*) Towards teachers	(*iii*) Projective techniques
(*iv*) Towards school property	(*iv*) Observation
(*v*) Towards school programme	(*v*) Questionaires

D. Physical Health. Once in each term.

(*i*) Height	(*i*) Medical check-up
(*ii*) Weight	(*ii*) Observations
(*iii*) Chest expansion	
(*iv*) Eye sight	
(*v*) Teeth	
(*vi*) Physical defects, if any	

III. CO-CURRICULAR ACTIVITIES

A. Literary and Scientific Activities. Twice a year.

(*i*) Creative writing	(*i*) Competitions
(*ii*) Debate	(*ii*) Observation
(*iii*) Reading habits (use of library)	(*iii*) Students diary
(*iv*) Recitation	
(*v*) Science Club	

B. Culturual Activities. Twice a year.

(*i*) Artistic embroidery	(*i*) Competitions
(*ii*) Dance	(*ii*) Observation
(*iii*) Drama	(*iii*) Rating scales
(*iv*) Drawing	
(*v*) Music	
(*vi*) Painting	
(*vii*) Sculpture	

C. Outdoor Activities. Twice a year.

(*i*) Community service	(*i*) Competitions
(*ii*) Games and sports	(*ii*) Observation
(*iii*) First aid	(*iii*) Rating scales
(*iv*) Girl Guiding and Scouting	
(*v*) N.C.C.	
(*vi*) Swimming	

D. Productive Activities. Three times a year.

(*i*) Competition

(*ii*) Exhibitions

Determination of the Periodicity and Other Elements of Evaluation

The following points may be kept in mind.

(1) Pupil's progress in most of the growth areas does not become tangible in a short time. Therefore, evaluations made too frequently may not give any significant new information each time about the progress made by the pupil.

(2) Every evaluation should be followed by remedial instruction. When pupils are evaluated too frequently, most of the school time is spent in evaluation and remedial work. Consequently, the instruction on new topics does not progress well.

(3) Too frequent evaluation means that the teacher has to maintain records of pupil progress very often. Maintenance of records in this situation becomes a time consuming and unmanageable job. Evaluation therefore, should not be done very frequently but necessarily at the end of every teaching unit.

(4) *Implementation of the programme.* A systematically planned and well-thought-out programme of evaluation is not difficult to implement by the teachers, specially when they themselves are actively involved in its development. However, supervisory and guidance facilities should be provided to implement the programme systematically and to help the teachers to cope with the unforeseen problems.

(5) *Recording of valuation results.* Systematic recording of evaluation results is as important as the evaluation itself. In the absence of such records, fruitful use of the results cannot be made. The form in which the evaluation results are to be recorded and reported should be determined at the planning stage itself. The records should be such that they can give a comprehensive picture of the progress of each pupil as well as the whole class in a simple manner. There should not be any unnecessary duplication and they should be manageable by the teachers.

(6) *Use of evaluation results.* The use of evaluation results for instructional decisions is the culminating point of the whole process of evaluation and unless it is reached the evaluation

process cannot play its role of being an integral part of instruction and a tool of improvement.

School Evaluation. (Based on the Programme suggested by NCERT—1978).

Weightage given to Periodical Tests and Annual Test : Academic Subjects

Test		*Approximate*
Monthly tests	(3)	30%
Term tests	(2)	20%
Annual tests	(1)	30%
Home assignments		20%
Total		100%

Weightage to Evaluation of Co-curricular Work

	Activity	*Appoximate weightage*
1.	Library work	20%
2.	Games and sports	30%
3.	Debates, study circle etc.	20%
4.	Community service	20%
5.	Visits (excursions etc.)	10%
	Total	100%

Weightage to Evaluation and Assessment of Personality Traits

In the assessment of personality traits, it is not possible to award scores. Various grades may be assigned to different traits. Grades may be on a five-point scale—A to E.

13.3. METHODS SUGGESTED BY THE EDUCATION COMMISSION (1964–66) TO OVERCOME THE SHORTCOMINGS OF INTERNAL ASSESSMENT

1. The results of the internal assessment and external examination should not be combined because the purposes and techniques of the two evaluations are different and because the results of the internal

assessment of the different institutions are not strictly comparable. The results of the external and internal assessment should, therefore, be shown separately in the certificate(s) given at the end of the course.

2. It should be an important point in the inspections of schools to review the internal assessment made and to examine the correlation between the internal and external assessments. Persistence in over-assessment should be regarded as a weakness in the school programmes. It should be taken due note of while classifying the schools and should also be related to grants-in-aid so that institutions which tend to over-assess their students persistently would stand to lose in status and finance. The grants-in-aid rules should also authorize the Education Departments to withdraw recognition for persistent irresponsible assessment.

Internal Assessment and a Challenge to Teachers. Internal assessment presupposes responsible teachers. It takes for granted that they will realise the sanctity of the trust reposed in them. They must discharge their responsibilities with impartiality and equity. They should rise above their prejudices and petty values. The success of the scheme depends upon their sincerity, honesty and integrity. They should have the moral courage to face the challenge of favouritism and nepotism. They should work honestly and should not cook figures. They should not create such impression that those students get high marks in the internal assessment who dance on the fingers of thier teachers according to their wishes.

Internal assessment should not be used as a tool of maintaining discipline in the institution. Discipline should not be secured by threatening the students to spoil their career or ruin their markings in case they question the authority of the teachers or the principal. No other crime can be more serious than this on their part. Internal assessment is likely to result in non-uniformity of standards of marking in different institutions. To mitigate this evil a general procedure of assessment and of different techniques must be laid down.

The entire staff should be associated with the different aspects of assessment of a single child. This would help in eliminating to a greater extent the subjectivity and misuse of power.

Sympathetic hearing must be given to the genuine grievances and complaints of the students. The students must be convinced of the awards. Of course, the success of this system of internal assessment depends on teachers themselves. They must justify the confidence reposed in them.

The role of Headmaster. According to the Group Report of the Short Term Training Course for the State Administrators of Basic Education, "The Headmaster plays an important role in the assessment work of the school. The headmaster should not only carefully observe the various records maintained by the children and the teachers but also devise his own records so that he may have a glimpse of the progress of work done in the school."

13.4. PROBLEMS OF INTERNAL ASSESSMENT AND SUGGESTIVE MEASURES FOR IMPLEMENTING THE PROGRAMME

The report of a Training Course on Evaluation (1991) discusses the following problems for the implementation of an internal assessment programme.

1. How to get acceptance of the programme of internal assessment by teachers, students, public and administration, etc ?
2. How to develop competence among the teachers to undertake internal assessment effectively?
3. How much of minimum facilities need to be provided in the schools for carrying out an effective programme of internal assessment ?
4. How to co-ordinate standard of different schools ?
5. What sort of machinery is required to be developed so as to keep up and progressively improve the standard of internal assessment ?
6. How to relate the external and internal marks ?

Problem 1. How to get acceptance of the Programme of Internal Assessment ?

(*a*) The analysis of the examination paper, answer books and examination marks to be made and the data to be placed before the people concerned to realise a need for the development of a more adequate measure of pupils growth.

(*b*) Experiments to be made in some selected schools to prove the superiority of the system of assessment which is advocated to be introduced.

(*c*) Developing a sound technique of internal assessment with the help of teachers and taking their full co-operation in the implementation of the scheme leading to their confidence in it.

Problem 2. Competence of Teachers.

(*a*) In the teacher's training courses, the concept of Internal Assessment in Evaluation, its problems and techniques should be included as an integral part of the training college programme.

(*b*) For teachers already in schools, special refresher courses or training camps may be held by way of in-service education.

(*c*) Periodic conferences of teachers and the principals atleast twice a year (in the beginning of each term) may be held so that the objectives of internal assessment are classified.

(*d*) A conference of teachers of different schools in the same region may also be held to evaluate and develop the system and form of maintaining records.

Problem 3. Problem of Minimum Facilities

(*a*) The curriculum should be detailed out adequately in the light of objectives of education.

(*b*) The curriculum should provide ample freedom to the teacher for planning his work in relation to his own environment.

(*c*) Any rigorous conformity to particular method of work as is generally advocated by the inspecting staff and other authorities should be avoided to be prescribed in order to allow teachers to develop their own initiative.

(*d*) Teacher-pupil ratio to be brought to a reasonable size of 1 to 30 at the maximum.

(*e*) Provision to be made for organizing class-libraries according to the standard of the class.

(*f*) Study and research in these aspects will help in developing maximum criteria for certifying accrediting schools, which will be necessary in course of time.

Problem 4. The Problem of Co-ordinating Standards among Different Schools and School Subjects to Internal Assessment

1. Advisory bodies of experts in different areas of knowledge may be appointed. These may issue suggestions to different institutions from time to time and also in the form of articles or books for the guidance of the teachers. A complete change in teacher's attitude will be necessary.

It shall have to be brought home to them that these experts are not official supervisors but only advisers to whom they may refer their problems in time of need.

2. A common core-curriculum may be provided for all schools. It shall be sufficiently flexible leaving enough scope for the teacher's ingenuity and skill.

3. Extensive facilities for the training of teachers in the new techniques of evaluation shall have to be made available and government grants to the institutions may be regulated by the qualifications of staff and other educational facilities available in the situation.

4. Assessors to check the teacher's estimates may be appointed and their identity may be kept confidential. They may compare assessments from different schools and also check them against other criteria which they may decide upon.

5. Teachers' estimates may be scaled against the results of external examination and co-ordination established, if possible.

Problem 5. What sort of a machinery is to be developed so as to keep up and progressively improve the standard of internal assessment?

The State Evaluation Unit will be one good agency for the purpose but it may work in co-operation with other agencies such as Curriculum Committee, Guidance Bureau, the Inspection Department, Central Evaluation Unit and the Research Bureau for the purpose.

Inspection of school by a team of subject experts may also prove helpful in this respect.

Problem 6. How to relate the internal assessment to the external examination marks ?

(*a*) Internal assessment should be in relation to the various aspects of pupil's growth such as his scholastic achievements, his interests, attitudes and personality traits etc.

(*b*) There should be some minimum standard of pass prescribed for both internal and external examinations in academic subjects and the result should be announced on the basis of pupil's record of achievement in both and mentioned separately.

(*c*) To make the result comparable it may be desirable to bring both internal assessment and external examination total marks at par so far as academic subjects are concerned.

(*d*) It should, however, be noted that internal assessment may be in symbols and grades or in qualitative description for assessing pupil's achievement in some fields, and therefore, external and internal results may not always be comparable.

(*e*) Certificates showing the achievement of students both at the external examination and internal assessment will provide better scope to the employer for making the choice.

(*f*) This type of certificate will provide the opportunity to carry on some studies to find out whether the internal or external result is more valid and reliable in respect of a particular school.

(*g*) This will also help in developing criteria for classifying and accrediting schools.

13.5. EXTERNAL EXAMINATIONS AND EVALUATION IN SCHOOLS — A COMPARISON

Aspects	*External Examinations*	*Evaluation in Schools*
Objective	Assessment of the level of achievement of the students	Improvement in the level of achievement of the students.
Coverage	Only scholastic aspects of student's growth (Proficiency in School subjects)	Scholastic and non-scholastic aspects of students growth–proficiency in subject fields alongwith physical, personal, moral and social development aspects.
Evaluation Techniques	Primarily written examinations and practical examinations	Psychological testing, interviews and observation in addition to written, oral and practical examinations.

Aspects	*External Examinations*	*Evaluation in Schools*
Evaluation Tools	Question papers	Inventories, rating scales and schedules in addition to question paper.
Periodicity	Generally after the end of a stage of education	A continuous process.
Organisational Structure	Top-heavy administrative structure (outside the school)	Teacher operated and an informal affair.
Uses of Results	Classification, grading, certification selection to admission to courses of higher education and jobs	Optimum development and growth of student's personality through feed-back for enrichment and remedial measures, academic prediction, in addition to classification and certification.
Examinee Status	Merely an incognito roll number	A human-being with a distinct personality.
Teacher Status	An insignificant and usually a mistrusted tool in the examination machinery.	A trusted and active individual involved in the student's development and growth.
Acceptability	Universal inspite of limitations	Limited.

Note : In this chapter, assessment and evaluation connote the same meaning.

Chapter 14

Cumulative Record Card

14.1. WHAT IS A CUMULATIVE RECORD CARD?

A cumulative record card is that card which contains the results of different assessments, evaluation, and judgements held from time to time during the course study of a student. A cumulative record is an account of the child's history in the school. It begins as soon as the child enters the school and continues till he leaves the school for good. Generally it covers three consecutive years. It contains information regarding all aspects of the life of the child—his physical, mental, social, moral and psychological. It seeks to give as comprehensive a picture as possible of the personality of a child. "Periodically the significant information gathered on students through the use of various techniques —tests, inventories, questionnaries, observation, interview, case study, case conferences and the like—should be assembled in summary form on a cumulative record," writes Jane Warters.

In the words of W.C. Allen, "The Cumulative Record is defined as a record of information concerned with appraisal of the individual pupil —usually kept on a card—kept in one place."

14.2. NEED FOR CUMULATIVE RECORD

The modern type of cumulative record was first made available in 1928 by the American Council on Education. The need of such a record was felt in view of the inadequate information that was contained in the various forms that were available. The Secondary Education Commission 1952-53 has made the following observations regarding the need for school records : "Neither the external examination, singly or together, can give a correct and complete picture of a pupil's all-round progress at any particular stage of his education; yet it is important for us to assess this in order to determine his future course of study or his future vocation. For this purpose a proper system of school records should be maintained for every pupil indicating the work done by him in the school from day to day, month to month, term to term and year to year. Such a school record will present a clear and continuous statement of the attainments of the child in different intellectual pursuits throughout the successive stages of his education. It will also contain a progressive evaluation of development in other directions of less importance, such as the growth of his interests, aptitudes, and personality traits, his social adjustments, the practical and social activities in which he takes part In other words it will give a complete career."

14.3. ADVANTAGES OF THE CUMULATIVE RECORDS

1. A good record contributes to guidance work in general in the following ways : (*a*) By providing a sound basis for understanding the individual, (*b*) By showing the significant experiences of individual, (*c*) By indicating his readiness for new experiences, (*d*) By pointing out the routes to new goals, (*e*) By pointing out his strengths and weaknesses.

2. It helps curriculum revision by revealing the needs of the students.

3. It helps in the improvement of the methods of teaching by revealing the needs of the students.

4. It provides a helpful basis for educational and vocational placement.

5. It is an aid in the search for talent. It assists the teacher to find out students who are gifted in abstract verbal ability, sciences, the arts and social relations.

6. It helps the teacher to find out the slow learners and accordingly he suggests measures.

7. It serves as a link between the teacher and the parents. The teachers find it convenient to write letters or descriptive reports to the parents on the basis of the information contained in the record.

8. The school authorities can make suitable recommendations to the prospective employers and college admission officers.

9. The cumulative records help in furnishing sufficient data for reports to the various authorities engaged in the student welfare field.

10. At the time of the transfer of a student form one school to another it helps the new school authorities to know about the child and to avoid mistake and to facilitate the adjustment of the child to the new environment

Writing about cumulative record Jane Warters rightly says, "It aids teachers in the study of the individual by making it possible for them to understand his present through an analysis of his past, by furnishing clues regarding the cause of his behaviour difficulties and failures, and by disclosing his strengths and weakness."

The Indian Education Commission 1964–66 discusses the importance of this card as "cumulative record cards play a vital role in indicating growth and development of the pupil at each stage, his academic and emotional problems and his difficulties of adjustment if any, and the directions in which remedial action is to be taken to solve his problems and difficulties."

14.4. METHODS OF POPULARISING THIS SYSTEM.

The use of the cumulative record in our educational institutions is still in its infancy. It cannot be imposed upon the teachers. The teachers must be familiarized with the advantages of this system. Talks and refresher courses should be organised for this purpose. Faculty meetings should be organised to discuss the nature of the information that these cards should contain. It must be remembered that the maintenance of cumulative records is a co-operative affair in which administrators, counsellors, teachers, clerical staff, students and their parents must participate and all of these must be convinced of the importance of such records. Teachers and counsellors must be provided with time to make necessary entries. The records should be placed at a place where all concerned may use them easily.

Forms of Cumulative Record Card. It is used in various forms such as card sheet, printed folders, cards or sheets contained in an envelope, booklet or some combination of these forms.

14.5. CONTENTS OF THE CUMULATIVE RECORD CARD

The card usually contains the following sections:

1. Personal Data.
2. Home Circumstances.
3. Health Information.
4. Psychological Report.
5. Scholastic Achievement.
6. Performance in Co-curricular Activities.
7. Educational and Vocational Plans.

8. Personality Characteristics.
9. General Overall Remarks.

14.6. SPECIMEN OF CUMULATIVE RECORD CARD

Name of the Pupil ....
Name of the Father ....
Occupation of Parent/Guardian ....
Address of Parent/Guardian ....
Date of Birth ....

SCHOOLS ATTENDED

Name of School	Month and year of enrolment	Class in which enrolled	Month and year of leaving	Reasons for leaving

HOME CIRCUMSTANCES

1. Economic status of the family..............................
   ....
2. Child's position in the family (whether only child, eldest or youngest child) ....
   ....
3. Type of family (whether Joint or unitary) ....
   ....
4. Education of the Parent/Guardian..............................
   ....
5. Special circumstances..............................
   ....

ATTENDANCE

Year	Possible	Actual	Nature of long absence, if any

PHYSICAL DATA

Year	Height	Weight	Any serious illness or physical disability

REPORT OF THE MEDICAL OFFICER

19.....	
19.....	
19.....	

PSYCHOLOGICAL REPORT (IF ANY)

19.....	
19.....	
19.....	

SCHOLASTIC ACHIEVEMENT

(Average percentage of marks or corresponding letter grade based on the result of periodical and annual tests).

Group	Subject	Class... 19.......	Class...... 19.........	Class..... 19..........
		Marks/Grade	Marks/Grade	Marks/Grade
Language and Literature				
General Science and Science				
Social Studies and Social Sciences				
Any other Group				
Craft/Work Experience				

PERFORMANCE IN CO-CURRICULAR ACTIVITIES

(Average Grade of the Child)

Activities	Class....... 19............	Class......... 19............	Class.......... 19...............
1. Sports and Athletics			
2. Personal Hygiene			
3. Literary (debating etc.)			
4. Dramatics			
5. Community service (sanitation drive, literacy campaigns etc.)			
6. Any other activity			

Notable Proficiency and skill in different fields or special merit obtained or position of responsibility held, if any

Years and class	In Scholastic Achievement	In Bal-Sabha	In Scouts Troop	In Sports	In Social Service	Any other
19........ Class...						
19........ Class...						
19........ Class...						

PERSONALITY CHARACTERISTICS

Nature	19........	19........	19..........
1. Honesty 2. Punctuality 3. Courtesy 4. Habits of work 5. Co-operativeness 6. Sociability 7. Self-confidence 8. Emotional stability 9. Leadership 10. Initiative			

GENERAL REMARKS

Year		Signature of the Class Teacher	Sign or Stamp of the Head
19........			
19........			
19........			

14.7. MAIN CHARACTERISTICS OF A CUMULATIVE RECORD

1. Validity. The facts recorded must be authentic. It is better not to write any information than to give untrue information.

2. Comprehensiveness. A cumulative record should contain informationn as complete and comprehensive as possible.

3. Accuracy. The information in the card should be accurately recorded from the original source. If instead of 105 one writes 150 as score of an individual in English let us say, one can imagine the difference in the educational guidance of that student.

4. Objectivity. Personal opinion and judgements should be reduced to the minimum.

5. Economy of space. The criterion of a good cumulative record form is that the maximum possible information is contained in the space available.

6. Recency. Any piece of information should be recorded as soon as it is obtained.

7. Outcome of a co-operative enterprise. It should be the result of group thinking.

8. Evaluation. It should be evaluated every year so as to know how far it serves the purpose.

14.8. PROBLEMS IN THE MAINTENANCE AND USE OF CUMULATIVE RECORD CARDS

1. Who should maintain the records? (*a*) *Functions of the class teacher.* The records may be kept by the class teacher and he should be responsible for getting the necessary entries made. Class teachers' responsibility is greater and he will not only ensure correct and up-to-date entries but also act as a liasion between the pupil and the subject teacher, and between the pupil and the parent.

(*b*) *Function of special teachers and teacher incharge of various activities.* This function is to assess the child's attainment from time to time to record the same and to pass it to the class teacher.

2. Where to keep them? This is a very formidable problem. Arrangement will have to be made so that a record card is easily accessible to the teachers. If possible it may be kept by the class teacher in his safe custody otherwise it may be kept in the Principal's Office. However, in either case, its contents should remain confidential.

3. When to fill up these records? Entries in the card should be made at the time of a particular event or test. It is advisable that every teacher should have a small note book to record his observations at the time of the incident about a particular pupil. He may record the significant entries according to his convenience. As a rule, other teachers may not record the entries on the card itself. They would pass on the entries to the class teacher. This would enable the class teacher to maintain the records neatly and scientifically. Too many hands may spoil the beauty and the neatness of the card.

4. **How to check the maintenance?** The Principal should check after every three months that the entries are regularly made and the records kept up-to-date. He may assign this work to one of his colleagues but must sign the record card himself.

5. **What should be the design of record cards?** Usually three types of cards are being maintained in schools.

(a) Folder type
(*b*) File type
(*c*) Envelope type

6. **The problem of new admissions and migrations.** The record card should move with the student in case he is transferred from one school to another. It should go with the pupil from class to class and from school to school.

7. **How to help the teacher in discharging the function ?**

(i) Teachers should be trained in the maintenance of these records.

(ii) The state authorities should get prepared model forms of records for the schools.

(iii) This work should be done by the teachers on the last working day of the month. There may not be any teaching work on that day. If we do not give adequate time to the teachers to fill up these cards, they will fill up these mechanically.

(iv) Adequate provision should be made for the safe custody of these cards.

(v) The supervisor should inspect the maintenance of these records at the time of the annual inspection of the school.

Chapter 15

Assessment and Measurement

15.1. CONFUSION REGARDING THE USE OF TERMS

We have already discussed the usage of various terms like evaluation, assessment, measurement and testing in Chapter 9 of this book. In this chapter we have used the terms assessment and measurement interchangeably as is done in several textbooks. However, a few select definitions of assessment and measurement are given here.

Definition of Assessment

In education assessment is the process by which one attempts to measure the quality of learning and teaching using various assessment techniques, assignments, projects, continuous assessment, objective type tests.

A Critical Dictionary of Education (1982)

As far as possible, the term assessment should be reserved for application to people. It covers activities included in grading (formal and non-formal) examining, certifying and so on. Students' achievement on a particular course may be assessed.

Panton, M.Q. (1985)

Students may be assessed for a number of different reasons and in a number of different ways. The range of types of assessment runs from the conventional written essays, through oral tests or practical projects to different types of objective tests.

A Critical Dictionary of Educational Concepts (1986)

Definitions of Measurement

In its broadest sense, measurement is the assignment of numerals to objects, or events, according to rules.

Stevens (1951)

Measurement as the assignment of numerals to entities according to rules.

Stuffebeam, D.L. (1968)

Act of firfding dimensions of any object and the quality found by each act.

International Dictionary of Education (1977)

Measurement implies assigning a numerical quantity. While instruments such as rulers and stopwatches can be used to determine height, speed, and so on, any intellectual capacities or other quantities of educational interest must be measured indirectly. Thus tests are typically used on measures such as dimensions and levels of intelligence. It may be included in an assessment.

Panton, M. Q. (1985)

Fundamentally, we can say that measurement entails certain rules and procedures for assigning numbers to attributes in such a way that the numbers represent the quantity of the attribute.

A Dictionary of Education (1981)

Propositions in measurement

Thorndike and Hagen (1979) list six propositions that seem to us to provide the foundations for a contemporary view of educational and psychological measurement procedures and their role in our schools and our society.

1. Various types of decisions have to be made.
2. The more relevant and more accurate the information, the better the decision.
3. Measurement instruments and procedures provide an important set of tools for improving the information available for decision making.
4. The use of any type of information for decision making needs to know what that information signifies and far it can be trusted.
5. The facts and values involved in any decision are complex.
6. The wisdom of the decider is crucial.

According to Thorndike and Hagen (1979), measurement in any field involves three common steps : (1) indentifying and defining the quality or attribute that is to be measured, (2) determining a set of operations by which the attribute may be made manifest and perceivable, and (3) establishing a set of procedures or definitions for translating observations into quantitative statements of degree or amount.

15.2. PERSONALITY ASSESSMENT AND MEASUREMENT

Significance and Meaning of Personality Assessment

The central task of the school is to bring about a harmonious and integrated development of the personality of the child. For this, a continuous assessment of the various aspects of the development of the personality is needed so that necessary changes in the programmes may be made for obtaining better results. Assessment, thus leads to follow up. Revised programmes are planned and implemented for the further development of the personality. In this way, assessment and development becomes a continuous processs which may be explained as:

Personality Development = Assessment → Follow up → Assessment → follow up → Development

Assessment is essential in the never ending cycle of formulating goals of development, measuring progress towards them and determining the new goals of development which emerge as a result of new warnings. Assessment implies that consideration has been given to certain traits, values, standards and that interpretation of the evidence has been made in the light of particular situation.

Assessment is a process of making judgements that are to be used for further planning. It is a procedure for improving the product, the process and even the goals themselves.

The purpose of assessment is to discover the needs of the individuals being assessed.

Assessment is an important and delicate process not only from the standpoint of determining the needs and growths of programmes and individuals but also from the standpoint of what it does to the individuals being assessed.

An assessment cannot adequately be made by using a single check-list, an isolated anecdotal record, or a battery of tests. A complete assessment will require the use of several techniques.

Assessment cannot be done in a vacuum. It is always with reference to the objectives of a particular system of education.

Assessment has to be very comprehensive in a system of education which aims at the many-sided development of the personality of a child. As observed by the Secondary Education Commission 1952-53, "The school of today concerns itself not only with the intellectual pursuits but also with the emotional and social development of the child, his physical and mental health, his social adjustment and other equally important aspects of life — in a word, with an all-round development of his personality." Assessment is a wider term than measurement. Measurement denotes quantity and assessment quality also. We measure cloth, height and weight but we assess personality traits and not cloth, height and weight.

Purposes of Assessment of Personality

1. To appraise the status of and changes in pupil's personality development.
2. To find out pupil's needs and possibilities of development.
3. To aid student-teacher planning.
4. To familiarize the teacher with the nature of pupil learning development and progress.
5. To serve as a means of improving school-community relations.
6. To facilitate the selection and improvement of assessment instruments.
7. To appraise the teacher's competence.
8. To serve as a guiding principle for the selection and application of supervisory techniques.

Difficulties in Assessing Personality

Several difficulties are encountered in the assessment of personality. Although for long psychologists have been trying to develop sound techniques for measuring personality yet even to-day they are far away from this goal.

There are three basic reasons for not arriving at exact conclusions.

1. Complex nature of the individual whose personality is to be assessed.
2. Complex nature of the person who assesses personality.
3. Nature of assessment instruments.

1. Complex nature of the personality of the individual. The personality of the individual being assessed is very complex. We may peep into the child's personality here and there in some detail but a total peep of the personality eludes us.

Assessment of personality does not remain stable because an individual is ever growing and he may not respond to the same situation in the same manner. There are several internal and external forces which influence him constantly.

An individual who is being assessed is capable of employing hundreds of ways to evade being assessed. Even if he cooperates willingly with the best of his intentions, he may be unable to tell about the elements hidden in his unconcious mind..

2. Complex nature of the assessor of personality. Subjectivity of the person who assesses can also influence assessment. Even when the same person assesses the same individual at different intervals under the same conditions, results may differ. It is also observed that when two or more persons assess the same person, results may not be identical.

3. Nature of assessment instruments. In measuring a piece of cloth, we can use units in terms of centimetres and inches. In measuring temperature, we have units in terms of degrees and so on but in psychological measurement, we do not have any regular unit of measurement. In personality assessment there is no starting point (zero) for reference. No child is born with zero personality. This also creates difficulties in the exact assessment of personality. Above all, tools of assessment of personality are not very exact, reliable and valid in terms of their results.

15.3. QUALITATIVE MEASURES FOR THE ASSESSMENT AND MEASUREMENT OF PERSONALITY

Qualitative measures are generally classified under the following heads:

1. Observational Techniques. Checklists, Rating Scales, Score cards etc.

2. Projective Techniques. B G Test, Blocky Picture Test, Children Apperception Test (CAT), Clay Modelling, Cloud Picture Test, Draw-a-Man Test, Graphology, Mosaic Test, Psychodrama, Rorschach Ink Blot Test, Sentence Completion Test, Socio-drama, Szondi Test, Thematic Apperception Test (TAT), Toy and Doll Playing Test, Word Association Test (Free and Controlled).

3. Self-Report Techniques. Anecdotal Records, Attitude Scales, Auto-biography, Diaries Interview, Inventories, Questionnaires.

4. Sociometric Techniques. 'Guess-who' Technique, Nominating Technique, Social Distance Scale, Sociogram.

5. Personal Inventories. Woodworth's Data Sheet. Bell Adjustment Inventory, Berneuter Inventory. Heston Personal adjustment Inventory Guilfod Temperament Schedule. Thurstone Temperament Schedule, Cattell's Inventory. The Minnesota Multiphasic Personality Inventory. The Guilford-Limmerman Temperament Survey. The Edward Personal and Preference Schedule.

Second Classification of Measures

Measures of Assessing Personality

Standardised Tests Objective Methods	Non-Standardised Tests or Subjective Methods	Projective Techniques
1. Achievement Tests	1. Anecdotal Records	1. BG Test
2. Aptitude Tests	2. Autobiography	2. Blacky Picture Test
3. Intelligence Tests	3. Case Conference or Case History or Case Study	3. Children or Apperception Test (CAT)
4. Interest Tests	4. Cumulative Record Card	4. Clay Modelling
5. Personal Inventories	5. Interview	5. Cloud Picture Test
	6. Observation	6. Draw-a-Man Test
	7. Parent's Views	7. Graphology
	8. Personal Data Blanks	8. Mosaic Test
	9. Questionnaire	9. Psychodrama
	10. Rating Scale or Attitude Scale	10. Rorschach Ink Blot Test
	11. Schedule	11. Sentence Completion
	12. Score card	12. Socio-drama
	13. Sociometry	13. Szondi Test
		14. Thematic Apperception Test (TAT)
		15. Toy and Doll playing
		16. Word Association (Free and Controlled)

15.4. OBSERVATIONAL TECHNIQUES

Meaning. Observation is one of the most ancient and widely used instruments of assessing personality.

Observation has been defined as, "measurement without instruments."

In education, observation is the most commonly employed of all measurement techniques. In the present as well as in the past, students have been labelled as good, fair or poor in achievement and lazy or diligent in study, etc., on the basis of observation. Similarly, teachers have listened to speeches and ranked students 1, 2, 3 and so on.

Rousseau wrote, "Watch nature long and observe your pupil carefully before you say a word to him."

The physicians and the psychologists depend heavily on what they observe of the patient's talk, gestures and facial expressions. Observation is one of the oldest techniques that man has made use of. Even today it is our common experience to notice that farmers feel the breeze, watch the sky, sun, moon and stars, all to determine what the weather is likely to be and what season is approaching.

Merits of Direct Observation

1. Being a record of the actual behaviour of the child, it is more reliable and objective.
2. It is a study of an individual in a natural situation and is therefore more useful than the restricted study in a test situation.
3. This method can be used with children of all ages; of course, the younger the child, the easier it is to observe him. This method has been found very useful with shy children.
4. It can be used with some training and experience and almost all teachers can use it. It does not require any special tools or equipment.
5. It can be used in every situation.
6. It is adaptable both to individuals and groups.
7. Frequent observations of a student's work and work habits can provide a continuous check on his progress.
8. The problems as they arise can be immediately detected and corrective action taken immediately.
9. Observational data provide teachers with valuable supplementary information.

Limitations and Demerits

1. There is a great scope for personal prejudices and bias of the observer.
2. Records may not be written with hundred per cent accuracy as the observation is recorded after the actions of the observed. There is some time-lag.

3. The observer may get only a small sample of student behaviour. It is very difficult to observe everything that a student does or says.

4. It reveals the overt behaviour only – behaviour that is expressed and not that is within.

Principles to be followed in Making Observations

1. Observe the whole situation.
2. Select one student to observe at a time.
3. Students should be observed in their regular activities, such as in classroom, on the play ground or in going from class to class.
4. Observation should be made over a period of days.
5. As far as possible, observations should be collected from several teachers.

Requisites of Good Observation.

As a research tool good observation is based on

1. Proper planning.
2. Proper execution.
3. Proper recording.
4. Proper interpretation.

Proper Planning of Observation

1. Specific activities or units of behaviour to be observed must be clearly defined.
2. An appropriate group of subjects be selected for observation
3. Scope of observation – whether individual or group – should be decided.
4. The length of each observation period, number of periods and interval between periods should be decided.
5. The form of recording should be decided.
6. The instruments to be used should be decided.
7. Physical position of the observer should be demarcated.
8. Proper tools for recording observation should be kept handy.

Proper Execution of Observation

An expert execution demands skill and resourcefulness on the part of the investigators. This depends upon

(*i*) Proper arrangement of special conditions for the subjects.
(*ii*) Assuming proper physical position for observing.
(*iii*) Focusing attention on the units of behaviour on the specific activities under observation.
(*iv*) Observing discreetly the length and number of periods and intervals decided upon.

(*v*) Proper handling of the recording instrument being used.
(*vi*) Utilising suitably the training received in terms of expertness.

Recording of Observation

Generally, two methods are employed for recording observation. Which of the two methods to use depends upon the nature of the activities or behaviour of the group to be observed. The skill of the observer also plays an important role in deciding upon the method.

The first method is to record the observation simultaneously. It is useful in the sense that a time-gap may distort facts. However, at times, this may not be feasible when the action or activity performed is very swift. Moreover, this is likely to distract the subject or subjects.

Facts may be recorded soon after the observation is over. This is helpful as this does not distract the mind of the subjects. But the investigator may not be able to recall facts accurately after the interval of a few minutes.

Devices Used in Observation are:

(*i*) Check-lists.
(*ii*) Rating Scale.
(*iii*) Score Cards.
(*iv*) Blank form of tallying frequencies.

Interpretation

Results should be interpreted cautiously and judiciously after taking into account various limitations of planning, sampling or procedure.

I. RATING SCALES

Meaning

Rating means the judgement of one person by another, "Rating is, in essence, directed observation," writes Ruth Strang. A.S. Barr and others define, "Rating is a term applied to expression of opinion or judgement regarding some situation, object or character. Opinions are usually expressed on a scale or values. Rating techniques are devices by which such judgements may be quantified." A rating scale is a method by which we systematize the expression of opinion concerning a trait. The ratings are done by parents, teachers, a board of interviewers and judges and by the self as well.

These rating scales give an idea of the personality of an individual.

Characteristics

There are two characteristics of a rating scale. (1) Description of the characteristics to be rated, and (2) Some methods by which the quality, frequency or importance of each item to be rated may be given.

Uses and Advantages of Rating Scales

1. Helpful in measuring specified outcomes or objectives of education.
2. Helpful in supplementing other sources of understanding about the child.
3. Helpful in their simulating effect upon the individuals who are rated.
4. Helpful in writing reports to parents.
5. Helpful in filling out admission blanks for colleges.
6. Helpful in finding out students' needs.
7. Helpful in making recommendations to the employers.
8. Helpful to the student to rate himself.

Limitations

1. Some characteristics are more difficult to rate.
2. Subjective element is present.
3. Lack of opportunities to rate students.
4. Raters tend to be generally generous.

The teacher or the counsellor may rate each individual on each quality on a three-point, four-point or five-point scale. In a five-point scale, the description of the qualities of an individual may be 'Outstanding', 'Very good', 'Good', 'Average' and 'Poor'

Principles Governing Rating Scales

1. The trait to be treated should be readily observable.

2. The specific trait or mode of behaviour must be defined properly. For example, we want to rate a child's originality in performing a task. First of all we must formulate a definition of 'originality' and then try to rate it.

3. The scale should be clearly defined, i.e. we are rating at a three, four or five-point scale.

4. Uniform standards of rating scale should be observed.

5. The rater should observe the rates in different situations involving the trait to be rated.

6. The number of characteristics to be rated should be limited.

7. In the rating scale card, some space may be provided for the rater to write some supplementary material.

8. The directions of using the rating scales should be clear and comprehensive.

9. Several judges may be employed to increase the reliability of any rating scale.

10. Well-informed and experienced persons should be selected for rating.

Errors in Rating

(*a*) *Generosity Error.* Sometimes raters would not like to bring down their own people by giving them low ratings. The result is that high ratings are given in almost all cases. Such an error is known as 'generosity error'.

(*b*) *Stringency Error.* The opposite of generosity error may be called stringency error. Some raters have a tendency to rate all individuals low.

(*c*) *The Halo Error.* 'Halo' means a tendency to rate in terms of general impressions about the rates formed on the basis of some previous performance.

(*d*) *The Error of Central Tendency.* There is a tendency in some observers to rate all or most of the rates near the mid-point of the scale. They would like to put most of the rates as 'Agerage,' etc.

(*e*) *The Logical Error.* Such an error occurs when the characteristic or the trait to be rated is misunderstood.

Types of Rating Scales

1. Descriptive. The rater puts a check (√) in the blank before the characteristic or trait which is described in word or phrase.

Example :Has this pupil initiative?

— Shows marked originality.
— Willing to take initiative.
— Quite inventive.
— On the whole unenterprising.
— Very dependent on others.

2. Numerical Scale. Here numbers are assigned to each trait. If it is a seven-point scale; the number 7 represents the maximum amount of that trait in the individual; 4 represents the average amount.

3. The Graphic Scale. This is similar to the descriptive scale and the difference lies only in the way it is written. This is also called

"Behavioural Statement Scale." The following two examples may be noted:

(*a*) *Example* — Responsibility for completing work

Very High	High	Average	Low	Very Low

(*b*) *Example* — Social attitude.

Anti-social	Self-centred	Has no positive attitude	Usually considerate of others	Strongly altruistic

4. **Percentage of Group Scale.** Here the rater is asked to give the percentage of the group that possesses the trait on which the individual is rated.

15.5. PROJECTIVE METHODS

Meaning

Projective methods are those methods in which we provide the subject with relatively indefinite and unstructured material and then allow him to structure the material in anyway he likes. The subject projects his feelings, attitudes etc. In doing so, he unconsciously projects himself and reveals his personality. Examples of such materials through which the subject reveals himself are: making a story, ink blots, drawing a picture, etc. The method is designed to penetrate somewhat below the peripheral personality and to disclose latent needs, images, and sentiments which the subject would be unwilling or unable to embody in direct communications.

"Typically, projective instruments also represent *disguised* testing procedures insofar as the subject is rarely aware of the type of psychological interpretation which will be made of his response. Projective techniques are likewise characterized by a global approach to the appraisal of personality. Attention is focused upon a composite picture of the whole personality rather than upon the measurement of separate traits."

According to Anne Anastasi, "it is expected that the test material of the projective techniqes" will serve as a sort of screen upon which the subject 'projects his characteristic ideas, attitudes, aspirations, fears, worries, aggressions and the like.'

"The label projective techniques has been applied to settings or materials designed to give a person a chance to reveal his thoughts and feelings while seemingly responding to something in the external environment," write Gates and others.

To quote Ruth Strang, "Projective techniques are a method of understanding the inner world of the individual. Rapport describes the aim of projective techniques as, "to elicit, to render observable, to record, and to communicate the psychological structure of the subject, as inherent to him at any given moment and without study of historical antecedents." An individual, it is recognised, reveals or 'projects' his personality in a free and unrestricted activity.

Murray writes, "The purpose of this procedure is to stimulate literary creativity and thereby evoke fantasies that reveal covert and unconscious complexes. The test is based on the well-recognized fact that when a person interprets an ambiguous social situation, he is apt to expose his own personality as much as the phenomenon to which he is attending."

L.K. Frank was the first person to use the term 'Projective Technique' in an article that appeared in 1939 though such methods had been in use for many years prior to that date.

Projective techniques are very useful with young children, illiterates and persons with language handicaps or speech defects. Non-verbal media is readily applicable to all these groups.

Common Characteristics of Projective Techniques

1. The stimulus material is ambiguous and weakly structured and the subject is expected to supply meaning, significance, organisation or in some other way leave the impression of his personality upon the underdefined stimulus of situation.

2. An attempt is made to explore the psychological reality or the underlying basic personality factors of the individual which consist of his hopes, aspirations, needs, motives, moods, attitudes, conflicts, complexes, fears, etc.

3. Projective techniques tap the implicit or unconscious aspects of the personality.

4. Projective techniques require sophistication in administration and interpretation.

Kinds of Projective Techniques

Some of the projective tests are standardized and are widely used.

They include Rorschach's Ink Blot Test, Thematic Apperception Test and various other picture tests like Children's Apperception Test, and Blocky Pictures, the Michigan Picture Test, Rosenzweig Picture-Frustration Study, etc. Out of these Rorschach's Ink Blot and Thematic Apperception Test (TAT) are very popular and widely used.

(*i*) *Free Association and Dream Analysis.* Freud used this method to find out the repressed unconscious desires, emotions and feelings of individual men and women. It has been recognised by many psychologists that day-dreams and even especially dreams are rather difficult to interpret but they do not just happen. They have their roots in the person's private world.

According to this method, the psychologist first of all develops rapport with the subject and then the subject is asked to take a comfortable position reclining on a sofa and is encouraged to talk about his troubles freely after a black cloth is tied over his eyes. The psychologist or the psychoanalyst records his responses and interprets them. After many such sittings, it becomes possible for him to have a clue of the personality of the subject.

(*ii*) *Incomplete Sentence Technique*. The method is very simple. Some incomplete sentences are presented to the child which he completes in anyway he likes. By reading the individual's responses, the counsellor records observations which indicate unhealthy or conflicting, positive or healthy attitudes, etc. Stimulus in the form of the following words may be presented to the child.

(*a*) A baby......
(*b*) The world .....
(*c*) My home ......
(*d*) My father.......
(*e*) Money.......
(*f*) My best friend.....

The child may complete these sentences in this manner:

(*a*) A baby is very lovely.
(*b*) The world is full of cruel people.
(*c*) My home is not a good place to live in.
(*d*) My father is very cruel.
(*e*) Money is everything in life.
(*f*) My best friend is very poor.

The psychologist, by going through these sentences, may get some clue of the repressed wishes of the child.

(*iii*) *Original Drawing and Paintings.* Original drawings and paintings of the children give an idea of the personality of the child. The theme or subject he chooses, the colour he uses, the masses and the open spaces that the paintings contain, the length, direction, curvature of the lines — all these give an indication of the various traits of the personality of the child.

(*iv*) *Play Situation.* Many dolls are given to the child to play with and observation is made of his reactions. These dolls represent a father, a mother, a boy and a girl. These dolls provide the medium through which the child might act out or reveal his thoughts, impulses and feelings about himself and others. Situation should be such as to give a free play to his ideas at the unconscious level. Controlled play techniques are also used.

In a free play a boy who happens to be jealous of his sister might assign the role of the sister to the baby doll and cause it punished by the father doll or mother doll, or shut the baby doll to a far corner of the room. This will indicate that the girl is preferred to him in the family.

A great variety of material may be used in play situations.

(*v*) *Rorschach Ink Blot Tests.* Rorschach was a Swiss Psychologist who experimented with the use of ink blots as a means of diagnosing mental disorders in 1921. Perceptual approach is the basis of this test. The perception of an individual is influenced by the emotional and social make-up when he is asked to perceive a figure which is not well defined.

Rorschach experienced for years together with thousands of ink blots and ultimately selected ten ink blots which proved to have the greatest diagnostic value. There are ten ink blots, five in black and white, two with splashes of red and three in other colours. These are printed on $7 \times 9\frac{1}{2}$ inch cards.

Each card is given to the subject in turn who is asked to tell what he sees in the ink blots, what that means to him and what that might be. The counsellor notes whatever the subject says. The counsellor then shows the card a second time and through well-worded questions he elicits answers. The success of the counsellor depends to a great extent upon his skill in asking questions that will clarify the free responses. Special techniques have been developed for recording the responses of the subject.

This technique has the following uses:

1. This helps to distinguish between 'normal' persons and persons in need of psychiatric treatment.

2. This helps to show the potential intelligence of an individual.

3. This helps to predict and plan for academic success and adjustment in college.

This may prove to be helpful in indicating personality tendencies significant for vocational success.

(*vi*) *Story-telling and Story-Completion.* An incomplete story may be told to the child and he may be asked to complete it. While completing the story, the child may reveal something about his feelings and desires. He may be asked to let this imagination go to show how imaginative he is. The situation selected should be such as touches the emotional life of the child whose personality traits we wish to assess. For instance, the child is asked to relate a story about an innocent child who was beaten by his father. The child is likely to depict his innermost feelings, wishes and thoughts while he narrates the story. Take another case when a child is told about the beginning of a story. Father is ready to take the childen to the Exhibition. All of a sudden a guest comes. The child may be asked to complete the story. As the child finishes the story, the psychologist comes to know the personality of the child.

This method is usually employed in the case of delinquent children.

(*vii*) *Thematic Apperception Test* (TAT). This test was designed by Morgan and Murray in 1935. The test involves a systematic use of pictures representing a number of dramatic events. The pictures are shown to the subject who identifies himself with some picture. The picture presents a stimulus to the child to talk freely. The child makes interpretations in accordance with his own past experience and present needs and attitudes. To quote Ruth Strang, "To some extent, he reads into the pictures his own experiences – the responses made in the test situation also reveal the person's attitudes and ways of thinking in life situations."

The pictures selected have the following characteristics:

First, no detail in the background is provided so that this may not limit the picture to a certain time or place.

Second, the theme of these pictures is vague.

Third, the action and expression of the characters in the pictures are not very clear and are rather vague and ambiguous.

Fourth, the contents of the pictures do not give the whole story. They are incomplete.

Fifth, home and social situations relate to the ordinary situations of life.

Sixth, characters in the pictures are such as the child can very easily identify himself.

The test can be employed suitably to persons over four years of age whose intelligence quotient is not lower than 80. The counsellor shows one or more of the pictures and puts questions like these. What does the picture mean to you? What can be the factors that have led to that situation? What will be the outcome?

In interpreting pictures, it is important to note not only turn of the thoughts the child injects into the situation, but also his mood.

Advantages of Projective Techniques

1. An individual reveals himself in various situations and sometimes he is not aware of this fact. Thus we get reliable information.

2. The connection between diagnosis and the situation is very close.

3. It is not possible for the individual to give readymade, habitual or conventional responses as the tasks presented are novel and unstructured.

4. These techniques encourage spontaneous responses.

5. These enable us to have a total view of the personality of an individual, rather than in piece-meal.

Limitations

First, they are very subjective.

Second, they require a lot of training in their administration. Only trained psychologists can administer them.

Third, they are time-consuming.

Fourth, they are very difficult to interpret.

Lastly, there are very few standardized tests.

Present Status of Projective Techniques

Anne Anastasi observes, "Such devices still represent only 'raw materials' rather than 'standardized tests. As such, they may serve as aids to the trained and experienced clinician. In his hands, they may provide effective means of/or establishing rapport, as well as a rich source of leads to be followed in the interview. At the same time, current research, such as that of Thurstone and Goodenough, suggests that the projective approach may eventually be utilised in the construction of instruments which can be properly designated as psychological tests."

15.6. SELF REPORTING TECHNIQUES

II. ANECDOTAL RECORD

Meaning

An anecdotal record is a running description of actual examples of behaviour of a student as observed by teachers and the counsellor. It is followed by his comments.

According to Brown and Martin, "Anecdotes are descriptive accounts of episodes or occurrences in the daily life of the student."

Anecdotal record has been defined by Randall as a record of some significant item of conduct, a record of an episode in the life of the student, a word picture of the student in action...., a word snapshot at the moment of the incident, any narration of events in which the student takes such a part as to reveal something which may be significant about his personality.

Raths Louis thinks that "an anecdotal record is a report of a significant episode in the life of a student."

Traxler thinks, "This record, as the name implies, involves setting down an anecdote concerning some aspect of pupil behaviour which seems significant to the observer."

Zann, D. Willard regards an anecdotal record "as a simple statement of an incident deemed by the observer to be significant with respect to a given pupil."

A Specimen of an Anecdotal Record

Name of the School

Name of pupil observed Class________ Subject________

Observer Date and place

Objective Description

Comments of the Observer

Objective Description. I have been finding Ram day after day in the library reading magazines, yet he never has time to correct error or to work carefully on Hindi assignments.

Comment. Ram does not like to write but likes to read. I have asked the librarian not to admit him during his free periods unless he hears from me that Ram has done his work.

Characteristics and Preparation of an Anecdotal Record

We cannot set any limit on the number of anecdotes to be recorded. It depends upon the time which is at the disposal of the teachers or guidance workers. The following points should be considered in connection with these records:

1. These supplement other records and should not be considered as substitutes.
2. The objective description of the behaviour should not be mixed up with the subjective comments.
3. Any significant behaviour, be it in the classroom, in the school or outside the school, should be recorded.
4. Behaviour, whether it is favourable, unfavourable or neither favourable nor unfavourable to the child, should be recorded.
5. The facts presented in all the anecdotes must be sifted and arranged so that they may be studied in relation to one another.
6. The record should be regarded as confidential. It should not fall into irresponsible hands.
7. What is written down is what was seen or heard. Inferences, guesses, assumptions are omitted unless they are clearly labelled as inferences, gussess, or assumption.
8. The observer observes only that aspect of the behaviour which has been earlier determined and records only that.
9. Only those words and phrases are used whose meaning is clear, and so far as possible, unequivocal.
10. Words and phrases are employed that are definable in terms of things rather than other words. Concrete statements are preferred to abstract ones. For example, "He became pale and his hands trembled," not "He was disturbed."
11. Words and phrases that have strong emotional connotations are avoided i.e. love, hate, insolvent, courteous, loyal, dishonest, etc.
12. Words and phrases are avoided which express the observer's judegement, or his opinion, and not his perception. Among the frequently encountered, "judgemental terms" that should be avoided are the following:

    (*a*) Well-behaved.
    (*b*) Delinquent.
    (*c*) Aggressive.
    (*d*) Did'nt try.
    (*e*) Industrious.
    (*f*) Nervous.
    (*g*) Happy.

Values and Uses of Anecdotal Records

1. They provide specific and exact description of personality and minimise generalisations.
2. They are very helpful in understanding the child's behaviour in diverse situations.
3. They provide a continuous recoru.
4. They provide data for pupils to use in self-appraisal.
5. A summary of these records is valuable for forwarding with a pupil when he is transferred from one school to another.
6. The new members of the staff may use these records and acquaint themselves with the students.
7. These records aid in clinical service.
8. They stimulate teachers to use the records and to contribute to them.

Limitations

1. Anecdotal records tend to be less reliable than other tools.
2. They are time-consuming to write.

Autobiography Technique

In this technique, a child gives an account of his life experiences from early childhood to the date of writing. This technique provides a lot of material to the teacher to measure the several aspects of the development of the presonality of the child. The autobiography is also a tension-releaser. It serves as a 'calbhassis' or 'psychic safety valve' and allows the child to express his pent-up feelings.

Organisation of Autobiographies

Following outline in writing an autobiography, may be used:

1. My Family
2. My first year before school
3. My years in the elementary school
4. Places I have lived
5. Vacations I have spent
6. Trips I have taken
7. The way I usually spend the afternoon when school is over
8. The way I spend my evening after supper
9. The way I spend my Sunday
10. Subjects I like the most, the least
11. Some subjects and activities I wish our school would provide

12. Things I should like to do well
13. The work I hope to do (three-choices) and reasons for the choices
14. Kinds of magazines and books I like to read, kinds of Radio and TV programmes I like to listen and watch, kinds of pictures I like to see
15. If I could have all the things I wanted by asking for them, I would ask for these things.

Principles of Using this Method

1. Rapport with the student should be established so that the child expresses his feelings freely.
2. He should be ensured that the information supplied would be kept confidential.
3. Detailed instructions may be given to the child as to the way in which autobiography is to be written.
4. Questions/hints may be given to the child so that he may reveal his history.

Limitations

1. Its scope is limited and it cannot be used when the child is unable to express himself correctly in speech.
2. The student may present facts in a distorted way.

Interpreting the Autobiography

1. First reading of the autobiography may be done in a general way.
2. Second reading should be more thorough.
3. The general appearance of the document; its neatness and contents would provide some clue to the understanding of the personality of the child.

III. INTERVIEW

Meaning and Classification

An interview may be defined as a face to face verbal exchange in which one person i.e., the interviewer attempts to elicit information on a variety of topics from the interview. Interviews are used for a variety of purposes and as such there are various types of interviews.

1. The assessment or evaluative interview for determining the fitness of a person for admission, for a job or for scholarship, etc.

2. The personality assessment interview of a student for finding out the status of development of his personality.
3. The diagnostic interview for getting some information about the home, environmental and school situations of the student or the client.
4. The introductory interview for preparing for further interviews.
5. The informative interview for giving some information to the students on subjects or careers, etc.
6. The research interview for collecting data about a problem.
7. The administrative or disciplinary interview for finding out the causes of indiscipline and taking further action.
8. The counselling interview for helping the counselee or the student in gaining insight into the problem and assisting him solving the same.

It is to be remembered that in educational institutions, the primary purpose of interview of personality assessment is to find out the existing status of the development of the various facets of personality and to take further measures for bringing about improvement in the learner.

Main Points in Successful Interviewing

1. Who is to interview? The interviewer must be clear in his mind of his strengths and weaknesses, so that prejudices or bias could be minimised.
2. Whom – He should understand his client thoroughly.
3. How – He should know the technique of interviewing.
4. Why – He should be very clear in his mind for the purpose of interview.
5. Where – Suitable place should be selected for this purpose.
6. When – Proper motivation should be developed in the child.
7. What to ask – He should prepare his questions thoughtfully.

Preparation for the Interview

1. A quiet and orderly place should be provided for interview purposes.
2. The teacher or the psychologist should prepare himself for the interview by gathering all the data concerning the student.
3. The teacher or the psychologist should prepare clear objective for the interview.
4. The teacher or the counseller should keep an open mind regarding the child.

5. Each interview should be considered as a step in the process of guiding pupil.

Techniques of Interviewing

Rapport should be established. Rapport is a technical term used to denote the feelings of friendliness, security and mutual confidence between the teacher and the child.

Davis and Robinson suggest the following techniques to increase rapport:

Sympathy – The teacher-counsellor expresses sympathy for the child.

Assurance – The teacher or the counsellor will try to ease the child's fear by encouraging him that this step is for his personality development.

Approval – The teacher or the counsellor expresses his approval with something that the counselee or the student has said or done.

Humour – The teacher or the counsellor attempts to ease tension in the mind of the counselee with humorous remarks.

Personal Reference – The teacher or the counsellor tells about some of his own experiences to illustrate his point by saying, 'I would do this'.

Non-Personal Reference – The teacher or the counsellor cites an example of the experience of another person.

Question Form – The teacher or the counsellor asks questions to stimulate the counselee to think further about his problem.

Threat – The teacher or the counsellor sometimes threatens the counselee that unpleasant results may occur if the counselee does not follow a certain specified course of action.

Merits of an Interview

1. It is the most dynamic way of understanding the individual.
2. It is natural-like conversation.
3. It can be made flexible so as to suit many situations.
4. It is relatively easy to conduct.
5. It is possible to get some most confidential information from the child, which otherwise he may hesitate to reveal through writing.

Limitations of an Interview:

1. It needs a trained and competent interviewer.
2. It is costly in terms of labour, money and time.
3. It suffers from the subjective bias of the interviewer.
4. The interviewee may not unfold himself.

5. The interviewee may have a language handicap to express his feelings freely.

IV. QUESTIONNAIRE

Meaning of a Questionnaire

Good and Hatt point out, "In general the word questionnaire refers to a device for securing answers to questions by using a form which the respondent fills in himself."

Barr, Davis and Johnson define questionnaire as a "systematic compilation of questions that are subject to a sampling of population from which information is desired."

Types of Questionnaires

A questionnaire may contain two kinds of items.

(*i*) The Closed or Structured Form.

(*ii*) The Open-End or Unrestricted Form.

The Closed Form. This form requires short and 'check' responses. It may provide the marking 'Yes' or 'No', or just a 'check' from a list of suggested responses.

Main advantages

(*i*) It is very easy to respond to such a questionnaire.

(*ii*) It takes a little time to answer.

(*iii*) It keeps the respondent on the subject.

(*iv*) It is relatively objective.

(*v*) It is fairly easy to tabulate and analyse.

Drawback of the Closed Form. The closed form does not provide any opportunity to the respondent to express his views very clearly as there is no scope for explanatory information.

The Open-End or Unrestricted Type or Free Responses or Unstructured Form. As the name of the form indicates, the respondent is at liberty to express his attitudes, interests, preferences, and decisions in his own words because no clues are provided. However, sometimes it becomes very difficult to tabulate, interpret and summarize such responses.

As far as possible, the questionnaire should be a balanced one and it should contain both the open and closed type items.

Questionnaire Compared with other Techniques of Research

(1) It is less expensive and less time consuming than interview or observation.

(2) Its construction needs less technical skills as compared with those required in conducting interviews and observations.

(3) Questionnaire do not permit variations in questions and as such they help in focusing the attention of the respondents on all the significant items. The interviewing situation, on the other hand, is rarely uniform.

(4) A Questionnaire places less pressure on the subject for immediate response. A subject has adequate time to think of the responses whereas in an interview the subject is expected to give his responses immediately.

(5) In an interview responses are recorded by the investigator whereas in the questionnaire, the responses are given in the language of the subjects. This brings validity to responses in the case of a questionnaire.

15.7. SOCIOMETRIC TECHNIQUES

Sociometry was designed by J.L. Moreno and Helen Jennings in 1946.

Through sociometric techniques we come to know what other members of the group feel about the subject whether they like him or not. The members of the group may be asked to name in order of preference one or two individuals with whom they would like to work or play.

According to Jennings, "Stated briefly, sociometry may be described as a means of presenting simply and graphically the entire structure of relations existing at a given time among members of a given group. The major lines of communication or the pattern of attraction and rejection in its full scope, are made readily comprehensive at a glance."

William J. Goode and others state. "These and other variants of sociometric techniques offer rather simple methods of ranking individuals on a continuum of 'acceptability' or 'outgoingness' on the part of group members. When their use is justified they may be powerful research tools since they meet the general problems of scaling very well."

Sociometric studies have been made of many types of social groups including classroom groups. Being peer-rating rather than rating by superiors, sociometry adds another dimension to the understanding of social relationships.

Example – Each group consisting of eleven students is asked to write his first choice about some significant and pertinent type of social setting. He may be asked questions like this:

1. Whom would you like to be the secretary of your debating society?
2. Whom would you like to sit next to you in the class or in the bus while going for a picnic?
3. With whom do you enjoy most ?

4. With whom would you like to work in the laboratory ?
5. With whom would you like to walk home ?

All those questions are positive questions and hence show social acceptances.

Negative questions may also be given to show social rejections.

In the above example, the individual has to name only one person of his choice.

Data may be tabulated as under:

(*i*) Let the members of the group be numbered from 1 to 10.

(*ii*) Write 'Choosers' in the vertical column and 'Chosen' in the horizontal column.

(*iii*) Total choices received by each member may be shown at the bottom.

(*iv*) In the cells, check marks may be shown.

(*v*) Add the number of each choice.

A similar table can be prepared for social rejections. In the vertical column will be listed the 'rejectors' and in the horizontal column 'rejected'.

An individual may be asked to name more than one person in order to preference.

Interpretation of a Sociogram

1. One person should be concentrated at a time.
2. A detailed study of the choices made and received should be made.
3. The 'isolates' and the 'stars' may be looked for. An 'isolate' is one whom nobody chooses. Of course he is not rejected. A 'star' is a member of the group who receives most of the choices.
4. Attempts should be made to discover the causes for such selections.

An individual may be isolated because:

(*i*) He is a new member of the group.

(*ii*) He is of a shy and withdrawing nature.

(*iii*) He does not try to make friendship with others.

(*iv*) He may belong to a lower or upper socio-economic level and therefore he is not acceptable in the group.

5. Look for individuals who select each other. This might be due to factors like:

(*i*) Close relations.

(*ii*) Neighbours.

(*iii*) Common interests and the like.

6. A triangle shows three persons selecting each other. This may be an evidence of cliques, or sharp divisions in the group.

Role of the Teacher and the Guidance Worker.

In general, he can work on three points:

1. Providing opportunities for developing friendly relations.
2. Improving social skills.
3. Building up competency for accomplishing something.

Reliable results can be achieved only when all the members consisting a group are fully acquainted with each other. The worker of the counsellor must establish friendly relations with the members of the group so that they may give their frank opinion about an individual or individuals.

SOCIOGRAM

Practical Work

Object. To find out the social structure of a group of 10 students.

Material. A Questionnaire asking students: Whom would you like to be the secretary of your club ?

Procedure. After taking the students into confidence, one-line questionnaire as indicated above was given to the students to mark against one of the 10 Roll Nos. Thereafter tabulation of the students responses was made.

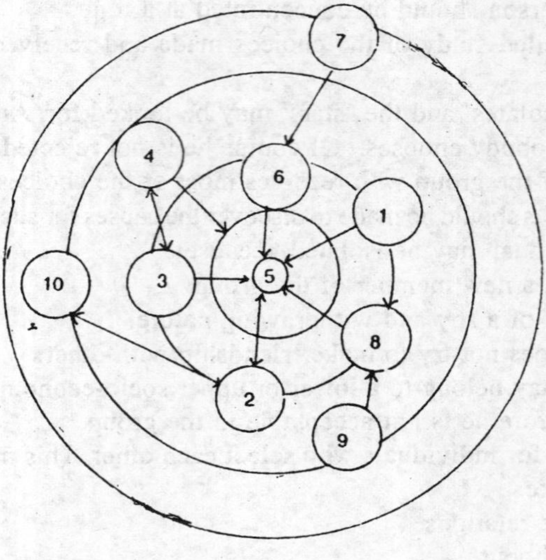

Fig. 15.1 Sociometric Matrix Showing who chooses whom

Interpretation

1. Roll no. 5 is the 'star' as he has been chosen by the maximum number of students.
2. Roll nos. 7 and 9 did not get any choice. This indicates that they tended to be isolated i.e. not being social.
3. Roll nos. 2 and 8 came next to roll no. 1.
4. Roll no 5 i.e. the star preferred roll no. 2.
5. Mutual choices were: 2 and 5; 3 and 4; and 2 and 10.

Notes 1. Students can be used to give their second and third choices also.
2. Choices are illustrated in Fig. 15.1
3. There are several ways of preparing a sociogram.
4. This seems to be the simplest form of a sociogram.

Using Sociometric Techniques

1. To study the relationships among members of the group and to improve them.
2. To organise classroom groups.
3. To assist those who have become isolates in the group.
4. To assign responsibility to the members off the group.

Limitations

1. The relationships are not necessarily stable.
2. Some members of the group may not reveal their real relationships on account of some fear or other considerations.

15.8. PERSONALITY INVENTORIES

Meaning

A personality inventory is essentially a standard set of questions about some aspects of the individual's life history, feeling preferences or activities presented in a standard way and scored with a standard scoring key. It resembles a questionnaire in several aspects like administration etc. However, a questionnaire is the general device and can be used for collecting all kinds of information but a personality inventory is specially designed to collect information about the personality of an individual.

The number of available personality inventories is very large. Here we shall be concerned primarily with a few of the most widely known inventories.

Woodworth's Data Sheet. The first name in this connection may be mentioned of the Woodworth Personal Data Sheet which was developed for use during World War I. This inventory was essentially an attempt to standardize a psychiatric interview and to adapt the procedure for mass testing. Inventory questions were formulated with reference to common neurotic and pre-neurotic symptoms and each question was to be answered in 'Yes' or 'No'. A questionnaire of 116 items was assembled on the basis that no item was retained if 25% or more of a 'normal' sample answered it in the unfavourable direction. The questions dealt with such behaviour deviations as abnormal fears, obsessions and compulsions, nightmares and other sleep disturbances, excessive fatigue and other psychosomatic symptoms, feelings or unreality, motor disturbance and the like. The individual score on the inventory consisted of the total number of items answered in the unfavourable direction. This was then compared with the mean scores obtained by neurotics and normals in the standardization sample. If the individual's score exceeded a certain number, it was considered to be indicative of possible neuroticism.

Cornell Index. This was developed during World War II and the civilian revision of this questionnaire contains 101 Yes-No items pertaining to feelings of fear and inadequacy, depression and other pathological mood reactions, nervousness and anxiety, etc. and several kinds of psychosomatic symptoms. The time required to complete the inventory varies from 5 to 15 minutes.

Bell Adjustment Inventory. In this inventory, 35 items are classified into separate categories and a score is provided for each category. Two forms of this inventory are available, one for high school and college students, the other for adults. However, the Student Form has been employed more widely. This form has been designed to measure adjustment in four areas: (1) Home, (2) Health, (3) Social, (4) Emotional. An additional score has been provided in the Adult Form to measure occupational adjustment. Answers are recorded by encircling 'Yes' or 'No'.

Allport A-S Inventory. This is also known as Ascendance Submission Inventory. This inventory seeks to assess the individual's tendency to dominate his associates or be dominated by them in face-to-face contacts of everyday life. Each item begins with a brief description of a situation which we usually encounter at a meeting, in school, on a bus or in other familiar settings. The subject is asked to indicate one of the two or four alternative ways listed for meeting the situation. Responses indicate the degree of ascendance or submission.

Separate forms of the tests are available for men and women.

This inventory has greatly influenced the development of many other inventories.

Bernreuter Inventory. It consists of 125 items and is designed to measure six scores: (1) Neuroticism, (2) Self-sufficiency, (3) Introversion, (4) Dominance, (5) Confidence, (6) Sociability. The last two were added by Flanagan.

This manual provides norms on all six scores for high school, college and general adult population.

The inventory appears to be more effective with normals and near normals than with psychotics.

Heston Personal Adjustment Inventory. This yields scores in Analytical Thinking, Sociability, Emotional Stability, Confidence, Personal Relations and Home Satisfaction.

Guilford Inventory. The latest inventory in the Guilford series consists of 300 items, 30 for each of the following 10 scores:

G. General Activity
R. Restraint
A. Ascendance
S. Sociability
E. Emotional Stability
O. Objectivity
F. Friendliness
T. Thoughtfulness
P. Personal Relations
M. Masculinity

Thurstone Temperament Schedule. It includes 20 items for each trait and these items pertain to the behaviour of relatively normal persons. Percentile norms are reported for high school and college students.

Thurstone lists seven major factors:

Active	(A)
Vigorous	(V)
Impulsive	(I)
Dominant	(D)
Stable	(E) (Emotionally Stable)
Sociability	(S)
Reflective	(R)

Cattell's Inventory. Cattell has devised the Sixteen Personality Factor Questionnaire. This inventory is available in two parallel forms, A and B each containing 187 items. The use of both forms is advocated for greater reliability.

The Minnesota Multiphasic Personality Inventory. Published in 1943, it consists of 550 items and is used for persons of 16 years of age and above. Each item is printed on a separate card. The subject has to sort the cards into 3 groups. True, False, and Cannot Say. The items are classified under 26 heads, such as health, religious attitudes, delusions, phobias, etc. Items can be grouped in separate scales to score nine personality traits. These are hypochondriasis, depression hysteria, psychopathic deviate, masculinity – feminity, paravoia, psychosthenia, schizophrenia, and hypomania. This inventory is used in clinical diagnosis.

Apart from its comprehensiveness, the MMPI is provided with several control keys meant for identifying untrustworthy responses. These keys give such scores as lie score (L) when the subject tries to fake good on socially approved behaviour, the 'K' score when the subject fakes bad to show himself in bad light; the question score when the subject gives a large number of 'cannot say' responses, and the 'F' score when the subject marks items with carelessness or misunderstanding.

The MMPI is one of the several most widely used inventories. A shortened version consisting of 336 items is also available for emergency use.

The Guilford-Zimmerman Temperament Survey. It is meant to identify ten different trait dimensions of personality. Some of these are general activity, friendliness, thoughtfulness, personal relations, and masculinity. The inventory is used with adolescents and adults. These traits have been included after factor analysis and are mutually exclusive. The sample used for standardization consisted of normal persons, and not of maladjusted or neurotics.

The Edward Personal and Preference Schedule. It consists of 210 items which assess the strength of 15 needs selected from among those listed by Murray. The items are presented to the subject in pairs and these are more or less equated for social desirability, so that the subject would respond as he really felt, and not in terms of what is the approved or desirable thing to say.

Evaluation of Personality Inventories

The construction and the use of personality inventories are beset with special difficulties in view of the following:

1. Complex nature of personality
2. Different definitions of personality
3. Greater specificity of responses in the sphere of personality.
4. Lack of adequate criteria for the determination of empirical validity.
5. Different actions by the same individual in different situations.

Guide to the Assessment of Personality Traits (Five Point Scale)

(The Secondary Education Commission 1952-53)

Personality Traits	*A*	*B*	*C*	*D*	*E*
Initiative	Shows marked originality and independence	Willing to take initiative.	Quite inventive, able to take initiative.	On the whole unenterprising.	Very dependent on others, diffident.
Integrity (Moral sense)	Completely trustworthy under all circumstances.	Of superior dependability, honest in face of punishment.	Usually dependable	Questionable at times.	Positively dishonest.
Persistence	Very persistent	Not easily stopped.	Works quite steadily.	Somewhat changeable, restless.	Gives up easily.
Leadership	Much drive, mild, impressive, steady, convincing, wide influence, acceptable to group, sought after by the group and takes the group with him.	Ready to take the lead, works quietly for leadership, accepts responsibility.	Sometimes leads in minor affairs.	Satisfied to have others lead.	Probably unable to lead his fellows.
Self-confidence (Poise)	Very self-confident, very resourceful, willing to take reasonable risks.	Self-confident, trusts his own ability, well-adjusted to others.	Normally confident in familiar circumstances. Does not need special assurance.	Cannot work for long without demanding attention or responds after special encouragement.	Always draws attention to self. Afraid of being overlooked or afraid to open out in presence of others, very nervous.
Emotional control	Unusual balance of responsiveness or control.	Well-balanced	Usually well-balanced.	Tends to be over-emotional.	Too easily moved to anger and fits of depression.
Social Attitude	Strongly altruistic, greater aesthetic sensibility.	Usually considerate of others, aesthetic sensibility	Has no positive attitude, neutral, conscious of his rights and those of others or indifferent.	Self-centred.	Anti-social.

Chapter 16

Tests and Testing

16.1. MEASUREMENT AND TESTING

Measurement plays a very important role in the teaching-learning process. Measurement of achievement of learners has been the major concern of the teachers and evaluators in the past. But to-day's teachers and evaluators are more concerned about student's learning and diagnosis of their weaknesses and inadequacies in instructional strategies for bringing about improvement in their learning than mere assessment of their achievement. One of the important instruments of measurement is testing. (See also chapters 9, 10 and 15).

16.2. DEFINITION OF A TEST

L.J. Cronbach, in his book *Essentials of Psychological Testing* (1970) defines a test "as a systematic procedure for observing and describing one or more characteristics of a person with the aid of either a numerical scale or a category system."

A Dictionary of Education (1981) gives the following definition: "A test is a compact task or series of tasks designed to ascertain the merit or quantity of something. Educational tests constitute a series of items for which a score is obtained. Depending on how they are constructed, they can serve a purpose."

The International Dictionary of Education (1981) explains Test "1. Any method by which the presence of quality or genuineness of anything is determined. 2. Examination to evaluate the performance and capabilities of a student or class (e.g. knowledge of a subject). 3. Procedure for eliciting responses upon which appraisal of the individual can be based (e.g. intelligence). 4. Process of detecting the presence of an ingredient in a compound, or of determining the nature of a substance."

16.3. MEANING OF A TEST

A test may be defined as a device or procedure confronting a subject with a standard set of questions or tasks to which the student is to respond independently and the results of which can be treated in such a way as to provide a quantitative comparison of performance of different students.

Following are the important elements of a test as contained in the above definition :

1. A test often implies the presentation of a standard set of questions to be answered for tasks to be performed by a student.
2. The student is to take the test independently.
3. The test results in a measure (a numerical value of a characteristic of the students).
4. The test often provides a quantitative comparison of the performance of students.
5. It is a technique that yields only a verbal description; for instance, an interview technique is not a test.
6. A test is to be completed in a given time.
7. Devices such as checklists and rating scales etc. are not included in the test classification even if they yield quantitative results, for they are typically filled in by the teacher and do not consist of questions to which the student is not to respond.

16.4. SIGNIFICANCE OF TESTS

According to Ebel and Frisbie (1991), "Tests can be and should be, among the most useful instructional tools for planning new learning activities and for monitoring student's progress in attaining the learning goals presented to them. Tests can be used to provide recognition and rewards for success in learning and teaching. They can be used to motivate and direct effort to learn. In short, they can be used to contribute substantially to effective instruction."

Main Purposes of Testing

1. To determine the achievement level and progress of the pupils.
2. To obtain data for diagnostic purposes.

3. To identify the interests of the students.
4. To identify the underachievers.
5. To determine the self concept, attitudes and personality pattern of the students.
6. To ascertain the extent and quality of social development of the students.
7. To identify the gifted.
8. To improve learning techniques.
9. To improve teaching techniques.

Relative Importance of Testing

Tests are used in the guidance programme as they have the following merits as compared with other techniques of guidance.

1. They are handy.
2. They are economical techniques of collecting information.
3. They are less time-consuming.
4. They are objective.
5. They provide significant means of comparing individuals.

Limitations of Testing

1. Heavy weightage to verbal ability in many tests.
2. Difficulty in obtaining level norms.
3. Relative narrowness of the traits measured by tests.
4. Indifference, lack of attention, low commitment and generally low motivation of the students, tending to invalidate the test results.
5. Difficulty to follow the directions of the tester by the testee.
6. Undue influence of socio-cultural conditions or environmental influences on the testees or the students.
7. Low validity and reliability in the case of some pupils.

Planning a Testing Programme

Following considerations may be kept in mind while planning a testing programme.

1. **Centralised Responsibility.** There should be one person in each school who will look after the administrative details given below:

(*a*) Ordering for relevant tests and test material.
(*b*) Arranging schedules of time.
(*c*) Arranging place for testing.

(*d*) Arranging scoring and recording results.

(*e*) Taking responsibility for the security and storage of tests when they are not being used.

2. Testing Schedule. Tests should be given under standard conditions that permit each testee to perform at his best level. Testing schedule should never be made too tight. The unit of time schedule for testing should be reasonably enough to permit its completion. It should provide a realistic allowance for distributing and collecting papers and for giving instructions.

3. Preparation by Testers. The testers should prepare themselves in advance especially for the following aspects of the testing programme.

(*a*) The tester should follow the manual verbatim.

(*b*) The tester should make the procedures and the tasks clear to the testee before administering the test.

(*c*) The tester should have a stopwatch and he should allow the subjects to work on a particular test for that much time only which is mentioned in its manual.

(*d*) The tester should go round the class and ensure that the students have followed the instructions carefully and are not copying.

4. Preparation of Students for Testing. Orientation talks on the usefulness of testing may be given to the students so that they are motivated to take tests and are convinced that tests are genuinely important.

5. Appropriate Environment for Testing. The desirable environment for testing should satisfy the following conditions:

1. Examinees are physically comfortable.
2. Examinees are emotionally relaxed.
3. Examinees are free from interruptions and distractions
4. Adequate space is provided to the examinees so that they are able to manipulate their test material conveniently.
5. Examinees are seated in such a way as to prevent copying.
6. Conditions of lighting and ventilation are adequate for testing.

6. Recording of Test Results. Results should be kept systematically so that these are made use of conveniently by the appropriate agency. Of course results should be kept confidential.

16.5. CLASSIFICATION OF TESTS

There are several ways of classifying tests. Some of these overlap. Here we take note of four types of classification of tests.

HENRY E. GARRET'S CLASSIFICATION OF TESTS

Henry E. Garret (1959) gives the following classification of tests:

I. Intelligence Tests

(*a*) *Individual* – administered to one examinee at a time.

(*b*) *Group* – administered like a school examination, to many examinees at the same time.

(*c*) *Performance* – make little or no use of language, in contrast with the paper and pencil tests in (*a*) and (*b*)

II. Educational Achievement Tests

(*a*) *Survey* – comprehensive examinations used to determine general academic standing.

(*b*) *Subject* – examination in specific fields — for example, English, Mathematics.

(*c*) *Diagnostic* – cover a wide range of academic skills (in reading or arithmetic, for example) and are designed to reveal specific weaknesses and strengths.

III. Aptitude Tests

(*a*) *General* – for example of:

(*i*) Mechanical ability.

(*ii*) Clerical ability.

(*b*) *Special* – aptitude for school subjects – for example, Chemistry, or foreign language.

(*c*) *Professional* – for example in:

(*i*) Law

(*ii*) Medicine

(*iii*) Engineering

(*iv*) Teaching

(*d*) *Talent* – aptitude in such fields as:

(*i*) Art

(*ii*) Music

IV. Tests of Various Aspects of Personality

(*a*) *Personal Adjustment Questionnaires* – survey of worries, fears, social inadequacies.

(*b*) *Attitude Surveys* – upon social, economic and political questions.

(*c*) *Interest Inventories* – related to various occupations.

(*d*) *Environmental Facts Related to Personality* – questionnaire covering socio-economic background and other variables.

(*e*) *Projective Techniques* – Subtle and direct measures of dominant personality trends.

NIKTO'S CLASSIFICATION OF TESTS

Anthony J. Nikto (1983) has classified tests as under:

1. By kind of Item.
2. By how observations are marked.
3. By degree of standardization.
4. By administrative conditions.
5. By language emphasis of response.
6. By emphasis on time.
7. By scoring referencing scheme.
8. By what attribute is measured.

1. By Kind of Item. Technically an item refers to a question, an exercise or a task on a test. When the tests are classified on the basis of item, they may take the following forms:

(*a*) *Choice Items or Recognition Items.* In choice items, the examinee selects a correct answer from two or more choices. The choice item may be in the form of true or false, multiple choice and matching. They are also called recognition items because the examinees attempt to recognise the correct answer among the given choices.

(*b*) *Completion Items.* Since the answer is given by the examinee by completion of sentence, it is known as completion items. Completion items may be open/free or closed. It is free when the examinee has the freedom to insert word or phrase for completion of the sentence or statement. In a closed item, the examinee has limited freedom for he has to choose the word or phrase from a given list. The given list may pertain to the entire set of sentences or to every sentence.

(*c*) *Short Answer Items.* For a short answer item, the examiner is required to supply the answer to a question. It may be in the form of just one word answer or in limited words.

(*d*) *Essay Item.* In an essay item, the examinee is required to structure a response, usually of some detail and length. The answer consists of some paragraphs. Essay item is used to measure capacity to generalise and analyse.

2. By How Observations are Marked. There are some skill areas and behavioural changes which can only be observed. For example the quality of pronunciation, intonation, emphasis etc. can be observed only when the students speak.

3. By Degree of Standardization. In *Essentials of Psychological Testing* (1970), L.J. Cronbach states that standardization refers to the degree to which the observational procedures. administrative procedures, equipment and material and scoring rules have been fixed in such a way that the same testing procedure occurs exactly at different times and places. Standardized tests possess the following characteristics:

(*a*) Items are fixed and not modifiable.

(*b*) The most common areas of the curriculum are included in the test.

(*c*) The rules for administering and scoring must be followed exactly as stated in the test manual.

(*d*) Norms are provided with the test to all teachers to compare performance of different age and class groups.

(*e*) Data on the quality of test are provided alongwith the test.

A standardized test does not fulfil all the requirements given above. It may also be stated that there is no test which is absolutely standardized test and there is no test which is absolutely non-standardized. It is a question of degree of standardization. Teacher made test, though considered as non-standardized test, they yet possess some of the characteristics of a standardized test.

4. By Administrative Conditions. Depending upon the administrative conditions, a test may be administered to an individual or a group. Thus on the basis of administrative conditions, the tests may be of two forms:

(*i*) *Individual Test.* An individual test is that test which is administered to one person at a time. It is generally administered by counsellors and psychologists and not by teachers. Gilbert Sax observes in *Principles of Educational Psychological Measurement* (1989), "Administering individual test generally requires much training and experience whereas the administration of group test is much less complicated."

Group Test. A group test is administered to several persons at a time. *In Educational Tests and Measurement* (1983), A. J. Nikto has observed, "Group tests sacrifice rapport, personalised testing conditions and clinical observation for increased efficiency and reduced cost. In the same time that it takes to administer and score an individual test, an entire class can be tested. Where large groups need testing, where finances are tight and where only coarse information is required, group testing becomes a more attractive option." Group tests are generally paper tests and students are asked to write their answers with a pencil. So sometimes they are called Paper and Pencil tests also.

5. By Language Emphasis on Response. The difference of emphasis of language given on response may also categorise tests. These are as under:

(*a*) *Verbal Tests.* In such tests, the emphasis is on the use of language as the primary means of responding to test items or questions. The form of language may be reading, writing or oral communication. Most of the school tests are verbal tests because schools stress verbal ability.

(*b*) *Non-Verbal Tests.* These tests de-emphasize the role of language in testing. They are usually given to illiterates or to very young children in the pre-primary and primary stages. They make extensive use of pictures to measure vocabulary, reasoning and other skills.

(*c*) *Performance Tests.* The performance tests require examinees to perform a task instcad of answering questions. These tasks include placing pegs in a board rapidly, assembling a puzzle, placing pictures in a correct segments etc.

(*d*) *Non-language Tests.* Such tests are administered by gestures and do not require language facility on the part of the examinee. They are generally used with deaf children or with children who do not understand language at all.

6. By Emphasis on Time. Emphasis on time test may take two forms:

(*a*) *Speed Test.* In a speed test, the content of students' responses is of less importance but the speed with which the examinees answer the test items is more important. The items of a Speed Test are of such nature that few students are expected to answer incorrectly.

(*b*) *Power Test.* A power test is that in which main emphasis is on assessing the knowledge and understanding and less emphasis on the speed with which the examinees answer the items of the test.

Thus it may be said that the speed test is limited in time and relatively easy in difficulty nature of items but power test is generous in time and relatively hard in difficulty.

7. By Scoring Reference Scheme. This category of classification is based not on the marks obtained by the examinee but it is referenced to something outside the test in order to interpret the marks. Two forms of mark referencing schemes generally used are :

(*a*) *Norm Referenced Test.* Gilbert Sax in *Principles of Educational and Psychological Measurement* (1989) states, "A norm-referenced test is designed to measure individual differences in achievement, intelligence, interests, attitudes or personality." For instance if an examinee scores 30 marks, on a test, it does not provide adequate information. If it is known that 75 per cent examinees score below 30 marks, then more information is found about the examinee. In this example, the marks of the individual examinee are being compared or referenced to the marks of other examinees. Percentile Ranks, Grade Equivalent Scores and Standard Scores are the examples of norm referenced test.

(*b*) *Criterion Referenced Test.* In the words of Gilbert Sax (1989), " Criterion referenced tests relate to a student's score on achievement test to a domain of knowledge rather than to another student's score." For example instead of saying that an examinee is "average", the examinee can be described as knowing 50% of some specific and educationally relevant tasks. This test is useful in those subject areas which are progressively more complex and the examinee might have to reach some level of proficiency on preceeding tasks before being advanced to a higher level. This test is also useful in diagnostic work also because it is more important to know what difficulty is being experienced by a student in a specific area of the curriculum than to know that the student is average in the class.

8. By What Attribute is Measured. There are a variety of human attributes which are measurable also. The tests are classified on the basis of attributes they measure. They may take the following forms on the basis of attributes they mainly measure:

1. Achievement Tests.
2. Aptitude Tests.
3. Personality and Adjustment Tests, which include:
   (*i*) Projective Techniques;
   (*ii*) Structural Personality Measurement Techniques;
   (*iii*) Interest Inventories;
   (*iv*) Attitude and Value Scales.

Yoak and Simpson's Classification of Forms of Tests

Tests vary according to form, use and type etc. Yoakaya and Simpson give the following classification of tests:

1. Form

(*a*) Oral examinations (*b*) Written examinations

2. Purposes

(*a*) Prognostic. (*b*) Diagnostic. (*c*) Power. (*d*) Speed.
(*e*) Accuracy. (*f*) Quality. (*g*) Range.

3. Organisation

(*a*) Essay. (*b*) Objective.

4. Period or Time of Administering

(*a*) Daily. (*b*) Weekly. (*c*) Monthly. (*d*) Term. (*e*) Year.

5. Duration

(*a*) Short. (*b*) Long.

6. Method of Scoring and Interpreting Results

(*a*) Non-standardized. (*b*) Standardized.

7. Abilities Involved

(*a*) Speed. (*b*) Comprehension. (*c*) Organization.
(*d*) Judgement. (*e*) Retention. (*f*) Appreciation etc.

8. Nature of Material Included

(*a*) Arithmetic. (*b*) Language. (*c*) Reading.
(*d*) Spelling. (*e*) Writing etc.

9. Mental Functions Involved

(*a*) Association. (*b*) Memory. (*c*) Recall. (*d*) Recognition.
(*e*) Problem-Solving.

10. Types of Response Involved

(*a*) Alternate response:
  (1) True – False
  (2) Yes – No
  (3) Plus – Minus.

(*b*) Multiple response:
  (1) Best Answer.
  (2) Correct Answer.

(*c*) Completion.
(*d*) Matching.
(*e*) Identification.
(*f*) Enumeration.
(*g*) Essay.

Sixfold Classification of Tests

Usually tests are classified under the following six broad categories:

1. Maximum Performance Tests and Typical Performance Tests.
2. Criterion-referenced Tests and Norm-referenced Tests.
3. Subjective Tests and Objective Tests.
4. Standardized and Non-Standardized Tests.
5. Speed Tests and Power Tests.
6. Select-Response Tests and Supply Response Tests.

Maximum Performance Tests

In maximum performance tests, the students are called upon to demonstrate their best in the cognitive as well as psychomoter areas. Tests of this nature are of the following kinds:

(*a*) Intelligence Tests.
(*b*) Achievement Tests.
(*c*) Aptitude Tests.

Typical Performance Tests

Typical performance tests deal with the affective domain of educational objectives. Common examples of this type of tests are:

(*a*) Adjustment Tests.
(*b*) Aptitude Tests.

(*c*) Interest Tests.
(*d*) Personality Tests.
(*e*) Preference Tests.
(*f*) Temperament Tests.
(*g*) Value Tests.

(Other types of tests are discussed separately).

Standardized Tests

Forms of standardized tests. Standardized tests have assumed such an important role in the guidance programme that the two terms 'Guidance' and 'Tests' have become synonymous terms.

The standardized tests may be classified as:

1. General Intelligence or scholastic aptitude tests.
2. Special abilities or aptitude tests.
3. Achievement tests.
4. Interest tests or inventories.
5. Personality tests or personal adjustment tests.

Importance of Standardized Tests. They are very useful for the following reasons:

1. They give us objective and impartial information about an individual.

2. Since they give us information in an objective manner, it becomes easier to convince the guardians of the assets and limitations of their wards.

3. They provide information in much less time than provided by any other device.

4. Since there is a definite way of expressing the results of these tests in the form of percentiles or standard scores, it has the same significance for all the guidance workers and all of them have the same interpretations.

5. These tests measure those aspects of the behaviour which otherwise could not be obtained.

6. In subjective observation we may overlook shy children but these tests discover such cases also.

Chief characteristics of a standardized test

1. A standardized test is constructed by test specialists or experts.

2. A standardized test generally covers a broad or wide areas of objectives and content common to the school system within a given geographical area.

3. Test items of a standardized test cover a large segment of knowledge and skills than the teacher-made test.

4. Before finalisation, a standardized test is tried out and administered on a number of subjects for the expressed purpose of refining its items by subjecting the performances of the 'standardization' sample to pertinent statistical analysis. The purpose is to ensure that items with adequate level of difficulty and which are capable of discriminating between the superior examinee and the inferior examinee have places in the test.

5. The validity and reliability of a standardized test are ensured right from the beginning of its construction.

6. A standardized test provides instructions and norms for the future users of the tests. Such norms usually include pertinent details about the following.

(*i*) The age, gender and academic background etc. of the sample used to lay down the norms.

(*ii*) The mean score of the sample on the tests.

(*iii*) The standard duration and variance of the sample on the test.

(*iv*) The size of the sample.

(*v*) Conversion tables for interpreting raw scores.

16.6. CLASSROOM TESTING

Teacher-made Tests. Teacher made tests are frequently the basis of evaluating the progress of students in the class. These tests are of great value to the teachers, the students and their parents and administrators and educators. Some of the important features of teacher-made tests are:

(*i*) They attempt to assess comprehensively the extent and degree of student's progress with reference to specific classroom activities.

(*ii*) They permit the teacher to ascertain an individual pupil's, strength and weaknesses and needs.

(*iii*) They provide immediate feedback for the teacher as to the effectiveness of his teaching methods and accordingly can make necessary adjustments and improvements.

(*iv*) They motivate the students.

(*v*) They are simple to use.

(*vi*) They provide information which is the basis for a report on the progress of students.

Limitations of Teacher-made Tests

1. Tests are often ambiguous and unclear.
2. Tests are either too short or too lengthy.
3. Tests do not cover the entire content.
4. Tests are usually hurriedly conducted.

5. Tests are cursory.
6. Supervision is not proper. There is a lot of scope for copying.
7. Tests are conducted as rituals only.
8. Answer books are not marked with care.

16.7. WRITTEN TESTS

The test in which students respond to the teacher in writing is called a written test. A written test has both merits and demerits.

Merits

1. A written test can provide us a reliable, stable and valid type of evaluation.
2. It can be planned carefully, hoping in view the objectives, contents and learning experiences.
3. With the help of a marking scheme and a scoring key, the answers can be assessed objectively.
4. Several students can be evaluated at a time and at various places.
5. Written tests help to evaluate the power of comprehension, critical, thinking, analysis and synthesis.

Demerits

1. Certain objectives such as skill in handling apparatus and speaking etc. cannot be evaluated.
2. Cramming and rote-memory predominate.
3. Attitudes and Values cannot be assessed.

16.8. TRAINING STUDENTS TO TAKE A TEST

1. Students should be trained to read or listen to attentively all the directions contained in the test and to follow them exactly.
2. Students should be impressed upon the fact that last minute cramming is a poor substitute for consistent effort throughout the course.
3. Students should pace themselves so as to have time to consider and respond to all the questions.
4. In answering an essay question students should take time to reflect, to plan, and to organize their answer before starting to write.
5. Students should decide carefully how much they can afford to write in the time available.
6. Students should attempt to answer all questions.
7. If possible, students should take time to reread their answers to detect and correct any careless mistake.
8. When an additional answer book is used, it should be made sure that it is properly attached with the main sheet and roll number written on it.

Ebel and Frisbie (1991) states that skill in test taking is called 'testwiseness' and students who are richly endowed with this attribute are supposed to be able to score well on any test.

16.9. FUNCTIONS OF A TESTING PROGRAMME

Thorndike and Hagen (1979) list the following functions of a testing programme:

Classroom functions	*Guidance functions*	*Administrative functions*
Diagnosing learning difficulties	Preparing evidence to guide discussions with parents about their children	Assigning students to classroom groups
Evaluating discrepancies between potential and achievement	Helping the student make immediate choices	Placing new students
Appraising gains or growth in achievement	Helping the student to set educational and vocational goals	Helping to determine eligi-bility for special groups
Grouping students for instruction within a class	Improving counsellor, teacher and parent understanding of problem cases	Evaluating curricula, curri-cular emphasis and curricular experiments
Planning instruc-tional activities for an individual		Improving public relations
Identifying students who need special diagnostic study and remedial instruction		Providing information for outside agencies
Determining reasonable achievement levels for each student		

16.10. DIAGNOSTIC TESTING

Meaning of a Diagnostic Test.

English and English (1958) have defined a diagnostic test in these words, "One designed to locate the particular source of a person's difficulties in learning, especially in school subjects, thus providing clues to what further measures of instruction, guidance, or study are needed." A diagnostic test is a test designed to locate specific learning deficiencies in case of 'specific individuals' at a specific stage of learning so that 'specific efforts' could be made to overcome those deficiencies. It helps the teacher in identifying the status of the learner at the end of a particular lesson, unit or course of learning as to what 'specific teaching or learning points' have been properly grasped by the learner. If such a deficiency is located in several students, it becomes obvious to the teacher to reflect upon whether something went wrong with his method of teaching. It is also possible that the entire group of students suffering from that particular learning difficulty might not have the basic knowledge required for benefitting from further learning. After administering a diagnostic test or a battery of diagnostic tests to students, a teacher takes remedial measures to overcome the deficiencies thus discovered.

Characteristics of an effective diagnostic test. Cook, Walter W. (1958) has stated the following characteristics of an effective diagnostic test:

1. It should be an integral part of the curriculum, emphasising and clarifying the important objectives.
2. Its test items should require responses to be made to situations approximating as closely as possible to be functional.
3. It must be based on experimental evidence of learning difficulties.
4. It should reveal the mental processes of the learner sufficiently to detect points of error.
5. It should suggest or provide specific remedial procedures for each error detected.
6. It should be designed to cover a long sequence or learning systematically.
7. It should be designed to check forgetting by constant review of difficult elements as well as to detect faulty learning.
8. It should reveal pupil progress in objective terms.

Steps in the Construction of a Diagnostic Test. The following steps are involved in the construction of a diagnostic step:

1. Indentifying learning deficiencies.
2. Analysing errors.
3. Analysing content.
4. Indentifying learning points to be covered emerging from above.
5. Developing test formats and their try-out.
6. Selecting items for inclusion in the test.
7. Assembling the test.

Administering the Test

The following points need to be kept in view:

1. The first task of the teacher is to win the confidence of the students and reassure them that the test is to help them in the improvement of their learning rather than for declaring pass or fail.

2. It should be administered in a relaxed environment.

3. Students should be seated comfortably.

4. Students should be asked not to consult each other while taking the test

5. If any student is not able to follow something, he should be allowed to seek a clarification from the teacher.

6. The teacher may ensure that the students taking the test attempt all questions.

7. Time schedule should not be enforced strictly. If any student takes a little more time, he should be allowed to do so.

16.11. TEST AND ITEM ANALYSIS

Like any other measuring instrument, each component of an evaluation instrument needs to be doing its proper job and functioning harmoniously with the other components in the system. One weak component and the performance of the instrument becomes suspect and its validity open to question. The major need for item analysis is to ascertain whether the questions/items do their job effectively. Usually a detailed test analysis and item analysis will have to be done before a meaningful and scientific inference about the test can be made in terms of its validity, reliability, objectivity, difficulty and discrimination. Let us now look at the outcomes of test analysis and item analysis before summarising the need for them.

According to a *Monograph on Test and Item Analysis for Universities* (1985), a systematic analysis aims at finding the following from the performance of a group:

(*a*) the central tendency of marks obtained by them. The mean, median and mode are usually found. The relative values indicate the type of distribution normal, or +ve or –ve skew. A high value of these within a range indicates that the test is very easy while a low value of these indicates that the test is very hard.

(*b*) The variability characterised by 'standard deviation'. This indicates the nature of spread of marks; the greater the spread, the greater will be the value of standard deviation. This is a very useful 'statistic' which allows us to use it for finding many other useful things.

(*c*) A coefficient of reliability for the test indicating the degree of consistency with which the test has measured the students' abilities. A high value of this means that the test is reliable and it produces virtually repeatable scores for the students. A low value indicates that the test cannot be trusted to give consistent results and marks obtained by various students cannot be automatically value judged.

(*d*) The error in marking an individual student. This is a function of its reliability and the nature of spread of marks. If the spread is large and the reliability is low, the standard error is pretty high. Usually the standard error is 0.3 to 0.8 times the standard deviation (or spread). This is particularly useful in making meaningful interpretations and value judgements about our marks. Amongst other things, the test analysis will provide us with information about the test and help us to design, for example, a suitable grading system in place of marks, to interpret the marks with caution, care and rationality.

At the same time, a detailed 'item analysis' will reveal the facility value of each of the items/questions and the discrimination index of these questions/items. It is through 'item analysis' that a teacher or a paper setter comes to know whether the question/items had the right level of difficulty and whether there was a discrimination between more able and less able students. Even though there is nothing like a right level of difficulty, it is usually accepted that values in the range of 20% to 80% are in order, for an achievement test or exam. However, the overall facility of the test for the entire population may have to be around 50%. A high facility value indicates that the item is 'very easy' for the group while a low facility value indicated a very difficult item. With a large number of items/questions available with known values of facility over a sample of population, it can be reasonably expected to enable test constructors to choose suitable item to yield desirable 'means'. Item analysis with the 'discrimination index' for every item and question will guarantee the use of item/questions that discriminate positively between 'higher' and 'lower' ability students. Usual acceptable values of discrimination are 0.2 to 0.6 for objective type and 0.5 and above for eassay (choice type) questions. Item analysis of the same items in successive years to similar groups will help.

(*a*) define standard of performance;
(*b*) maintain standard of performance;
(*c*) ensure comparability of standards.

Test and item analysis carried out by teachers for all their class tests will help them.

(*a*) understand the behaviour of their questions.
(*b*) become better item writers;
(*c*) become more scientific, professional and competent.

16.12. DIFFICULTY LEVEL/FACILITY LEVEL OF A TEST

Difficulty/facility level of a test is an index of how easy or difficult the test is from the point of view of the testees. The index is a ratio of the average score of a sample of subjects on the test to the maximum possible score on the test. It is usually expressed in percentage. Thus, the difficulty/facility level of a test is expressed as :

$$P = \frac{\text{Average score on the test}}{\text{Maximum possible score}} \times 100$$

P denotes the difficulty/facilty level. The following table illustrates this.

Table : Difficulty/Facility level

No. of Tests	*Mean score*	*Maximum Possible score*	*P-Value*	*Comments*
1.	10	100	10%	Extremely difficult test
2.	20	100	20%	Very difficult test
3.	30	100	30%	Difficult test
4.	40	100	40%	Not so difficult test
5.	50	100	50%	Easy test
6.	80	100	80%	Very easy test
7.	90	100	90%	Extremely easy test

16.13. CRITERION OF GOOD TEST

A good test should have the following qualities:

1. Validity
2. Reliability
3. Objectivity
4. Predictability
5. Administrative ease.

1. Validity. By validity we mean the degree to which a test or examination measures what it is intended to measure. In geography if the aim is to test the reasoning power of the student, the questions should be framed in such a manner as to elicit replies which may assist in judging the reasoning and argumentative power of the student. Spelling or handwriting should not be taken into account while assessing the paper. Perhaps this factor of validity is the most baffling one in regard to our essay type of examinations.

Following points regarding validity may be noted:

(*i*) The validity of a test cannot be reported in general terms.

(*ii*) No test can be said to have 'high' or 'low' validity in the abstract. Its validity must be determined with reference to the particular use for which the test is being considered.

(*iii*) The validity pertains to the results of a test or evaluation instrument and not to the instrument itself. We sometimes speak of the validity of a test for the sake of convenience but it is more appropriate to speak of the validity of the test results or more specifically of the validity of the interpretation to be made from the results.

(*iv*) Validity is a matter of degree. It is best considered in terms of categories that specify degree such as higher validity, moderate validity and low validity.

Types of validity. There are four main types of validity.

(*i*) Content Validity
(*ii*) Productive Validity
(*iii*) Concurrent Validity
(*iv*) Construct Validity.

(i) Content Validity. The content validity relates to the degree to which a test samples the content area which is to be measured. All major aspects of the content area must be adequately covered by the test items and they must be in the correct proportions.

(ii) Predictive Validity. It refers to the extent to which a test can predict the future performance of the students/learners. This type of validity is important for those tests which are used for classification

and selection purposes. The degree to which a test can predit the future performance of the individuals depends upon the degree of relationships between the two variables – the test and the criterion. The higher the relationship between these variables, the greater will be the predictive validity of a test. The most important and difficult task in this method is to determine the criterion which is the index of future performance. Predictive value is reported through a coefficient of correlation obtained when predictor and the criterion data are correlated.

(iii) Concurrent Validity. Concurrent validity refers to the relationship between scores on a measuring tool and a criterion available at the same time. It differs from predictive validity only on time factor. Concurrent validity is appropriate for those tests which are employed for diagnosis of existing status of the individual rather than predicting about his future outcome.

(iv) Construct validity. Construct validity refers to the extent to which a test reflects constructs presumed to underlie the test performance and also the extent to which it is based on theories regarding these constructs.

Reliability

By this term we mean the degree of accuracy with which an examination measures what it seeks to measure. The greater the number of questions in an examination the more reliable is the result. New type objective tests are considered to be more reliable as the sampling is more extensive.

Methods of Determining Reliability. Four methods for determining the reliability of a test are :

1. Test-Retest
2. Equivalent Form
3. Split-half
4. Inter-item Consistency

Test-Retest Method. For establishing reliability through this method, the same test is administered twice to the same group of students/learners/subjects with a given time intervals between the two administrations of the test. With the help of these two sets of scores, correlation is computed. This correlation coefficient provides a measure of reliability. It indicates how stable the test results are over the given period of time. Thus, this correlation coefficient can also be referred to as a correlation of stability.

There are certain assumptions made when we compute a coefficient of stability. First, the characteristics being measured by the test is stable over time. Second, practice or forgetting does not affect significantly the trait being measured by the test. Third, no differential learning should occur between the two administrations.

Equivalent Form Method. Determination of reliability by means of equivalent form method involves the use of two different but equivalent forms of the test. These forms are also called alternative or parallel forms. Equivalent forms cover the same content, use same types of items instructions, time limits and formats are of equal difficulty. The two forms of the test are administered to the same group of students/learners/subjects in close succession or with minimum time lag. The correlation coefficient is computed from the two sets of scores. This correlation coefficient provides a measure of equivalence. It indicates the degree to which both forms of the test measure the same aspects of behaviour. Inconsistencies in scores in this method can be attributed to difference in content sampling or item sampling. Long intervals between the two administrations will lower the reliability.

Split-Half Method. For determination of reliability by means of the split-half method, the test is to be administered once to a group of selected students. The test is split in nearly comparable halves. There are several ways of dividing a test. In most cases the first half and the second half of a test would not be comparable on account of difference in nature and difficulty level of items as well as in the cumulative effects of warming up, practice, fatigue and any other factor varying progressively from the beginning to the end of the test. If the items are arranged in an approximate order of difficulty, then the test can be split into two halves by using odd-numbered items in one half and even-numbered items in the second half. Then this method would provide two comparable halves. Once the two comparable halves are obtained, the two half-scores can be obtained for each student of the group. From thest two sets of scores, the correlation can be computed by following the usual method of correlation.

Inter-item Consistency Method. (Homogeneity - Kuder - Richardson Reliability Method). For determining reliability through this method, the test is to be administered once and is based on the consistency of students' responses to all items in the test. The inter-items consistency is influenced by two sources of error variance: (*i*) Content sampling (*ii*) Heterogeneity of the behaviour domain sampled. The more homogeneous the domain, the higher the inter-item consistency. For example, if one test includes only subtraction items, another test includes addition, division and multiplication items, the former test will most probably show greater inter-item consistency than the latter. In the latter test which is more heterogeneous, one student may perform better in addition than in any of the other arithmetic operations, another student may score reliably higher on the division items but low on addition and multiplication and so on. Thus, in the latter test there might be little or no relationship between a student's performance on the different types of items. Therefore, the inter-item consistency means that every item in the test has high correlation with every other item of the test.

The most common method of finding inter-consistency is the one developed by Kuder and Richardson.

Interpretation of a reliability coefficient. There are three considerations which must be kept in mind while interpreting reliability. First, the reliability of a test as estimated by one technique in one situation and with one example will not be the same as an estimate obtained with a different technique, in a different situation, or with a different sample.

Second, a reliability co-efficient situation is only an estimate of the magnitude of inconsistency in test scores and it does not indicate the causes of the inconsistency. Third, reliability is not the be-all and end-all of a measuring tool. It is not an end in itself rather a step on a way towards that goal.

Factors affecting reliability. The following factors affect reliability:

(*i*) *Length of the test* – The longer the test, the greater its reliability.

(*ii*) *Difficulty of the test* – The tests which are too easy or too difficult for the group members taking it will tend to provide scores of low reliability.

(*iii*) *Heterogenity of the group* – The reliability increases with the spread of heterogenity of the members of the group who take the test.

Objectivity

Objectivity refers to the extent the opinion or judgement of the scorer is eliminated from the scoring process. Objectivity is high in most of the standardized tests of achievement, aptitude, creativity and intelligence, etc. The test items are of objective type – fill in the blanks, multiple choice, true-false, etc. Objectivity is usually attained by

(*i*) stating the items precisely and specifically.

(*ii*) requiring short and specific answers

(*iii*) scoring the test by the use of a previously determined scoring key or providing specific guidelines for scoring.

Predictability

The test should be such as can give a forecast of the possibilities of the future achievement of the students.

Administrative Ease

A test should be easy to administer in all its three stages i.e. setting, answering and scoring.

16.14. A WORD OF CAUTION

A word of caution may be said in the use of tests. Tests are tools and should be used as such. It would be a great error to use tests as the sole basis for evaluating pupil needs and abilities. Ross writes, "Guidance is always more than the giving of tests, no matter how extensively or carefully done."

Tests, when correctly used, yield more accurate and speedy information that the subjective techniques, such as the interview, observation and questionnaire. However, these have their own limitations. They fail to provide comprehensive measurement. There are factors like cultural and social backgrounds, emotional stability etc. which play their own role and these tests fail to measure them.

Chapter 17

Achievement Tests

17.1. DEFINITION AND MEANING OF AN ACHIEVEMENT TEST

An achievement test has a great significance in all types of instructional progress of the individual. A classroom teacher depends upon the achievement tests for measuring the progress of his students in his subject area. Several educational and vocational decisions about students are taken on their performance in the achievement tests. It is, therefore, necessary that the teachers should be well-versed with the meaning and characteristics of achievement tests.

Following definitions throw adequate light on the nature and role of achievement tests.

Thorndike and Hagen (1969) observe, "The type of ability test that describes what a person has learned to do is called an achievement test."

Gronlund (1977) defines an achievement test as "a systematic procedure for determining the amount a student has learned through instruction."

Popham (1981) states, "The achievement test focuses upon an examinee's attainments at a given point in time."

Gronlund, N.E and Linn, R.L. in their book *Measurement and Evaluation in Teaching* (1990) have observed, "There typically have been norm-referenced tests that measure the pupil's level of achievement in various content and skill areas by comparing their test performance with the performance of other pupils in some general reference group."

In the words of Wiersma, W. and Jurs, S.G. (1990) achievement test "is a measure of knowledge and skilis in a content area."

Popham, W. James, in his book *Modern Educational Measurement* (1990) provides the description of achievement tests in these words, "Tests in the cognitive or psychomotor realm are often focused on an examinee's attainment at a given time; these tests are usually referred to as achievement tests."

17.2. CHARACTERISTICS OF A GOOD ACHIEVEMENT TEST

Gronlund and Linn (1990) have identified the following characteristics of a good standardized achievement test:

1. A good achievement test is tried out and selected on the basis of its difficulty level and discriminating power.
2. It should have a description of measured behaviour.
3. It should contain a sufficient number of test items for each measured behaviour.
4. It should be divided into different knowledge and skills according to behaviours to be measured.
5. Its instructions in regard to its administering and scoring are so clear that they become standardized for different users.
6. It is accompanied by norm which are developed at various levels and on various age groups.
7. It provides equivalent and comparable forms of the test.
8. It carries with it a test manual for its administering and scoring.

17.3. PRACTICAL USES OF ACHIEVEMENT TESTS

I. ADMINISTRATOR'S USE

1. Tests help to evaluate the extent to which the objectives of education are being achieved.

2. Tests help to classify school objectives.

3. Tests discover the type of learning experiences that will achieve these objectives with the best possible results.

4. To evaluate, revise and improve the curriculum in the light of these results.

5. To discover backward children who need help and to plan for remedial instruction fo: such students.

6. To select talented pupils for special classes and courses.

7. To decide proper classification of students.

8. To get a better understanding of the needs and abilities of pupils.

9. To select students for the award of special merits or scholarships.

10. To group pupils in a class so that students are put in such a way that individual differences are as slight as possible.

11. To help the parents in recognising the strengths and weaknesses of their children so that they direct their energies on suitable goals only and do not put heavy demands on them.

12. To determine the efficiency of one school with the others.

13. To determine the general level of achievement of a class and thus to judge the teaching efficiency of the teacher. The level of achievement of a class may be judged on the basis of the achievement of the class in the beginning and at the end of the school year.

II. THE TEACHER'S USE

1. The teacher will come to know the general range of abilities of students in the class.

2. In the light of above, he will select appropriate materials of instruction so that all individuals benefit from instruction to the maximum.

3. The teacher will determine and diagnose the weakness of the students in various subjects.

4. The teacher will spot out brilliant and backward children.

5. He will determine the progress of the group in a particular subject over a period of time.

6. By studying the results of the students on achievement tests and intelligence tests, the teacher will determine whether or not the students are working at their maximum capacity.

17.4. PLANNING OF AN ACHIEVEMENT TEST

Shipman, M. in his book *School Evaluation* (1979) suggests the following stages which can be helpful in planning an achievement test:

1. Stating the objectives in such a form that it will enable their achievements to be verified.

2. Spelling out the actions that are necessary for the attainment of objectives.

3. Spelling out the criteria by which the attainment of objectives is to be assessed.

4. Spelling out personnel whose judgments are involved in each component of the plan.

5. Stating the arrangements for any standardization procedure and the forms of reports and records which are to be maintained.

Wiersma, W. and Jurs, S.G. (1990) have identified the following stages for planning an achievement test:

1. Deciding purposes of the test.
2. Listing educational objectives of different areas of knowledge.
3. Preparing table of specifications.
4. Determining practical considerations.

Gronlund and Linn (1990) discuss in detail the following steps in classroom testing:

1. Determining the purposes of testing.
2. Developing the test specifications.
3. Selecting appropriate type of items.
4. Preparing relevant test items.
5. Assembling the test.
6. Administering the test.
7. Scoring the test.
8. Appraising the test.
9. Using the test results.

1. Determining the purpose of the test. According to purpose, tests may be divided into the following five categories:

(*i*) Pre-testing which includes
- (*a*) Readiness pre-test
- (*b*) Placement pre-test

(*ii*) Testing during placement
- (*c*) Formative test
- (*d*) Diagnostic test
- (*e*) End testing - summative test.

2. Developing test specifications. Specifications of the test include the following:

- (*a*) A list of instructional objectives.
- (*b*) An outline of the course contact.
- (*c*) A two-way chart.

Following chart explains the specifications of the contents of the test as for weightage to different areas is concerned.

Each level of thinking and number of test items.

% Content	*Knowledge*	*Comprehension*	*Application*	*Analysis*	*Total*
Topic No. 1	7	5	4	4	20
Topic No. 2	6	6	4	4	20
Topic No. 3	6	6	3	3	18
Topic No. 4	2	5	5	2	14
Topic No. 5	4	5	5	2	16
Topic No. 6	5	6	1	0	12
Total	30	33	22	15	100

3. Selecting appropriate types of questions. There should be a balanced selection of essay type, short-answer type and objective type questions.

4. Preparing relevant test items. This includes the following steps:

(*i*) Matching the test items with the learning outcome.

(*ii*) Selecting most representative items.

(*iii*) Preparing test items which are of proper difficulty level.

(*iv*) Avoiding all possible barriers in test items which prevent examinees from responding.

(*v*) Avoiding providing any clues to answers which may help examinees to answer correctly even if they lack the necessary achievement.

5. Assembling the test. After preparing relevant test items, the test constructor should follow the process as indicated below:

(*a*) Writing each item on a separate card.

(*b*) Reviewing the test items by the test constructor himself and also by some other teacher.

(*c*) Arranging the test items according to a well defined criteria.

(*d*) Providing proper instructions to the examinees.

6. Administering the test. Following suggestions are made while administering the test.

(*i*) Long announcements before or during the test should not be made.

(*ii*) Instructions, if any, should be given in writing so that uniformity is maintained and all the examinees get the same opportunities.

(*iii*) The test administrators should not respond to the individual problems of the examinees, otherwise any hint on their part may provide unfair chance to some examinees.

(iv) Test should be administered in an appropriate physical and psychological environment.

7. Scoring the test. Scoring may be done mechanically or manually; depending upon the situation.

8. Appraising the test or item-analysis. After scoring, the test should be appraised for each item.

9. Using the test results. Test results are used primarily for the following purposes.

(*a*) For making decisions about the promotion of students to the next higher grade.

(*b*) For bringing about improvement in teaching methods and techniques.

17.5. GENERAL PRINCIPLES TO BE OBSERVED IN TESTS

E.W. Menzel observes that whether old-type or new-type, we observe among others the following principles:

1. It will be general and comprehensive enough to test thoroughly the pupil's mastery of the desired skills or grasp of a subject-matter. It will make it impossible for a pupil to get a good mark just because he got a few 'lucky questions' and will not fail a good pupil just because of a few 'unlucky questions'. Very few examinations in India are adequate in this respect.

2. It will reliably grade the pupils into at least six to ten (or more) different classifications according to their ability.

3. It will be as objective as practicable. Some questions of a discussional nature can be given to advantage but there should also be some work which pins pupil and examiner down to answers which can be quite objectively scored. Even in the essay type of examination, the objectivity can be greatly increased with study and care.

4. Other things being equal, the test which examines most intensively or extensively in the least time and with the least fatigues on the part of the pupil is the best.

5. The test should encourage creative and self-reliant work and discourage mere mechanical rote-memory work.

6. The test should encourage the pupil to put forth his best effort.

7. The test should convincingly reveal to the pupil his deficiencies and encourage him to remove them.

8. The test should examine exactly what it pretends to examine and not handicap pupils for deficiencies in unrelated subjects. The more

a test tries to examine in subjects extraneous to the avowed subject, the less efficiently it examines its own.

9. The standards of a test should be based on actual performance and not upon mere opinion of what a standard should be or on an arbitrary percentage work.

10. The more a test makes it possible to compare the performance of a certain group of pupils to that of other pupils the more revealing it is.

11. Keep in mind that no test is infallible. The daily work of the pupil and an observation of his habits of work are equally important in appraising the work and ability of a pupil.

12. Keep in mind that poor results on the part of a group of pupils indicate a faulty test or one that is not graded to the ability of the pupils or deals with matters the children have not been taught.

Chapter 18

Criterion-Referenced Test (CRT) and Norm-Referenced Test (NRT)

18.1. SIGNIFICANCE

Revolutionary changes have taken place in the field of teaching and learning processes in the last four decades. Individual instruction is emphasised. So designing of the tests should be such as to reflect the changes in what the individual has learned. Again as an individual progresses through a programme of instruction educators want to know at various junctures, precisely what the student knows and whether he knows enough to proceed further. CRT and NRT are used to measure the attainment of the learner. The fundamental distinction between NRT and CRT is based on the manner in which one interprets the results of the learner's test performance. In the case of NRT one interprets learner's test performance according to the performance of 'others'. In case of CRT, one interprets learner's performance in relation to well defined class of knowledge, skills, attitudes and the like. The following presentation provides details of CRT and NRT.

18.2. CRITERION REFERENCED TEST

Glaser (1963) first used the term CRT to highlight the need for tests that can describe the position of a learner on a performance continuum, rather than the learner's rank within a group of learners.

The word 'criterion' in the CRT refers to a domain of behaviours and in criterion referencing one is interested in referencing of an examinee's test performance to a well defined domain of behaviour measuring an objective or skill.

Definition of CRT

Hambleton and others (1978) point out that there are almost as many ideas about a CRT as there are contributors to the field. However, of all the definitions and explanations of CRT, Pophan's definition has been preferred in general.

1. Popham, W.J. and Husek, T.R. in their paper, "Implications of Criterion - Referenced Measurement" published in *Journal of Educational Measurement* Vol. VI (1969), define criterion-referenced measures as, "Those which are used to ascertain an individual's status with respect to some criterion i.e. performance standard. It is because the individual is compared with some established criterion, rather than other individuals, that these measures are described as criterion-referenced. The meaning of an individual score is not dependent on comparison with other testees. We want to know what the individual can do, not how much he stands in comparison to others."

2. Ivon (1970) defines a Criterion-Referenced Test as "One consisting of items keyed to a set of behaviour objectives.

3. Harris and Stewart (1971) define CRT as "One consisting of a sample of production tasks drawn from well defined population of performance."

4. Glaser and Nitko, in their paper "Measurement in Learning and Instruction" in the book *Educational Measurement* (1971) edited by R.L. Thorndik write, "A criterion-referenced test is one that is deliberately constructed to yield measurements that are directly interpretable in terms of special performance standards."

5. In the words of Gronlund, N.E. (1985), criterion-referenced test is "a test designed to provide a measure of performance that is interpretable in terms of a clearly defined and delimited domain of learning tasks."

6. Sex Gilbert (1989) writes, "Criterion-referenced tests relate a student's score on an achievement test to a domain knowledge rather than to another student's score."

7. Hopkins, Stanley and Hopkins (1990) observe, "These tests have the purpose of identifying individuals who have or have not acquired certain basal competencies, Different consequences for instruction such as remediation, may result."

8. Wiersma, William and Jurs, Stephen G. (1990) write "Criterion-referenced tests describe the performance of the student in terms of actual skills or tasks that are included in the test."

From above definitions it is concluded that Criterion-Referenced Test is meant to measure the achievement of an examinee on a certain domain to find out his level of achievement in that domain. It has nothing to do with the achievement level of other examinees.

Characteristics of Criterion-Referenced Test

1. Its main objective is to measure student's achievement of curriculum based skills.
2. It is prepared for a particular grade or course level.
3. It has balanced representation of goals and objectives.
4. It is used to evaluate the curriculum plan instruction progress and group student's interaction.
5. It can be administered before and after instruction.
6. It is generally reported in the form of
   (*i*) Minimum scores for partial and total mastery of main skill areas.
   (*ii*) Number of correct items.
   (*iii*) Percent of correct items.
   (*iv*) Derived score based on correct items and other factors.

Uses of Criterion-Reference Testing

(*i*) to discover the inadequacies in learner's learning and assist the weaker section of learners to reach the level of other students through a regular programme of remedial instruction.

(*ii*) to identify the master learners and non-master learners in a class.

(*iii*) to find out the level of attainment of various objectives of instruction.

(*iv*) to find out the level at which a particular concept has been learnt.

(*v*) to better placement of concepts at different grade levels.

(*vi*) to make instructional decisions of what to do with a learner in individually prescribed instruction programme.

Limitations of Criterion-referenced Testing

Chase (1974) lists the following limitations:

1. Criterion-referenced tests tell only whether a learner has reached proficiency in a task area but does not show how good or poor is the learner's level of ability.
2. Tasks included in the criterion-referenced test may be highly influenced by a given teacher's interests or biases, leading to general validity problem.
3. Only some areas readily lend themselves for listing specific behavioural objectives around which criterion-referenced tests can be built and this may be a constructing element for teachers.

4. Criterion-referenced tests are important for only a small fraction of important educational achievements. On the contrary, promotion and assessment of various skills is a very important function of the school and it requires norm-referenced testing.

Reliability of Criterion-Referenced Tests

Reliability can be increased by the following:

1. Paying proper attention to the construction of test items.
2. Paying proper attention to the test-setting.
3. Paying proper attention to the examinees.
4. Making the items similar.
5. Using appropriate wording.
6. Increasing the number of items.
7. Increasing the number of discriminating items.
8. Giving clear directions to the examinees.
9. Giving clear directions to the evaluations.
10. Motivating students to perform better.

Interpretation of Criterion-Referenced Test

1. Interpretation should be based on what the items actually measure.

2. There should be sufficient items for each type of interpretation. In case these are less than 10 items, they should be combined with other items through lengthening content items.

3. The test should contain easy as well difficult items otherwise it would be difficult to describe what low achievers could do.

Guidelines for Constructing, Administering and Evaluating Criterion-Referenced Tests

Ronald Hambelton and Daniel Eignor (1978) have suggested the following guidelines.

Objectives

1. The purposes of the test should be stated clearly and concisely.

2. Objectives should be written in such a way that each item could be identified with one objective.

3. There should be appropriate rationale for the inclusion of each objective in the test.

4. The classroom teacher should be in a position to adapt the test to meet local situation.

5. The set of objectives of the test should be a true representative of content domain.

Test Items

1. The test items should be free from any bias.
2. The test items should be free from technical flaws.

3. The set of test items should measure an objective for which it has been included in the test.

4. The test items should be valid indicators of the objectives for which they have been prepared.

5. The test items should be in appropriate form to measure the objectives for which they have been selected.

6. A heterogenous sample should be used in the test items.

7. Item analysis should be used to detect flawed items.

8. The item review process should be described.

Administration

1. The test manual should specify the role and responsibilities of the examiner.

2. The test administrators should have adequate information relating to the purpose, time limits, answer sheets and scoring of test.

3. The directions of the test should be clear.

4. The test should be easy to score.

Test Layout

1. Test booklet should be attractively printed.

2. The layout of test booklet should be convenient for examiners.

Reliability

(*i*) The test length should be sufficient enough to find out test score reliability.

(*ii*) The sample of examinees used in finding out reliability should be adequate and representative.

(*iii*) The reliability information should be provided in the test for each intended use of the test score.

(*iv*) The reliability information provided in the test should be appropriate for the use of the score of the test.

Cut Off Scores

1. There should be a rationale for the selection of the method for determining cut-off scores.

2. There should be evidence for the validity of the chosen cut-off marks.

Validity

1. The validity evidence should be adequate for the intended use of the test score.

2. The test manual should provide an appropriate discussion on the factor affecting the validity of the scores.

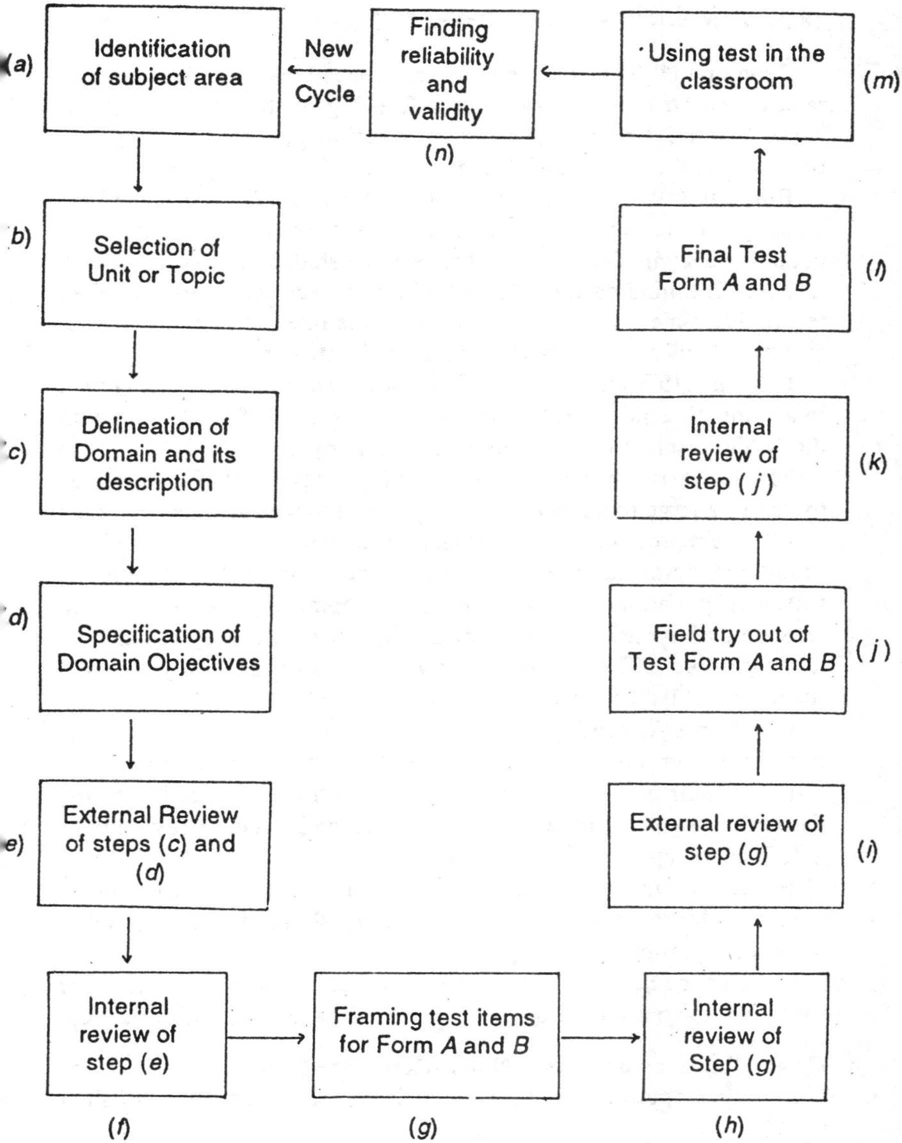

Fig. 18.1. Flow chart showing various steps in development of criterion referenced tests
(*Source* : Singh, Pritam, *Criterion-Referenced Testing: A Monograph*, NCERT, New Delhi, 1983)

18.3. NORM-REFERENCED TEST (NRT)

Gronlund (1976) states that non-referenced tests are "designed to rank students in order of achievement, from high to low, so that decisions based on relative achievements (e.g., selection, grouping, grading) can be made with greater confidence."

Bormuth (1970) writes that a norm-referenced test is designed "to measure the growth in a student's attainment and to compare his level of attainment with the levels reached by other students and norm group."

N.R. Gronlund defines Norm-Referenced Test as "a test designed to provide a measure of performance that is interpretable in terms of an individuals relative standing in some known group."

Bormuth (1970) writes that a NRT is designed "to measure the growth in a student's attainment and to compare his level of attainment with the levels reached by other students and norm group."

This test is used primarily for comparing achievement of an examinee to that of a large representative group of examinees at the same grade level. The representative group is known as the 'Norm Group'. Norm group may be made up of examinees at the local level, district level, state level or national level. Since the development of norm-referenced tests is expensive and time consuming. They are produced by commercial test publishers. The following derived scores are generally reported for these published tests.

(*a*) *Percentile Rank:* A number telling the percentage of examinees in a defined group scoring lower than the particular raw score.

(*b*) *Linear Standard Score:* A number telling the location of the particular row score in relation to the mean and standard deviation of a defined group.

(*c*) *Normalized Standard Score:* A number telling the location of the particular raw score in relation to a normal distribution defined in terms of a particular group.

(*d*) *Grade Equivalent Score:* A number telling the grade placement for which the particular raw score is the average for a defined group.

Chief Characteristics of a Norm-Referenced Test

1. Its basic purpose is to measure student's achievement in curriculum based skills.
2. It is prepared for a particular grade level.
3. It is administered after instruction.
4. It is used for forming homogeneous or heterogeneous class groups.

5. It classifies achievement as above average, average or below average for a given grade.

6. It is generally reported in the form of Percentile Rank, Linear Standard Score, Normalized Standard Score and Grade Equivalent Score.

Process for Developing Norm-Referenced Achievement Test

According to L.M. Carey (1988), the process for developing Norm-Referenced Test may be divided into the following stages:-

1. **Design Stage.** It is done through
   (*i*) Curriculum analysis
   (*ii*) Selecting objectives to be measured
   (*iii*) Analysing objectives for determining pre-requisite skills.
   (*iv*) Developing table of specifications for test.
   (*v*) Determining specifications for items.
2. **Development Stage.** This consists of
   (*i*) Writing items according to specifications.
   (*ii*) Developing needed art work and illustrations.
   (*iii*) Writing response directions and examples.
   (*iv*) Writing administrative directions.
   (*v*) Reviewing items illustrations and directions.
   (*vi*) Developing test lay-out.
   (*vii*) Developing simple test.
3. **Conducting Field Test.** At this stage, test is tried out through
   (*i*) Selecting representive group.
   (*ii*) Administering test.
   (*iii*) Scoring
   (*iv*) Analysing information.
   (*v*) Analysing data and selecting items
   (*vi*) Developing final test form.
4. **Developing Test Norm.** Norms of the test are developed through:
   (*i*) Describing characteristics of population.
   (*ii*) Selecting representative norm group.
   (*iii*) Administering test to norm group.
   (*iv*) Scoring.
   (*v*) Converting raw scores to standard scores.
   (*vi*) Creating norm tables.
5. **Writing Test Manual.** The test manual is written through
   (*i*) Describing the design process and skills measured.
   (*ii*) Describing the field test process.
   (*iii*) Describing the development process.

(*iv*) Describing criteria used to select items.
(*v*) Describing norm group selection procedure.
(*vi*) Describing norm group characteristics.
(*vii*) Describing test characteristics — reliability and standard error of measurement.
(*viii*) Describing standard administrative procedures.
(*ix*) Describing scoring procedures and derivation of standard scores.
(*x*) Describing score interpretation procedures.

Reliability of Norm-Referenced Test

Test length affects reliability. Other things being equal, the reliability of the test can be increased by increasing its length. Items of similar content also increase reliability. Items of moderate difficulty increase reliability over the items which are either too easy or too difficult. Increased range of performance of the examinees being tested tends to increase reliability.

Validity of a Norm-Referenced Test

The validity of a norm-referenced test can be increased by

(*i*) Constructing items of proper difficulty level.
(*ii*) Increasing the test length.
(*iii*) Increasing the heterogeneity of the group which is being tested.
(*iv*) Administering the test under proper conditions.

Suggestions for interpreting examinee's scores on Norm-Referenced Test

Bescott, G.A., Balow, J.H., Hogan, T.P. and Far, R.C., in their book *Metropolitan Achievement Tests* (1978) suggest the following points for score interpretation on norm-referenced tests:-

(*a*) Generally students should obtain the same scores which are expected from them by a regular classroom teacher. If it does not happen and the students obtain too high or too low scores, the teacher should explore by instructional implications.

(*b*) Generally any student should score within the same range in all the subjects. If there is too much gap in the score of one subject in comparison with the other subject, the teacher should try to locate the reason for it in motivation, special interests and special difficulties, etc.

(*c*) Generally the test results should be according to the expectation of the teacher for individual students. If it is not so, the validity of the test is threatened.

(*d*) Small differences in sub-test scores may be due to chance error also for which the standard error of measurement should be used.

(*e*) Information collected from various tests should be used to explain performance on other tests.

Uses of Norm-referenced Testing

N. Vasantha Ram Kumar and K.N. Lalithamal (1990), state that N.R.T. is useful—

(1) in aptitude testing for making differential prediction;
(2) to get a reliable rank ordering of the pupils with respect to the achievement we are measuring;
(3) to identify the pupils who have mastered the essentials of the course more than others;
(4) to select the best of the applicants for a particular programme;
(5) to find out how effective a programme is in comparison to other possible programmes.

Drawbacks of Norm-referenced Testing

According to the above mentioned authors some of the criticisms raised against these tests are:

(1) Test items that are answered correctly by most of the pupils are not included in these tests because of their inadequate contribution to response variance. They will be the items that deal with important concepts of course content.
(2) There is lack of congruence between what the test measures and what is stressed in a local curriculum.
(3) Norm-referencing promotes unhealthy competition and is injurious to self-concepts of low scoring students.

18.4. CRITERION-REFERENCED TESTING (CRT) *vs* NORM-REFERENCED TESTING (NRT)

According to Popham, W.J. (1978) a criterion-referenced test is used to ascertain an individual's status with respect to a well defined behaviour domain. By defined behaviour we mean the learning of a specific skill like the ability to multiply 4×8 (most specific) or the ability to multiply any pair of single number (class of behaviour). In the words of Stanley J.C. and Hopkins, K.D. (1972) the word criterion in CRT denotes, "an instructional objective, an expected post-instructional outcome, an intended level of a student's performance, an acceptable level of learner's achievement or a desired standard of product of performance". By norm-referenced testing is meant the measurement of student's achievement in terms of a group, a class, a school or a state which is taken as a referent for interpreting student's scores and for passing judgements. Thus the typical performance or norm of a group is used as the basis for judging individual student's learning.

In CRT, the emphasis is on improvement of student's achievement and in NRT, emphasis is on measurement of achievement.

Similarities between NRT and CRT

1. Validity and reliability are needed in both.
2. Achievement domain is measured in both.
3. Sample of test items should be relevant and representative in both.
4. Same types of items can be used in both.
5. Same rules are followed for writing items in both excepting the item of difficulty.

Differences in NRT and CRT

NRT	*CRT*
1. NRT covers a large domain of learning task with just a few items measuring each specific task.	1. It focuses on a delimited domain of learning tasks with a relatively large number of items measuring each specific task.
2. It stresses discrimination among individuals.	2. It stresses what examinees can do and what they cannot do.
3. It contains items of average difficulty.	3. It contains easy as well as difficult items.
4. In this test, interpretation needs a defined group.	4. Interpretation needs defined as well as delimited achievement domain.

Student in NRT and CRT

NRT	*CRT*
1. A student is tested after each unit (usually large) of the new material presented.	1. A student is tested after each unit for mastery of objectives.
2. A student is assigned the marks or grades to indicate his performance.	2. A student is allowed to proceed to the new material if mastery is obtained.
3. A student is allowed to go to the next unit along with the whole class.	3. A student is given remedial instruction if the material presented is not mastered.
4. A student is presented with the new materials of the next unit.	4. A student is tested again after remedial work to check for mastery of the material.
5. A student is tested for the new material and assigned marks.	5. A student is tested for mastery of objectives.
6. A student is allowed to go to the next unit.	6. A student is allowed to proceed to the next unit if mastery is obtained after remedial instruction.

In India work on Criterion-referenced testing is yet in the stage of infancy. There seems to be more emphasis on norm-referenced measurement in the evaluation of students. The terminal examination system which is based on norm-referenced measurement still holds good.

Chapter 19

Psychological Tests and Measurement

19.1. BRIEF HISTORY

Sir Francis Galton. An English biologist, was primarily responsible for launching the testing movement on its course. In 1882, an anthropometric laboratory was established by him in South Kensington Museum, London. In this laboratory individuals could be measured in certain physical traits by the payment of a small fee. Galton himself devised most of the simple tests. Galton also paved the way for the application of rating scale and questionnaire methods etc. One of his disciples, *Karl Pearson* carried forward his work.

James McKeen Cattell of America occupies a prominent position in the development of psychological testing. He used the term "mental test" in an article in 1890. This article related to a series of tests which were being administered annually to college students in the efforts to determine their intellectual level. Cattell like Galton felt that a measure of intellectual functions could be obtained through tests of sensory discrimination and reaction time.

Binet and Post-Binet-Era. The early experiments of Wundt were all concerned with sensory discrimination and motor ability. His worthy pupil *Cattell* did much useful work in America. However, the credit of scientific mental testing goes to Binet and Simon. The names of *Terman, Cyril Burt* and *Wechsler* may also be mentioned who did very useful work in mental testing. In India, *Dr. V.V. Kamat* and *Dr. C.H. Rice, Pt. L.S. Jha, Prof. S. Jalota* and *Principal R.R. Kumria* have contributed a lot to this.

19.2. BINET-SIMON TEST

The father of intelligence testing is Alfred Binet, a French educator. Binet disagreed with some of his contemporaries who tried to measure general intelligence by testing reaction time, rote memory, sensory activity, or muscular movements. According to him, intelligence could be estimated, only by test of higher faculties like reasoning, comprehension, judgement, adaptability, persistence, and self-criticism. Binet worked on these lines and in collaboration with Thephile Simon, published the first intelligence test in 1905. This test had thirty items arranged in order of increasing difficulty. It took about 15 years to complete the test.

Binet tried out these items on children and in 1908, brought out a revised scale which divided the test items into age groups from 3 to 11 years. At some age levels, only 3 questions were asked, at others 5 or 6. With this scale Binet introduced the concept of mental age. If a child's (whose chronological age is 8) score on a test is equal to the average score of children of 9 years of age, then his mental age will be nine in spite of the fact that his chronological age is eight.

In 1911, shortly before his death Binet published a second revision of his scale. It omitted some old items and introduced some new ones. He also brought the scale upto adult level. In this revision, he included 5 tests for each age except the 4-year level.

Revised Test 1916

The first serious revision of Binet-Simon Scales was prepared by Terman at Stanford University and was published in 1916. This revision introduced great many alternatives and new additions. The entire scale was restandardized on an American sample of about 1,000 children and 400 adults. For the first time the term I.Q. or "Intelligence quotient" was introduced, I.Q. has been defined as the ratio of Mental age to Chronological age. To avoid fraction, it is multiplied by 100. Thus:

$$\text{I.Q.} = \frac{\text{Mental Age}}{\text{Chronological Age}} \times 100$$

or simply $\text{I.Q.} = \frac{\text{M.A.}}{\text{C.A.}} \times 100$

In the 1916 revision, the number of questions was 90.

1937 and 1960 Revisions

In 1937 and 1960, the Stanford University Test was revised by Merril and Terman. It is also known as Stanford-Binet Individual Test of

Intelligence. It contains 129 questions suitable for a child of 2 years, $2\frac{1}{2}$ years, 3 years, $3\frac{1}{2}$ years, 4 years, $4\frac{1}{2}$ years and then for 5, 6-14 years of ages. There are no questions for $5\frac{1}{2}$ as it is thought that there is not much difference in I.Q. of 5 years and $5\frac{1}{2}$ year old child.

19.3. THE WECHSLER SCALES 1939 AND 1955

The 1937 Stanford-Binet Scale in spite of its merits was not considered particularly well-suited for adults. It was not standardized on any individual over 18 years of age in obtaining the I.Q. The Wechsler Scale was published in 1939 for this purpose. The scale was revised in 1955 and a new version Wechsler Adult Intelligence Scale (WAIS) came into existence. The age ranges are from 16 to 64 years.

The Scale comprises the following sub-tests which fall under two broad categories: (*a*) Verbal Tests and (*b*) Non-Verbal Tests.

Verbal Tests. These contain the following types: (*i*) Vocabulary; (*ii*) Information; (*iii*) Arithmetic items; (*iv*) Comprehension; (*v*) Similarities; (*vi*) Digit span.

Non-Verbal Tests. These include (*i*) Block design; (*ii*) Picture arrangement; (*iii*) Object assembly; (*iv*) Mazes; (*v*) Picture completion.

Comparison between Binet Test and Wechsler Scale

Binet Test	*Wechsler Scale*
1. It is primarily for children.	1. Age ranges are from 16 to 64 years.
2. It is a mental age scale. Items are grouped in terms of mental age.	2. It is a point scale. Points are given for correct responses.
3. Selection is made by relation of success by age.	3. Selection is made by function measured.
4. Items are ungraded and unrelated.	4. Items are graded.
5. The test is inflexible.	5. The test is flexible.
6. It is qualitative in evaluation.	6. It is quantitative in evaluation.

19.4. INTELLIGENCE TESTS

These may be classified under three categories:

1. Individual Tests. These tests are administered to one individual at a time. These cover age group from 2 years to 18 years. These are: (*a*) The Binet-Simon Tests, (*b*) Revised Tests by Terman, (*c*) Mental Scholastic Tests of Burt and (*d*) Wechsler Test.

2. Group Tests. Group tests are administered to a group of people Group tests had their birth in America—when the intelligence of the recruits who joined the army in the First World War was to be calculated. These are: (*a*) The Army Alpha and Beta Test, (*b*) Terman's Group Tests, (*c*) Otis Self-Administrative Tests. Among the group tests there are two types: (*i*) Verbal and (*ii*) Non-Verbal.

Verbal tests are those which require the use of language to answer the test items.

Non-Verbal tests do not require the use of language to respond to the item.

3. Performance Tests. These tests are administered to the illiterate persons. These tests generally involve the construction of certain patterns or solving problems in terms of concrete material. Some of the famous tests are: (*a*) Koh's Block Design Test, (*b*) The Cube Construction Tests, and (*c*) The Pass Along Tests.

19.5. COMPARISON OF INDIVIDUAL TESTS AND GROUP TESTS

Individual Test	*Group Test*
1. It is administered to an individual at a time.	1. It is administered to a group at the same time.
2. It is costly in terms of administration and time.	2. It is less costly in terms of administration and time.
3. A trained tester is required to administer it.	3. No trained person is required to administer it.
4. There is face to face interaction between the individual and the tester.	4. There is no such face to face interaction.
5. Individual test is more reliable. Guidance can be provided to the individual on the basis of its results.	5. Group test may be influenced by several factors.
6. It is useful for small children.	6. It is suitable for older children and adults.
7. The tester can motivate the individual by means of praise and encouragement as he can adapt to the needs of the individual child.	7. It is not possible to do so.

Individual Test	*Group Test*
8. There is very little scope for cheating.	8. Cheating on a large-scale is possible.
9. There is no competition in individual testing.	9. Speed and reading ability may influence the test score.
10. No special formalities are observed in individual testing.	10. Several formalities are observed in administering.
11. Instructions can be made clear before testing.	11. A few members of the group may not clearly understand the instructions.

Measuring Special Ability. The I.Q. obtained as a result of peformance on an intelligence test indicates general status only. It does not point to the size of strength or weakness in each of the particular mental abilities that are being measured. For example, two students showing an I.Q. of 120 on a particular test may have different positions on different sub-tests; one may do very well on arithmetic and poorly on vocabulary, while the other may do well on vocabulary and poorly on arithmetic; yet both score the same total.

Primary Mental Abilities Test (PMA Test). To correct this sort of error we need tests which indicate differential success of a subject on various mental abilities. The tests of primary mental abilities prepared by Thurstone meet this need. The PMA test for ages 11 to 17 is based on the group factor theory of mental ability which postulates that intelligence is made up of certain distinct and more or less independent mental functions which Thurstone called the primary mental abilities.

The primary abilities measured by this test are:

1. Number facility.
2. Verbal comprehension.
3. Spatial perception.
4. Work fluency.
5. Reasoning.
6. Rote memory.

Differential Aptitude Test Battery (DATB). Another test to measure the special abilities is Differential Aptitude Test Battery (DATB). This comprises eight tests:

1. Verbal Reasoning.
2. Numerical Ability.
3. Abstract Reasoning.

4. Space Relations.
5. Mechanical Reasoning.
6. Clerical Speed and Accuracy.
7. Language Usage: Spelling.
8. Language Usage: Grammar, punctuation and word usage.

General Aptitude Test Battery (GATB). Another test of the differential aptitude type is the General Aptitude Test Battery (GATB), developed by the United States Employment Service. It consists of 15 tests which cover 9 factors, such as intelligence, verbal aptitude, numerical aptitude, spatial aptitude, form perception, clerical perception, motor-coordination, finger dexterity and manual dexterity.

These sophisticated test batteries mentioned above give a much more clear picture of what special abilities a person has than the general intelligence tests.

19.6. LANDMARKS IN THE DEVELOPMENT OF TESTS

Robert Owen's Rating Scale	1826
Seguin's Form Boards	1842
Binet-Simon Scale	1905
Goddard Translation of Binet's Scale	1908
Courtis Practice Test in Arithmetic	1909
Thorndike Handwriting Scale	1910
Healy and Fernald Performance Test	1911
Hillegas Composition Scale	1912
Buckingham Spelling Scale	1915
Yerkes Point Scale	1915
Stanford Revision of the Binet-Simon Scale	1916
Army Group Tests, Stenquist Assembly Tests	1917
Seashore Tests of Musical Ability	1919
Rorschach Test	1921
Strong Vocational Interest Inventory	1927
Hildreth Readiness Test	1933
Murray Apperception Test	1935
Stanford-Binet Revision Scale	1937
Thurstone Primary Abilities Test	1938
Wechsler Scale	1937
Wechsler Adult Intelligence Scale	1955
Revised Version of Stanford Binet Test	1960

19.7. INTELLIGENCE TESTING IN INDIA: A BRIEF HISTORY OF EARLY TESTS

Verbal Individual Tests

1. Dr. H.C. Rice's Hindustani Tests. Dr. H.C. Rice of the Forman Christian College, Lahore, was one of the first to start this work in India in 1921. His is an adapted scale of the Binet scale in Urdu. These tests were published by Oxford University Press in 1929.

2. Dr. Kamat's Age Scale Revision Tests. In 1935, Dr. V.V. Kamat of Belgaum Training College followed up the Binet-Simon system with the Stanford Revision and adapted it in the age scale for Indian children knowing Kanarese and Marathi languages.

3. Stanford Hindustani Revision by Patna Training College, Patna.

4. Allahabad Intelligence Test for 11+ (in Hindi) by Dr. Sohan Lal, published by Kitabistan, Allahabad.

5. C.I.E. (Central Institute of Education) Test of Intelligence by Shri Udai Shanker, Central Institute of Education, Delhi, 1953.

Verbal Group Tests

1. Dr. J. Morays Test, 1927.

2. The Pasrur Group Intelligence Test (Urdu) by Prof. R.R. Kumria, of Central Training College, Lahore.

3. Group Test of Intelligence (Test No. 12), Bureau of Psychology, Allahabad.

4. Sohan Lal's Test, 1946.

5. Samuhik Manasik Yogyata Pariksha by Prof. S. Jalota, Banaras Hindu University, 1951.

6. Buddhi-Mapak Pariksha by Shri V.G. Jhingram, Dharam Samaj College, Aligarh, 1952. The test has been prepared both in Hindi and Urdu scripts.

7. C.I.E. Group Test of Intelligence by Prof. Udai Shankar of the Central Institute of Education, Delhi, 1953.

8. Jha's Group Tests by R.B. Pandit Lajja Shankar Jha, the late Principal of Teachers Training College, Banaras.

Non-Verbal Group Tests

1. Hindi adaptation of Dr. R.A.C. Oliver's Test for East Africa by E.A. Menzel, Bisrampur (M.P.)

2. Non-Verbal Group Test by T.C. Vicary and M. Draper, Union Christian Training College, Berhampore, Orissa.

Performance Test.

Dr. C.M. Bhatia's Battery of Performance Tests of Intelligence, 1945.

19.8. PROMINENT INSTITUTIONS AND ORGANISATIONS IN THE FIELD OF TESTING IN INDIA

1. National Council of Educational Research and Training (NCERT), New Delhi.

Types of tests developed by NCERT, may be broadly classified as under:

(1) Mental Ability Tests.
(2) Standard Achievement Tests.
(3) Teacher-Made Achievement Tests.
(4) General Aptitude Tests.
(5) Special Aptitude Tests.

2. Department of Education, Delhi University/Central Institute of Education, University of Delhi.
3. Departments of Education and Psychology of Indian Universities.
4. Agra Psychological Research Cell, Belanganj, Agra.
5. Directorate of Psychological Research, Ministry of Defence, Government of India.
6. State Institutes of Education, State Bureaus of Educational and Vocational Guidance.

19.9. I.Q. OF SOME FAMOUS MEN

(**Note:** Assumed and estimated on the basis of different measures since I.Q. tests were not available. Authenticity not confirmed. Still indicative of intelligence. Very Superior Intelligence)

John Stuart Mill: 1806-1873 (English economist and philosopher)	190
J.W. Von Goethe: 1749-1832 (German poet and dramatist)	185
S.T. Coleridge: 1772-1834 (English poet)	175
J.Q. Adams: 1767-1848 (6th U.S. President)	165
Alfred Tennyson: 1850-1892 (English poet)	155
David Hume: 1711-1776 (Scottish philosopher and historian)	155
William Wordsworth: 1770-1850 (English poet)	150
Francis Bacon: 1561-1626 (English philosopher)	145
Thomas Jefferson: 1743-1826 (3rd President of the U.S.A.)	145
John Milton: 1608-1674 (English poet)	145
Daniel Webster: 1782-1852 (American statesman and orator)	145

(No such study on India's famous men is readily available.)

19.10. USES OF INTELLIGENCE TESTS

1. Selection of student to a school.
2. Classification of students.
3. Selection of students to different courses.
4. Detection of superior and inferior intelligence.
5. Selection of suitable occupations.
6. Award of scholarships.
7. Determination of the optimum level of work.
8. Discovery of unusual cards.
9. Diagnosis of backwardness.

It may be remembered that intelligence tests are not all in all in measuring the capability of an individual and such should be used along with other instruments of measuring personality traits.

19.11. APTITUDE TESTS

According to Bingham and Freeman, aptitude tests are tests that will predict success to some degree. It may be mentioned here that aptitudes are relatively constant.

Aptitude tests help us to measure the probability of success in an activity such as playing at piano, learning a language, etc.

Any definition of aptitude should be in terms of these characteristics: (*a*) ability to acquire the skill, information, etc., necessary for success, (*b*) readiness to acquire, (*c*) constancy, and (*d*) satisfaction in the job.

In many countries, tests of aptitudes for specific school subjects have been developed.

Tests of clerical aptitude, of mechanical aptitude and dexterity, of aptitude in art and music, aptitudes in professions have also been devised.

Aptitude tests are made by analysing the particular occupation or activity for which aptitude is to be measured and test items are then devised for revealing the component abilities. Tests of aptitude for law will include items which measure accurate recall, reading comprehension of legal material, skill in logic, and reasoning by analogy and by analysis.

Uses of Aptitude Tests

Aptitude tests serve the following functions.

Admissions. Aptitude tests can be used in admitting candidates for various types of professional training such as engineering, medicine and training etc.

Guidance. Aptitude tests can be used for the purpose of guidance in selecting subjects for studying in educational institutions.

Selection for Jobs. The employer can use aptitude tests for selecting persons for jobs. Perhaps for the time in India, selection of teachers on the basis of aptitudes (one of the measures) was envisaged by the Delhi Administration.

Specific Areas of Aptitude Tests

Among these may be mentioned as under:

1. Art Aptitude Test.
2. Clerical Aptitude Test.
3. Manual Aptitude Test.
4. Mechanical Aptitude Test.
5. Medical Aptitude Test.
6. Musical Aptitude Test.
7. Scholarly Aptitude Test.
8. Scientific Aptitude Test.
9. Teachers Aptitude Test.

Scholastic Aptitude Tests. Scholastic aptitude tests are helpful in giving educational and vocational guidance to students. *Froehick* and *Benson* think that we can use the results of scholastic aptitude tests in counselling students regarding vocational opportunities. Reading, writing and speaking abilities are invloved in various jobs and a student's scholastic aptitude is a fair measure of his chances for success in such jobs.

Students with superior scholastic aptitude should be preferred in admitting to colleges.

Scientific and classical courses require a higher level of scholastic aptitude on the part of the student.

Many scholastic aptitude tests have been constructed in America.

How to Measure Scholastic Aptitude

1. School Marks and Scholastic Aptitude. This is the traditional method of measuring aptitude.

2. Occupation of Parents and Scholastic Aptitude. McNemur tested the I.Q.s of children of parents following different occupations. He found that children of professional people (engineers, doctors, lawyers, etc.) got higher I.Q. at all age levels than children of clinical, skilled trade and retail business people. The lowest I.Q. was of the children of day labourers. This study indicated a positive relationship between the intelligence of the child and the occupational status of the father.

3. Teacher's Observation and Scholastic Aptitude. The following points may be observed:

(*i*) Rapidity in comprehending material of study.
(*ii*) Rapidity and accuracy in reading.
(*iii*) Ability in attaching new problems.
(*iv*) Large vocabulary.
(*v*) Eagerness to answer questions.
(*vi*) Deficiency in one or more skills.
(a negative criterion.)

4. Scholastic Aptitude Tests

The Yale Educational Aptitude Test. The battery contains tests designed to measure a person's relative aptitude or ability in the areas of: (1) Verbal facility; (2) Linguistic ability; (3) Verbal reasoning; (4) Quantitative reasoning; (5) Mathematical aptitude; (6) Spatial visualising; and (7) Mechanical ingenuity. On the basis of these aptitude tests, students are admitted to courses like social sciences, pure sciences, mathematics and applied sciences.

Mechanical Aptitude Tests. These tests are designed to measure fundamental aptitudes of tool usage, space visualization and shop arithmetic in the area of mechanical ability. In general there are two types of mechanical aptitude tests: (1) Performance tests in which the subject is expected to do something with special equipment and (2) Paper-and-pencil in which the responses are given on paper.

19.12. INTEREST TESTS

It is not possible to measure interest as an independent entity as it is related to general intelligence and special aptitudes and is determined partly by social environment of an individual and his opportunities to find out different kinds of activities. Interest is not as consistent as aptitude.

Educational interest inventories are intended to help pupils to choose their courses, curricula, and co-curricular activities. There are also vocational interest inventories. The names of Kuder and Strong may be mentioned in this field.

19.13. TABLE SHOWING THE CLASSIFICATION OF OCCUPATION ON THE BASIS OF INTELLIGENCE

Sl. No.	*Standard of Occupation*	*Names of Occupation*	*Intelligence Required*	*I.Q.*
1.	High professional and executive occupations	lawyer, principal (University and Secondary), manager of big concern, professor, scientist, successful politician.	genius, very superior, intelligence	Over 150
2.	Lower professional, technical and executive work	executive of a moderately large business, doctor, engineer etc.	superior intelligence	130 to 150
3.	Clerical, technical and highly skilled work	shorthand typist, bank clerk, salesman, photographer, etc.	high average intelligence	115 to 130
4.	Skilled work	typist, file clerk, carpenter, dress-maker, cashier.	average intelligence	100 to 115
5.	Semi-skilled occupations	number sorters, delivery man, Painter, baker, barber.	below average intelligence	85 to 100
6.	Unskilled repetition work	manual labour, packer.	backward and very backward	70 to 85

19.14. SUMMING UP

Many labels are attached to tests and lack of clarity in the naming of tests has created a lot of confusion. J. Rothney and B. Rones draw our attention to this fact when they remark, "Certain testing terms have traditionally been used together, thus, testers speak of clerical, mechanical, musical, and (more recently) scholastic aptitude, but they also use the term mental abilities, academic achievement, and subject—field performance or prognosis—frequently the same instrument is described as both a test of mental ability and a scholastic aptitude." They go on to point out that lack of clarity in definitions of terms makes a very great difference in actual counselling procedure. They stress that the label on the test is derived from the use to which the test is to be put.

According to Froehlick and Darley, three kinds of tests are needed nearly with all the students-tests of scholastic aptitude, achievement and interests. To quote Jane Warters, "Inclusion of intelligence tests is practically always recommended, that of achievement tests and of interest tests is usually recommended, that of personality tests is not often recommended and that provision for individual tests of intelligence and measures of special aptitudes is recommended for use with special cases when the training of workers and the financial resources of the school make their use practical."

Chapter 20

Presenting Measurement Results

20.1. STATISTICAL CONCEPTS

A variety of statistical concepts and techniques are used to interpret scores. When a test has been given, statistical procedures help to describe the performance of the learners. The same statistical methods provide information about the effectiveness of the test instrument. The purpose of this chapter is not to provide a comprehensive statistical treatment but to describe statistical ideas that form a foundation for the measurement concepts.

Population and Sample. In statistics population refers to an aggregate or group of people in a particular setting. For example, we are studying the Study Habits of 12th Grade Students in Delhi. Now for this investigation we are not likely to take all the students studying in the 12th grade in all the schools of Delhi for our study. Instead we would take only a limited number of cases representative of the total group and base our findings on that group (limited), for drawing inferences about the total group. All the students in the tenth grade studying in all the schools of Delhi, in this case would comprise the population, whereas a limited representative section of the total lot would constitute the sample.

Measurement. In educational psychology, we study differences in respect of student's personality traits, abilities, aptitudes etc. and we assign numbers according to some scale. This assigning of numbers in called measurement. There are two purposes of measurement. First purpose is to know the magnitude or quantity of the trait or thing possessed. The second purpose is to compare the quantities possessed.

For measuring we need a scale i.e. the rule according to which we assign numbers. Different types of scales are followed.

Variables and Constants. The term variable refers to a property whereby the members of a group differ from one another. The members of a group may differ with regard to sex, age, social status, intelligence, personality traits, attitudes towards certain issues, interest patterns etc. Such properties are termed as variables. The term constant, on the other hand, indicates a property whereby the members of a group do not differ from one another.

Classification. Classification implies that related data or facts or observations are grouped into categories or classes. Classification is of two types:

(*i*) Qualitative (*ii*) Quantitative.

Tabulation and Tables. Tabulation is the process of summarising data in the form of a table so that it is easily understood and a researcher or an individual interested in the data is quickly able to locate the desired information.

A statistical table is the logical listing of related quantitative data in vertical columns and horizontal rows of members with sufficient explanatory and qualifying words, phrases and statements in the form of titles, headings and notes to make clear the full meaning of the data and their origin.

An ideal table consists of the following main parts:

(1) Table No. (2), Title of the table, (3) Caption, (4) Stubs – brief and self-explanatory headings of horizontal rows, (5) Body of the table containing the numerical information, (6) Footnotes for explanation of any fact, and (7) Source or sources of information.

Discreete and Continuous Series. In discrete series data are presented in a way that exact measurements of units are clearly indicated. Data on facts like per family children, or per house rooms etc. are given in discrete series.

In continuous series measurements are only approximations and are expressed in class i.e. within certain limits. An example of continuous series is given below:

Marks Obtained (Class interval)	0-20	20-40	40-60	60-80	80-100
No of students *(Frequency)*	15	20	15	10	10

Score. Most of the educational measurements are on a continuous scale. The position of an individual on a test is generally indicated by a certain number. In statistics this term is called a score. Thus a score is the numerical statement of the position of an individual on a test. Suppose we want to know our student's performance in Social Studies. We would administer a test in social studies and assign marks to students. For the term marks in statistics, the term usually used is scores.

Frequency Distribution. When the scores of numerical data of a large number of individuals have been obtained, the scores must be arranged in some order so that useful results may be derived. Frequency distribution is an arrangement of numerical data according to size or magnitude. Frequency means the number of cases in a particular class interval or the number of objects or scores or individuals in a category when data are tabulated. For example we have marks of fifty students– 40, 43, 43 etc. Here frequency of 43 scores is 2 i.e. two students getting 43 marks each.

Re-arrangement of Test Scores for Position and Ranking Purposes. Let us study the set of thirty raw scores with repeated scores derived from a test given to a class of thirty students – 68, 80, 90, 90, 51, 69, 80, 75, 80, 50, 62, 74, 70, 70, 45, 68, 95, 58, 54, 40, 60, 90, 59, 55, 36, 40, 60, 55, 38, 35.

The array of scores ranges between a score of 35 to a maximum score of 95. The question is how any of the scores be conveyed to a parent in a manner that he would understand the academic standing of his child in relation to the peers. This is the crux of test scores interpretation.

Let us first re-arrange the scores in a descending order of magnitudes for purposes of ranks as shown in the table below:

Table 1: Rearrangement of Test Scores for Ranking Purposes

Scores	*Positions*	*Ranks*	*Scores*	*Positions*	*Ranks*	*Scores*	*Positions*	*Ranks*
95	1st	1	69	12th	12	54	22nd	22
90	2nd	3	68	13th	13	51	23rd	23
90	2nd	3	68	13th	13	50	24th	24
90	2nd	3	62	15th	15	45	25th	25
80	5th	6	60	16th	16.5	40	26th	26.5
80	5th	6	60	16th	16.5	40	26th	26.5
80	5th	6	59	18th	18	38	28th	28
75	8th	8	58	19th	19	36	29th	29
74	9th	9	55	20th	20.5	35	30th	30
70	10th	10.5	55	20th	20.5			
70	10th	10.5						

It will be seen from the above table that positioning of scores differs slightly from their ranking when such scores contain scores that occur more than once on the distribution of scores. For positioning, scores of equal magnitude are seen as ties and thus are given the same position, as in the scores of 90, 80, 70, 68, 60, 55, and 40. However, the next score is put in a position that would have taken care of the repeated scores of the higher scores as if they occur in different positions. So the score of 80 has a position of 5th rather than 3rd. In ranking the average of the different positions the repeated scores would have taken as individual scores in their own right is taken as the rank for the score. Thus, the score of 90 is ranked 3rd. This is arrived at by finding the average of the positions, 2nd, 3rd and 4th i.e. $\frac{2+3+4}{3} = 3$ which would have normally been 3 occupied by the three scores of 90. Further, the score of 80 which also occurs. Thrice, receives a rank of 6 from the average of the position, 5, 6 and 7 i.e. $\frac{5+6+7}{3} = 16$. However, in general, we use the term positioning which is also taken as ranking.

20.2. CENTRAL TENDENCY AND MEASURES OF CENTRAL TENDENCY

If we take the achievement scores of the students of a class and arrange them in a frequency distribution, we can easily find that there are a few students who either score very high or very low. The marks of most of the students lie somewhere between the highest and the lowest scores of the entire class. This tendency of a group of distribution is called as the central tendency of distribution and the typical score lying between the extremes and shared by most of the students is referred to as *measure of central tendency.*

In the frequency distribution the items tend to cluster about a point somewhere in between the extremes.

A measure of central tendency may be defined as *single expression of the net result of a complex group.* It serves two purposes. Firstly, it gives the concise picture of a large group. Secondly, it provides the basis of comparison with other groups.

Measures of Central Tendency. Following are the measures of central tendency (i) Mean; (ii) Median; (iii) Mode; (iv) Geometric mean; (v) Harmonic mean. However mean, median and mode measures of central tendency are commonly used.

The mean (M). It is the most simple and useful measure of central tendency. It may be defined as the sum of all the values of the items in a series divided by the number of items. It is designated by the symbol *M*.

Formula for the Calculation of the Mean. Using $X_1, X_2, X_3, \ldots X_N$ to represent N items the definition be written as:

$$M = \frac{X_1 + X_2 + X_3 + X_N}{N}$$

In brief it can be written as

$M = \frac{\Sigma X}{N}$ where Σ stands for sum of the values of the items and N for the number of items.

It is very easy to calculate mean for short series. For example six students secured 40, 45, 50, 55, 60, 68 scores in an arithmetic test. Here N is six and ΣX is equal to 40+45+50+55+60+68 = 318. Now apply formula $M = \frac{\Sigma X}{M}$; we have 318/6 = 53. But the calculation is laborious when the series is long. It is, therefore, necessary that we should have some short-cut method for calculating mean.

Calculation of Mean of Ungrouped Data. The score of 28 students in economics are given in the following table. The number of students having each score is shown in column f.

Table 2:

Scores X	f	fX	Scores X	f	fX
72	1	72	55	2	110
69	1	69	54	1	54
68	1	68	53	2	106
64	1	64	52	1	52
63	1	63	51	1	51
62	1	62	50	1	50
60	1	60	49	3	147
59	1	59	47	1	47
58	1	58	44	1	44
57	2	114	41	1	41
56	2	112	38	1	38
			$\Sigma f = 28$		$\Sigma fX = 1541$

In the above table column X shows scores; column f shows the number of students securing each score and column fX shows the product of column X and f. Applying the formula $M = \frac{\Sigma fX}{N}$ we get

$$M = \frac{1541}{28} = 55.03.$$

Table 3. Calculation of Mean in Grouped Data

Scores X	Mid. Value X	f	fX'
71 - 80	75.5	1	75.5
61 - 70	65.5	5	327.5
51 - 60	55.5	14	777.0
41 - 50	45.5	7	318.5
31 - 40	35.5	1	35.5
		$\Sigma f = 28$ $\Sigma fx' =$	1534.0

Substituting the values in formula $M = \frac{\Sigma fX'}{N}$ we have

$$M = \frac{1534}{28} = 54.70$$

Short-Cut Method for Calculating Mean. In the above method, calculating the mean involves considerable work of addition when the series is large and each number has several digits. Therefore, for saving labour and time, the short-cut method is used. For using this method mid-point of any class interval is taken as assumed mean and deviations in terms of class intervals are found out from this interval of assumed mean. Proper algebraic signs are put down with the deviation. Algebraic sum multiplied by class interval is divided by the number of cases. When this is added to assumed mean, it gives the required mean.

Symbolically $M = AM + \frac{\Sigma d}{N} \times i$

Where AM = Assumed Mean

Σ stands for sum of

d is the deviation in terms of class intervals from the interval in which the AM lies.

i = Size of class interval
N = Σt = Total number of Cases
Calculation of mean by this method is as follows:

Table 4: Calculation of Mean by Short Cut Method

	Scores X	f	d	fd
	71 - 80	1	2	2
	61 - 70	5	1	5
Let AM be 55.5	61 - 60	14	0	0
	41 - 50	7	–1	–7
	31 - 40	1	–2	–2
		28		–2

Now according to formula $M = AM + \frac{\Sigma fd}{N} \times i$.

$M = 55.5 - 2 \times 10/28 = 55.5 - 5/7.$
$= 55.5 - 0.714$
$= 55.5 - 0.7 = 54.8$

Calculation of Mean : Example No. 2 — Calculate the mean from the following data:

Table 5: Calculation of Mean by Short Cut Method

Class interval	*Frequency*
195 - 199	1
190 - 194	2
185 - 189	4
180 - 184	5
175 - 179	8
170 -174	10
165 - 169	6
160 - 164	4
155 - 159	4
150 - 154	2
145 - 149	3
140 - 144	1
	N = 50

Table 6: Solution

Class Interval Scores	*f*	*d*	*fd*
195 - 199	1	5	5
190 - 194	2	4	8
185 - 189	4	3	12
180 - 184	5	2	10
175 - 179	8	1	8
			+43
170 - 174	10	0	0
165 - 169	6	−1	− 6
160 - 164	4	−2	− 8
155 - 159	4	−3	−12
150 - 154	2	−4	− 8
145 - 149	3	−5	−15
140 - 144	1	−6	− 6
			−55

Assumed Mean = 172.0

According to Formula $M = AM + \frac{\sum fd}{N} \times i$

Here i 5 $\frac{Fd}{-12}$

$$AM = \frac{-55+43}{50} \times 5 = \frac{-12}{50} \times 5 = -.24 \times 5 = 1.2$$

Ans. M = 172 - 1.2 = 170.8

Merits of the Use of Mean

1. It is easy to understand.
2. It is easy to calculate.
3. It utilizes the entire data in the group.
4. Aggregate can be calculated if the number of items and the mean are known.
5. It is amenable to algebraic manipulation. It is useful in computing standard deviation and correlation, etc.
6. It provides a good comparison.
7. It is rigidly defined.

Limitations

1. It can hardly be located by inspection while the median can be located.

2. In the absence of actual data it can mislead.

3. Abnormal difference between the highest and the lowest score would lead to fallacious conclusions.

4. If a single item of a series is missing, the mean cannot be calculated.

5. A mean gives greater importance to the bigger items of a series and less importance to the smaller items.

6. A mean sometimes gives such results as appear almost absurd, e.g. 4.3 children.

7. A mean can be used only in distributions that give absolute scores. It cannot be used with scores expressing grades or ranks qr order of students, such as A, B, C, D....

8. As the skewness of the distribution increases, the reliability of the mean decreases.

Median. It is the score or value of that central item that divides the series into two equal parts. It is the value of the item, in the series above and below which, lie 50 percent cases. If 13 students stand in order of height, the 7th student from either side shall be one whose height will be called median height.

Computing Median in Ungrouped Data. There are two situations n computing the medium from the ungrouped data (*i*) where N is 'odd' and where N is 'even'.

Example of odd data. Below are given mental ages of 9 students in a class. We are required to locate the median.

Mental Ages – 7, 10, 6, 8, 13, 9, 10, 11, 6

Solution. As a first step, we arrange the given data in the ascending order of values.

6, 6, 7, 8, 9, 10, 10, 11, 13

Now Median = N+1/2th item $= \frac{9+1}{2} =$ 5th item

Therefore median is 5th item i.e. 9. Clearly 9 is also the mid point in the above arrangement as four observations are below and four above this point.

Computing Median of 'even' items of Ungrouped Data. Mental age of 8 students is given and we are to find out the median mental age.

Mental ages 7, 10, 6, 8, 3, 9, 10, 11

Solution. First we arrange the data in the ascending order as under

6, 7, 8, 9, 10, 11, 13

Since the number is even, there will be two middle values in the array and their average will be the median.

Therefore Median = 4th Value + 5th Value/2 = $\frac{9+10}{2} = 9.5$

Clearly the number of observations below and above the median would now be four.

Table 7. Computing Median in a Frequency Distribution

Class intervals Scores	*Mid point X*	*f*
195-199	197	1
190-194	192	2
185-190	187	4
180-184	182	5
175-179	177	8
170-174	172	10
165-169	167	6
160-164	162	4
155-159	157	4
150-154	152	2
145-149	147	3
140-144	142	1
		N= 50
		N/2 = 25

Formula of Median = $l + \left(\frac{\frac{N}{2} - F}{fm}\right) i$

l is the lower limit of the class interval upon which the median lies.

$\frac{N}{2}$ is one half of the total number of scores

F is the sum of the scores on all intervals below l

fm is the frequency (number of scores) within the intervals upon which the median falls.

i is the length of the class interval.

Now let us illustrate the formula in Table 7

x = 169.5: $\frac{N}{2}$ = 50/2 = 25, F = 20, fm = 10 and i = 5

$$\text{Median} = 169.5 + \frac{25-20}{10} \times 5 = 169.5 + \frac{5}{10} \times 5 = 169.5 + 2.5 = 172.0$$

Table 8. Computation of the Median : Example from Garrett

Intervals	*f*
40-44	3
35-39	4
30-34	8
25-29	10 - 25
20-24	9 - 15
15-19	6
	N=40

Take $\frac{1}{2}$ of N. Count the distribution from the lower end until the interval containing the median is reached. In the above Table N/2 = 20. Count the distribution from interval 15-19. We locate the median in the interval 25-29. The two lowest intervals contain 6+9 or 15 fs. It is clear from this cumulated frequency that the 20th score must fall on interval 25-25.

Apply the formula for median in which

(i) l = lower limit of interval on which median lies i.e. 24.5

(ii) N/2 = 1/2 of the number of scores i.e. 40/2 = 20

(iii) f=Sum of scores on intervals below l i.e. 6 + 9 = 15

(iv) fm=frequency on the interval containing the Median =10

(v) i = length of the interval i.e. 5

Substituting the formula $l + i \dfrac{\left(\frac{N}{2} - f\right)}{fm}$

$$\text{Median} = 24.5 + 5\left(\frac{20-15}{10}\right)$$

$$= 24.5 + 5 \times \frac{5}{10} = 24.5 + \frac{5}{2}$$

$$= 27.00$$

Merits of the Median

1. It is rigidly defined. Therefore, it is an ideal average.
2. It is not influenced by extreme variations.
3. It is easily understood.
4. It is possible to determine it without the knowledge of the magnitude of extreme item provided the member of items is known.
5. It can be used not only with distribution that give absolute scores

such as 30, 32, 35 etc., but also with scores expressing grades or ranks or order of students, such as A, B, C, D...

6. Median is preferable when the units of measurement are unequal. Median does not assume equality of units, whereas the mean does assume it.

7. Median never gives absurd or fallacious results.

Limitations of the Median

1. It is not suitable for algebraic treatment.
2. The arrangement of the items in the ascending or descending order becomes very tedious sometimes.
3. A median is more likely to be affected by the fluctuations of samples than the mean.
4. A median may not be the representative of the series when there are wide variations between the values of different items.
5. It cannot be used for computing other statistical measures such as S.D. or coefficient of correlation.

Mode. Mode is the value of the score which occurs the largest number of times in a distribution i.e. the score obtained by the maximum number of students. To illustrate this, let us suppose that 10 students take a test and their scores are 47, 47, 49, 50, 52, 65, 70, 70, 70 and 80. Here the mode is 70 and it occurs thrice and the other scores occur once or twice.

Computation of the Mode. Mode = 3 Median – 2 Mean

In a particular distribution, if median is 26 and mean is 26.5, then the mode is $= 3 \times 26 - 2 \times 26.5 = 78 - 53 = 25$

In an ideal (normal) distribution, all the three i.e. mean, median and mode have the same value.

Merits of the Mode

1. It can easily be located by mere inspection.
2. It eliminates extreme variations.
3. Knowledge of extreme item is not necessary. It can be determined even when the distribution is open-ended.
4. For the determination of mode, it is not necessary to know the values of all the items of a series.
5. It is commonly understood.

Limitations of the Mode

1. It is not based on all the observations of a series.
2. It is affected by changes in the grouping scheme.
3. It may be unrepresentative in many cases.

4. It is not capable of further mathematical treatment.
5. It is ill-defined and indefinite and so untrustworthy.

Table 9. Calculation of Mean, Median and Mode from a given distribution

Class Interval	*Frequency*
95 - 99	1
90 - 94	6
85 - 89	8
80 - 84	33
75 - 79	40
70 - 74	50
65 - 69	26
60 - 64	14
55 - 59	10
50 - 54	4
45 - 49	6
40 - 44	2

Table 10. Solution

Class interval	*f*	*d*	*fd*	*cfc*
95 - 99	1	5	5	200
90 - 94	6	4	24	199
85 - 89	8	3	24	193
80 - 84	33	2	66	185
75 - 79	40	1	40	152
70 - 74	50	0	0	112
65 - 69	26	-1	-26	62
60 - 64	14	-2	-28	36
55 - 59	10	-3	-30	22
50 - 54	6	-4	-24	12
45 - 49	4	-5	-20	6
40 - 44	2	-6	-12	2
	200		$\Sigma fd = 19$	

Mean = Let the assumed mean (A.M.) to be 72 i.e. midpoint of class intervals 70-74

$$\text{Mean} = \text{A.M.} + \frac{\sum fd}{N} xi$$

$$= 72 + \frac{19x3}{200} = 72 + 0.475 = 72.475 = 72.5$$

Mean = 72.5

(Note : We can take the A.M. in any class interval.)

Calculation for Median. We have already worked out the cumulative frequencies for this purpose

$$\text{Median} = l + \frac{\left(\frac{N}{2} - C\right)}{fn} \times 2$$

(*i*) l is the lower limit of class interval, where median lies.
(*ii*) fn is the frequency of median class
(*iii*) N is the total number of cases
(*iv*) C is the cumulative frequency upto the median class

In the case Median i.e. $\frac{N}{2}$ or $\frac{200}{2}$ = 100 or 100th case will lie in the class interval 70 – 74 which becomes our median class

$$\text{Therefore Median } 69.5 + \frac{\left(\frac{200}{2} - 62\right)}{50} \times 5$$

$$= 69.5 + \frac{100 - 62}{50} \times 5$$

$$= 69.5 + \frac{38}{50} \times 5$$

or 69.5 + 3.8 or 73.3

Median = 73.3
Mode = 3 Median – 2 Mean
= 3 × 73.3 – 2 × 72.5
= 219.9 – 145.0
= 74.9

Ans. Mean = 72.5; Median = 73.3; Mode=74.9

WHEN TO USE THE MEAN, MEDIAN AND MODE

When to use the Mean

1. We compute mean for the given data when a reliable and accurate measure of central tendency is needed.
2. We use mean for the computation of various statistics like Standard Deviation and Co-efficient of Correlation etc.
3. We calculate mean when the series have no extreme items and each score carries equal weight in determining the central tendency.

When to use the Median

1. Median is used when the exact mid-point of the distribution is desired.
2. We use median when a series contains extreme scores.
3. Median is the most reliable measure in case of an open end distribution (incomplete distribution 80 and above or 20 and below etc.)
4. We compute median when we have suitable graphs like frequency curve, polygon etc.

When to use the Mode

1. Mode is used where quick and approximate measure of central tendency is desired.
2. Mode is used when we need to know the most often recurring score or value of the item in a series.
3. We compute mode when we have a graphical representation of the distribution.

20.3. MEASURES OF VARIABILITY OR DISPERSION

Measures of central tendency – mean, median and mode provide central value or typical representative of a set of scores as a whole. But the central value or an average alone cannot describe the distribution adequately. By comparing typical representative of the different sets of scores we can compare the achievement of two groups. But these representative numbers do not show how the individual scores are spread out. For example, let us consider the scores of two groups of students on the same test.

Scores of first group : 20, 80, 60, 45, 40, 55

Scores of second group : 50, 45, 45, 40, 55, 65

Here both groups have the same mean score of 60. But a close examination reveals that the two sets of scores differ widely from one another. The scores in the first group range from 20 to 80 while in the second group, they range from 40 to 65. This difference in range shows that the students in the second group are more homogeneous in scoring than those in the first. The scores fall around the same point on the scale, and the *variability, dispersion* or *scatteredness* of scores is relatively less. Thus measures of variability or *dispersion* help us in studying the extent to which observations are scattered about the average or the central value.

Following four measures are commonly used for measuring the variability or dispersion.

1. The Range (R)
2. The Quartile Deviation (Q)
3. The Average or Mean Deviation (AD)
4. The Standard Deviation (SD)

Range. Range is the simplest measure of variability or dispersion. It is calculated by subtracting the lowest score in the series from the highest score. Range may be defined as the difference between the values of the extremes i.e. the highest and the lowest value of the data under consideration.

Quartile Deviation. Quartile deviation or Q is also called Semi Interquartile Range. It may be defined as one-half the distance between Q_3 or 75th percentile and Q_1 or 25th percentile in a frequency distribution. If we know Q_3 and Q_1 we can find out the quartile deviation or Q by the formula $Q = \frac{Q_3 - Q_1}{2}$

Average Deviation (A.D.) or Mean Deviation

Quartile deviation is based on quartiles and affords a general idea of the variability of a group without taking account of each and every item. When we want to take account of all the items we use Average Deviation. It can be defined as the average of the deviation of the group measured from an average (Mean, Median or Mode) taking all the deviations as positive. In actual calculation we find some of the deviations positive and some negative. But for the purpose of calculation of Average Deviation we take all the deviations as positive. Average Deviation for ungrouped data can be calculated with the help of following formula :

Average Deviation or AD = $\Sigma |x|$ where Σ stands for sum and $|x|$ for deviation from mean, median or mode, ignoring the sign.

Table 11. Calculation of Average Deviation for Ungrouped Data

%Scores X	*lxl*
72	3.5
70	1.5
70	1.5
69	0.5
69	0.5
68	0.5
67	1.5
67	1.5
67	1.5
66	2.5
$\Sigma =$ 685	15.0

$$\text{Mean} = \frac{685}{10} = 68.5$$

To find out Average deviation we apply the formula $AD = \frac{\Sigma\, lxl}{N}$ substituting the values in the formula we have

$$AD = \frac{15}{10} = 1.5$$

Table 12. Calculation of AD for Grouped Data

% Scores	*Md. val*	*f*	$\|x\|$	$f\,\|x\|$
91—100	95.5	3	23.00	69.00
81—90	85.5	5	13.00	65.00
71—80	75.5	15	3.00	45.00
61—70	65.5	18	7.00	126.00
51—60	55.5	3	17.00	51.00
		44		356.00

Mean = 72.5

Here we apply the formula for AD $- \frac{\Sigma\, flxl}{N}$ substituting the values

we have, $AD = \frac{356}{44} = 8.1$

Using A.D.

(i) When it is desired to weigh all deviations from the mean according to their size.

(ii) When extreme deviations would influence SD unduly.

Standard Deviation or SD

While calculating the Average Deviation we ignore the signs. An alternative method for eliminating the signs is to square up each deviation. We employ this method for the calculation of standard deviation. For the calculation of SD one thing is certain that it is calculated from mean alonc. Conventional symbol used for SD is Greek letter sigma (σ). Standard deviation may be defined as the square root of the sum of the squares of the deviations calculated for each item.

Formula used for the calculation of SD for ungrouped data is

$\sqrt{\frac{\Sigma d^2}{n}}$ and for grouped data $\sqrt{\frac{\Sigma f d^2}{n} - \left(\frac{fd}{n}\right)^2} \times i$

wherc d is the deviation from the mean.

Table 13. Calculation of Standard Deviation for Ungrouped Data

Scores	*d*	d^2
72	3.5	12.25
70	1.5	2.25
70	1.5	2.25
69	0.5	.25
69	0.5	.25
68	–0.5	.25
67	–1.5	2.25
67	–1.5	2.25
67	–1.5	2.25
66	–2.5	6.25
	0	30.50

M 68.5

Substituting the values in the formula $\sqrt{\frac{\Sigma d^2}{n}}$ we get

SD or $\sigma\sqrt{\frac{305}{10}} = \sqrt{3.05}$

1.75

Table 14. Calculation of Standard Deviation for Grouped Data

Scores	*f*	*d*	*fd*	fd^2
91—100	3	2	6	+12
81—90	5	1	5	+ 5
71—80	15	0	0	0
61—70	18	−1	−18	+18
51--60	3	−2	− 6	+12
	44		−13	47

Substituting the values in the formula $\sqrt{\frac{\Sigma fd^2}{n} - \left(\frac{\Sigma fd}{n}\right)^2} \times i$

$$\sigma = \sqrt{\tfrac{47}{44} - \left(\tfrac{-13}{44}\right)^2} \text{x} 10$$

$$= \sqrt{1.07 - (-.3)^2} \text{x} 10$$

$$= \sqrt{1.07 - 0.09} \text{x} 10$$

$$= \sqrt{0.98} \times 10$$

$$= 0.999 \times 10$$

$$= 9.9$$

Use the SD

(1) When the statistic having the greatest stability is sought.

(2) When the extreme deviations should exercise a proportionally greater effect upon the variability.

(3) When coefficient of correlation and other statistics are subsequently to be computed.

Percentiles and Percentile Ranks. Robert L. Ebel and David A. Frisbie explain the term percentile rank as under.

The percentile rank of a particular test score can be defined in three similar but significantly different ways. It is the percentage of scores in a distribution of scores that:

1. is below the given score, or
2. is the same as or below the given score, or
3. is below the midpoint of the score interval of the given score.

Table 15 shows the effects of using each of these different definitions to compute the percentile ranks of 5 hypothetical scores. The highest score gets a percentile rank of only 80 under definition 1. The lowest score gets a percentile rank of 20 under definition 2. The median score gets a percentile rank of 40 under definition 1 and of 60 under definition 2. But under definition 3 the median score gets a percentile rank of 50, as it should in a symmetric distribution of scores. In addition, the highest and lowest scores are both the same distance from the extremes of the percentile rank scale, as they also should be. For these reasons, definition 3 is preferred and we will use it here.

There are seven steps in the process of computing the percentile rank of a given score in a particular distribution using definition 3.

Table 15. Effect of Different Definitions of Percentile Ranks

Score	*1*	2	*3*
5	80	100	90
4	60	80	70
3	40	60	50
2	20	40	30
1	0	20	10

1. Prepare a frequency distribution.
2. Beginning with the lowest score, add successive frequency values to obtain a column of cumulative frequencies.
3. For the given score, identify the cumulative frequency upto but not including, the score.
4. For the same given score, divide its frequency by 2.
5. Add the values from steps 3 and 4
6. Divide the sum from step 5 by the total number of scores.
7. Multiply the result by 100 to obtain a percentile rank (rounded to the nearest whole number).

Table 15 illustrates the computation of percentile ranks for the spelling scores from the table of spelling. Notice that the score scale extends from one score below the lowest score obtained to the highest score obtained. And the scale always includes all possible scores between the extremes, even when no student may have actually obtained some of those scores. The number of students who received each of the scores is shown in the second column of the table.

The third column gives a cumulative frequency for each score. It is calculated by counting the number of scores lower than the given score and adding the frequency at that score point. Consider the score 19, for example. There are 11 scores lower than 19 and four scores of 19. So we get a cumulative frequency of 15.

Table 16. Scores of 30 students on a 25 – item Spelling Test and Computation of Percentile Ranks

Aruna	16	Deepa	20	Jagdish	20
Sita	19	Gary	17	Pant	17
Ram	20	Kishan	18	Vedi	23
Sohan	17	Sarita	21	Biala	23
Sham	21	Suman	14	Biswas	19
Carmille	24	Shruti	19	Surindra	22
Donald	15	Smridhi	22	Ravindra	21
Satish	18	Sanjay	18	Kiran	19
Aslam	20	Aarti	21	Nidhi	21
Singh	16	Pramila	20	Rajat	15

(Adapted from Robert L. Ebel and David A. Frisbie)

To obtain the percentile rank for a score of 19, the value in the fourth column, we proceed as follows. Take the cumulative frequency of scores below 19 (which is 11) and add to it half of the frequencies at a score of 19 (one-half of 4 is 2). The sum, 13, is divided by 30 (the number of scores) to yield 0.433. That quotient is multiplied by 100 (43.3) and then rounded to obtain 43. In summary, we take half the scores at the given score value plus all the scores below, we divide that sum by the total number of scores, and we change the result to a rounded percentage value.

Table 17. Computation of Percentile Ranks

Score	*Frequency*	*Cumulative Frequency*	*Percentile Rank*
24	1	30	98
23	2	29	93
22	2	27	87
21	5	25	75
20	5	20	58
19	4	15	43
18	3	11	32
17	3	8	22
16	2	5	13
15	2	3	7
14	1	1	2
13	0	0	–

20.4. COEFFICIENT OF CORRELATION

When we have two sets of scores from the same group of students, it is desirable to know the degree to which the groups are related. A teacher may be interested in the relationship between:

(*i*) The Science test scores and the scores in other school subjects;
(*ii*) The ability of a student to play a game and his scholastic achievement;
(*iii*) Student's physical fitness and the scholastic achievement;
(*iv*) Student's scholastic achievement and intelligence;
(*v*) The shape of student's head and intelligence;
(*vi*) Student's speed in reading and ability for abstract thinking;
(*vii*) Student's ability to memorise and chronological age; and so on.

The relationship among abilities can be studied by the method of correlation. It is a method of summarising the relationship between two sets of data.

Correlation may be defined as the relationship or interdependence between two variables.

The relationship between two sets of test scores can be described mathematically by the co-efficient of correlation. Coefficient of correlation is expressed by a decimal fraction called 'r' which may vary along a scale from .00 to ±1.00

A coefficient of correlation is a single number indicating the *going togetherness* of two variables.

Nature of Relationships: Positive, Negative and Zero

(*a*) If the relative position of each student in a sample is exactly the same in one test as in the other, the relationship is perfect and positive and the coefficient of correlation is 1.00. Here, the two variables vary together in the same direction.

(*b*) If the relative position of each student in a sample is exactly in the reverse order in one test as in the other, the relationship is perfect but negative and the coefficient of correlation is – 1.00.

Here, the two variables vary together in the opposite direction.

(*c*) If in two tests, there is no correspondence between the two sets of the scores achieved by students in a sample, there is no systematic relationship and the coefficient of correlation is zero.

Degrees of Correlation. The coefficient of correlation varies from +1.00 (perfect positive) to – 1.00 (perfect negative) through .00 (zero correlation). The extreme values and zero correlation are rarely obtained in behavioural sciences; but high (such as .9, .80 – .75 etc.) and low (such as .2, –.15, .10 etc.) values are common. Positive coefficients range from .00 upto 1.00 and negative coefficients from –1.00 upto .00. Coefficients of – .30, – .50 – .80, or – .90 indicate increasing degrees or negative or inverse relationship, while coefficients of .30, .50, .80 or .90 indicate increasing degrees of positive relationship.

Interpreting the Correlation Coefficient. While interpreting the coefficient of correlation, the following points need to be considered:

(*i*) Sign — the direction of relationship;
(*ii*) Size or Magnitude — the degree or closeness of the relationship;
(*iii*) Significance.

The positive sign indicates a direct relationship. It shows that there is a tendency for the two series (variables) to vary in the same direction. The negative sign indicates an inverse relationship. It shows that there is a tendency for the two series (variables) to vary in the opposite directions.

It is the size or magnitude and not the sign of the coefficient which gives us a clue to the closeness or degree of relationship. A zero coefficient indicates no consistent relationship whatsoever, while – .95 and .95 both indicate equally close relationship.

The coefficients of correlation are computed in order to determine whether there is *any* correlation (over and above chance relationship) between two variables and, if so, to determine the significance of the degree or closeness of relationship.

The following classification may be useful in interpreting a coefficient of correlation.

(*i*)	r from ± .00 to ± .20	denotes an indifferent, negligible relationship;
(*ii*)	r from ± .20 to ± .40	denotes a definite but low, slight relationship;
(*iii*)	r from ± .40 to ± .70	denotes a substantial, marked relationship;
(*iv*)	r from ± .70 to ± .99	denotes a high to very high relationship;
(*v*)	r of ± 1.00	denotes a perfect relationship.

This classification is broad and tentative, and can only be accepted as a general guide with certain reservations. A correlation coefficient is always to be judged with reference to the conditions under which it is obtained and the objectives of the experiment.

Uses of Correlation Coefficient

1. It indicates the nature of the relationship between two variables.
2. It predicts the value of one variable from another. We can often predict from a battery of aptitude tests the probable success of an individual who plans to enter a given trade or profession. Advice on such a basis is measurably better than subjective judgement.
3. It is useful in validating a test; e.g., a group intelligence test.
4. It is useful in determining the reliability of a test.
5. It gives us an indication of the degree of the objectivity of a test.
6. It can answer the validity of arguments for or against a statement or a belief; e.g., Men are more intelligent than women.
7. It is helpful in educational and vocational guidance, prognosis, in the selection of workers in office or factory, and in educational decision-making.

Calculation of Correlation. Coefficient of correlation is denoted by the letter r. These are several methods of finding the coefficient of correlation between two series of measures. However, two methods are commonly used. One is Karl Pearson's Product Method and the other is Spearman Rank-Difference Method.

Karl Pearson calculated the coefficient by dividing the product of all the deviations of each pair of observations or scores from their respective means by the product of the standard deviations of the two variables and the number of items. His formula can be written as

$$r = \Sigma\, xy / n\sigma x\sigma y$$

(whereΣxy stands for the sum of the product of the deviation of each pair of scores). n is the number of items and, σx, σy are the standard deviations of both variables.

Example. Calculate the coefficient of correlation for the Scores of 10 students in Physics and Maths.

(Deviation calculated from actual mean).

Table 18. Calculation of Coefficient of Correlation

Students	*Scores (X) Physics*	*x*	*x^2*	*Scores (Y)*	*y Maths*	*y'*	*xy*
A	88	8	64	65	5	25	40
B	87	7	49	69	9	81	63
C	85	5	25	71	11	121	55
D	84	4	16	59	– 1	1	– 4
E	81	1	1	55	– 5	25	– 5
F	79	–1	1	40	–20	400	20
G	76	–4	16	61	1	1	– 4
H	75	–5	25	60	0	0	0
I	73	–7	49	57	–3	9	21
J	72	–8	64	63	3	9	–24

$\Sigma X = 800$ $\Sigma x^2 = 310$ $\Sigma Y = 600$ $\Sigma y^2 = 672$ $\Sigma xy = 162$

Mean X = 80 $\sigma x = 310/10$, Mean Y = 60 $\sigma y = 672/10$

Substituting the value in Karl Pearson's formula

$$r = \frac{\Sigma\, xy}{n\sigma x\sigma y} \text{ weget}$$

$$r = 10x \frac{162}{\sqrt{\frac{310}{10}}\sqrt{\frac{672}{10}}}$$

$$= \frac{162}{10x\sqrt{31}x\sqrt{67.2}}$$

$$= \frac{162}{10 \times 5.56 \times 67.2}$$

$$= \frac{162}{455.4} = 0.355$$

When we calculate deviations from the assumed mean we use the following formula for the calculation of coefficient of correlation.

$$r = \frac{\frac{\Sigma xy}{n} - \frac{\Sigma x}{n} \times \frac{\Sigma y}{n}}{\sigma x \times \sigma y}$$

Table 19. Calculation of coefficient of correlation for the data of previous table from the deviations taken from assumed mean.

%Boys	Scores (X) Physics	x	x^2	Scores (Y) Maths	y	y^2	xy
A	88	7	49	65	4	16	28
B	87	6	36	69	8	64	48
C	85	4	16	71	10	100	40
D	84	3	9	59	– 2	4	– 6
E	81	0	0	55	– 6	36	0
F	79	–2	4	40	–21	441	42
G	76	–5	25	61	0	0	0
H	75	–6	36	60	– 1	1	6
I	73	–8	64	57	– 4	16	32
J	72	–9	81	63	2	4	–18
N=10		–10	320		–10	682	172%

Substituting the value in the formula

$$r = \frac{\frac{\Sigma xy}{n} \frac{\Sigma x}{n} \frac{\Sigma y}{n}}{\sigma x \times \sigma y} \text{ weget}$$

$$= \frac{172}{10} - \left(-\frac{10}{10}\right)\left(-\frac{10}{10}\right)$$

$$r = \sqrt{\frac{320}{10}} - \left(-\frac{10}{10}\right)^2 \times \sqrt{\frac{682}{10}} - \left(\frac{-10}{10}\right)^2$$

$$= \frac{17.2 - (-1)(-1)}{\sqrt{32 - (-1)^2} \times 68.2 - (-1)^2}$$

$$= \frac{17.2 - 1}{\sqrt{32 - 1}\sqrt{68.2 - 1}}$$

$$= \frac{16.2}{\sqrt{31} \times \sqrt{67.2}}$$

$$= \frac{16.2}{5.56 \times 8.19}$$

Ans. $r = \frac{16.2}{455.4} = 0.355$

Correlation Coefficient by Rank Differences. In this method we rank the individual scores on both the scores. In both the variables we give 1 to the student who gets the highest scores. Then we find the difference for the ranks.

$$P = 1 - \frac{\Sigma D^2}{N(N-1)}$$

where Σ stands for the sum and D^2 is the square of each rank difference. N is the number of items. Let us consider the following example.

Table 20. Calculation of Correlation Coefficient by Rank Difference Method

Students	*Scores in Maths*	*Rank*	*Scores in Music*	*Rank*	*Rank Dif. D*	*Square Dif. D^2*
A	5	6	21	4	2	4
B	15	4	14	5	1	1
C	10	5	28	3	2	4
D	20	3	7	6	3	9
E	25	2	35	2	0	0
F	30	1	42	1	0	0
						18

Substituting the values in the formula

$$= 1 - \frac{\Sigma D^2}{N(N-1)}$$

$$\text{we have} = P = \frac{18}{6(6-1)}$$

$$= 1 - \frac{18}{6 \times 5}$$

$$= 1 - \frac{18}{30}$$

$$= 1 - \frac{3}{5}$$

$$= 1 = 0.6 = 0.4$$

20.5. NORMAL PROBABILITY CURVE (NPC)

If we observe the frequency distribution of students marks in any examination, we will find that the maximum frequencies are in the middle while towards the end and the beginning, the frequencies are low. For example, in an examination result of English, we find that only a few students will get marks very high or very low, while a great majority have their marks in the middle of the range. If we examine a very large number of students we will find that the distribution of these scores will be very similar to a mathematical normal curve. On account of this, we say that the achievement of students in English is normally distributed. Almost every human trait – height, weight, intelligence, speed of work, even errors in measurement—are normally distributed.

The normal probability curve is a perfect bell-shaped bilaterally symmetrical curve wherein the measures are concentrated closely around the centre and taper off from this central high crest to the left and right. These are relatively few measures at the low-score-end of the scale; an increasing number upto a maximum at the central position and a progressive falling-off towards the high-score of the scale.

The following figure shows the Normal Probability Curve

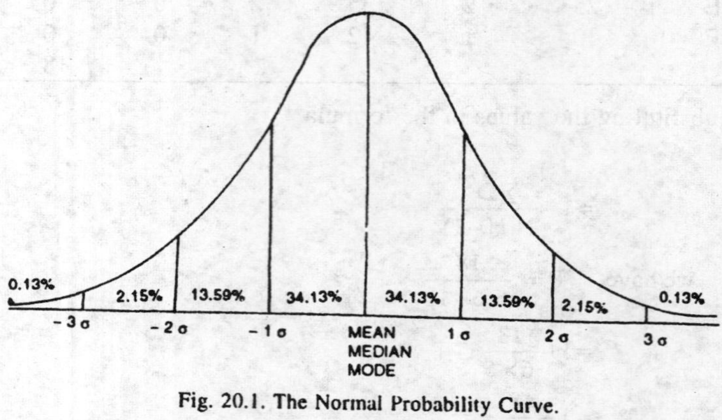

Fig. 20.1. The Normal Probability Curve.

Properties of Normal Probability Curve

(*i*) It is perfectly bilateral symmetrical about the mean, the median and the mode; i.e., all these coincide exactly in the middle of the Normal Probability Curve.

(*ii*) From the maximum point at the mean of Normal Probability Curve, the height of the curve declines as we go in either direction form the mean. This falling-off is slow, then rapid and then slow again.

(*iii*) Theoretically, the curve never touches the base line. Its tails approach but never reach the base line. Hence the range is unlimited.

(*iv*) The points of inflection (the points where the curvature changes its direction) are each ±1 SD from the mean ordinate.

(*v*) The height of the curve at a distance of 1 SD, 2 SD and 3 SD from the mean on both sides is 60.7%, 13.5% and 1.1% respectively of the height at the mean.

(*vi*) In a normal distribution, the mean equals the median exactly and the skewness is zero.

Areas Under the Normal Probability Curve

The distances, always in units of SD, are measured on the base line of the normal curve from the mean as origin.

The number of cases in the normal distribution between the mean and the ordinate erected at the distances of $\pm 1\sigma$, $\pm 2\sigma$ and $\pm 3\sigma$ is shown below:

(*i*) Between mean and 1σ	: 34.13%	i.e., 3413 cases in 10,000
(*ii*) Between mean and -1σ	: 34.13%	i.e., 3413 cases in 10,000
(*iii*) Between 16 and 2σ	: 13.59%	i.e., 1359 cases in 10,000
(*iv*) Between -1σ and -2σ	: 13.59%	i.e., 1359 cases in 10,000
(*v*) Between 2σ and 3σ	: 2.15%	i.e., 215 cases in 10,000
(*vi*) Between -2σ and -3σ	: 2.15%	i.e., 215 cases in 10,000
(*vii*) Beyond 3σ	: −13%	i.e., 13 cases in 10,000
(*viii*) Beyond -3σ	: −13%	i.e., 13 cases in 10,000
	100.00%	10,000

Application of the Normal Probability Curve

1. The percentage of cases in a normal distribution within given limits can be determined.
2. The limits in any normal distribution, which include a given percentage of the cases, can be found out.
3. Two distributions in terms of *overlapping* can be compared.
4. The relative difficulty of test questions, problems and other test items can be determined.
5. Using a Normal Probability Curve a given group can be separated into sub-groups according to capacity, when the trait is normally distributed.
6. The area relationship under the Normal Probability curve to derive important information about any normal distribution of measures.
7. A given histogram or frequence polygon may be compared with an NPC of the same area, mean and S.D.

Skewness. When the dispersion or scatter of the scores in a series is greater on one side of the point of a central tendency than on the other, the distribution is skewed.

A distribution is said to be skewed when—

(*i*) The mean and the median fall at different points in the distribution;

(*ii*) The balance or centre of gravity is shifted to one side or the other.

Positively Skewed Distribution. When most of the scores pile up at the *low end* (*or left*) of the distribution and spread out more gradually towards the *high end* of it, the distribution is said to be *positively skewed.*

In a positively skewed distribution, the mean falls to the right of the median.

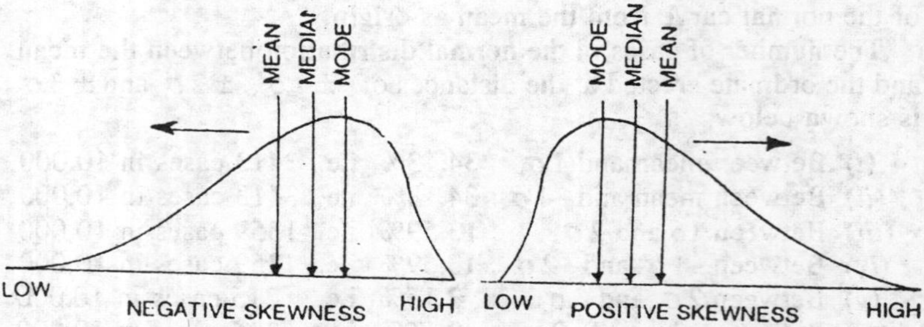

Fig. 20.2. Skewed Curves.

Negatively Skewed Distribution. When most of the scores pile up at the *high end (or right)* of the distribution and spread out more gradually towards the *low end* of it, the distribution is said to be *negatively skewed.*

In a negatively skewed distribution, the mean falls to the left of the median.

Following points may be remembered that in a skewed curve :

(*i*) The mean and the mode fall on opposite sides of the median;

(*ii*) The mean is pulled more towards the skewed end of the distribution than is the median;

(*iii*) The greater the gap between the mean and the median, the greater the skewness. The closer together are the mean and the median, the less is the skewness.

Detection of Skewness. For detecting skewness, we may put one of the following questions to ourselves.

(*i*) Do the mean, the median and the mode coincide?

(*ii*) At points of equal deviations on either side of the mode, are the frequencies equal?

If the answer is *No,* the distribution is skewed.

Index of Skewness

A useful index of skewness is given by the following formula

$$SK = \frac{3\ (\text{Mean} - \text{Median})}{SD}$$

The formula clearly states that —

(*i*) The skewness is zero, when the mean = the median;

(*ii*) The skewness is positive, when the mean > the median;

(*iii*) The skewness is negative when the mean < the median.

When the percentiles are available, the following formula is used to find the skewness:

$$SK = \frac{P_{90} + P_{10}}{2} - P_{50}$$

For a normal curve, the skewness is zero.

Kurtosis

The term *Kurtosis* refers to the peakedness or flatness of a frequency distribution as compared with the normal.

A frequency distribution more peaked than the normal is said to be *leptokurtic*. A frequency distribution, which is flatter than the normal, is said to be *platykurtic*. A normal curve is also called *mesokurtic*. The following figure shows these three types plotted on the same diagram around the same menu.

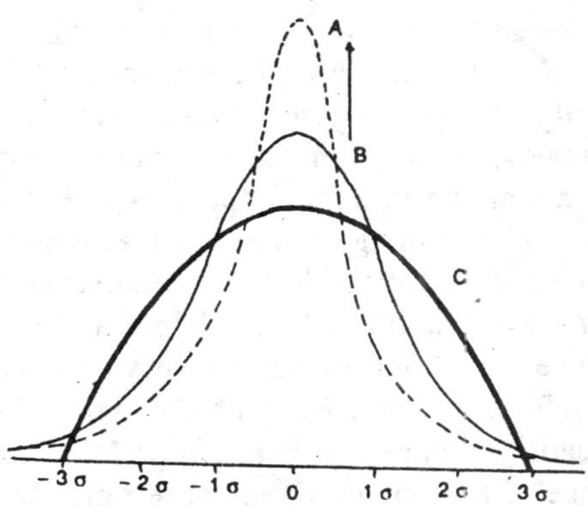

Fig. 20.3. Kurtosis: Leptokurtic (A); Normal or Mesokurtic (B); Platykurtic (C).

The formula for measuring Kurtosis is

$$Ku = \frac{Q}{P_{90} - P_{10}}$$

Chapter 21

Examination, Evaluation and Measurement : Comparative Study of Selected Countries

21.1. INDIA

Background. In Ancient India, the Vedic texts were often the subjects of study and examinations in their recitation were the normal practice. The examinee making a single mistake or two mistakes in the recitation was classified as a pupil of one error or two errors, and in this way grading went upto 12 lapses. The stress was on memorization as inevitably knowledge had to pass from man to man largely through oral instruction. With the advent of the British rule though there was a specific shift in the educational system, the stress on memory continued. Education was mainly for recruitment to services and depended upon the results of examination in terms of *pass* or *fail.* The universities started primarily as examining bodies and teaching was introduced later. In 1858, 66% of students failed in the entrance examination and 85% in the B.A. examination of the Calcutta University. Some universities, however, prided of having very low pass percentage indicative of their high standard. But such a high rate of failure became a matter of educational concern rather than pride as it was conducive to a great wastage of human and financial resources.

Examination ridden education system. Commissions and Reforms. Immediately after independence, the University Education Commission (1949) convincingly said, "If we are to suggest any single reform in university education it should be that of examinations". The Secondary

Education Commission (1953) recommended a new approach to school evaluation and made a number of concrete proposals for the improvement of external examination and the methods of internal assessment.

As a result, the examination reform movement started. The movement gathered momentum with the establishment of Central Examination Unit of trained evaluation officers by the Government of India in 1958 and the subsequent establishment of Evaluation Units in different States during Third Five Year Plan. The work of N.C.E.R.T. in this direction is also of great significance.

The Report on Examination Reform (1962) published by the University Grants Commission dealing with reforms in methods of evaluation, marking and ranking asserted that no reform would reduce the failure rate unless the prevailing admission procedures were improved.

Discussing the new concept of evaluation, the Education Commission (1964-66) said: "As the common method (and often the only method) of evaluation used at present in India is the written examination, a natural corollary of the acceptance of the new approach will be to improve the written examination in such a way that it becomes a valid and reliable measure of educational achievement ..... Other methods such as observation techniques, oral tests and practical examinations, have to be devised for collecting evidence for the purpose." The Commission also recommended that classes I to IV should be treated as an ungraded unit, weightage should be given to oral tests upto the higher primary level and external examinations should be improved by raising the technical competence of paper setters, orienting question papers, improving the nature of questions, adopting scientific procedures and mechanising the processing of results.

The Committee on Examination (1971) appointed by the Central Advisory Board of Education examined the prevailing situation and made recommendations to counteract malpractices and to give protection to those concerned with the conduct of examinations.

Present position and recent developments in the system of examinations in India

There are both internal and external examinations in India. External examinations are held at the end of the school stage in all the States. For this purpose there are different State Secondary Boards, Departments of Education or Universities, besides the Central Board of Secondary Education whose services may be availed of by any educational institution in India. In some States the external examinations are held at the end of class X (High School or High School Leaving Certificate Examinations) and in some States at the end of class XI (Higher Secondary or Secondary School Certificate Examinations). With the introduction of the 10+2+3 pattern of education, external examinations are conducted at the end of class X and XII by the State Boards and at the end of three year degree course by the Universities.

The main purpose of these examinations is certification which enables students either to go to the University or get some employment. In the past there used to be two other external examinations, one at the end of the primary stage, and another at the end of the middle school stage but now these are not a common feature. In some States an external examination is held at the end of class VII or VIII. This examination, as a general practice, is not compulsory and students can pursue their studies to higher classes without passing this examination. In addition, in some States special examinations are held at the end of classes IV or V and VII or VIII for award of scholarship. There is another examination conducted at the national level for the award of merit scholarships for the age groups 9 to 11 and 11 to 13.

Internal examinations are conducted by schools. Generally there are three quarterly examinations and one annual or comprehensive examination every year. In some areas there may be monthly or weekly tests in place of or in addition to the quarterly examinations. Usually in the eyes of both the school authorities and the pupils, the most important of these internal tests and examinations is the annual examination. On the results of this examination the annual promotions are decided so that it dominates all other tests and examinations.

National Policy on Education 1986 and as modified 1992 on Examination and Evaluation Reform

In part VIII, entitled 'Reorienting the content and process of Education' the NPE has set the following directions:

1. Assessment of performance is an integral part of any process of learning and teaching. As part of sound educational strategy, examinations should be employed to bring about qualitative improvement in education.

2. The objective will be to recast the examination system so as to ensure a method of assessment that is a valid and reliable measure of student development and a powerful instrument for improving teaching and learning. In functional terms, this would mean:

(*i*) The elimination of excessive element of chance and subjectivity;
(*ii*) The de-emphasis of memorisation;

(*iii*) Continuous and comprehensive evaluation that incorporates both scholastic and non-scholastic aspects, of education, spread over the total span of instructional time.

(*iv*) Effective use of evaluation process by teachers, students and parents;

(*v*) Improvement in the conduct of examinations;

(*vi*) The introduction of concomitant changes in material and methodology;

(*vii*) The introduction of the semester system from the secondary stage in a phased manner, and

(*viii*) The use of grades in place of marks.

3. The above goals are relevant both for external examinations and evaluation within educational institutions. Evaluation at the institutional level will be streamlined and the predominance of external examination reduced.

A review of the present situation would reveal that by and large, follow up work on the directions of the NPE is rather very negligent. The Central Board of Secondary Education, Delhi, which affiliates about 4,500 secondary and senior secondary schools out of a total of about 80,000 schools in the country, started multiple set of question papers at the Senior Secondary stage (class XII) in the year 1992 with the objective of checking copying and the use of unfair means in the examinations.

21.2. U.K.

State of examination and evaluation before the Introduction of National Curriculum 1988

Examination-ridden System in England. One lifelong observer of the examination systems in England has said, "The desire to submit to public examination is endemic to English education. Many English educationists would also agree that their school system is the most 'exam-ridden' in the world. It is true that many students before obtaining the university degree might have gone through atleast four major public competitive examinations, at the ages eleven, sixteen, eighteen and twenty-one. In contrast many American students might have taken no public examination before obtaining similar degree, though others might have been through an examination in the form of the College Boards or standardized tests. In England, at the primary level, there is a selection examination for secondary education conducted by the local education authorities and taken by students between 10 or 12, but the use of such selection is rapidly decreasing. At the secondary level, unlike continental system, there is no naturally administered examination. The two major examinations in the secondary field are the General Certificate of Education (G.C.E.) administered by 8 boards (to some extent regional in their clientele), and the Certificate of Secondary Education (C.S.E.) administered by 14 regional boards. Thus there are 22 boards approved by the Department of Education and Science instead of one national board.

G.C.E. The G.C.E. is the most important of the two. The number of students taking the G.C.E. has increased though still nearly two-thirds of the children in English schools do not attempt it. It is regarded as a competitive device serving the functions of a leaving, a matriculation and a qualifying examination. Briefly defined G.C.E. is a voluntary, two-level, public, written examination of the essay type, prepared and graded externally. Unlike the Indian school leaving examinations with their compulsory group of subjects, G.C.E. is a separate-subject examination in which a candidate may offer any number of subjects, but these need not all be taken at the same time. Thus a students does not 'fail' or 'pass' the G.C.E., he fails or passes in individual subjects. The ordinary (or O Level) is usually taken at the age of 15-16 at the end of the fifth form, and the Advanced (or A level) at 17-18 at the end of the upper sixth form. At O Level, 9 numbered grades are awarded, grades 1 to 6 being pass grades. These grades are unofficial and are not entered on the certificates awarded. They are, however sent to the school where the headmaster makes them known to the students. At 'A' Level seven lettered grades are officially awarded, grades A to E being pass grades. Besides A grade, O is awarded to candidates who do not reach the lowest pass mark but are judged to have reached the standard of O Level. The best students often take and pass three subjects at A Level. The pass rates of different Boards differ, the national average being about 58% of O Level and 68% of A Level.

G.C.E. critically considered. Heads and the staff of selective secondary schools, the Department and the Inspectorate of Schools give their support to the G.C.E., while the non-selective secondary schools and colleges and institutes of education are critical of the system. One Director of Institute of Education remarked, "the Grammar School's curriculum is largely dominated by these examinations...teaching becomes a business of filling up pupils with information as if a school were a petrol station." Much of the controversy stems from the fact that G.C.E. is an external examination, prepared and graded by agencies outside the school.

C.S.E. C.S.E. was the outcome of the Beloe Report (1958) which recommended that : the examination should be on a subject basis; it should be appropriate for pupils at the end of the fifth year; it should be designed to suit the needs and interests of a range of pupils covering approximately the 40th to the 80th percentiles of ability and finally the examinations were to be controlled by the teachers themselves. It attempts "a new reconciliation of freedom and order by placing upon the teachers themselves full responsibility for syllabus content and methods of examining. A favourite slogan is that the C.S.E. is to follow and not to dictate the curriculum. Unlike the G.C.E., the C.S.E. is not a pass/fail examination. It uses five grades I—V to record performance in all subjects. The examinations are held in any one of the three modes: In Mode I, papers are based upon a prescribed syllabus and are externally set and marked; in Mode 2, papers are based upon school's own syllabus but are externally set and marked; in Mode 3, papers are based upon school's own syllabus and are set and marked by the school to external moderation by the concerning board. Modes 1 and 2 are already used by the G.C.E. Mode 3 is an exiting new departure.

Absence of Research. Educationists have pointed out the comparative absence of research report on G.C.E. The majority of C.S.E. boards have been processing their results on computers from the very start. Four G.C.E. boards have also started using computers. Greater availability of statistical information will make more research possible. "Informed discussion on the many problems associated with secondary school testing in England and Wales is essential if solutions are to be devised for them."

State of Examinations and Evaluation in U.K. since 1988

The Curriculum— England and Wales. Under the Education (No. 2) Act 1986, head teachers in England and Wales have been made responsible for determining and organising the curriculum within their schools, taking into consideration the policy of their local education authority and that of their governing body. The Government favours widening educational opportunities as much as possible through a broad and balanced curriculum which is differentiated to meet the individual needs of pupils and is relevant to the requirements of the modern world.

Under the Education Reform Act 1988, the introduction of a National Curriculum in primary and secondary schools in England and Wales began in 1989, (a) There are four key stages — Key stage I — upto age 7 (Infants). Key stage II — 7 to 11 years (Juniors). Key stage III —

11 to 14 (Pre— GCSE) and Key Stage IV — 14 to 16 (Preparation for GCSE). (b) For the first 3 key stages for children between the ages of 5 and 14, which the Government believes should occupy not less than 70 per cent of teaching time, consists of the 3 core subjects of english, mathematics and science, as well as 6 other foundation subjects of history, geography, technology, music, art, physical education. Besides these, at the key levels III and IV for secondary level children, aged 11 to 16, a modern foreign language is also compulsory. At key level IV music and art are not compulsory and children can take either history or geography or short courses in both. Economic and industrial awareness are important cross-curricular themes in the National Curriculum.

In Wales, the Welsh language constitutes a core subject in Welsh-speaking schools and a foundation subject elsewhere under the National Curriculum. In the primary sector 80 per cent of schools either use Welsh as a teaching medium or teach it as a second language, while nearly 90 per cent of secondary schools teach Welsh as a first or second language.

Attainment targets have been devised to establish what children should normally be expected to know, understand and be able to do at the end of each of four key stages, *i.e.*, at the ages of 7, 11, 14 and 16 the end of each of four key stages, *i.e.*, at enabling the progress of each child to be measured against national standards. Pupils' performance in relation to attainment targets will be assessed and reported on at the four key stages. Regulations have been introduced covering the manner and form in which assessments of individual pupils are to be made available to parents and others.

Religious education, already compulsory under the Education Act 1944, is required for all pupils as part of the basic curriculum, although parents have a right to withdraw their children from religious education classes. The content of religious education courses is determined locally.

Attainment Targets. Attainment targets are set for each National Curriculum subject. In English, for instance, there are 5 basic targets: speaking and listening; reading; writing; spelling and hand-writing. For each attainment target, there are ten levels of attainment. Towards the end of each of the first three stages children are assessed against attainable targets using both teacher assessment and 'standard assessment tasks'. At the end of key stage II, GCSE or equivalents form the basis of the National Curriculum Assessment.

School Tests

The Statement of the Secretary of State for Education, Mr. John Patten to the House of Commons on 11 May 1993, illustrates fully the importance of tests. The Government's commitment to tests this summer for seven and 14 year-olds had, he said, already been confirmed, 'There is abundant evidence of the importance of testing the progress of our children. Our main competitor countries do so as a matter of course. So should we. It would be a betrayal of a future generation of pupils to postpone what are acknowledged on all sides to be much needed educational reforms.

'Tests for seven-year-olds are in their third year. We know that they work. Tests in 1991 and 1992 have improved standards of teaching and learning. Last year's pilot tests for 14-year-olds were well received.

'Children have been working towards the tests for several years. Abandoning the tests would leave conscientious teachers, concerned parents and the wider community in the dark about our schools, depriving them of vital information about the attainments of individual pupils. The Government have therefore decided on the following for 1994. First, mandatory tests in 1994 for seven and 14-years-olds should concentrate on the core subjects English, Mathematics and Science, and on Welsh as a first language in Wales. We shall decide later whether to add technology at the age of 14, in the light of this summer's tests.'

Examinations

The principal examinations taken by secondary school pupils in England, Wales and Northern Ireland around the age of 16 are those leading to the General Certificate of Secondary Education (GCSE). This replaced the General Certificate of Education (GCE) Ordinary (O) level and the Certificate of Secondary Education (CSE) in 1988. GCSE courses were introduced in 1986 with a view to raising standards of performance. GCSE examinations are usually taken after five years of secondary education and have a seven-point scale of grades denoted by the letters A to G. The Government intends the GCSE to be the principal means for assessing attainment at stage 4 of the National Curriculum.

The GCE Advanced (A) level is normally taken after a further two years of study. New examinations, Advanced Supplementary (AS) levels, were introduced for the first time in 1989 and provide an opportunity for sixth-form pupils to study a wider range of subjects than before. Students specialising in the arts and humanities, for example, are able to continue to study mathematics and technological subjects at the new level.

The Certificate of Pre-Vocational Education, awarded for the first time in 1986, is intended for those at school or college who wish to continue in full-time education for a year after the age of 16 to prepare either for work or for vocational and other courses. In common with other Business and Technician Education Council (BTEC) qualifications, it can serve as a stepping stone into higher education. The Certificate is devised by BTEC and the City and Guilds of London Institute.

School Examinations and Assessment Councils. All GCSE and other qualifications offered to pupils of compulsory school age in maintained schools in England and Wales must be approved by the Government. Associated syllabuses and assessment procedures must comply with national guidelines and be approved by the School Examinations and Assessment Council.

The Council keeps under review all aspects of examinations and assessment in England and Wales and carries out research and development. It co-operates with the National Curriculum Council for England and the Curriculum Council for Wales on work connected with the National Curriculum in schools.

The Northern Ireland School Examinations and Assessment Council was established in April 1990.

Progress Reports. A system of school reporting of individual pupils' achievement was introduced in April 1990, under which parents in England and Wales receive a yearly progress report on their child's National Curriculum achievements and results in public examinations. In Scotland the report card system has been reformed to give parents a clearer view of their children's progress. In Northern Ireland there is a commitment for all pupils to be issued with a record of their performance on leaving primary and secondary school.

Educational Standards. Her Majesty's Inspectors report to the Government on the quality of education provided in all schools and in most further and higher education establishments outside the universities, and advise education authorities and schools as well as the Government. They also report on the youth service and education provision in hospitals, prisons and youth custody centres, and the armed services. Their reports on individual establishments are published. Local education authorities employ inspectors or advisers to guide them on maintained schools.

The Evaluation and Monitoring Unit, which is part of the School Examinations and Assessment Council, is mainly concerned with the evaluation of the assessment arrangements for the National Curriculum. In England, Wales and Northern Ireland programmes of monitoring have been carried out in English language and mathematics at the ages of 11 and 15, in science at the ages of 11, 13 and 15, and in the first foreign language at the age of 13. A survey of performance at the age of 15 in design and technology was undertaken in 1988. In Scotland the Assessment of Achievement research programme has surveyed attainments of pupils in English and mathematics at ages 8, 12 and 14.

21.3. U.S.A.

In contrast to Indian and English system, the American system is distinguished by the absence of external examinations. The educational achievement is usually evaluated by daily class work, test results, project or committee work, and pupil growth over a long period of time. Tests are prepared and given by subject teachers. In addition, standardized achievement tests are used periodically in many schools. Normally "promotion is based on the earning of a required number of units of credit, and not upon a comprehensive examination at the close of secondary school year. To achieve credit for a subject at the end of the school year, a student in most schools needs a D or above on a letter scale of A, B, C, D and F. A represents the highest achievement and F unsatisfactory performance. Graduation from high school ordinarily occurs after a student has completed the 12th grade, the normal age of graduation being 17 or 18. No special examination given by the State or external agency is taken as a requisite for passing the high school. The United States is the only one among the advanced nations in the world which lacks a school leaving public (or external) examination.

Regents Examinations. There are, however, some exceptions. The Regents Examinations of New York State are the closest thing to a school leaving examination in the United States. This State-wide examination system has evolved over a hundred years. It combines many internal and external factors. The syllabus is prescribed externally by the State. The question papers are set externally by committees of teachers. The answers of students are graded internally by their teachers, though a certain amount of external moderation is exercised by the State Education Department. It is the responsibility of the principal of each school to maintain grading standard according to the rating scales based on State-wide norms and issued by the State. It appears that the external moderation is not much in practice. "Unless external moderation is more effective than I believe it is in New York State, standards will almost certainly be low in many schools, in spite of rating scales or anything else," says Koerner. There are major differences between the Regents Examinations and the G.C.E. or C.S.E. "The Regents is a group-subject exam, in which the student is required to have completed a stipulated preparatory course throughout high school and to pass simultaneously in a number of both mandatory and elected subjects. The exam is aimed at the upper half of the high-school population and is usually taken at age eighteen, whereas both the C.S.E. and the O Level of the G.C.E. are taken at sixteen."

SAT and GRE Tests

In the USA, two important examinations conducted are : Scholastic Assessment Test (SAT) and GRE. The US Educational Testing Service (ETS) administers the Programme of the College Board. The College Board is a national non-profit association in the USA that champions educational excellence for all students through the collaboration of nearly 2,900 member schools, colleges, universities educational systems and organisations. The Board promotes universal access to high standards of learning, equality of opportunity and sufficient financial support so that every student is prepared for success at college and works through responsive forums, research, programmes and policy developments.

SAT-I is a three-hour test comprising seven sections: two 30-minute and one 15-minute verbal and similar mathematical reasoning ability sections. It also has another 30-minute verbal or mathematical reasoning equating section. The verbal questions test one's ability to understand and analyse what one reads, recognise relationships between parts of a sentence, and establish relationships between pairs of words. The emphasis is on critical reading passages, while mathematical questions test the student's ability to solve problems involving arithmetic, algebra and geometry.

Questions on the "equating" section in SAT-I do not count towards scores. There are two reasons for this. First, some questions are framed to ensure that scores on new versions of SAT-I are comparable to scores in earlier versions. Secondly, some questions are new and they may be used in future SAT-I tests. The mere fact of trying them out ensures that future tests contain, the right type of questions and are about just as fair as the test a student is taking.

The US Educational Testing Service (ETS) administers the Scholastic Assessment Test (SAT), programme of the College Board. The College

Board is a national non-profit association in the USA that promotes universal access to high standards for all students through the collaboration of nearly 2,900 member schools.

SAT-I provides colleges with an opportunity to compare the academic ability and preparation of students who apply for admission. This is because, although a student's high school record — his grades, class rank etc. — are a fair indicator of how well he will rate in college, high schools can be very different in the courses they offer and in the way they award grades. While the same work might fetch a student an "A" in algebra in one school, another might award a "B". SAT-I only gives students an opportunity to show colleges what they know and how they can be independent of school grades.

SAT-II is a one-hour test that evaluates student knowledge and skills in a particular subject and his ability to apply that knowledge. This test offers 16 subject areas. SAT-II scores on subject test used in combination with high school record and results of SAT-I, teachers' recommendations and other supplementary background information provide a reliable measure of a student's academic achievements.

GRE

GRE is a three-and-a half hour general test of a higher level in the US, offering subject tests in 16 areas. GRE General Test questions are designed to measure skills and knowledge gained over a long period of time. GRE scores provide a common measure for comparing the qualifications of applicants who come from a variety of colleges and universities with different standards.

The GRE General Test is only one of the several means of evaluating likely success in graduate school. It is not intended to measure inherent intellectual capacity or intelligence. Neither is its aim to measure creativity, motivation, perseverance or social worth. The test only makes it possible to compare students with different backgrounds. Thus, a GRE score of 500 holds the same meaning irrespective of whether it is earned by a student at a small, private liberal arts college or at a large public university.

21.4. EXAMINATIONS AND EVALUATION IN U.S.S.R. (FORMER)

External Organization. In the U.S.S.R. Ministries of Education of the Union Republics organized and supervised the examinations in a centralized manner. Examination cards were prepared under their guidance and approved by them. Local departments of education had the responsibility to see that examinations were properly organized to approve the examination commissions headed by the Headmasters and to arbitrate in case where the commissions failed to take unanimous decision. The Soviet school system had a uniformity of curricula which resulted in uniformity of expectation in pupils' knowledge and skill. It was possible, therefore, to compare the results of examinations in different schools in various parts of the country, and to observe the shortcomings in the results of teaching, so as to determine and implement measures for eradication of these shortcomings.

Internal Assessment of everyday work. The examination by itself was not everything though it provided a 30 to 40 per cent weightage in the final marking. The pupils' knowledge was assessed throughout the year. It was assessed by the teacher in everyday work by calling on the pupils to give oral answers, by periodic written tests and by seeing how the students are able to work in the classroom and at homes. Based on these regular check-ups, marks were allotted for the year. The final marking was based on the year's mark and examination mark. This final marking was entered in the school leaving certificate. Since 1944, a five point system had been used for marking, 5 being the highest and 1 being the lowest mark. The pupil's conduct was also assessed on a five-point system and was taken into consideration in awarding the school-leaving certificate. In classes where no examination was held (school leaving or annual), final marking was based on terminal marks which in turn were based on everyday work. All students above 2 marks were promoted. Students with 1 or 2 marks were also promoted but on condition that they would show better results at the next chance. They got assignments for the summer months and summer consultations with teachers were organized. The number of repeaters was 3 to 5 per cent.

Oral and Written Examinations. The amount of material tested in the school leaving examinations was not great. The examination at the end of the 8th class consisted of mathematics and Russian language (also regional language in the non-Russian schools) and at the end of 10th class it consisted of literature, mathematics, physics, chemistry, social sciences and a foreign language. Examinations were both oral and written. Written examinations were held only in the Russian language (and regional language in non-Russian school) for 8th class, mathematics for 8th and 10th classes and literature (composition) in class 10th. More stress was laid on oral examination. At the oral examinations, students chose one from 25 to 35 examination cards (tickets) containing two or three questions. These questions for the examinations were issued to schools 4 or 5 months before the examinations. This practice helped the students to see in what direction they should prepare, systemise and revise their subjects.

Soviet examination system was predominantly based on a year round regular internal assessment. Even in school leaving examinations the knowledge and skill of the students were assessed by their own teachers, though the questions cards were externally prepared. Regularity of everyday checking of pupil's work, flexibility of an individualized approach through oral examination and objectivity of an examination commission comprising a group of teachers made the system more reliable and realistic. The system induced the pupils to study diligently and relieved them from unnecessary surprises and fears. Since teacher's individual work got revealed before his colleagues in the commission, it was only natural that he should work to the best of his ability.

Chapter 22

Committees and Commissions on Examinations, Evaluation and Measurement

INTRODUCTION

This Chapter includes detailed observations and recommendations of the following Committees and Commissions which have guided the reform movement in the field of examinations, evaluation and measurement.

1. University Education Commission (1948-49)
2. Secondary Education Commission (1952-53)
3. U.G.C. Examination Committee (1957)
4. Education Commission or Kothari Commission (1964-66)
5. Committee on Examination Reform in Central Universities (1966)
6. Committee on Examinations Appointed by the Central Advisory of Education, Ministry of Education and Social Welfare, (1970-71)
7. Report of the Training Course on Evaluation (1971)
8. National Seminar on Research in Examination (1978)
9. National Seminar on the Management of Public Examinations (1978)
10. National Seminar on Evaluation (1979)
11. Challenge of Education : A Policy Perspective (1985)
12. National Policy on Education – NPE (1986)
13. Programme of Action (1986) on NPE (1986)
14. National Seminar on Oral Examinations (1987)
15. National Seminar on Scaling of Examination Results (1987)

16. UGC Guidelines for Teaching and Related Matters (1984-88)

17. Committee for Review of National Policy on Education (NPE 1986) or Ramamurti Report (1990)

18. Central Advisory Board of Education Committee (CABE Committee) on Policy or Janardhana (Committee 1992)

19. Revised Policy Formulation (1992)

20. Programme of Action (1992)

21. Conference of Chairmen of Boards of School Education on Semesterisation and Examination Reform (1992)

22.1. UNIVERSITY EDUCATION COMMISSION (1948-49)

(From Chapter X, Examinations of the Commission's Report),(1) Special state examinations for recruitment to the various services should be open to whosover cares to take them. This would remove one of the chief evils of the educational system.

(2) No credit is, at present, given for class work in courses except sometimes in the case of practical work. We recommend, therefore, that one-third of the marks allotted to each subject be reserved for work done during the course of instruction and that this be adopted forthwith in the teaching universities for the B.A. and B.Sc., M.A. and M.Sc. examinations. The affiliating universities should also take immediate steps to evolve a method of more or less uniform marking for this internal award at the affiliated colleges. An effective machinery for the supervision and inspection of affiliated colleges to ensure uniformity of standards should be devised. In post-graduate courses, term papers could be required as a part of this course credit. The progress tests will be of great use in this connection.

(3) Three years will be invloved for the first degree. It is not desirable that all the work should be subjected to the one examination at the end of the period. That would entail unnecessary mental strain. Sections of the course which are more or less self-contained can be made the subject of periodical examinations spread over the three years' duration. A scheme of such self-contained units of work should be prepared by each university and the student should be required to pass in all the units before getting the degree.

(4) Examiners should be selected with great care. No one should serve as an examiner in a subject which he has not taught for atleast five years. Three years should be the limit of continuous service as an external examiner for the first degree examination. After a break of three years, they may be permitted again.

(5) Every examining authority should have a careful study made on the work done in other countries to discover methods of minimising

the outstanding defect of the essay type examination, the subjectivity of marking; and should take all necessary precautions to see that marking is done under closely controlled conditions.

(6) The standards for success at the examination should, as far as possible, be uniform in the various universities and should be raised. We suggest that a candidate should get 70% or more marks to secure a first class, 55% to 69% for a second and at least 40% for a third. The students will be arranged in alphabetical order in each of the three classes.

(7) In view of the other recommendations made by us, especially the one requiring due regard being paid to work during the course, we recommend that the system of awarding grace marks be abolished for the first degree and all higher examinations.

(8) Viva voce examinations should be employed only for post-graduate and professional degrees. They should be designed, however, to test the candidate's competence in the fundamentals of the field of study to which the problem of his research belongs.

22.2. SECONDARY EDUCATION COMMISSION 1952-53

(Chapter XI of the Report)

A New Approach to Examination and Evaluation

The subject of Examination and Evaluation occupies an important place in the field of education. It is necessary for parents and teachers to know from time to time how the pupils are progressing and what their attainments are at any particular stage. It is equally necessary for society to assure itself that the work entrusted to its schools is being carried on satisfactorily and that the children studying there are receiving the right type of education and attaining the expected standards. This kind of check up of the school work is essential in the interests of all concerned—pupils, teachers, parents and the public. Examinations are the usual means adopted for this purpose.

Examinations, Internal and External

Examinations may be either internal or external. Internal examinations are conducted by schools from time to time and atleast once during the school year, for evaluating the progress of the pupils, for grading them and, when the time comes, for selecting and promoting them to a higher class. Of the purposes for which examinations are held, certainly the first, namely, the evaluation of progress is the most important. On it depends not only grading and promotion but even the method of instruction.

Annual examinations are a common feature of our schools. Some schools also hold terminal examinations, i.e., examinations at the end of each term. A few also hold weekly or monthly tests. Usually in the eyes of both the school authorities and the pupils, the most important of these internal tests and examinations is the annual examination. On the results of this examination the annual promotions are decided so that it dominates all other tests and examinations. A few schools have replaced the annual examination by the cumulative results of periodic tests and examinations.

The external examination comes generally at the end of the school stage. Its purpose is two-fold-selective and qualifying, selecting those who have successfully completed a course and qualifying them from among many for the next higher stage. At one time besides the matriculation or University entrance examination (or its equivalent, the School Final or the School Certificate Examination) there used to be in some parts of the country, two other examinations, one at the end of the primary stage and another at the end of the middle school stage; and all these were regarded as public examinations. We are told that still these are prevalent in some States. We are convinced that our system of education is very much examination-ridden.

Scope and Limitations of the Present System of Examinations in India

Both the internal and the external examinations in this country are more or less modelled on similar lines and they follow the same general pattern. Both are intended to test mainly the academic attainments of a pupil and his progress in intellectual pursuits. These do not test the other aspects of the pupils development; or if they do, it is only indirectly.

The twentieth century has witnessed a widening of the meaning and scope of education. The school of today concerns itself not only with intellectual pursuits but also with the emotional and social development of the child, his physical and mental health, his social adjustment and other equally important aspects of his life—in a word, with an all-round development of his personality. If examinations are to be of real value they must take into consideration the new facts and test in detail the all-round development of pupils.

Even as a test of the intellectual attainments of pupils, the validity and usefulness of the present pattern of examinations have been widely questioned. It has been urged that the present system of examining by means of essay-type questions leaves so much scope for the subjectivity of examiner that it cannot be relied upon to any great extent. In this connection reference may be made to the findings of the Hartog Report on an Examination of Examinations which clearly proves the foibles of such a system. It may therefore be fairly inferred that as conducted at present,examinations do not help us to evaluate correctly even the intellectual attainments of the pupils.

The Effect of the Examination System on our Education

We have already referred to the new concept of education. Unfortunately our present system of education still lays exclusive emphasis on the intellectual attainments of the pupils and this has been due mainly to the influence of our examination system. The examinations determine not only the contents of education but also the methods of teaching—in fact, the entire approach to education. They have so pervaded the entire atmosphere of school life that they have become the main motivating force of all effort on the part of pupil as well as teacher. It is not often clearly realised that a pupil's effort throughout his education is concentrated almost wholly on how to get through the examinations. Unless a subject is included in the examination scheme the pupil is not interested in it. If any school activity is not related directly or indirectly to the examination, it fails to evoke or enlist his enthusiasm. As regards methods, he is interested in only those which secure an easy pass rather than in those which may be educationally more sound but which do not directly concern themselves with examinations. He is more interested in notes and cribs than in textbooks and original works; he goes in for cramming rather than for intelligent understanding since this will help him to pass the examination on which depends his future.

As has already been stated it is not only the pupil but the teacher also who is affected by this examination craze. To the teacher the system of examination affords an easy solution to many of his problems. While it is difficult, if not impossible, to show immediate, tangible and measurable results with regard to those intangible efforts of a good education such as character training, well rounded personality, a wholesome social adjustment and a proper development of appreciation of the finer values in life it is much easier to show results in intellectual attainments and academic progress. And if society sets greater store by these attainments than by what is conductive to character building and sound citizenship, how can the teacher help paying attention to the former attainments. Moreover examinations are, comparatively speaking, an easy method of grading pupils and pronouncing judgement on their work. Again, and this is most unfortunate, his success as a teacher is very often measured by the results of his pupils in the examinations. It is not uncommon to hear statements such as, so and so is a good teacher because his pupils show a high percentage of success in the final examination. Headmasters in presenting their reports at the annual gatherings lay emphasis on the results of examinations and on the brilliant success of some of their pupils, thus provoking the criticism that the report resembled a profit and loss account presented to shareholders of an industrial concern. To judge the work of a teacher by the pass percentage of his pupils in the examination, is to keep alive the old and exploded system of payment by results.

The attitude of the parents also lends support to this state of affairs. Because of the close connection between employment and the passing of external examinations, the average parent is more interested in his child passing that examination than in anything else. Even the authorities who provide higher courses or employ young people are guided almost solely by the certificates awarded on the results of the external examinations. To this may be added the unfortunate trend in recent times to utilise the marks obtained at public examinations as the sole criterion for admission of students to most colleges.

Thus all circumstances conspire today to put an undue and unnatural emphasis on examinations, specially the external examinations and they have come to exercise a restricting influence over the entire field of Indian education to such an extent as almost to nullify its real purpose. Many complained of the hampering effect of examinations. They said and we generally agree with them, that the examinations today dictate the curriculum instead of following it, prevent any experimentation, hamper, the proper treatment of subjects and sound methods of teaching, foster a dull uniformity rather than originality, encourage the average pupil to concentrate too rigidly upon too narrow a field and thus help him to develop wrong values in education. Pupils assess education in terms of success in examinations. Teachers, recognising the importance of the external examination to the individual pupil, are constrained to relate their teaching to an examination which can test only a narrow field of the pupil's interest and capacities and so inevitably neglect the qualities which are more important though less tangible. They are forced to attend to what can be examined; and to do that with success they often have to 'spoon-feed' their pupils rather than encourage habits of independent study. We were told that in some schools notes are dictated even in the lower classes and after some time the children feel unhappy and helpless if this is not done. This system is not so uncommon as we would wish to imagine.

The Place of Examinations

Nevertheless examinations—and specially external examinations—have a proper place in any scheme of education. External examinations have stimulating effect both on the pupils and on the teachers by providing well defined goals and objective standards of evaluation. To the pupil the examination gives a goal towards which he should strive and a stimulus urging him to attain that goal in a given time, thereby demanding steady and constant effort. This makes the purpose clear and the method of approach definite. He is judged by external and objective tests on which both he and others interested in him can depend. And finally, it gives him a hallmark recognised by all.

For the teacher, too, it is helpful to have a goal and stimulus. Without these his work may lose in precision and direction. The external examination gives him standards common for all teachers and therefore, universal and uniform in character. It also releases him from the responsibility of making wrong judgements about the work of his pupils. Finally, the external examination has another great advantage, namely, that it helps a school to compare itself with other schools.

Suggestions for the Improvement of the Present System

In view of all these considerations it would appear that the external examination cannot be altogether done away with. Certain steps however have to be taken to minimise its undesirable effects. Firstly, there should not be too may external examinations. Secondly, the subjective element which is unavoidable in the present purely essay-type examination should be reduced as far as possible. The essay-type examination has its own value. It tests certain capacities which cannot be otherwise tested. But it cannot be the only test for measuring the attainments of pupils. One of its greatest disadvantages is that it gives undue weight to the power of verbal expression in which so many individual differences exist. In order, therefore, to reduce the element of subjectivity of the essay-type tests, objective tests of attainments should be widely introduced side by side. Moreover, the nature of the tests and the type of questions should be thoroughly changed. They should be such as to discourage cramming and encourage intelligent understanding. They should not deal with details but should concern themselves with a rational understanding of the problems and a general mastery of the subject matter. In this connection we consider that it is undesirable to set two papers of three hours each on one and the same day. Lastly, the final assessment of the pupil should not be based entirely on the results of the external examination; other things such as internal tests and the school records maintained by teachers should be taken into consideration and due credit should be given to them. With these safeguards and changes, we feel the external examination can serve a useful purpose.

With regard to the prevalent system of internal examinations also certain changes are necessary. The emphasis on all-important annual examination should be reduced. A few schools have abandoned such examinations. They use the results of peiodical tests and of weekly or monthly examinations for purposes of promotion. A few other supplement the annual and periodical examinations by more elaborate records of work done by pupils throughout the year. We commend these steps which will give the annual examination its proper place. The promotion of a child should depend not only on the results of the annual final examination but also on the results of periodic tests and the progress shown in the school record. The pattern of internal examination should also be changed. The objective type of tests should be widely used to supplement the essay-type tests; other steps suggested with regard to the eyternal examination should also apply in the case of internal examinations.

Need for School Records

But neither the external examination nor the internal examination, singly or together, can give a correct and complete picture of a pupil's all-round progress at any particular stage of his education; yet it is important for us to assess this, in order to determine his future course of study, or his future vocation. For this purpose a proper system of school records should be maintained for every pupil indicating the work done by him in the school from day-to-day, month-to-month, term-to-term and year to year. Such a school record will present a clear and continuous statement of the attainments of the child in different intellectual pursuits throughout the successive stages of his education. It will also contain a progressive evaluation of development in other directions of no less importance, such as the growth of his interests, aptitudes, and personality traits, his social adjustments, the practical and social activities in which he takes part. In other words it will give a complete career. We have seen such records being maintained in some schools but their number is few. We recommend that these should be a common feature of all schools all over the country. Schools may devise their own forms on the lines indicated therein.

Maintenance of Cumulative Record Card

This cumulative record will be maintained by the class teacher. The class teacher who will maintain it (he may also be a specialist in charge of a particular subject) is specially placed in charge of a class of pupils for one school year. He teaches them one or two important subjects and thus spends more time with them than other teachers do. He gets to know them personally and individually. His responsibilities as far as his class is concerned are not confined to the four walls of the class-room; they extend over the pupil's entire life in the school. He is thus the right person to maintain the record.

In some schools a class teacher remains incharge of a class for one year at the end of which he hands over the charge of his pupils to the class teacher of the next higher class. In some other schools the class teacher follows his class from year to year till the class goes out of the school. Both systems have their advantages. Whether a teacher remains in charge of a class for one year or for a number of years, the important thing is that he gets the opportunity to establish personal contacts with a group of pupils. Such personal contacts, specially with adolescent pupils have great value, and their importance cannot be exaggerated.

In most schools some sort of class-teacher system prevails; but it is not fully exploited because of the supposed importance of teaching by specialist teachers. Often the class-teacher's responsibilities consists of only in maintaining the class register and collecting monthly school fees from the pupils. There is no inherent contradiction between the class-teacher system and the subject-specialist system. The two can be easily combined in the same system and the class-teacher can function in *loco parentis* for the pupils under his care with great advantage for all concerned.

Teachers and School Records

It has been said that the introduction of cumulative records will increase the responsibilities of teachers and add to their work. This is no doubt true. But the advantages would outweigh the personal disadvantage to teachers. And once they become used to the system they themselves will come to appreciate the advantage of such school records. The cumulative records will greatly influence their work in the classroom specially their methods of teaching and handling children, so much so that the entire character of their work will change.

Doubts have been expressed whether teachers will be able to discharge this added responsibility satisfactorily; in maintaining the records will they not be swayed too much by their personal predilections and judgements thereby nullifying greatly the value of these records? Maintaining the records would need a certain amount of training. We have no doubt that arrangements will be made by the State Departments of Education to provide such training, perhaps in the Training Colleges for teachers. With such training and a certain amount of practice and with an occasional checkup by the head of the institution and by the Inspectorate, we have no doubt that the teachers will be able to discharge these duties to the satisfaction of all. There may be occasional lapses here and there, but these should not cause any anxiety or loss of faith in the teachers. In his sense of responsibility the average Indian teacher does not yield to any teacher in any other country. What he needs is clear direction, encouragement and sympathy.

Need for Research

In order to maintain the cumulative records properly the teachers will have to use a number of tests of different kinds—intelligence tests, attainment tests, aptitude tests and others. We expect that the State Bureau of Education which will devise the forms of cumulative records will also prepare these tests in collaboration with the Training Colleges. There is need for continuous research in these fields. The Training Colleges should also organise short courses of training in the use of these forms and tests.

Evaluation and Marking

At this stage it is necessary to indicate the actual means to be adopted in evaluating and grading the work of pupils whether in the external or internal examinations and in maintaining the school records. The present system of evaluating by percentiles *i.e.* by numerical marks, out of a hundred, may have certain advantages but the disadvantages seem to outweigh the advantages. Firstly, it introduces too many subdivisions which are not only useless but cumbersome; and secondly, it is indeed difficult to distinguish between two pupils one of whom obtains, say, 45 marks and another 46 or 47. This system no doubt gives the semblance of accurate judgement which for most of the pupils it is hardly worthwhile to exercise and is beset with many errors. In this connection we would again invite attention to the Hartog Report on 'An Examination of Examinations' which fully reveals the limitations and errors of the system. A simpler and better system is the use of the five-point scale to which 'A' stands for excellent. 'B' for good. 'C' for fair and average, 'D' for poor and 'E' for very poor. In this system pupils are grouped in broad divisions which are more easily distinguishable than the differences indicated by percentile marks. We recommend that this system be adopted for school records.

For written examinations, whether external or internal, the same scale may be used with this modification that here D and E will be combined to indicate 'failure'. Here 'A' will indicate 'Distinction', B 'Credit' and C 'Pass' and D and E 'Failure' or 'Cases Referred Back'. The values of these categories in terms of percentile marks may be determined by the examining authority. Individual examiners in different subjects may even use the percentile system and then convert the percentile scores in terms of categories. The system recommended here will work in almost all cases except where the distinctions are to be made for the award of scholarships and prizes. In these cases (whose number will always be limited) the system may be modified to introduce a finer scale which may show the difference between two cases which may be almost similar. It must however be admitted that a difference of a few marks on the percentile scale is more often a matter of chance than of exact determination. We note that changes have been introduced in recent years in several universities where candidates who have secured a first or second class are arranged in the alphabetical order of their names and not as hitherto according to the percentile scale.

We have discussed at some length the general principles of evaluation of school work in view of its extreme importance in education. We now come to offer certain specific and firm recommendations on the subject.

A Single Final Examination

We have referred to the desirability of reducing the number of external examinations. We recommend that there should be only one public examination to indicate the completion of the school course. It may be either the High School Final Examination or the Higher Secondary Examination depending on the nature of the School where the pupil completes his course. There should be no other public examination before it. The certificate to be awarded to indicate the completion of the Middle School or any other school class will be given by the school itself and it will be based entirely on the school records which will include the results of periodic and annual tests.

School Certificates

Even the final public examination need not be compulsory for all; that is, if pupils so desire they need not take it. However every pupil who completes the school course will get a school certificate based on school records testifying to his progress and attainments in different directions in school.

The point has been raised that the school certificate may not be reliable and that standards will vary. As regards reliability, with all the provisions we have mentioned previously we have little apprehension on that score. The only way to make the teachers' judgements reliable is to rely on them. In the beginning there may be stray cases of wrong judgement, but before long they will come to be more and more reliable and trustworthy. "No one can examine better than the teacher who knows the child, and a method of examination by the teacher, combined with school records, would be devised which would furnish a certificate giving information of real importance to employer or college or profession, and yet would preserve in tact the freedom of the school and would rid teacher and pupil of an artificial restrain imposed from without. As for uniformity of standards, even under the present conditions, two apparently similar certificates mean very different things and illusory uniformity can be brought too dearly." (Norwood Committee Report on Curriculum and Examination in Secondary Schools. H.M.S.O. 1941, p.32).

Examination Certificate

Pupils who complete the school courses and take the final examination will get certificate to be awarded by the authorities holding the examination.

The form of these certificates needs also to be changed. Some States award a bare certificate mentioning only the division obtained by the pupil without mentioning in detail the courses taken by him. Such certificates are not very helpful either to the colleges or to the employing authorities. In one or two States, however, a more elaborate form of certificate is used which incorporates not only the results of the school tests in these and other subjects which are not included in the public examination but also contain extracts from school records.

Examining authorities should prescribe a form wherein the schools could fill in the details of the school record of the pupil concerned. At the time of the public examination the school will forward the record to the examining authority. The examining authority in its turn will enter therein the results of the public examination and return it to the school to be forwarded to the pupil concerned. Every candidate who appears for the examination will get a certificate, showing the school record and the public test record. The system of evaluation to be adopted by the school and the examining body has already been described.

For the final examination a candidate will ordinarily take six subjects. He may also take an additional subject, but the result should be decided on the performance of the six subjects only. A pass in six subjects should be deemed sufficient for the satisfactory completion of the certificate. Of these six passes atleast four should have been obtained at the public examination, while two others may be passes obtained in the school records. If such school record passes are taken into consideration candidate should have obtained atleast one credit among the four passes of the public examination. In such a scheme due notice would also have been taken of the school record of the pupil.

We have indicated in a general way of the tests to be observed for certifying satisfactory completion of the school courses. It is, however, open to those concerned with the selection of pupils for higher education, university, technical or otherwise, or for those authorities which recruit public services to determine the exact standard of achievement required of candidates in the several subjects.

We are of opinion that as far as the final public examination is concerned the compartmental system should be introduced. If a candidate fails in one or more subjects of the public examination he should be allowed to take these subjects of public examination at a subsequent examination but in such cases the school records will not be taken into account. He need not again sit for subjects in which he has obtained a pass. He will be given not more than three chances to appear at subsequent examinations.

A candidate who has passed the examination in the required six subjects and wishes to qualify in any additional subject, may appear at a subsequent examination. The result thus obtained will be entered by the examination authority in the certificate already obtained by the candidate.

The scheme recommended by us here for the reform of the entire system of examination and evaluation of school work should be tried for a reasonably long period of time. It takes time for such fundamental changes to be assimilated before they can work satisfactorily and before any judgement can be pronounced on them.

22.3. UGC EXAMINATION COMMITTEE (1957)

The Committee was appointed by the University Grants Commission in 1957 under the Chairmanship of Shri S.R. Dongerkery.

Terms of Reference

A. To examine the problems relating to examinations, and

B. To advise the Commission on the steps that may be taken to improve the methods of examination in our universities.

Main Recommendations (Extracts)

1. No reform in the system of examinations will reduce the failure rate in our universities and colleges, unless the prevailing admission procedures are improved. We have, therefore, to see that only those candidates are admitted to universities who can profit by higher education. One of the feasible ways by which this could be done is to introduce in the School Leaving Examination two additional papers, one to test competence in the use of the language of the university and one to test intellectual maturity, for those who wish to enter the university.

2. Teaching work should be done not only through lectures but through tutorials, seminars, etc. It will be desirable to hold periodical short tests on the work done in the tutorials and to maintain a record of the assessments made. This should be regularly evaluated. Even university may decide what weightage should be given to this. In order to make room for tutorials, lectures may be cut down (it should be possible to reduce them by 50 per cent) and the teaching work divided between tutorials and lectures.

3. The U.G.C. should encourage seminars, discussions and conferences of university and college teachers for defining the objectives of teaching and examinations in different subjects at various levels. A clear conception of the aims of teaching will facilitate good teaching and bring about a greater conformity between examinations and teaching.

4. Research should be undertaken in regard to both the educational and technical aspects of examinations. It should be possible for the departments of education in universities to undertake such work as a part of their normal activities. Perhaps the newly created National Council of Educational Research and Training would also be able to assist in this. There would be arrangement in the University Grants Commission to coordinate the research work of the different universities and to disseminate information and conclusions with regard to the studies undertaken in the country.

5. Where the courses are spread over two years or more, convenient spacing of the examinations should be arranged, so that the examination is not concentrated at the end of the final year.

6. Use of methods of evaluation other than essay type examination such as multiple-choice tests, short answer tests, open-book tests, viva voce, etc., may be tried wherever necessary.

7. The present methods of marking examination scripts and of combining and tabulating marks in university examination without reference to recognised statistical procedures are not satisfactory. The procedures will have to be developed to make marking and combining of marks more objective.

8. In view of the difficulty of achieving objectivity and precision in the marking of papers, it may be desirable to rank students classwise rather than marks-wise. In general, only two classes may be awarded for Master's Degree, *viz.*, the first and the second, provided the standards of the present first and second classes are maintained.

9. In universities where more than one media of examination exists, the examiners in the different media (atleast head examiners) should meet and define the standards and spread of marks to be adopted in the evaluation work undertaken by them, in order to avoid variation in the marking of scripts.

10. Ways and means must be found for avoiding wastage of time in the administrative work of examinations resulting in late publication of results and consequent difficulties to students.

22.4. EDUCATION COMMISSION OR KOTHARI COMMISSION ON EDUCATION (1964–66)

(Chapter 9, Paras 9.65 to 9.89)

The New Programme of Evaluation

9.65. *The evils of the examination system in India are well known to everybody.* The baneful effects of the system on education in general, and secondary education in particular, have been discussed in the reports of several committees and commissions. The Secondary Education Commission, after reviewing these defects at the secondary education stage, recommended a new approach to school evaluation and made a number of concrete proposals for the improvement of the external examination and the methods of internal assessment. As a result of these proposals, a movement was started for examination reform, which gathered momentum with the establishment of the Central Examination

Unit of trained evaluation officers by the Government of India in 1958. The outstanding feature of the new reform movement is the emphasis laid on the modern concept of evaluation which has found increasing acceptance in educational circles in India in recent years.

9.66. *The New Concept of Evaluation.* It is now agreed that evaluation is a continuous process, forms an integral part of the total system of education, and is intimately related to educational objectives. It exercises a great influence on the pupil's study habits and the teacher's methods of instruction and thus helps not only to measure educational achievement but also to improve it. The techniques of evaluation are means of collecting evidence about the student's development in desirable directions. These techniques should, therefore, be valid, reliable, objective and practicable. As the common method (and often the only method) of evaluation used at present in India is the written examination, a natural corollary of the acceptance of the new approach will be to improve the written examination in such a way that it becomes a valid and reliable measure of educational achievement. There are, however, several important aspects of the student's growth that cannot be measured by written examinations, and other methods such as observation techniques, oral tests and practical examinations, have to be devised for collecting evidence for the purpose. These methods need to be improved and made reliable instruments for assessing the student's performance and educational development.

9.67. *Progress of the Movement for Reform.* During the seven years of its existence the Central Examination Unit has made a multipronged attack for the popularization of the new concept and techniques of evaluation. It has worked with thousands of secondary school teachers in seminars and workshops, introduced hundreds of training college lectures to the new techniques, established a very large pool of test items, trained paper-setters attached to different Boards of Secondary Education, published a good deal of literature on evaluation and carried out or sponsored several studies and investigations on various practical problems in examinations. As the work of the Unit expanded, the Government of India approved of the establishment of Evaluation Units in different States during the third plan period. So far, State Evaluation Units have started functioning in 12 States and one Union Territory.

9.68. But the task is a stupendous one, and it will take considerable time for the new measures to make their impact on objectives, learning experiences and evaluation procedures in school education. The improvements already made in the external examination by the different Boards have not removed all its major defects. The objectives have not yet been enlarged to include the testing of application and problem-solving abilities. The character of the school examinations, atleast in the senior classes, is determined largely by that of the external examination, and the new techniques of evaluation are not readily adopted in these internal examinations. Moreover, all the efforts in the direction of reform have been confined to the field of secondary education. No attention has been paid to the improvement of examinations at the primary stage, and hardly any to the problems in this area at the university stage.

9.69. *Evaluation at the Lower Primary Stage.* One of the main purposes of evaluation at the primary stage is to help the pupils to improve their achievement in the basic skills and to develop the right habits and attitudes with reference to the objectives of primary education. These objectives and their implications for evaluation should be made clear to the teachers. As has been suggested in an earlier chapter, it would be desirable to treat the lower primary stage covering Classes I to IV as an ungraded unit, because this would help the children coming from different backgrounds to advance at their own pace. As the conditions in most primary schools, however, are not favourable to the general adoption of this procedure, we have recommended that the experiment should be tried out in the beginning in Classes I and II, which should be regarded as a single ungraded unit. This will put an end to the existing practice of detentions in Class I and the drop-outs and wastage resulting therefrom, and will also provide for continuity and flexibility in the educational programme of the first two classes. The two-year block may be divided into two groups, one for slow-learners and the other for fast-learners to enable different pupils to proceed at the level of their ability and move from one unit to another. Such a division, however, will be practicable only in a large-sized school with more than one section in each class. If the experiment regarding the ungraded unit succeeds in Classes I and II, it may be extended to the remaining classes of the lower primary stage.

9.70. Teachers should be prepared for the ungraded system through the regular training courses and orientation programmes and should be helped with a supply of diagnostic tests and remedial material. The orientation may be given by the State Institutes of Education. Observation techniques, which are more reliable for assessing the pupil's growth at this stage than mere formal techniques of evaluation, should be used by teachers in a planned and systematic manner.

9.71. *Evaluation at the Higher Primary Stage.* At present evaluation in these classes is carried out largely by means of written examinations. We believe that due importance should be given here also to oral tests, which should form a part of the internal assessment. The teacher should be helped in such assessment with a rich supply of evaluation materials prepared by the State Evaluation Organizations, including standardized achievement tests. Diagnostic testing is necessary here and indeed throughout the school stage. In most cases, such testing will be through simple teacher-made diagnostic tests. Cumulative record cards play a vital role in indicating the growth and development of the pupil at each stage, his academic and emotional problems, and his difficulties of adjustment, if any, and the directions in which remedial action is to be taken to solve his problems or difficulties. We are of the opinion that cumulative record cards intended for the primary classes should be very simple, so that primary teachers can use them with just a little training. In the first instance, the cards should be introduced from Class IV onwards in about 10 percent of selected schools as an experimental measure; but once the majority of teachers are trained in evaluating certain important aspects of the child's personality and the proper maintenance of the records, the use of the cards may be gradually extended to all the higher primary and as a next step, even to lower primary schools.

9.72. *Is a Primary External Examination Necessary?* An external examination at the end of the primary stage (Class VII or VIII) to be taken compulsorily by all pupils was strongly recommended by some witnesses who appeared before the Commission. We were informed that some of the States which had abolished the external examination at the end of this stage had either reintroduced it or proposed re-introducing it in the near future. It was pointed out that an external examination was necessary for (1) maintaining certain uniform standards at the end of the stage; (2) providing a basis for choice of courses at the secondary stage and (3) creating incentives for better teaching and learning. But all these arguments do not establish a case for an external examination of the formal type to be compulsorily taken by all the pupils in Class VII or VIII. Though we have recommended elsewhere that the first national standard of attainment should be defined at the end of the primary stage, we do not think it necessary or desirable to prescribe a rigidly uniform level of attainment for all the primary school pupils in a State or even in a district, through an external examination. Moreover, instead of treating incentives for better teaching, the external examination intended for all will saddle teachers with standardized programmes and encourage the process of rote memorization, which is the besetting evil of teaching and learning methods in our schools to-day. Again, since full-time education at the lower secondary stage will provide, by and large, general education without any streaming, the argument regarding the choice does not hold good; and for the diversion of pupils to full-time vocational courses to be made available at this stage, an examination which will merely test intellectual ability and academic attainment will not be of much help. We, therefore, recommend that no compulsory external examinatioon should be held at the end of the primary school stage.

9.73. While we are not in favour of a compulsory external examination, we believe that for the proper maintenance of standards, periodic surveys of the level of achievement of primary schools is necessary. We recommend that such surveys should be conducted by the district educational authorities to assess the standard of performance of the schools in a given area by means of standardized or highly refined tests prepared by specialists in the State Evaluation Organizations. This procedure will enable the education officers to pick out the weaker schools and help them to improve their performance. It will also assist the schools in finding out the weakness of their pupils for purposes of remedial work.

9.74. *A Common Internal Examination for Inter-School Comparability.* By making use of the standardized or refined test material referred to above, the district educational authorities may, if they so desire, arrange for a common examination to be taken by the pupils of all the schools in a district at the end of the primary stage. This common school leaving examination will be different from the school certificate examination now held in many States, because though the question papers will be set by the district educational authorities or by special paper-setters appointed by the State Evaluation Organization, the performance of the pupils of each participating school will be assessed by the teachers of the school themselves, and not by any external examiners. The advantages are obvious. As the question papers will contain standardized tests and highly refined and professional test items, the evaluation will be more valid and reliable than what is possible through the kind of annual and final examinations conducted in the ordinary primary school. Moreover, through such common tests inter-school comparability with regard to levels of performance in the district can be obtained, and this would be helpful as shown above, both to the education officers, and to the schools. We would like to emphasize that the question papers in the different subjects at this common examination should be of short duration each of not more than one hour or one hour and a half, so that the entire examination should be completed in two or three days.

9.75. The whole purpose of the proposal is to reform the existing examination by making it less formal, reducing its burden on the pupils' minds, and increasing its validity as a measure of educational attainment. The school at the primary stage plays the determining role in the total assessment of such attainment. The certificate regarding the completion of the course should be given by the school and not by the external agency, and this certificate should be accompanied by a statement showing the results of the common final examination if any, together with the results of the internal assessment made by the school of the pupils' performance throughout the year, as shown in his cumulative records.

9.76. In addition to the common examination, special tests may be held at the end of the primary course for the award of scholarships or certificates of merit or for the purpose of identifying talent and pupils may appear for these tests on a voluntary basis. The evaluation of the pupil's performance in these tests will be done by external examiners.

9.77 *Improvement in External Examination.* At present in the case of the higher secondary class or the intermediate classes located in the school, the external examination is held by the State Board of Secondary (or Higher Secondary) Education, and in the case of pre-university class, the examination is held by the university concerned. We have recommended that the pre-university classes now located in affiliated colleges should be transferred to schools as higher secondary classes in a phased programme spread over ten years, and that the duration of the higher secondary course should be extended to two years everywhere by 1986. When these classes are located exclusively in the schools, the Board of School Education will conduct the external examination at the end of Class XI (or Class XII) as well as that at the end of Class X. In the transitional period the present dual control will continue.

What we state below applies to all external examinations at the school stage, whether they are at present conducted by the Boards or by the universities.

(1) Most of the weaknesses in the present system of external examinations are due to defects in the questions and the question papers set for the examination. The paper-setters are, by and large, appointed on the basis of seniority, subject competence, and experience in teaching. Very few of them possess the necessary knowledge and skill in the construction of valid and reliable tests. We are of the opinion that no major break-through towards the improvement of external examinations is possible unless (*a*) the technical competence of paper-setters is raised through an intensive training programme sponsored by the State Boards; (*b*) the question papers are oriented to testing not merely the acquisition of knowledge but the ability to apply knowledge and the development of problem-solving abilities; and (*c*) the nature of the questions asked is improved.

(2) Apart from the improvement of questions and question papers, many other procedures of the external examinations need to be made more systematic and scientific. For example, the marks of different subjects are added without being standardized. The determination of cut-off points, the award of grace marks and other similar methods are also not based on any sound rationale. All these factors tend to make the examination scores less and less reliable. It is essential that scientific scoring procedures should be devised so that there may be optimum reliability in the assessment of the candidate's performance.

(3) With the ever-increasing number of students appearing for the Board examinations, the task of getting the answer scripts properly valued and of processing the results efficiently within a given time is becoming more and more difficult. It is necessary that this process should be mechanized so as to make it more accurate and expeditious.

9.78. *Large Incidence of Failures.* The matter about which the public at large is most deeply concerned is not the irrationality of the scoring procedures or the inefficiency of the administrative processes, but the large incidence of failures in the external examination at the end of the school stage. An analysis of the results of the different Board examinations for the last five years show that about 55 per cent of the candidates appearing for the high school examination and about 40 per cent of those appearing for the higher secondary school examination fail regularly every year. In the case of the private candidates the percentage soars upto 70 or even more. Failure often has a demoralizing effect on the unsuccessful candidate. The failure of such large numbers of students, particularly after they have been screened year after year by means of annual and other school examinations, is a sad reflection on our methods of education as well as on our system of examination.

9.79. There is no doubt that if the measures suggested above for the reform of the external examination are properly implemented the situation will gradually change in the years to come. We also believe, that with the proposed improvement in the curriculum, instructional materials and methods of teaching and the reorientation in the training of teachers, the incidence of examination failures will be reduced. But we do not think that a student should be branded as a total failure, if he passes in certain subjects but is unable to make the grade in others. There is no reason why he should carry with him the stigma of being declared an unsuccessful candidate if he has partially succeeded in his educational effort.

9.80. *Certificates Given by the Board and the School.* We recommend that the certificate issued by the Board on the basis of the results of the external examination at the end of the lower or higher secondary stage, should give the candidate's performance only in those subjects in which it has passed, but there should be no remark to the effect that he has passed or failed in the whole examination. The Board, however, should issue a statement along with the certificate showing his marks or grades in all the subjects. We further recommend that the candidate should be permitted to appear again, if he so desires, for the entire examination or for separate subjects in order to improve his performance.

9.81. On the completion of the course at the end of the lower or higher secondary stage, the student should receive a certificate from the school also giving the record of his internal assessment as contained in his cumulative record card. This certificate may be attached to that given by the Board in connection with the external examination, but we are of the opinion that the external examination need not be compulsory for all the students of Class X or Class XI/XII. A student may choose to leave the school with the school certificate only without appearing for the external examination, and seek a job or even an entry into some vocational course on the basis of the certificate and the school records. It must be recognised, however, that since admission to institutions of higher secondary education as well as of higher education will be selective, the authorities controlling such institutions will lay down their own rules of eligibility for admission. A student seeking entry into these institutions may have not only to pass the external examination in the subjects laid down and secure the prescribed grades but also submit himself if necessary to certain admission tests required by the institutions.

9.82. *Establishment of Experimental Schools.* We have suggested certain measures above for reducing the domination which the external examination exercises over school education. In order to lessen its importance still further, we recommend that a few selected schools should be given the right of assessing their students themselves and holding their own final examination at the end of Class X, which will be regarded as equivalent to the external examination of the State Board of School Education. The State Board will issue the certificates to the successful candidates of these schools on the recommendation of the schools. A committee set up by the State Board of School Education should develop carefully workedout criteria for the selection of such schools. The schools should not only be freed from the requirements of an external examination but should be permitted to frame their own curricula, prescribe their own textbooks, and conduct their educational activities without departmental restrictions.

9.83. This is a bold step in the direction of freedom and of educational experimentation. But the right given to the experimental schools should be reviewed periodically as institutions invested with such powers should continuously earn their privilege. We hope, however, that after the experiment is tried out successfully in a few schools, more and more schools will be released from the restrictive influence of the external examination and given the freedom to work out their own ideas in education.

9.84. *Methods of Internal Assessment.* We shall now pass onto the question of internal assessment to which a reference was made earlier in this section. This internal assessment or evaluation conducted by individual schools is of great significance and should be given increasing importance. It should be comprehensive, evaluating all those aspects of the student's growth that are measured by the external examination and also those personality traits, interests and attitudes which cannot be assessed by it. Internal assessment should be built into the total educational programme of the school and should be used for improvement rather than for certifying the level of achievement of the student. It must be pointed out that all items of internal assessment need not follow qualified scoring procedures. Some of them may be assessed in descriptive terms. The results should be kept separately and not be combined artificially with other results to form aggregate scores.

9.85. The written examinations conducted in schools should be improved on the same lines as the external examination. The use of standardized achievement tests wherever available, is strongly recommended. There is need for developing other types of evaluation tools for improving internal assessment such as interest inventories, aptitude tests and rating scales. They should be prepared by specialists and made available to schools, and the teachers should be trained to use them through a network of in-service programmes. Teachers should also be trained to make simple tests of their own on the models supplied and use them for the assessment of the performance of their pupils.

9.86. We are aware that the experience of introducing internal assessment has not been very happy so far and that there has been persistent over-assessment by the weaker schools. This has led some critics to suggest that the system should be abandoned altogether. We cannot agree with this view. Internal assessment has to continue and its importance will have to be increasingly emphasized. To overcome the shortcomings discovered, we make the following recommendations:

(1) The results of the internal assessment and external examination should not be combined because the purposes and techniques of the two evaluations are different and because the results of the internal assessment of the different institutions are not strictly comparable. The results of the external and internal assessment should, therefore, be shown separately in the certificate(s) given at the end of the course.

(2) It should be an important point in the inspections of schools to review the internal assessment made and to examine the correlation between the internal and external assessments. Persistence in over assessment should be regarded as a weakness in the school programmes. It should be taken due note of while classifying the schools and should also be related to grants-in-aid so that institutions which tend to over-assess their students persistently would stand to lose in status and finance. The grant-in-aid rules should also authorise the Education Department to withdraw recognition for persistent irresponsible assessment.

9.87. *Higher Secondary Examination during Transition.* We have recommended above that the first external examination should be held at the end of Class X or the first stage of school education, and the second examination should come after Class XII which will be the end of the higher secondary stage. At present, the higher secondary stage in all the States except Uttar Pradesh and Kerala ends with Class XI after which there is the higher secondary school examination. This will continue to be the position till the duration of the course is extended to two years. During the transitional period, therefore, most students in the higher secondary school will have to appear for two successive external examinations, at the end of Class X and Class XI, within the period of a year. This is undesirable but cannot be avoided, particularly where the course of Class IX, X and XI is not integrated. When the P.U.C. class gets transferred from the affiliated colleges to the high schools, the course will be a non-integrated one.

9.88. As a number of existing higher secondary schools with integrated courses are already in existence in some of the States, we do not insist that this integration should be broken up and the students of the schools should be made to appear for two public examinations within a year. There may be only one public examination for such students—the higher secondary school examination at the end of Class XI. However, we would like to invite attention in this connection to the procedure that is followed in some areas, where the higher secondary school examination is staggered over a period of two years, the core subjects being offered for examination at the end of Class X and the electives at the end of Class XI. This procedure may be adopted with suitable modifications in other places. It must be remembered that the problem is a temporary one and will disappear when schools are organized on the 10 plus 2 pattern.

9.89. The comprehensive programme of evaluation that we have described in the preceding paragraphs requires for the implementation a well-organized machinery both at the State and the Central levels. The Secondary Boards of School Education that now conduct external examinations at the secondary stage will be converted into State Boards of School Education with enhanced powers and functions. At the Centre, there will be a National Board of School Education that will be responsible for evaluation programmes at the national level.

22.5. COMMITTEE ON EXAMINATION REFORM IN CENTRAL UNIVERSITIES (1966)

The Committee was appointed by the University Grants Commission with Prof. F.C. Auluck as its Chairman. Its terms of reference were:

1. To study the examination system of the Central Universities; and
2. To make suitable recommendations for examination reform.

Recommendations (Extracts)

1. One of the chief characteristics of the present examination system of the Central Universities is that it is of the 'essay type' which means that the student has the freedom to build up his theme, examine the facts critically and elaborate his ideas freely and fully. However, evaluation of such answers tends to become subjective, there being no precise tool of measurement in the hands of individual examiners. It would be an advantage if some questions are introduced of the objective type having separate time allotted to them. This may not be feasible in all the subjects but it should be possible in a number of subjects to introduce some specific questions of the short answer type if not the multiple choice.

2. It would be advantageous if in sessional tests which all the four Central Universities have introduced in one form or the other, evaluation is done not only on the basis of written tests but through quizzes, viva-voce, practicals, problem-solving exercises, reports of field work, project reports, prescribed readings, etc. thereby giving the student the necessary practice in writing, thinking and expression and encouragement to do independent reading and hard sustained work..

3. One practical method of checking any possible abuses of the system of sessional assessment is to review the marks in sessional tests and university examinations and to scale the former whenever there is a large disparity between the two.

4. It is also important that marks awarded for sessional work should be known to the student immediately after the test. This would be a possible check on biased marking on the part of the teacher which may happen in some cases.

5. The system of external examinations should be gradually replaced by internal and continuous evaluation by the teachers themselves, if the experience of the Central Universities with sessional marking encourages them to do so.

6. The size of the tutorial groups should be comparatively smaller than what obtains at present in the Central Universities.

7. The universities should also be assisted to create examination cells under the guidance of an evaluation expert. The association of university professors in advisory capacity would also be desirable. The function of the cells would be to carry out studies in correlation between sessional records and university examinations, item analysis of question paper and other studies pertaining to examinations.

8. The appointment of external examiners may perhaps be justified in examinations where the number of examinees is very large.

9. It is important that universities should think of arranging examinations in parts and space them conveniently.

10. Paper-setting is one crucial area of examination reform which calls for radical changes. For example, the question paper might contain at least one question which does not belong to the syllabus. This could be tried at post-graduate examinations since at this level the student is expected to have a certain degree of maturity and access to the sources of knowledge.

11. It would also be useful to have a large number of short-answer type questions rather than few other kinds of questions.

12. The practice of giving a large number of optional questions should also be restricted as far as possible.

13. The U.G.C. might convene a series of seminars of teachers in the Central Universities to discuss the important problem of reframing the question papers to make them balanced as well as problem-oriented.

14. In the interest of uniformity of evaluation, the paper-setter may be asked to prepare a tentative outline of answers to the questions set by him together with detailed instructions regarding marking and distribution of marks as done by the Delhi University. The outline should be circulated to all the examiners working under the guidance of the head-examiner. The examiners should also be requested to keep in view the distribution of marks, *i.e.* the marks to be awarded for an excellent answer, good answer, fair answer, poor answer, etc.

15. The examiners should also prepare detailed reports on the performance of students together with their suggestions for improving methods of study and instruction. The reports should be circulated to the teachers concerned and discussed at meetings of the boards of studies.

16. There should be ceiling on the number of scripts that an individual examiner may examine.

17. The present system of moderation being entrusted to boards with vast discriminatory powers as in the Benaras Hindu and Delhi Universities or the award of grace marks leaves much to be desired.

22.6. COMMITTEE ON EXAMINATIONS APPOINTED BY THE CENTRAL ADVISORY BOARD OF EDUCATION, MINISTRY OF EDUCATION AND SOCIAL WELFARE, GOVT. OF INDIA (1970-71)

Appointment of the Committee and Terms of Reference. At the 35th meeting of the Central Advisory Board of Education, held at New Delhi on the 2nd and 3rd of May, 1970, most members expressed considerable concern about the malpractices, eruption of violence, etc., during the progress of our public examinations held in the different parts of the country. The Board, therefore, passed the following resolution which appears as resolution 12 in the minutes of the 35th meeting of the Board :

> "The Board requests the Chairman to set up a Committee on Examinations which will examine the present situation and make recommendations to counteract malpractices and to give protection to invigilators and others concerned with examinations."

Pursuant to the above resolution, the Chairman of the Central Advisory Board of Education appointed a Committee with Union Education Minister as Chairman and Director, NCERT as the Member Secretary.

MAJOR RECOMMENDATIONS

A. Legislation

The State and Central Governments should immediately take suitable measures to get amending legislation passed in the relevant laws pertaining to the following matters :

(*a*) Empowering the Board/University to grant autonomous status to well-established institutions.

(*b*) Empowering the examining authorities to check students and prohibit those with weapons from entering the examination halls.

(*c*) Making the assembly of persons within a certain distance from the examination hall a cognizable offence.

(*d*) Making the indulgence in malpractices by employees and authorities of the universities/boards a cognizable offence.

(*e*) Empowering the examining authorities to take out risk insurance for the invigilators and examiners.

(*f*) Making the assault on an examiner or an invigilator or other person connected with examination, a cognizable offence.

B. Conduct of Examinations

1. Paper-setters should be appointed atleast six months prior to the commencement of Public Examination and they should be given at least eight weeks to draft questions. The papers should be finalised at a meeting of the paper-setters.

2. Where the number of candidates in public examination is very large, there should be decentralisation with separate examinations for each group of 10,000 school students or 1,000 college students.

3. A Public Examination should be conducted in the institution in which the students study. The majority of the invigilators and superintendents should be drawn from the institution concerned.

4. Admission to the centre of a Public Examination should be through one main entrance. Only bonafide candidates with identity cards should be admitted in the examination centre after thorough checking.

5. Model answers should always be prepared and supplied by the paper-setters.

6. Copies of the question-papers set should be made available to the teachers in the schools and colleges on the day of the examination but after it is over, so that the teachers could comment on the paper to the authorities quickly.

7. The method of spot valuation at a central place to which all the examiners are called, should be adopted.

8. The result should be declared subject-wise and furnished in the form of grades. The 'raw' marks given by the examiners should never be made available.

9. Subject-wise passing should be introduced and the Public Examination certificate should be given on the candidates passing in the minimum number of subjects.

10. The certificate issued by an examining authority should have two columns, *viz.* one giving the result of Public Examination and the other giving the result of the internal assessment by teachers.

11. For the awarding of prizes and scholarships to a candidate who stands first in an examination or in a subject, a separate test should be conducted and admission to the same limited to those who secure the highest grade in the Public Examination.

12. There should not be too many Public Examinations. There should be one at the end of the upper primary/middle school stage, another at

the end of the secondary stage and the third at the first degree stage. All others should be internal assessments only.

C. Use of Examination Results

1. Recruitment to the services should be made on the basis of tests/examinations conducted by the Public Service Commissions and the maximum age for appointment for clerical posts be reduced to 19 years.

2. Admission to colleges including professional colleges should be on the basis of an entrance test conducted specifically for assessing the aptitude of a student for a particular course. Eligibility to appear at these tests should alone be determined by the results of the Public Examination.

D. Budgeting for Education

In future, both the Central and State Governments should earmark funds separately for guidance and studies and research on examinations.

E. Research

There should be continued study and research on examinations, both at the State and Central levels and in the boards/universities in a co-ordinated manner. Necessary funds for the same should be provided on a priority basis.

F. Novel Ideas

Novel ideas for the organisation and conduct of Public Examinations should be encouraged.

22.7. REPORT OF THE TRAINING COURSE ON EVALUATION (1971)

Refer to Chapter 13.

22.8. NATIONAL SEMINAR ON RESEARCH IN EXAMINATION (1978)

Refer to Chapter 7.

22.9. NATIONAL SEMINAR ON THE MANAGEMENT OF PUBLIC EXAMINATIONS (1978)

Refer to Chapter 6.

22.10. NATIONAL SEMINAR ON EVALUATION (1979)

Refer to Chapter 10.

22.11. CHALLENGE OF EDUCATION : A POLICY PERSPECTIVE (1985)

Introduction. Before the formulation of the New Policy on Education, 1986 (NPE, 1986), the Ministry of Education (now known as Ministry of Human Resource Development), Government of India, prepared a status paper called *Challenge of Education* which contained the status of education in India. The contents of this documents were discussed at various levels and at different educational forums in the country. Ultimately this document paved the way for NPE, 1986.

Contents of the Document on Examinations and Evaluation (Chapters 1 and 4)

1.23 No description of the contemporary educational scenario can be complete without a reference to the examination system since it decides, not only the fate of students, but also the content, orientation as well as the quality of education at all levels. Apart from evaluating examinees on the basis of rote learning and memorising, their annual periodicity creates an environment in which students tend to while away their time for most part of the year and gear themselves to work for the last three or four months. For obvious reasons, lack of continuity in application results in the building up of unbearable pressures at the end of the year which find expression in boycott of examinations, leakage of question papers, mass-copying, payment of bribes to evaluators and other unethical practices. Consequently, degrees and grades do not generally command credibility as a whole with the public as well as employers in the public and private sectors and the whole process of higher education has become warped, disoriented and dysfunctional, producing a large number of unemployable young men and women.

4.126 In a system in which everything has been sub-ordinated to examinations and grading, the characteristics of quality (education) will receive no attention unless these too are evaluated and credits are also awarded for them. However, before this is done, the course curricula, textual materials and the teaching-learning processes will have to undergo a radical transformation. Who can undertake this task and how it might be done are issues which need careful and immediate attention. In this context, it appears self-evident that the present system of annual examinations will have to be modified since these, more than any other factor, have contributed to the deterioration in quality. A stage has now been reached when neither those who conduct examinations nor those responsible for teaching and academic management are scandalised by the very poor grades and pass percentages in examinations. This is largely because the curricula as well as evaluation systems are out of tune, not only with the teaching methods and time disposition in the learning process, but also with the attitudes, limitations and potentials of students. Diagnostic studies, systems analysis, simulation exercises and action research are by and large, conspicuous by their absence, in the field of curriculum development.

22.12. NATIONAL POLICY ON EDUCATION, 1986 (Paras contained in Part 8 of the Policy)

The Evaluation Process and Examination Reform

Assessment of performance is an integral part of any process of learning and teaching. As part of sound educational strategy, examinations should be employed to bring about qualitative improvement in education.

The objective will be to re-cast the examination system so as to ensure a method of assessment that is a valid and reliable measure of student development and a powerful instrument for improving teaching and learning. In functional terms, this would mean:

(*i*) The elimination of excessive element of chance and subjectivity;

(*ii*) The de-emphasis of memorisation;

(*iii*) Continuous and comprehensive evaluation that incorporates both scholastic and non-scholastic apsects of education, spread over the total span of instructional times;

(*iv*) Effective use of evaluation process by teachers, students and parents;

(*v*) Improvement in the conduct of examinations;

(*vi*) The introduction of concomitant changes in introductional material and methodology;

(*vii*) The introduction of the semester system from the secondary stage in a phased manner, and

(*viii*) The use of grades in place of marks.

The above goals are relevant both for external examinations and evaluations within educational institutions. Evaluation at the institutional level will be streamlined and the predominance of external examinations reduced.

22.13. PROGRAMME OF ACTION (1986)

Introduction. After the formulation of the National Policy on Education

(1986), Department of Education, Ministry of Human Resource Development, Government of India, prepared a programme of action for the implementation of the NPE.

Chapter XVIII 'Evaluation Process and Examination Reforms' of the *Programme of Action* contains the following:

1. Reforms in examinations have been a subject of serious discussion for long. Some changes have been introduced in the system at the initiative of the NCERT in school examinations and the UGC in university examinations. On the whole, however, the impact of these reforms have not been too significant.

The Policy And Strategies For Implementation

2. The policy visualises integration of the assessment of performance with the process of learning and teaching, and utilising the process of evaluation to bring about qualitative improvement in education (para 8.23). In order to ensure that the method of assessment of students' performance is valid and reliable, the following short-term measures are proposed:

(*a*) **At the School Level:**

- (*i*) Public examinations will continue to be held only at the levels of Classes X and XII;
- (*ii*) Decentralisation of the operations involved in the conduct of examinations to make the system work more effectively.
- (*iii*) School Boards in certain States have set up a number of sub-centres to decentralise the conduct of examinations. Adoption of similar measures by other States will be pursued.
- (*iv*) In the event of decentralisation as indicated above, the State Boards of School Education would continue to get the question papers set and printed, consolidate the results of examinations and also undertake test checks on random basis of the functioning of the subcentres; and
- (*v*) Spot evaluation of answer scripts.

(*b*) **At the University Level:**

- (*i*) Continuous institutional evaluation will be introduced at the post-graduate level, to begin with, in Unitary Universities, Deemed Universities and Autonomous Colleges;
- (*ii*) Students' performance will be indicated through letter grades, and assessment of overall performance will be on the basis of cumulative grade point average;

(*iii*) Provision will be made for improvement of performances through subsequent appearances without involving anv disadvantage to the candidates;

(*iv*) External examinations will continue to be held by universities which have a large number of affiliated colleges and efforts will be made to improve the conduct of examinations through effective decentralisation as indicated for school level examinations;

(*v*) Modifications in the qualifying recruitments for admissions in the universities and colleges will be examined to accelerate the process of change in the school level examinations.

(*c*) **Conduct of Examinations:**

(*i*) The possibility of introducing legislation to define various malpractices connected with examinations and to treat them as cognizable and unbailable offences will be considered;

(*ii*) Such laws will also, when enacted, make provision to prescribe the nature and type of punishments for various offences under the law, and to include within its scope persons engaged in various operations connected with examinations and also to provide protection to them; and

(*iii*) Innovations and experiments in the conduct of examinations, like printing and distribution of question papers with questions arranged in different sequences to avoid copying and other unfair means in the examination halls.

3. In order to attain the objective of integrating the process of evaluation with teaching and learning, several long-term reforms will be necessary. For this purpose, the following programmes would be considered:-

(*a*) **At the School Level:**

(*i*) The Boards of Education will lay down the levels of attainment expected at classes V, VIII, X and XII;

(*ii*) The Boards will also prescribe the learning objectives corresponding to these levels of attainment in terms of knowledge and comprehension, communication, skills in the application of knowledge, and the ability to learn;

(*iii*) Schemes of evaluation consisting of examinations to test those aspects of learning which can be assessed through formal examinations, and the procedure for assessing those aspects which cannot be tested through such an examination, will be developed. Abilities and proficiencies which can and should be assessed through institutional evaluation will be identified and procedures evolved for such evaluation;

(*iv*) The development of schemes of evaluation is a continuing process. To provide professional support to this process, the Boards of Education will consider setting up a Consortium for initiating research and development in evaluation procedures and in the conduct of examinations;

(*v*) For performing this task, the Consortium will adopt selected schools as pilot centres and will hold examinations and award certificates for the students of such schools;

(*vi*) Before question papers are set, a detailed design will be evolved indicating the weightage to be given to various areas of content, types of questions and the objectives of teaching/learning;

(*vii*) Alongwith external examinations, continuous institutional evaluation of scholastic and non-scholastic aspects of education will be introduced;

(*viii*) Evaluation of students' performance will move towards cumulative grading system;

(*ix*) In the big States, the possibility of establishing more than one Board of Education will be considered, so that the number of students to be examined by one Board does not exceed one lakh; and

(*x*) Procedures will be developed for the appointment of Chairmen/ Secretaries of Boards of Education and Controllers of Examinations to inspire confidence among public.

(*b*) **At the University Level:**

(*i*) The possibility of developing alternate system of evaluation in place of external examinations for affiliated colleges will be explored;

(*ii*) The question of some universities functioning only as examining bodies for a number of colleges will be examined;

(*iii*) Academic reforms visualised in the policy like flexibility in the combination of course, modular structure, provision for accumulation of credits, redesigning of courses, etc. will lead to considerable decentralisation in the evaluation process. Detailed schemes will be evolved to facilitate transition to new evaluation procedures concurrently with the changes in the content and structure; and (*iv*) An agency will be developed either as part of the AIU (Association of Indian Universities) or independently, for continuous research and development in evaluation procedures.

(*c*) **General:**

(*i*) Integrity of the examiner is crucial to the credibility of the examination system.

This credibility can be established by the openness of the examinations. It has to be recognised that students have the inalienable right to scrutinise their answer scripts and its evaluation and also compare them with those of others:

(*ii*) The practice of declaring results in terms of over-all divisions and pass/fail may be reviewed and substituted by a system of declaration of results in terms of marks/grades in each subject separately;

(*iii*) Candidates should have the opportunity to improve upon their grades through subsequent attempts;

(*iv*) Provisions should be made for clearing examinations in parts, in conformity with the modular pattern of courses;

(*v*) The practice of scaling marks of different subjects which are not at par may be adopted in determining the grades;

(*vi*) Intensive training programmes will be organised for paper-setters;

(*vii*) Question banks will be developed to assist paper-setters;

(*viii*) A detailed marking scheme will be developed to ensure objectivity in scoring answer scripts;

(*ix*) Innovative ideas like open book examination, diagnostic evaluation etc. may be experimented with;

(*x*) Separate certificates will be awarded showing the results of institutional evaluation and external examinations;

(*xi*) The certificate of institutional evaluation may cover academic achievements as well as non-scholastic aspects.

(*xii*) Attempts will be made to move towards a situation in which only those who teach will evaluate their students;

(*xiii*) Integration of evaluation with the process of teaching and learning will help diagnose the weaknesses and deficiencies in education. This diagnostic aspect will be utilised to develop remedial programme for weaker sections.

(*xiv*) Facilities will be provided in schools and colleges for maintenance of students' records to facilitate continuous institutional evaluation; and (*xv*) Programmes of training and orientation of teachers will give special attention to new evaluation methodologies, setting of question papers, measurement of performances, etc.

(*d*) **National Testing Service**

A National Testing Service will be established and developed as a quality control mechanism to organise nation-wide tests on a voluntary basis so that norms can be evolved for comparability of performance and also for conducting independent tests.

22.14. NATIONAL SEMINAR ON ORAL EXAMINATIONS (1987)

Refer to Chapter 2.

22.15. NATIONAL SEMINAR ON SCALING OF EXAMINATIONS (1987)

22.16. UGC GUIDELINES FOR TEACHING AND RELATED MATTERS (1984-88)

Mininum Programme of Examination Reform

Every university/deemed to be university shall have to adopt the following minimum examination reform.

Syllabus/Question Paper

(*a*) The syllabus in each paper should be demarcated into well defined units/areas of content alongwith a topicswise breakdown. The units may be numbered.

(*b*) Examiners should be free to repeat questions set in a previous examination. This is necessary in order to ensure that students do not leave out important portions of the syllabus. Instructions to paper-setters should be amended accordingly.

(*c*) There is often a very wide choice given to students for answering questions, say 5 out of 10. Such overall choice restricts the area of knowledge with which a student can pass an examination and is therefore undesirable. If there is choice, it may be provided by alternate questions in each unit of the syllabus.

(*d*) No examination should be held without fulfilling the requirement of a minimum number of lectures/tutorials/laboratory sessions, etc. which should be clearly laid down by the university.

(*e*) Examinations should be conducted in fair and impartial manner. Cheating in examinations is a cognizable offence. Universities must take all steps for the proper conduct of examinations such as effective security measures, proper supervision and invigilation, cordoning off the examination centres from the range of loudspeakers and other interference, flying squads and stern action in all cases involving copying and use of unfair means.

22.17. COMMITTEE FOR REVIEW OF NPE 1986 OR RAMAMURTI REPORT (1990)

Introduction. The Committee for Review of National Policy on Education (NPE) 1986, popularly known as Ramamurti Committee, after the name of its chairman, which was appointed by the Janata Government, reviewed the implementation of the NPE and made its observations and recommendations on all aspects of education including examinations and evaluation.

EXTRACTS FROM CHAPTER 12 ENTITLED 'CONTENT AND PROCESS OF EDUCATION'

Examination Reforms

12.10.1. Examination reform has been a subject of almost consistent consideration by various committees and commissions appointed by the Government of India from time to time. The justification for examination reforms arises from academic considerations. Examinations alongwith teaching and learning, in fact, constitute the trinity of functions in the educational process. Examinations over the years have tended to be an instrument for testing memory. Learning has become a rather mechanical process of acquiring skills and teaching has been largely a process of coaching for examinations. The relationship between examinations and standards of teaching and learning are intimate. Improvement in any one of these aspects results in improvement of other aspects as well. Therefore, the objective of examination reform is to make it an instrument of good education.

12.10.2. The Indian University Commission (1902) observed that the teaching in Indian education stood subordinated to examination and not examination to teaching. The Hartog Committee (1929) deprecated academic bias of examinations at the school level, geared as they were to the needs of the majority who did not have access to the university system and were to enter life. Similar criticism was voiced by the Sargent Plan 1944. The Radhakrishnan Commission (1948) pointed out that examination reform was a matter of very high priority in education reform as a whole. The Mudaliar Commission (1952-53) made elaborate recommendations on examination reform and called for reduction in the number of external examinations, conduct of objective tests, assessment of attainments of the students through a proper system of school records, weightage for in-school tests, symbolic rather than numerical marking for purposes of evaluation and grading etc. The Education Commission (1964-66) considered the question of examination reform at all stages of education and called for evaluation being construed as a means to assess learner development on an objective basis. The CABE Committee on Examination Reform (1970), also made wide ranging recommendations. The National Policy on Education, 1986, envisaged evaluation as a continuous process so that the student would be helped to improve his level of achievement, as distinct from certification of the quality of his performance at a given moment of time. The National Policy on Education, 1986 also considered examinations as a means for improvement of quality of education. Specifically, it called for removal of subjectivity in examinations, de-emphasis of memorisation, continuous and comprehensive internal evaluation of scholastic and non-scholastic achievements of students, improvement in the conduct of examinations, introduction of concomitant changes in instructional material and methodology introduction of the semester system from the secondary stage in a phased manner and use of grades in the place of marks. The Programme of Action (POA) suggested several sepecific short-term and long-term measures for carrying out examination reform at the school level as well as the university level.

12.10.3. Following up on NPE, 1986, NCERT conducted a National Seminar on Examination Reforms and issued certain guidelines to the States, principally covering the subjects of scaling and grading, continuous comprehensive internal evaluation, setting up of balanced question papers etc.

12.10.4. The CABE, in July, 1989, also recommended that the State Boards should take effective steps in the areas of grading and scaling, continuous comprehensive internal evaluation of scholastic and non-scholastic achievements of students etc. The 19th Annual Conference of the Council of Boards of School Education in India, (COBSE) recommended the following in September, 1990:

- Comprehensive and continuous internal evaluation should be introduced in a phased manner, initially at the elementary stage;
- A letter grading system on a nine point scale should be introduced for declaration of individual results by the State Boards by 1995 at the elementary stage.

- The State Boards should work towards abolition of public examinations, particularly at the end of class X subject to credibility of continuous and comprehensive internal evaluation, stage of reforms effected in grading system and introduction of entrance test for admissions in institutions for higher learning.
- Introduction of semester system in a phased manner from the secondary stage so that the students are enabled to progress at their own pace.

Despite Efforts

12.10.7. Despite efforts at reforms the present day situation is one of tail wagging the dog *i.e.* the system of examination dictating the character and quality of education itself. The schools have come to be construed as some kind of a giant conveyer belt, transferring students from stage to stage leading to the university, rather than institutions equipping the students for life and working in society. The centralised public examination system, as distinct from evaluation at the institutional level results in the majority of the examinees getting thrown off the conveyor belt, in effect making education discriminatory and elitist. (It is the comparatively more well-to-do who are able to afford the coaching materials and guidance through tuitions required for success in examinations.). The importance given to the marks in public examinations obtained by students either for admission to higher courses or for selection of jobs has resulted in marks-based value system. The universities also have tended to jack up their marking system to compete with good universities, not necessarily mindful of standards. Universities are also under severe strain on account of the burden of holding examinations at the under-graduate level. It is desirable that universities are relieved of the load of administering examinations. The students have to take several admission tests for entry into engineering and medical institutions. Apart from being a strain on the students, parallel tests by different institutions are an avoidable waste of resources.

Recommendations

1. The question of examination reform should be construed as a package of all the following factors:
   - Introduction of semester system.
   - Continuous internal evaluation; and maintenance of integrity of such evaluation (and examinations in whatever form and scale they may be conducted) within the same classes, in

primary stage, diaggregated evaluation of groups of students to cater to individual differences.

- Teachers playing the key role, the principle being "He or she who teaches shall lay down the syllabus and also evaluate".
- Facilities for students to move from one stage of education to another by appearing in entrance tests.
- Facilities for students to have the freedom of choice of modules rather than whole course packages.
- Provisions for credit accumulation by students and facilities for transfer of grade from one institution to another; facilities of multiple entry and exit for students which in effect facilitates *opening* to and *non-formalising* the school system.

It is this *package* as a whole which should be brought under implementation and not merely individual elements that too in a piecemeal or *ad hoc* fashion.

2. In the present context of our educational system, however there are serious apprehensions basically about the concept of the teacher playing the key role. In the responses received in pursuance of the perspective paper on education, these apprehensions have been voiced by a large number of respondents. The main reason for these apprehensions is that the authority vested in the teacher in this regard might be abused in various ways. Respondents have also expressed the opinion that experiments in this regard in the past have not necessarily been successful. Another view expressed is that the teachers themselves might not be prepared to accept the onerous responsibilities going with examination reforms. It is natural that any attempt at reforms for the purpose of changing the *status-quo* means resistance from the established order. However, the call for examination reforms on the part of experts over the years having been very consistent and several states and universities already having taken up examination reforms in fact, though in a piecemeal way, there is undoubtedly need for orderly progress towards examination reforms in terms of the above package. Implementation of this package, however, bristles with several practical problems, diversities in the education system in the country being vast. Therefore, there is need for an Examination Reforms Commission. This should also be a permanent body which will facilitate monitoring of progress in examination reforms from time to time until the task is fulfilled in stages. The terms of reference for this Commission may be:

(*i*) Review of the status of examination reforms from time to time.

(*ii*) Phasing of examination reforms, indicating time frame within which, and levels at which, the reforms are to be effected.

(*iii*) Introduction of fair and objective systems of grading/scaling.

(*iv*) Laying down norms for continuous comprehensive internal evaluation and suggesting safeguards against abuse of this evaluation system.

(*v*) Advising on minimum levels of learning to go with internal evaluation system.

(*vi*) Laying down modalities for semesterisation and modularisation.

(*vii*) Advising on inter-institutional linkages to secure comparable standards.

(*viii*) Teacher orientation for successful implementation of examination reforms.

It is obvious that the Examination Reforms Commission will have to go into problems relating to the reforms in each State, fully involving the State level authorities so that problems at the state level as well as the sub-state levels are fully taken into consideration. Functionaries of UGC, AIU, AICTE, NCERT, NIEPA, state resource institutions. State Boards of Education and other expert bodies at the national and other levels, apart from teacher and student organisations will also have to be consulted from time to time by the Commission. The Commission may be headed by an eminent educationist with the rank of Minister of State, Government of India. The Commission may be a compact body consisting, apart from the Chairman of experts in the areas of school, university and technical education. The Chairman and members may be full time functionaries.

22.18. CENTRAL ADVISORY BOARD OF EDUCATION (CABE) COMMITTEE OR JANARDHANA COMMITTEE (1992)

Introduction. The CABE Committee was appointed to review the implementation of NPE and the recommendations of the Ramamurti Committee. Shri Janardhana Reddy, Chief Minister and Minister of Education, Andhra Pradesh was its Chairman. The Committee made its recommendations on examinations in Chapter 16 entitled 'Content and Process of Education.'

EXTRACTS ON EXAMINATION REFORMS FROM CHAPTER 16

16.10 The reading of the recommendations as a whole would make it appear that NPERC (National Policy on Education Review Committee or Ramamurti Committee 1991) was itself undecided about the immediate feasibility or acceptability of the package suggested by it. Given the diversity of the educational institutions, it would not be realistic to prescribe a single package of reforms across the board. Some of the reforms like introduction of semester system may be relevant for higher education rather than for school stage. Facilities for multiple entry and exist, and transfer of grade from one institution to an other are not immediately feasible, atleast in the school stage, and call for a degree of uniformity in curriculum and medium of instruction, which are difficult to achieve in a continental nation like ours. Therefore, the endeavour should be to strive for the best achievable results rather than plan for the best unobtainable package. Examination reforms have necessarily to be contextual and evolutionary.

16.11 The essentiality of examination reforms cannot be overstated. We do feel that rather than leaving examination reforms to the individual initiatives and inclinations of the examination bodies a strong and coordinated effort should be made by the Centre and the State Governments in this area. The idea underlying the Constitution of an Examination Reforms Commission is appealing. However, rather than creating yet another institution, we suggest that the NCERT and the UGC should play a lead role in promoting and guiding examination reforms in school and higher education systems respectively. *Inter-alia,* the following measures are suggested:

1. Preparation of a status report of examination reform measures undertaken by the examining bodies.
2. Preparation of a National Examination Reform Frame work to serve as a set of guidelines to the examining bodies which would have the freedom to innovate and adapt the frame work to suit the specific situation.
3. Developing an effective mechanism for coordination, monitoring and evaluation of the implementation of the examination reforms by different examining bodies.
4. Documentation and dissemination of innovations and measures for examination reform.

22.19. REVISED POLICY FORMULATION (1992)

(Revised Para 8.25 of the NPE)

The above goals (as mentioned in NPE 1986) are relevant both for

external examinations and evaluations within the educational institutions. Evaluation at the institutional level will be streamlined and the predominance of external examinations reduced. A National Examination Reform Framework would be prepared to serve as a set of guidelines to the examination bodies which would have the freedom to innovate and adapt the framework to suit the specific situations.
(Note: Other paras of NPE (1986) remain unchanged)

22.20. PROGRAMME OF ACTION (1992)

Introduction. The NPE (1986) was slightly revised in 1992 in the light of experience gained from its implementation and also the recommendations made by the Ramamurti Committee (1990) and Janardhana Review Committee (1992) of the Central Advisory Board of Education. The revised formulation called for a new programme of action. Accordingly the Ministry of Human Resource Development, Government of India issued the document entitled *Programme of Action* (1992).

OBSERVATIONS AND RECOMMENDATIONS
(Chapter 21)

21.1.1 Reforms in examinations have been a subject of serious discussion for long. The NPE 1986, postulated that the examination system should be recast so as to ensure a method of assessment that is a valid and reliable measure of student development and a powerful instrument for improving teaching and learning. In functional terms, this would mean:

(*i*) The elimination of excessive element of chance and subjectivity;
(*ii*) the de-emphasis of memorisation;
(*iii*) continuous and comprehensive evaluation that incorporates both scholastic and non-scholastic aspects of education, spread over the total span of instructional time;
(*iv*) effective use of the evaluation process by teachers, students and parents;
(*v*) improvement in the conduct of examinations;
(*vi*) the introduction of concomitant changes in instructional materials and methodology;
(*vii*) the introduction of the semester system from the secondary stage in a phased manner; and
(*viii*) the use of grades in place of marks.

21.1.2. The NPE, 1986, held that the above goals were relevant both for external examinations and evaluation within educational institutions. It envisaged that evaluation at the institutional level will be streamlined and the pre-dominance of external examinations reduced.

21.1.3. Whatever changes that have been introduced in the school and university examination systems at the instance of the NCERT and the UGC respectively, their impact on the developments indicated above is not perceptible. Inspite of the initiatives of the NCERT and the UGC in this field, only limited awareness has been created on the issues arising from the policy statement on examination reform.

21.1.4 Taking note of this situation the Revised Policy Formulations (RPF) called for preparation of a National Examination Reform Framework to serve as a set of guidelines to the examining bodies which would have the freedom to innovate and adapt the framework to suit the specific situations.

Broad Parameters

21.2.1 To formulate a national examination reform work the Department of Education would, *inter-alia,* constitute an inter-institutional committee with representations from UGC, NCERT, AICTE and State level organisations including Boards of Secondary Education. The framework can be expected to be formulated by December, 1993.

21.2.2 While the specifics of the framework cannot be postulated at this stage the broad parameters seem to envisage the following:

(a) *Elementary Stage.* Specification of minimum levels of learning in the remaining areas and classes, their adaptation at the State and District levels, designing flexible procedures of evaluation to suit a variety of school conditions, and use of evaluation in teaching and learning.

(b) *Secondary Stage.* Specification of expected levels of attainments in curricular subjects, designing flexible schemes of continuous and comprehensive evaluation considering introduction of semester system at secondary stage in a phased manner.

(c) *Higher Education Stage.* Gradual switching over by postgraduate departments of all universities to semester, grading, continuous evaluation and credit systems. Exploring possibilities of introducing validation tests at the first degree and postgraduate levels.

(d) *The Higher Technical and Professional Stage.* Preparing guidelines of evaluation for institutions by each university, replacement of external examination by internal institutional evaluation and All India testing programmes for admission to professional and technical courses; and

(e) *At all Stages.* Devising procedures for setting up of appropriate administrative and technical support mechanisms, and a review of legislation.

Strategies For Implementation

21.3.1 While the inter-institutional committee would work out the detailed feature of strategy the following strategies are envisaged at this stage:

(a) *Elementary Stage:*

- The minimum levels of learning (MLLs) in language (mother tongue), mathematics and environmental studies for classes I-V have been developed by MHRD at the national level. Similar exercise to develop these in the remaining areas and classes of elementary curriculum will be carried out.
- These MLLs will be adapted/adopted by the concerned agency in each state and district to suit the local conditions.
- Since no detention policy is envisaged at the primary stage, the main function of evaluation will be diagnostic in nature so as to provide remedial help to the pupils.
- The concerned agency in each state will prepare a flexible scheme of Continuous Comprehensive Evaluation (CCE) at the elementary stage so as to make the evaluation process an integral part of teaching and learning at this stage. The CCE will cover cognitive, affective and psychomotor areas of pupils' growth and will employ a variety of tools and techniques of evaluation for collecting evidence on different dimensions of pupils' growth. These evaluations will be reported in the form of grades on a comprehensive proforma. Appropriate procedures for ensuring reliability, validity, objectivity and transparency of the evaluation will be suggested by the concerned agency in each state.

(b) *Secondary Stage:*

- Each State Board will lay down expected levels of attainments at classes IX to XII and prescribe appropriate courses of studies to accomplish these levels in terms of knowledge and/or comprehension, communication skills, understanding, application analysis, synthesis, judgments, etc.

In each State the concerned agency will prepare a flexible scheme of CCE for the secondary/senior secondary stage to suit a variety of specific situations obtaining in different regions and types of schools. Certain models have been developed by NCERT and other agencies which could be looked into for guidance.

(c) *Higher Education Stage:*

- Selection tests for admissions to all professional and technical courses will be conducted on an all India basis.
- Each University will prepare broad guidelines for grading to be followed by individual colleges, institutions and departments under its jurisdiction. Orientation programmes may be organised to familiarize the teachers with the grading system.
- The movement towards entrance tests for admission to institutions of higher education will be encouraged and promoted by UGC and State Governments. The services of the National Evaluation Organisation (NEO) should be utilized by the university system for developing, designing and administering entrance tests for admission.

(d) *Strategies common for all Stages:*

- The emphasis will be laid on testing of expected levels of achievement of a variety of learning objectives in order to ensure due importance to higher abilities of understanding, application, analysis, synthesis, judgment and parallel parameters and not only to memory.
- The semester system when introduced at the secondary stage and onwards should, *inter-alia* provide for;

  (*a*) flexibility in the combination of courses; and

  (*b*) accumulation of credits to enable the pupils to proceed at their own pace resulting in upward and horizontal mobility of the students across the country.

- Appropriate courses in examination reform will be developed by Indira Gandhi National Open University through distance education mode in collaboration with NCERT for the large scale training of different kinds and levels of personnel.
- An Examination Reform Centre will be established at the UGC for coordination, documentation and dissemination of information on examination reforms in higher education. Similarly, NCERT would perform this function at school stage.

(*e*) *External Examinations : Nature and Conduct*

The possibility of introducing legislation to define various malpractices connected with examinations and to treat them as cognizable and unbailable offences will be considered. Such laws will, when enacted, make provision to prescribe the nature and type of punishments for various offences under the law, and to include within its scope persons engaged in various operations connected with examinations and also to provide protection to them.

(*f*) *National Evaluation Organisation*

- The National Evaluation Organisation will be developed as a quality control mechanism to organise nation-wide tests on a voluntary basis so that norms can be evolved for comparability of performance and also for conducting independent tests.

(*g*) Monitoring and Evaluation:

- Rather than leaving examination reforms to the individual initiatives and inclinations of the examining bodies, a strong and co-ordinated effort should be made by the Centre and State Governments in this area. It is, therefore, desirable that the monitoring and evaluation of the reforms in examinations and evaluation in a State is also done by the State Department of Education or an agency so designated by it.

22.21. CONFERENCE OF CHAIRMEN OF BOARDS OF SCHOOL EDUCATION ON SEMESTERISATION AND EXAMINATION REFORM (1992)

Introduction. The National Conference of Chairmen of Boards of School Education and Directors of selected SCERTs was organised by the NCERT in collaboration with the Council of Boards of School Education (COBSE) from 6-8 July 1992 at the Mussorie International School, Uttar Pradesh.

Objectives of the Conference

1. To clarify the various aspects of restructuring the curriculum from the point of semesterisation at the secondary stage.
2. To discuss the various academic and administrative problems that could arise as a result of semesterisation being implemented by the Boards of School Education and to suggest solutions to those problems.
3. To suggest a suitable strategy for learner's evaluation as a necessary element of adopting semesterisation.
4. To suggest and plan for the immediate follow up action for the Boards to be taken up in this connection.

Recommendations on the conceptual Aspects of Semester System

(*i*) Division of academic year into two terms of 16-18 week's duration, i.e. having 90-100 working days (500-600 hours);

(*ii*) Restructuring the existing courses into units, modules of different credits semesterwise;

(*iii*) Flexibility to choose the semester courses, according to pupils' needs, future requirements, satisfying the minimum credit requirements for certification;

(*iv*) Carrying forward of the credits earned in different semesters;

(*v*) Reforms in instructional technology;

(*vi*) 15 hours of instruction in theory per week in a semester may carry one credit and in case of practicals, 21 hours of practicals may carry one credit;

(*vii*) About 108 credits may qualify a pupil for the award of the certificate, and

(*viii*) Assessment of each course at the end of a semester which shall include continuous and comprehensive internal evaluation, will ensure conduct of periodical tests and organise remedial instructions so that all students attain optimal levels of achievement.

For introduction of semester pattern of education at the +2 level, detailed action in respect of the above parameters is required to be undertaken for which expert committees be constituted so that necessary models are prepared.

Inter-Board flexibility within the national structural framework in respect of semesterised curricula will have to be an essential pre-requisite for successful implementation of the new system. The Boards will monitor the curriculum transaction in the affiliated institutions.

The group also recommended arranging semesterisation appreciation programmes in different parts of the country in which the personnel of the Boards, the SCERTs and the higher secondary schools, should participate.

RECOMMENDATIONS ON OPERATIONALISATION OF THE SEMESTER SYSTEM AT THE SECONDARY/HIGHER SECONDARY STAGE

The NPE 1986 speaks of the evaluation process and examination reform. It recommends recasting the examination system so as to ensure a method of assessment that is valid and reliable for measuring student development and improving teaching and learning. It suggests streamlining evaluation at the institutional level and reducing predominance of external examinations.

The revised policy formulations 1992 endorse the above approach. It further states that a 'National Examination Reform Framework' would be prepared to serve as a set of guidelines to the examining bodies which would have freedom to innovate and adopt the framework to suit the specific situation. Thus we are now committed to strengthening evaluation at the institutional level and reducing predominance of external examinations. The working group constituted by the conference for suggesting the strategy of implementing the semester system has considered the pros and cons of the issue and it recommended the following strategy for implementation of the reform :

> Semesterisation at the school level is relatively a new concept for all those who are going to implement it and they have to participate in the process. Semesterisation is a major deviation from the traditional approach to assessment and it needs a carefully planned and designed strategy, if it is to succeed in a valid, reliable and objective assessment of the competencies achieved by students at various levels. Modified semester system will include both internal and external assessment.

Since the objectives of both types of assessments are different, the internal and external assessment may have to be separately reflected.

There are some issues which may create certain difficulties to those who are going to implement semesterisation. The difficulties are listed below.

Difficulties of Teachers:

1. Evaluation of answer books of every semester examination and internal assessment work is going to increase the work-load of teachers. The syllabi will, therefore, have to be revised unitwise in such a way that teaching of evey unit has an inbuilt provision for regular continuous evaluation and remedial teaching.
2. With more emphasis on internal assessment, the subjectivity of internal assessment by teachers is likely to increase. Students may also exert pressure on teachers for subjective assessment.
3. Teachers may find the available time for covering the prescribed syllabi to be inadequate.
4. Additional load of semester and internal assessment may take the student's time away from extracurricular activities.

Difficulties of Students:

1. Students may complain about too many examinations.
2. They may not find adequate time for indepth study.
3. Subjectivity in internal assessment may give extra advantage to some and disadvantage to others.
4. The student's time for extracurricular activities is likely to be reduced.
5. There will be less teaching and more examinations as a student would look at it.

Difficulties at the Institutional Level:

1. Schools may find excess load of work on account of making arrangements for recurrent examinations, maintaining studentwise record of internal assessment over a long period of time.
2. Schools will be busy with making correspondence with students, teachers, Boards, etc.

Difficulties at the Board Level:

1. Excessive work increase on account of the increase in the number of examinations.

2. Late and irregular receipt of internal assessment marks.
3. Mistakes in the internal assessment record submitted by the schools.
4. Increase in correspondence with the schools.

It is necessary to consider all the above issues carefully and evolve solutions/alternatives/justifications for each one of them before implementing the reform.

Two Alternatives for Introducing the Reform

The group suggested two alternatives for implementing the reform:

1. To introduce semester system for all schools at both levels (secondary and higher secondary) in all courses covering all subjects.
2. To introduce semester system at both levels in selected courses in a number of selected schools in selected subjects.

It is necessary to identify activities that will have to be taken up at various levels. They are summarised below.

Activities at the Level of the State Board:

1. Undertaking action researches on the existing system including external and internal evaluation and feeding to the school the information about effective teaching/learning methods and efficient assessment procedures.
2. Giving guidance to teachers on assessment and evaluation and encouraging teachers to evolve new techniques of evaluation.
3. Maintaining quality control.

Activities at the Level of Board's Semesterisation Cell:

1. Preparation of question bank/blueprints/sample question papers.
2. Collecting information from schools regarding their experiments in the area of evaluation.
3. Preparing and circulating guidelines for continuous comprehensive internal evaluation.
4. Conducting orientation training programmes for state level resource persons, teacher-educators, office-bearers of teachers' organisations (subject teachers), administrators, supervisors.
5. Analysing results of Board's external examinations.
6. Analysing evaluation work of schools and giving them feedback for improvement.
7. Preparing guidelines for teachers in respect of formative evaluation.

Activities at the District Level Units of the Board

It is necessary to evolve a district level set-up for monitoring, controlling, guiding and evaluating the work done at the institutional level. The state level body can suitably delegate some of their functions to the district level bodies.

Activities at the Institutional Level:

1. Liaison with the Board.
2. Spelling out the syllabi.
3. Orientation of teachers.
4. Test checking of internal assessment.
5. Familiarisation of students and parents about the semester system.
6. Recording progress in internal assessment and other tests.
7. Holding seminars for academic improvement of teachers.
8. Drafting a programme for internal assessment of semester tests.
9. Development of question papers, question pools, record sheets.

Initial steps for semesterisation will include involvement of all those who are going to implement the programme. It is also necessary to educate parents, teachers, headmasters, supervisors and administrators on the subject. This can be done by building up public opinion through mass media and seminars.

Information regarding implementation of the reform must reach all the concerned well in advance.

Restructuring of the Curriculum

Coursewise, subjectwise restructuring of the syllabi will have to be taken up so as to identify the areas for external and internal evaluation. The curriculum will also have to be appropriately graded. A modular approach will have to be taken in restructuring the curriculum.

Various Other Issues Which Need Attention before Implementing the Reform

1. Implications of semester courses in respect of vocationalisation.
2. Procedure for certification.
3. Role of different agencies which are concerned with the reform (State Boards of Education, COBSE, NCERT, district level unit, institutions). The support to the system could be extended by various agencies including the Government of India, NCERT, NIEPA, COBSE and state level organisations like SCERTs, etc.

4. Strengthening of district level units for enabling them to perform their role effectively.

5. Dialogue with the UGC and the AIU, etc. especially at the higher secondary level.

6. Adoption of the semesterisation pattern by the Open School System (if not already done).

Financial Aspect

In addition to the academic and administrative support the reform needs financial support which can be mobilised through grant-in-aid from the Central/State Government.

RECOMMENDATIONS ON EVALUATION IN THE SEMESTER SYSTEM

The group did not discuss the examination reforms in general, but focused its attention only on the evaluation system which can be considered necessary for the introduction of semesterisation as an immediate measure. However, the need for reforming examinations was reiterated.

In its deliberations, the group discussed different scenarios and the alternatives which would need to be matched with the reports of the other groups.

(*i*) Since the public examinations are still occupying a prominent position in the education system, more particularly at the school stage, any consideration of semesterisation has got to be linked with the public examination system.

(*ii*) Elements of internal and continuous evaluation may be added to this process at a subsequent stage when the semesterisation system has achieved some degree of stabilisation.

(*iii*) It is presumed that there will be two semesters per year and four semesters in the total duration of the course, i.e. classes XI and XII.

(*iv*) The end of each semester should mark a definite stage of instruction and evaluation.

(*v*) The first and third semesters of the two years' course should end with final examination to be conducted by the institutions internally, while the second and fourth semesters will end with public examinations to be held by the Board. Consequently, the Board will now be required to conduct two examinations a year and the system of supplementary examinations will then be dispensed with.

(*vi*) The marks or the grades, as the case may be, obtained in the first and third semesters may be shown parallel to the achievement in the Board's (second and fourth semesters) examinations in the certificate issued by the Board.

(*vii*) In order to maintain a broad uniformity in standards of assessment, the Boards may also consider either supplying question papers or providing detailed specific guidelines for evaluating achievement in the first and third semesters to be examined internally.

(*viii*) As an extenstion of this idea further, at an appropriate stage, the Boards may consider scaling the marks/grades of the first and third semesters in the light of performance level obtained in the second and fourth semesters at the state level.

(*ix*) Since, in this structure, it is being proposed that marks of public examinations and internal assessment in each semester have to be shown side by side, it seems practically not feasible to conduct any internal or continuous evaluation for private candidates. Hence, the responsibility of the private candidates should be taken over by the Open Learning System in due course. The Open Learning System could also be the part of the State Board's functions.

Select Bibliography

Aggarwal, J.C., *Survey of Educational Documents in the World Since 1983.* Doaba House, Delhi, 1991.

Aggarwal, J.C., *Documents on Higher Education in India (1781-1992).* Doaba House, Delhi, 1992.

Aggarwal, J.C., *Documents on Primary Education in India* (1772-1992). Doaba House, Delhi, 1992.

Aggarwal, J.C., *Documents on Secondary Education in India (1781-1992).* Doaba House, Delhi, 1992.

Aggarwal, J.C., *Education Policy in India, 1992: Retrospect and Prospect.* Shipra Publication, Delhi, 1995.

Aggarwal, J.C., *Landmarks in the History of Modern Indian Education.* Vikas Publishing House Pvt. Ltd., New Delhi, 1994.

Aggarwal, J.C. and Agrawal, S.P., *Second Historical Survey of Educational Documents in India. Select Documents* 1985-90. Concept Publishing Company, New Delhi, 1991.

Aggarwal, J.C. and Agrawal, S.P., *Third Historical Survey of Educational Documents in India. Select Documents 1990-92.* Concept Publishing Company, New Delhi, 1994.

Aggarwal, J.C. and Bhatt, B.D., *Educational Documents in India.* Arya Book Depot, New Delhi, 1987.

Aggarwal, J.C. and Biswas A., *Comparative Education.* Arya Book Depot, New Delhi, 1995.

Agrawal, Mamta, *Handbook of Evaluation in English.* NCERT, New Delhi, 1988.

Ahmann, J.S. and Block, M.D., *Measuring and Evaluating Educational Achievement.* Allyn and Bacer, Inc., Boston, 1975.

All India Council for Secondary Education, *Proceedings of the First Conference of the Chairmen and Secretaries of the Boards.* AICSE, New Delhi, 1957.

Arora, P.N., *Open Book Examination System.* NCERT., New Delhi, 1982.

Arora, P.N., *Oral Examinations: A Theoretical Framework.* NCERT., New Delhi, 1988.

A.I.U., *Monograph on Moderation of Examination Results.* The Author, New Delhi, 1981.

Block, J.H. (Ed.), *Mastery Learning: Theory and Practice.* Holt, Rinehart and Winston, New York, 1971.

Brown Sally, *What Do They Know? A Review of Criterion Referenced Assessment,* Her Majesty's Stationery Office, Edinburgh, 1981.

Central Board of Secondary Education, New Delhi, *Improving Question Papers in Schools.* Author, New Delhi, 1991.

Central Advisory Board of Education, Ministry of Education and Social Welfare, India, *Report of the Committee on Examinations.* NCERT, New Delhi, 1971.

Choppin, B. and Postlethwaite, T. (Eds.), *Evaluation in Education, Vol.3,* Pergamon Press, Oxford, 1974.

Gene R. Howes and Lyne Salop Howes, Van, *The Concise Dictionary of Education.* Nostrand Reinhold Company, New York, 1982.

Derek Rowtree, *A Critical Dictionary of Education,* Harper and Raw Publishers, London, 1981.

Carter V. Good (Ed.), *Dictionary of Education,* McGraw-Hill, New York, 1973.

P.J. Hills (Ed.), *A Dictionary of Education.* Routledge & Kegan Pal, London, 1982.

Faster Waston, *The Encyclopaedia and Dictionary of Education.* Sir Issac Pitaman & Sons, London, 1921.

Lee C. Deighton (Editor-in-Chief), *The Encyclopaedia of Education.* Macmillan Company and The Free Press, London, 1971.

Harlod E. Mitzel (Editor-in-Chief), *Encyclopaedia of Educational Research.* The Free Press, London, 1982.

Harry N. Rivlon (Ed.), *Encyclopaedia of Modern Education.* Philosophical Library, New York, 1943.

Torsten Husen and T. Neville Postlethwaite (Eds.), *The International Encyclopaedia of Education Research and Studies.* Pergamon Press, Elmsford, New York, 1985 (10 Vols.)

Michael J. Demkin (Ed.), *The International Encyclopaedia of Teaching and Teacher Education.* Pergamon Press, Oxford, 1987.

Dave, P.N. and Murthy, C.G. Venkatesha, *Educational Research and Innovations* (1988-1992), NCERT, 1993.

Dave, R.H. and Srivastava, H.S., "*Examinations in Secondary Education in the Fourth Indian Year Book of Education*", NCERT, New Delhi, 1973.

Department of Education and Science and The Welish Office, *Report of the National Curriculum Task Group on Assessment and Testing.* U.K. London, 1988.

Federal Ministry of Education, *A Handbook on Continuous Assessment.* Heinemaon Educational Books Ltd., Ibadan, 1995.

Frathwohl, D.R. and Payne, D.A., "Defining and Assessing Educational Objectives" in R.L. Thorndike, (Ed.). *Educational Measurement.* American Council on Education, Washington, D.C., 1971.

Government of India, Ministry of Education, *Challenge of Education: A Policy Perspective.* New Delhi, 1985.

Government of India, Ministry of Education, *Learning To Do.* New Delhi, 1978.

Government of India, Ministry of Human Resource Development, *Minimum Levels of Learning at the Primary Stage* (Report of the Committee). NCERT, New Delhi, 1991.

Government of India, Ministry of Human Resource Development, *National Policy on Education (NPE),* New Delhi, 1986.

Government of India, Ministry of Human Resource Development, *NPE: Programme of Action,* New Delhi, 1986.

Government of India, Ministry of Human Resource Development, *National Policy on Education* (NPE), 1986, *Revised Policy Formulation,* New Delhi, 1992.

Government of India, Ministry of Human Resource Development, *NPE: Programme of Action,* New Delhi, 1992.

Government of India, Ministry of Human Resource Development, Committee for Review of National Policy on Education, 1986, *Towards an Enlightened and Human Society* (Ramamurti Committee Report), New Delhi, 1990.

Government of India, Ministry of Human Resource Development, *Report of the Committee for Review of National Policy on Education, 1986, Recommendations,* New Delhi, 1992.

Gronlund, M.E., *Readings in Measurement and Evaluation* Collier, Macmillan Ltd., London, 1971.

Harper, A., Edwin. Jr. and Misra, V.S., *Research on Examinations in India.* NCERT, New Delhi, 1975.

Hill, Walter H., *Improvement of Examinations.* University of Calicut, Calicut, 1972.

Inter University Board of India and Ceylon, *Examinations in Higher Education :* Report of a Seminar, Author, New Delhi, 1971.

Martuza, V.R., *Applying Non-Referenced and Criterion-Referenced Measurement in Education.* Allyn & Bacon, Boston, 1977.

Mathews, J., *Examinations : A Commentary.* George Allen & Unwin, London, 1985.

Mehreas, W.A. and Cohmenn, I.J., *Measurement for Educational Evaluation,* Holt Rinehert and Winston, Inc., New York, 1973.

Mascarenhas, M., *Examinations: An Informative Update.* Doaba House, Delhi, 1991.

Misra, V.S., *Discrimination Value of Essay Type Questions,* Examination Research Unit, Gauhati University, 1976.

Narain, S., *Examinations in Ancient India.* Arya Book Depot. New Delhi, 1993.

Natarajan, V., *Monograph on Semester System for Universities* A.I.U., New Delhi, 1979.

NCERT, *The Concept of Evaluation in Education.* NCERT, New Delhi, 1960.

NCERT, *Contemporary Issues in Public Examinations.* Author, New Delhi, 1985.

NCERT, *Curriculum for the Ten-Year School-A Framework.* Author, New Delhi, 1976.

NCERT, *Guidelines on Scaling and Grading for Examinations Conducted by Boards of Secondary/Higher Secondary Education.* NCERT, New Delhi, 1988.

NCERT, *National Curriculum for Elementary and Secondary Education: A Framework, Revised Version.* Author, New Delhi, 1988.

NCERT, *Open Book Examination Questions in Economics.* Author, New Delhi, 1986.

NCERT, *Report of the Conference of Chairmen of Boards of School Education on Semesterisation and Examination Reform.* Author, New Delhi, 1992.

National Literacy Mission Authority, *Modalities of Total Literacy Declaration and Evaluation of Learning Outcomes.* Report of the Expert Group. Directorate of Adult Education, Ministry of Human Resource Development, Government of India, New Delhi, 1992.

Natrajan, V., *Monograph on Grading for Universities.* A.I.U., New Delhi, 1977.

Nikto, A.J., *Educational Tests and Measurement: An Introduction.* Harcourt Brace Joyanovich, New York, 1983.

Noll, V.H., Scanel, D.P. and Craig, R.C., *Introduction to Educational Measurement.* Houghton Mifflin Company. Boston, 1979.

Ogunniyi, M.B., *Educational Measurement and Evaluation*, Longman, London, 1989.

Passi, B.K. and Sansanwal, D.N., "Educational Evaluation and Examinations : A Trend Report". In M.B. Buch (Ed.) *Second Survey of Research in Education.* Society for Educational Research and Development, Baroda, 1979.

Payne, D.A., *The Assessment of Learning Cognitive and Affective.* D.C. Health and Company, New York, 1974.

Pophan, W.J., *Criterion-Referenced Measurement.* Prentice Hall, New York, 1978.

Popham, W.J., *Educational Evaluation.* Prentice Hall, New York, 1975.

Popham, W.J., *Modern Educational Measurement.* Prentice Hall, New York, 1981.

Qamar Uddin, *Sample Unit Tests in History For classes XI-XII.* NCERT, New Delhi, 1985.

Rao, K. Sudha, *Influence of Continuous Evaluation on Learning.* NCERT, New Delhi, 1986.

Ross C.C. and Stanley, Julian C., *Measurement in Today's Schools.* Prentice Hall, Inc., New York, 1954.

Roid, Gale H. and Haladyna, Thomas M., *A Technology of Test Item Writing.* Academic Press, New York, 1982.

Schofield, H., *Assessment and Testing: An Introduction*, George Allen and Unwin Ltd., London, 1972.

Singh, Pritam (Ed.), *Criterion - Referenced Measurement* (Selected Readings). NCERT, New Delhi, 1990.

Singh, Pritam, *Criterion Referenced Testing: A Monograph.* NCERT, New Delhi, 1983.

Singh, Pritam (Ed.), *Evaluation At the Elementary Stage : A Book of Readings*, NCERT, 1986, New Delhi.

Singh, Pritam, *Evaluating Students in Elementary Schools*, NCERT, New Delhi, 1983.

Singha, H.S., *Modern Educational Testing.* Sterling, New Delhi, 1974.

Singha, H.S., *Public Examinations.* Vikas Publishing House Private Ltd., New Delhi, 1984.

Srivastava, H.S. *Comprehensive Evaluation in Schools.* NCERT, New Delhi, 1989.

Srivastava, H.S., Arora, P.N. and Shourie, J.P., *Unit Tests in Economics.* NCERT, New Delhi, 1976.

Srivastava, H.S. and Shourie, *Instructional Objectives of School Subjects*, NCERT, New Delhi, 1988.

Srivastava, H.S., Singh, Pritam and Anand, V.S., *Reforming Examinations Some Emerging Concepts.* NCERT., New Delhi, 1978.

Stodola, Quentin and Stordah, Kalmer, *Basic Educational Tests and Measurements.* Thomson Press (India) Ltd., New Delhi, 1972.

Stufflebeam, D.L., *Educational Evaluation and Decision Making in Education.* Peacock, Itascea, Illonis, 1971.

Taiwo, Adediran A., *Fundamentals of Classroom Testing.* Vikas Publishing House Pvt. Ltd., New Delhi, 1995.

Thorndike, Robert L & Kagen, Elizabeth, P., *Measurement and Evaluation in Psychology.* Western-Eastern Limited, New Delhi, 1979.

Thyne, James M., *Principles of Examining.* University of London, London, 1974.

Travers, Robert M.W., *Educational Measurement.* Odyssey Press, New York, 1990.

Tuckman, B.W., *Measuring Educational Outcomes. Fundamentals of Testing.* Harcourt, Brace, Jovanovich, Inc., New York, 1975.

UGC, *Evaluation in Higher Education.* Author, New Delhi, 1971.

UGC, *Examination Committee.* Author, New Delhi, 1957.

UGC, *Examination Reform : A Plan of Action.* Author, New Delhi, 1976.

UGC, *Principles and Mechanics of Semester System.* The Author, New Delhi, 1971.

University of London, *University Entrance and School Examinations Council.* Conference Report, No 3. 1970.

University of Mysore, *Report of University Examinations.* Author, Mysore, 1975.

Vernon, Philip E. , *The Measurement of Ability.* University of London, London, 1972.

Weiss, D. (Ed.), *New Horizons in Testing.* Academic Press, New York, 1982.

Index